# THE SCROLLS
## AND THE NEW TESTAMENT

# THE SCROLLS

## AND THE NEW TESTAMENT

*Edited by Krister Stendahl
with James H. Charlesworth*

*Christian Origins Library*
CROSSROAD • NEW YORK

1992

The Crossroad Publishing Company
370 Lexington Avenue, New York, NY 10017

Printed in the United States of America

*Library of Congress Cataloging-in-Publication Data*
The Scrolls and the New Testament / edited by Krister Stendahl with
James H. Charlesworth
p.    cm. — (Christian origins library)
Originally published: New York : Harper, 1957. With new introd.
Includes bibliographical references and index.
ISBN 0-8245-1136-0 (pbk.)
1. Dead Sea scrolls—Relation to the New Testament.   2. Bible.
N.T.—Criticism, interpretation, etc.   I. Stendahl, Krister.
II. Charlesworth, James H.   III. Series.
BM487.S36   1992
296.1'55—dc20                                        91-35661
                                                        CIP

# CONTENTS

The Timelessness of *The Scrolls and the
New Testament*        vii
*James H. Charlesworth*

New Preface        x
*Krister Stendahl*

Contributors

 I. The Scrolls and the New Testament:
   An Introduction and a Perspective   1
   *Krister Stendahl*

 II. The Significance of the Qumran Texts for
   Research into the Beginnings of Christianity  18
   *Oscar Cullman*

 III. John the Baptist in the New Light
   of Ancient Scrolls       33
   *W. H. Brownlee*

 IV. The Two Messiahs of Aaron and Israel  54
   *Karl Georg Kuhn*

 V. The Lord's Supper and the Communal Meal
   at Qumran        65
   *Karl Georg Kuhn*

 VI. New Light on Temptation, Sin, and Flesh
   in the New Testament      94
   *Karl Georg Kuhn*

VII. "Peace among Men of God's Good Pleasure"
Lk. 2$_{14}$                                                      114
*Ernest Vogt, S.J.*

VIII. The Sermon on the Mount and the
Qumran Texts                                        118
*Kurt Schubert*

IX. The Dead Sea Manual of Discipline and
the Jerusalem Church of Acts                 129
*Sherman E. Johnson*

X. The Constitution of the Primitive Church
in the Light of Jewish Documents           143
*Bo Reicke*

.XI. Paul and the Dead Sea Scrolls: Flesh and Spirit   157
*W. D. Davies*

XII. The Qumran Scrolls and the Johannine
Gospel and Epistles                             183
*Raymond E. Brown, S.S.*

XIII. The Qumran Scrolls, the Ebionites, and
Their Literature                                  208
*Joseph A. Fitzmyer, S.J.*

XIV. Hillel the Elder in the Light of the
Dead Sea Scrolls                                232
*Nahum N. Glatzer*

Abbreviations; Editions of Qumran Texts          245

Notes                                                           249

Index of Authors                                          303

Index of Passages                                        306

Selected Bibliography:
The Scrolls and the New Testament              309

# THE TIMELESSNESS OF
## *THE SCROLLS AND THE NEW TESTAMENT*
### *James H. Charlesworth*

*The Scrolls and the New Testament* is a classic. It was the first major collection of articles on the importance of the Dead Sea Scrolls (frequently seen to be "Essene") for understanding the New Testament. Most experts in the field today have been significantly influenced by the thoughts published in this volume.

The articles cover most aspects of New Testament research. Cullmann suggests that "a bridge between the Essenes and the early Christians is to be found in the Hellenists who are mentioned in the Book of Acts." Brownlee focuses on the intriguing relation between that mysterious figure John the Baptizer and the Dead Sea Scrolls; he concludes in favor of "some Essene associations." Kuhn points to the odd messianism in the Scrolls, helps "sharpen our vision" of Jesus' last supper with his disciples, and throws new light on Jesus' 'temptation.' Vogt claims the Scrolls prove that Luke 2:14 means peace among those of "God's good pleasure." Schubert shows how important the Scrolls are for understanding the Sermon on the Mount, and that Jesus refers to Essene practices and presumes widespread acquaintance with their regulations. Johnson reveals how these Jewish documents help us recreate the history of Jesus' followers in Jerusalem after the Easter event of 30. Reicke shows how the rules in the Scrolls clarify the development of Christian ecclesiastical organization. Davies indicates that any attempt to understand Paul must take seriously his Jewish roots, although Paul is closer to the streams leading from the Old Testament to Rabbinics than to the Scrolls. Brown demonstrates that the author of the Gospel of John was generally acquainted with the thought and style of expression found in the Scrolls. Responding in part to Cullmann's chapter, Fitzmyer suggests that the Essenes did not become Ebionites, but that Qumranites "influenced the Ebionites in many ways." Glatzer concludes that Hillel the Elder knew about the Qumranites or Essenes and that some personal contact with them is conceivable.

These scholars were, and those who are still alive remain, leaders at the forefront of research. They appear in any celebration of the ways the Dead Sea Scrolls have revolutionized our approach to and understanding of Judaism before 70 C.E., when the Roman soldiers destroyed Jerusalem, and of Jesus and his followers. These scholars dominate a who's who of research on the Scrolls and the New Testament.

While published in 1957 these chapters remain informative, pioneering, and suggestive. In the nineties, we are seeing a resurgence of interest in Dead Sea Scrolls research; numerous articles have appeared in 1990 and 1991 in the *New York Times*, most leading newspapers, and news-oriented magazines. None of the recently published Scrolls, or about-to-be-published fragments, can be said to be more important than the Scrolls cited in the chapters of this book.

The *Rule of the Community* (1QS) is the manual of discipline for the Qumran Covenanters, and along with the *Cairo Damascus Document* (CD) is the major document for understanding the life of the Community and its concept of the human. The *Hodayot* or *Thanksgiving Hymns* (1QH) is the hymnbook of the Qumran Covenanters; it is a repository of thoughts on salvation, forgiveness, and God's grace, along with probable reflections on the life and suffering of the Righteous Teacher, the founder of the Community. *The War Scroll* (1QM) is one of the major documents for understanding the Qumranites view of the Endtime. The *Habakkuk Pesher* (1QpHab) is one of the most important writings for assessing and comprehending the means for interpreting scripture that sets the Qumran Covenanters out as unique within the world of Early Judaism.

The following chapters are based on the Scrolls preserved in Cave I and on CD (see p. 247). Added to the brilliant insights, many of which have become definitive for New Testament study, is the freshness and excitement couched in the early work on the Scrolls (and now beginning to reappear in light of new challenging discoveries). These together make this book attractive to all who are interested in early Jewish thought and the origins of Christianity.

The scholars demonstrate the Jewish origins of Christianity. They also indicate the contours within which the uniqueness of Jesus and Christianity become obvious and can be explored.

Krister Stendahl, the editor, has enjoyed numerous prestigious positions of leadership, including a chair at Harvard, the Dean of Harvard Divinity School, and Bishop of Stockholm. His contributions to a better understanding of the Bible are impressively diverse: advocating the place of leadership for women in the Bible and the Church, appealing for a recognition of the Jewish roots of Christianity, honoring the Jew in our midst, and studying Paul and the gospels (especially Matthew) in light of their own historical context.

His two main contributions to Dead Sea Scrolls studies were in biblical interpretation. He argued that the concept of non-retaliation along with hate characteristic of the Qumranites was a development of traditional elements in scripture (it was not something novel), and that Qumran eschatology clarifies Paul's theology.[1] He demonstrated that those who produced the Gospel of Matthew interpreted scripture in a way similar to, and perhaps influenced by, the authors of the Dead Sea Scrolls.[2]

With Stendahl I wish to stress "that both the Pauline and Johannine literature can be understood in their Jewish background and that many of the odysseys of scholars some decades ago over the deep waters of Hellenistic philosophy and religion were more fascinating than they were rewarding" (p. 5). Stendahl also helps us explore the meaning of Christianity and "its true foundation in the person and the events of its Messiah" (p. 17).

1. K. Stendahl, "Hate, Non-retaliation, and Love 1QS x, 17–20 and Rom. 12:19–21," *Harvard Theological Review* 55 (1962) 343–55. Stendahl's argument receives support from some insights published by J.L. Kugel; see his *In Potiphar's House: The Interpretive Life of Biblical Texts* (San Francisco: Harper, 1990) see especially pp. 214–25.

2. Stendahl, *The School of St. Matthew and its Use of the Old Testament* (Philadelphia: Fortress, 1968 [a reprint of the 1954 edition with a new introduction]). Also, see Stendahl's "Quis et Unde? An Analysis of Mt 1–2," in *Judentum, Urchristentum, Kirche: Festschrift für Joachim Jeremias*, ed. W. Eltester (Berlin: Töpelmann, 1960) pp. 94–105.

# NEW PREFACE

There is no end to the list of things that could be said when this collection of essays now reappears. Those of us who wrote about the Dead Sea Scrolls in the mid fifties had a unique feeling of freshness. Imagine biblical scholars—of all things—writing without having to cut through and evaluate layers of secondary literature. Of course it was risky, but it seems to me that on the whole we guessed right. And I hope that it is not for not having kept up with the field of Qumraniana that I feel pretty satisfied with my introductory assessment of the significance of the scrolls for the understanding of Christian origins and for the diversity of Judaism prior to the parting of the ways of Church and Synagogue.

There is only one thing, however, that I feel needs to be added before it is forgotten, and that is the homage and the gratitude I owe to the person who suggested way back then that I bring something like this together, and who paved the way for its publication. His name was Jacob Taubes, then of Harvard, later at Columbia, and from 1965 until his death in 1987 Professor of Jewish Studies and Hermeneutics at the Free University in Berlin.

Jacob Taubes was one of the mind-blowing experiences during our—Brita's and my—first years at Harvard, and we kept in touch with him sporadically during the ensuing years.

Imagine the commentaries and conversations at our first Seder ever. It was in Cambridge (Mass.) with Jacob and Susan Taubes. The other guests were Herbert Marcuse, Susan Sontag, and Philip Rieff. Nor shall I ever forget going with Jacob Taubes to the Jewish Theological Seminary in New York City for the most un-Lutheran service of all, the Simchat Torah (rejoicing in the Law).

I do miss getting drunk on sheer intellectual exuberance together with that man, with that restless mind that made him describe himself as Erzjude/Urchrist (Authentic Jew/Pristine Christian). It sounds just as heretical as Jacob wanted to sound in order to realize his vision of ultimate orthodoxy.

I have read in Jan Assmann's obituary of Jacob Taubes how two books followed him on all his travels: Walter Benjamin's *Illuminations* and Erik Peterson's *Theological Tractates*. Two brilliant scholars despising the then equivalents of p.c. thinking. My teacher Anton Fridrichsen had steered me toward Erik Peterson as "someone who thinks"—so I was somewhat prepared.

Jacob Taubes' only booklength work, from 1947 when he was 24, will be republished this winter. *Abendlandische Eschatologie* is a philosophy of history focussed on the categories "Revelation and Apocalyptic through Western Culture," with heavy attention to Hegel, Marx, and Kierkegaard.

Philosophy as it bordered on theology of history remained the turbulent center of Jacob Taubes' thought and ongoing conversations—sometimes, but far from always, rather monologues. I remember a penetrating—typically unpublished—paper on messianism that gave life to one of my seminars in the 1980s. And I have read in one of the obituaries* that when he knew that he had only months left, he returned to his studies of Paul's letter to the Romans, for in it he saw a text which encapsulated the explosive power of "the Eschatology of Western Culture."

As this collection of essays on the Scrolls reappears, I respond to the urge of expressing thanks for the catalytic brilliance of Jacob Taubes.

The Christian prayer for the dead reads traditionally: Requiescat in pace—may he rest in peace. Perhaps in Jacob's heaven the blissful greeting rather reads: May he be enlivened by ever new dialectic.

If that be the case—so be it.

*Krister Stendahl*
Brandeis University
At the Jewish High Holy Days 5752 and the
middle weeks of the Christian Trinity Season 1991.

*Neue Züricher Zeitung, March 24, 1987, Fernausgabe, p. 27.

# Contributors

Raymond E. Brown, S.S.
St. Mary's Seminary, Baltimore, Maryland

W. H. Brownlee
Duke University Divinity School

Oscar Cullmann
University of Basel and l'Ecole des Hautes Etudes in Paris

W. D. Davies
Princeton University

Joseph A. Fitzmyer, S.J.
Woodstock College, Maryland

Nahum N. Glatzer
Brandeis University

Sherman E. Johnson
Church Divinity School of the Pacific

Karl Georg Kuhn
University of Heidelberg

Bo Reicke
University of Basel

Kurt Schubert
University of Vienna

Krister Stendahl
Harvard Divinity School

Ernest Vogt, S.J.
The Pontifical Biblical Institute, Rome

# I

# The Scrolls and the New Testament: An Introduction and a Perspective

Archaeological discoveries are always fascinating, and they often attract a considerable interest even outside the exclusive guilds of the specialists. They easily find their way to the front pages of our newspapers. If this is true in general, it is especially true about the finds in the caves at the Dead Sea. The details of how these caves were found and the strange mixture of co-operation and competition between the archaeologists and the unauthorized Bedouin hunting for new scrolls adds to the excitement of the reports from this hot and unfriendly landscape in the time of the scroll rush, which—as far as the Bedouin are concerned—is a veritable gold rush as well. Institutions all over the world are pooling their resources and putting kind and desperate pressure on prospecitve benefactors in order to raise the necessary funds for purchasing what the Bedouin have found during their free enterprise raids in the area.

Nevertheless, there can be no doubt that it is the very problem to which this volume addresses itself—the Scrolls and the New Testament—which has been the catalyst responsible for the wide interest in the Qumran discoveries. It is as a potential threat to Christianity, its claims, and its doctrines that the Scrolls have caught the imagination of laymen and clergy. It may also be said that this interest is far more intense and widespread in the United States than anywhere else in the world, and we all know why that is so. It is due to Edmund Wilson's article in *The New Yorker*, in 1955, on "The Scrolls from the Dead Sea," later published in a slightly enlarged form as a book which enjoyed a top rating on book lists for quite some time. With an astonishing ability to grasp the material and the problems involved, and with the eye of a journalist for what is hot in the news, Wilson introduced the Dead Sea Scrolls to the American public.

But the success of his book was due not only to his skill to tell the story but also to his intimations that these Scrolls had drastic ramifications for Christianity—"that the rise of Christianity should, at last, be generally understood as simply an episode of human history rather than propagated as dogma and divine revelation."[1] Wilson also managed to give the impresssion that Christian scholars all around the world now were stunned and afraid and that this fact accounted for the slowness of communicating their findings to a larger public. On this latter point, Wilson was certainly wrong, since the pace of publication has obviously been higher in the case of the Scrolls than is usual in these areas of research. One example may suffice. Hardly anything of the magnificent discovery of a Gnostic library in Egypt in 1945, which will have considerable bearing  on the origin of Christian doctrines, is yet available, "in spite of" the fact that the publication is in the hands of men who take a rather radical view on religious matters.[1a] Apparently the time-table of scholarship and that of journalism are somewhat different.

The framework of a challenge to Christianity is, however, most significant, and not only as a device which can always arouse interest. Even the casual reader of arguments and counterarguments in the discussion about the Scrolls must soon recognize that there is more to such a debate than meets the eye. The more popular discussion about the Scrolls and the New Testament has brought into the open the tragic fact that very little of the spirit and the results of modern biblical studies has reached outside the walls of our seminaries and divinity schools. It is not only due to the professional ties of the clergy that they generally have felt less alarmed by the findings from Qumran than have their parishioners. While in seminary, the majority of our clergy have been exposed to a considerable number of rather close parallels to New Testament ideas and concepts. But it may be a fair criticism to say that this exposure has not materialized into a thorough attempt to come to grips with the basic problem of what such parallels actually mean to the theological enterprise in general, and to the preaching and teaching in the parish in particular.[2] Thus we are badly prepared to receive the good news from the Qumran Scrolls.

The first area where this insufficient preparation for a sound judgment is striking is in dealing with the New Testament itself. Modern scholarship is well aware of the fact that the New Testament text cannot be taken at face value, but that it shows the marks of theological, missionary, and catechetical interests of the early church. It is also obvious that the New Testament bears witness to different stages and conflicting tendencies and practices within the primitive church. It is only with these facts in mind that one can proceed from general impressions of similarities to a more accurate comparison between the Scrolls and the New Testament. It is also only on this basis that one has the right to dismiss some of the alleged dissimilarities as irrelevant for the stage or segment of primitive church life which may be subjected to comparative study. What this means in concrete terms for, e.g., the eschatology of Qumran and the New Testament we shall try to show.

It is for this very reason that we are turning to the scholars who have contributed to this volume. Most of them belong technically to the field of New Testament studies, and all of them are approaching their topics within the framework of the discipline of such studies. The last of the essays, dealing with Hillel in the light of the Scrolls, widens the perspective by indicating how the Scrolls may add to our insight into the history of Judaism regardless of their relations to Christianity. In some of the essays, it becomes particularly clear that it is only by way of a rather elaborate critical analysis of the New Testament material that a comparative study can be carried out with some precision. This becomes especially clear in Dr. Kuhn's study of the relation between the Lord's Supper and the communal meals of the Essenes. The strange mixture between a naïve use of the New Testament and a sophisticated interest in its relation to the Scrolls—a blend which is found also in Wilson's book—thus calls for contributions like those presented here.

The second area in which the discussion of the Scrolls has revealed great confusion in our presuppositions and our terminology is a more philosophical one. Everybody recognizes similarities between the Qumran material and the New Testament. But the way in which arguments and counterarguments just do not meet one another indicates that parallels in the field of religion have very different significance for different people. In the long run, the most important impact of the Scrolls may be a theological one. It is here that Wilson's statement, which we just quoted, about Christianity "as simply an episode of human history" has to be taken seriously. The question about the relation between the "episode" and the "revelation" has been the basic theological problem of Christian theology from its very beginning. In the first century the main concern of Christian thinking was to preserve the episode dimension against all tendencies to transform Christianity into a system of timeless truth. "Crucified under Pontius Pilate" is not only a piece of historical information, but within the creed it stands to safeguard the historical aspect of Christianity, its character of an episode of "secular" history. Thus the tension between the episode and the dogmatic claims is a more complex feature than is often recognized. Let us try to see how this tension affects the issues raised by the Scrolls.

The usual approach is one of emphasis: i.e., one emphasizes either the similarities or the dissimilarities. This can be done just by counting how many of each can be found. Or some similarities/dissimilarities are considered so fundamental that the rest can be more or less discounted.

Here one could mention the name which Wilson uses as a symbol of truth and integrity: Ernest Renan. Following Dupont-Sommer,[3] he refers to Renan's famous statement that "Christianity is an Essenism which has largely succeeded."[4] One could point out, however, that this quotation is often used out of context, since Renan goes on to criticize those who want to "explain Christianity as almost totally derived from Essenism. . . . A direct communication between Christianity and Essenism is doubtful." Thus Renan is not so clearly on one side of the discussion as Wilson and Dupont-Sommer give us to believe. On the other hand—and that is of greater interest in our context—Renan's comparison of the two movements must be considered radically misleading, since for him—as for many of our contemporaries—the point of comparison is only that of moral philosophy. Speaking about the differences, he points to the legalism of the Essenes and then goes on to say that "for Christianity the messianic ideas were only the leaven necessary for raising the dough.

Once this ferment was thrown away, there was left a rule of life far superior to Essenism."[5] Here the modern discussion is much more to the point, when it centers on the messianic ideas of the two movements as one of the pivotal points in the comparative study. To Renan, religion was basically ethics with religious overtones, and this liberalism has made him a poor historian at this point.

Once the messianic claims and tenets of the two movements are brought into focus, most Christian apologists have been repeating an argument which seems rather clear and strong: To the Essenes the Messiah was yet to come, but the Christians knew and believed that he had come, that he had died, and that he is risen. The arguments of Dupont-Sommer[6] and J. M. Allegro[7] amount to an identification of the Teacher of Righteousness who was tortured to death and the priestly Messiah who was expected to return in the time of ultimate consummation; but this argument still leaves a difference between the Christian claim of a risen Messiah and the Essene expectation of a Messiah yet to come. A closer study of the New Testament reveals that the religious attitude of early Christianity had a stronger note of expectancy than we usually recognize, and this fact makes the comparison between the two movements a more crucial one.[8]

It has often been said that the Dead Sea Scrolls add substantially to our knowledge of the Jewish background of Christianity. On this point there is universal agreement. This is significant enough. It means, among other things, that both the Pauline and the Johannine literature can be understood in their Jewish background and that many of the odysseys of scholars some decades ago over the deep waters of Hellenistic philosophy and religion were more fascinating than they were rewarding. The essays of W. D. Davies and R. E. Brown in this volume are most revealing at this point. At the same time the Scrolls, in spite of being thoroughly Jewish in character, are not understandable as a straight development of Old Testament[9] religion, but witness to the fact that once more the impact of neighboring cultures of the Near East has fertilized Jewish religion. At this juncture the Iranian influence has been especially strong.[10] Th. H. Gaster's edition of *The Dead Sea Scriptures*[11] gives ample evidence of how the Scrolls are rooted in the Near Eastern patterns of thought.

To end a comparative study on the note of "good for the background" sometimes awakens the suspicion of the reader that the writer has taken the easy way out. In the case here under discussion, we must pursue the study further and ask whether the background does not really help us to see the material itself in a different light and perspective. It has always been known that Christianity emerged out of Judaism, and to the early church this was not only a historical but a theological fact. The fight against Marcion's attempts to do away with the Old Testament and the Jewish legacy of Christianity makes this clear once for all.

Marcion's intentions were, however, rather close to the unconscious attitudes of modern man. He wanted Christianity to be a new religion, just as it is to us. Whereas the New Testament sees Jesus as the fulfillment of the prophecies, we are apt to see him as the founder of a new religion. And our paramount problem is to prove that there is something new in Christianity, something never heard of before. Our pattern of thought is that of natural science: Jesus is the inventor of Christianity and the church is the guardian of his patent and his copyright. In the New Testament the major concern is the diametrically opposite one: to make clear that all is "old," in accordance with the expectations of the prophets. The golden rule is not promulgated as the terrific achievement of an ethical thinker; it is recommended by the remark, "This is the Law and the Prophets."

Thus the issue between the Essenes and the early Christians was not one of "originality," but a searching question about who were the legitimate heirs to the prophetic promises and who could produce the most striking arguments for fulfillment. This is the issue which gives the Qumran commentaries their form: to the words of Scripture they attach a reference to what has happened with their Teacher or their community, and the link is the word *pishro*, "its meaning is . . ." And so do the Gospels, most extensively the Gospel of Matthew: "This happened in order to fulfill that which was said by the Prophet. . . ."[12]

It may be significant that the New Testament does not coin the word "Christianity." It occurs in the second century (Ignatius), but the New Testament writers did not feel any need for such an abstraction. They spoke about the gospel, the good news, that now the promises had come true, and they spoke about the church as the true people of God, who had been worthy to be counted as the chosen ones of God since they had accepted the messianic claims of Jesus and the church.

For more than fifty years the term "eschatology" has been the key word in biblical studies. Albert Schweitzer's *The Quest of the Historical Jesus* (1906, first Eng. edition, 1910), has become a symbol for this new approach, although the reorientation had been brought about more than a decade earlier by scholars like· Joh. Weiss (*Die Predigt Jesu vom Reiche Gottes*, 1892). Eschatology had up to that time been the technical term for the last c.1apter of traditional systematic presentations of Christianity: the doctrines about the "last things" and the hereafter. Now eschatology was discovered to be the climate and the frame of reference for the ·appearance and the teaching of Jesus from beginning to end; the original setting of primitive Christianity within the messianic and eschatological expectations of its time was recaptured. This insight came to stay; and to say the least, it has been underscored far beyond any expectations by the discovery of the Qumran Scrolls. We are now for the first time in a position where we can compare the messianic expectation of the Jewish sect called the Christians with another Jewish sect, already on the scene in the time of Jesus.

We use the term "sect" deliberately. Josephus' presentation of the Pharisees, the Sadducees, and the Essenes as philosophies (*Ant.* 18, 1, 2) or as parties is somewhat misleading (*hairesis: Bell.* 2, 8, 2; cf. Acts 5₁₇, 15₅; and 24₁₄ about the Christians: ". . . the Way, which they call a party"—RSV: "sect"; cf. 24₅). The structure of the Pharisees and the Sadducees differs from that of the Essenes in one respect which is of crucial importance. The former may adequately be described as parties. From the standpoint of their different opinions they tried to influence the life of the Jews. The Pharisees were apparently better organized[13] and more effective than were the Sadducees. It may also be true that the Pharisees took a dim view of the chances for publicans and sinners to have a part in the Age to Come, but there is nothing that leads us to believe that membership in these parties was given a theological or eschatological significance. This was, however, precisely what happened with the Essenes. They did not form a party; they formed the Community of the New Covenant. Through initiation and obedience, they were the elect ones.

It is this feature of the Essene Community which makes it important to distinguish it as a sect over against the parties of the Pharisees and the Sadducees.

Once we have this distinction in mind, it is clear even to a casual reader of the New Testament that the primitive church must be described as a sect in this sense and not as a party. Already the terminology by which the Christians call themselves ("the holy ones," "the chosen ones," etc.) points in this direction, and so does the practice of baptism for the purpose of initiation. The Manual of Discipline (1 QS) contains two columns of minute regulations for "church discipline," and shows that it was not a discipline for educational purposes. The punishment is described in terms of "exclusion from the Purity" (vi, 25 etc.), i.e., from the common meals.[14] As we shall see later, the meals are not arbitrarily chosen as the focal point of the holiness of the sect, but were the anticipation of the Messianic Banquet, and he who is not worthy of that banquet is consequently excluded from its counterpart in the community.

The chapters by S. Johnson and B. Reicke in this volume present the material on discipline in its proper Qumran and New Testament context. Yet it may be pertinent to point out how much more severe the primitive church handled, e.g., "a man who lies in the matter of wealth" (1 QS vi, 25), than do the Qumran rules. At Qumran such a sinner was excluded from the Purity for one year and was deprived of a fourth of his food ration. But in the case of Ananias and Sapphira (Acts 5₁₋₁₁) no casuistry applies. Peter pronounces a curse, a kind of healing miracle in the reverse. Ananias and Sapphira are virtually killed. Their sin is a sin against the Holy Spirit and there is no place for repentance. There is a note of ultimate seriousness in the New Testament which does not leave room for the gracious casuistry and second chance which the Qumran sect practices in all cases except those of downright apostasy or disloyalty.[15] This difference is significant for our attempt to assess what we may call the degree of anticipation of the two sects.[16]

The distinction between the sect and the party is also crucial for the proper understanding of another of the striking parallels between the Scrolls and the New Testament. In the hymnal section of the Manual of Discipline we find some words of a quite Pauline ring: "As for me, if I slip, God's mercy (hesed) is my salvation for ever, and if I stumble in the iniquity of flesh, my vindication (*mish-pat*) through the righteousness (*sedaqah*) of God will stand eternally" (xi, 11 f.). This is really a concept of justification by the righteousness of God, usually referred to as the heart of Pauline theology. The fact that it stands side by side with the stern legalism of the Qumran Community just adds to its significance, and is not much different from the way in which Paul adds his ethical exhortations to his setting forth of the gospel of salvation.

The parallel from Qumran indicates in what direction we can find the key to Paul's use of the term "righteousness of God." In the Song of Deborah, presumably the oldest piece of tradition incorporated in the Old Testament, we read: ". . . they rehearse the 'righteousnesses' (*sidqoth;* King James Version: "righteous acts"; RSV: "triumphs") of Yahweh, the 'righteousnesses' of his peasantry in Israel" (Judg. 5₁₁). Our literal translation gives us the basic meaning of God's righteousness: that which, according to the covenant, vindicates his chosen people and destroys its foes and enemies. As long as the unsophisticated self-consciousness as the chosen ones was applied to the whole people, God's righteousness was synonymous with his salvation, with his giving of victory and triumph to his own. As the history went on and the prophets had reason to challenge the claims of a chosen people for the whole of the nation, God's righteousness becomes a judge of Israel as well as its vindicator: the dividing line is drawn within Israel itself. But in a sect which claims to constitute the holy remnant, and whose members are the gathering of the elect ones, the old terminology becomes meaningful again. God's justification can now mean only one thing: vindication and salvation. The day of judgment is the day of glory and grace for the holy ones, and the early church prayed confidently: "Let grace come and let this world pass away!" (Did. 10₆).

Thus it is the sect structure, and the high eschatology of the community, which brings out—or brings back—the term "justification" as a synonym for salvation and as a thing which the members are sure to profit by. The difference between Paul and Qumran is not a conceptual one. Their discussion would rather have centered around what valid motivation could be produced for applying the concept. For Paul the answer was: through the cross of Jesus Christ; for the Qumran Community: through the revelation which ordered us to gather as the New Covenant. Once this is said, we may add that in Paul's theology this concept has transformed the whole structure of thought and practice to a much greater extent than ever happened at Qumran.[17]

The concept of the sect which we have stressed so far fits well into the framework of promise·and fulfillment. The character of the sect is defined by the promises and its right to existence takes the form of a claim of fulfillment. Yet there is always something more to come. The sect is an *anticipation*. The idea of anticipation is the necessary correlate to the promise—fulfillment pattern of biblical eschatology. It is in the terms of anticipation that the Qumran material and the New Testament must be compared with each other if we are interested in capturing the issue in its original dimensions.

In a fragment from Cave I (*Serek ha-edah*, 1 QSa) we have a description of what is going to be the rule and the procedure when both the royal and the priestly Messiah (see Kuhn's essay in this volume on "The Two Messiahs of Aaron and Israel") are present. To this description of the Messianic Banquet is added the sentence: "And they shall follow this prescription whenever the meal is arranged, when as many as ten meet together."[18] Thereby the actual meal of the Essene Community (cf. 1 QS vi, 4-6) is defined as an anticipation of the Messianic Banquet.[19] In its central religious act the sect understands itself as an anticipation of the Age to Come.

The idea of the Messianic Banquet is well known from the Gospels: ". . . many will come from east and west and sit at table with Abraham, Isaac and Jacob in the Kingdom of Heaven" (Mt. 8₁₁), cf. Lk 22₃₀ ". . . that you may eat and drink at my table in my kingdom . . . ," a saying which is found in the context of the Last Supper. The theological interest which the Gospels display when reporting on the meal-fellowship with Jesus and the feeding of the multitudes points to the same concept, but more striking in our context is the fact that the account of the Last Supper in all its editions—Mark, Matthew, Luke, Paul (and the Didache)—has a strong note of anticipation: Jesus will not taste of the meal until it comes to its fulfillment in the Kingdom of God, and by the celebration of the meal Christ is proclaimed until his coming again; the prayer *marana tha*, "Our Lord, come!" belongs to the eucharistic liturgy.[20]

At this point it is rather tempting to raise the old question about the meaning of the Greek word (*epiousios*) behind our translation of the Lord's Prayer, "our *daily* bread give us today." The apocryphal Gospel to the Hebrews says: "our bread for tomorrow give us today"; this meaning is more in accordance with the precise meaning of the Greek word (in-standing) and may be supported by the only instance in secular Greek where it is found (the ration allotted for the next day).[21] Furthermore, the context of the Lord's Prayer is strongly eschatological; it is basically a prayer about the coming of the Kingdom, the relief from the trial of the ultimate catastrophe, the deliverance from evil. In such an original setting and in the light of the anticipation structure of the Qumran meal a prayer for participation in the heavenly meal already here and now gives perfect sense: "Our bread for tomorrow give us today."

The application of the category of anticipation has, however, far more drastic ramifications for our study. We mentioned already in passing how the clear-cut distinction between the Christian view of a Messiah who has come and the Essene expectation of the two Messiahs yet to come seems to overlook the futuristic accent of New Testament Christianity. The primitive church did not live in a nostalgic retrospection to the glorious days when Jesus walked on earth. It is one of the striking features in the Epistles and in Acts that the earthly ministry plays so small a role. In the light of what had happened later and what was yet to come it was a prelude, not the climax. "Even if we had known Christ in the flesh, we do not know him that way now" (2 Cor. 5₁₆). "Ours is a commonwealth in heaven and from it we await a savior, the Lord Jesus Christ" (Phil. 3₂₀). This future is one of hope: "In hope we are saved, but a hope which one sees fulfilled is no hope any more" (Rom. 8₂₄). There is, however, something which makes this hope more than mere longing or expectation intensified by the immediate hope for fulfillment. The Spirit has been poured out as the earnest, the down payment of the future consummation (2 Cor. 1₂₂, 5₅; Eph. 1₁₄),[22] as a firstfruit of the Spirit in its ultimate and transforming power (Rom. 8₂₃). This is what gives the primitive church its joy and nurtures its expectancy. The Spirit is the anticipation which bridges the tension between the two tenses: we are saved—we will be saved.

We have so far chosen our examples from the Pauline Epistles but this futuristic attitude is certainly not confined to Paul, nor is it to be understood as a defense, construed by Paul to overcome his inferiority complex vis-à-vis the other apostles who had been the disciples of Jesus from the beginning. Modern New Testament studies have rather made us inclined to see even Jesus himself in this light of future expectations. The hot debate about whether Jesus actually did make any claims to be the Messiah or not has, through the healthy influence of Weiss and Schweitzer, been purged of one false alternative. The question is not whether Jesus intended to be a teacher, a rabbi, to the increase of religious insight and moral quality of life or if he thought of himself as the Messiah, the Son of God. The two real alternatives are now totally within the framework of promise and fulfillment: Was he the Messiah or was he only his forerunner, the prophet who came to announce that the Kingdom was at hand? It is in the light of this alternative that the messianic ideas of the Qumran texts become significant parallels.

The Teacher of Righteousness appears to have been the founder of the Qumran sect. He was certainly more than a "teacher," he was the one who had received authority to reveal "the final phase of the end which was not made known to the prophet Habakkuk himself" (1 QpHab vii, 1 f.). The publication of some fragments from Cave IV has now made it clear that this Teacher, called the "Interpreter of the Law" in the Damascus Document (vi, 7; vii, 18), may be identified with the priestly Messiah to be raised in the last days.[23] Regardless of this tenet, the messianic character of the Qumran community is obvious. They are the ones to receive the two Messiahs and the messianic Prophet. In one of the hymns (1 QH iii, 9f.) we may even find a closer description of the relation between the community and a Messiah: "For through deathly contractions she brings forth a male child, and through hellish pains there burst forth from the womb of her who is pregnant a Wonderful Counsellor with his might."[24] The woman in travail appears to be the community itself which through tribulations brings forth the Messiah, as the woman in Rev. 12 is a symbol for the church.

Thus we find that although the Messiahs are yet to come the Qumran sect must be called a messianic community in a far more specific sense than Judaism in general could be referred to as messianic. The messianic events have started to happen in an anticipating way; the community is a manifestation of the New Covenant of the Age to Come. The Teacher of Righteousness was not and is not but will come back as a Messiah.

When we turn to the gospel records with this messianology in mind the alternative between Jesus as the messianic Teacher and Prophet or as the Messiah in person becomes a more intriguing one. At the same time, we receive an indirect confirmation that such an alternative is the natural one in its historical context. It is a well-known fact that there is no case in Mark where Jesus applies the title "Christ" (the Greek translation of the Hebrew "Messiah," both meaning "the anointed one") to himself, and that Mark has the word only seven or eight (1₃₄?) times. In the other Synoptic Gospels the use of the title increases, but the reluctancy to use "Christ" in the Gospels still contrasts with its frequency in the Epistles and in Acts.[25] The difference between Luke and Acts is most significant since here one and the same author apparently holds a view which urges him to preserve such a difference.

On the other hand, the term used by Jesus—and only by Jesus—is "the Son of Man" (and consequently this term is not found elsewhere in the New Testament, except in three instances which have the character of an allusion to the Book of Daniel: Acts 7₅₆; Rev. 1₁₃, 14₁₄). We cannot here deal with the entangled discussion about the Son of Man.[26] The popular understanding has been that Jesus avoids the title "Messiah" because it carried with it the idea of a worldly leadership, a warrior-king who should help the Jews to throw off the humiliating yoke of Roman occupation.[27]

Already apart from the Qumran texts we had enough insight into Jewish messianology in the time of Jesus to know that the difference between Jesus and Jewish expectations could hardly be that of spiritual *vs.* mundane.[28] It seems more plausible that this shift in terminology has something to do with a messianology of anticipation. Even within the Gospels the Son of Man is often spoken of with reference to the future. The title also has an enigmatic character in that it actually may mean only "man" in a most casual sense, and used by the person speaking it could mean "I" or "me." Thus it was a suitable term to be used in the stage of anticipation, an anticipation which was at the same time the first act of the messianic events themselves.

The futuristic emphasis of the New Testament has found one of its expressions in what we usually refer to as the Second Coming, the *Parousia*. This concept appears strange in its apocalyptic and mythological intensity and has created much confusion in Christian theology and in church history. But the reason for this strangeness may be that the "First Coming," the earthly ministry of Jesus, has become too much of a "coming." Its character of anticipation, of overture, has been forgotten and covered over, mainly due to the influence of philosophies to which the idea of anticipation was too alien to be considered meaningful enough.

Jews and Christians, Essenes and Pharisees, all knew of the Coming, the Advent at the end of time, the *Parousia*. But to the messianic sects like the Christians and the Essenes the *Parousia* had started to unfold itself on the stage of history; the futuristic element is rather heightened than lessened thereby. In one of the speeches in Acts, we find an expression with the ring of a very original type of messianology—or christology. We read, as words of Peter to the Jews: "Repent and turn again so that your sins may be blotted out, in order that times of refreshment may come from the face of the Lord and that he may send the Messiah which is appointed for you, Jesus, whom heaven must receive until the times of ultimate consumation, concerning which times God spoke through the mouth of his holy prophets" ($3_{19-21}$).[29] Here Jesus is identified as the Messiah (or should we say that the Messiah is identified as Jesus?). He is the Messiah to come in the time of the *Parousia*. But there can be no doubt that he is also considered to have been the Messiah himself in all respects in the time of his first coming. He is the Prince of Life, killed by these Jews (v. 15) who now are invited to make better use of their second chance.

Here we come across a clear difference between Qumran and the New Testament, a difference which stays within the framework of promise and fulfillment and could be described as a difference in the degree of anticipation. While the Qumran texts identify the Teacher of Righteousness as the Messiah to come (as does Acts $3_{20-21}$), there seems to be no attempt to say that the Teacher *is* or *was* the Messiah. This may appear to be a thin line to draw, but even if we should find such a saying at Qumran, the reason for the Christian application of the full messianic terminology to Jesus—even to the extent that Jesus Christ becomes just a name in the Greek-speaking church—is a specific one, which clarifies what we call a different degree of anticipation.

The Teacher of Righteousness was expected to be raised as the priestly Messiah together with The Anointed One of Israel. This was a future event. But the Christian claim was a stronger one. Jesus, the Messiah *designatus,* was risen. A new and great step had been taken toward the ultimate messianic consummation; the Christian church was one act ahead of the Essenes.

Let us take time to emphasize that also the resurrection of Jesus must be seen as an anticipation. To modern man—believer and unbeliever alike—the resurrection is an extreme miracle. We are paralyzed by the *phenomenon* as such. But all Jews—except the Sadducees in this case—were used to looking forward to resurrection as one of the aspects of the end of time. The phenomenon did not bother them as such. To them the message about the resurrection of Jesus—if they accepted the witnesses as trustworthy—meant that now the events of the glorious Age to Come really had started to unfold themselves. Jesus was risen as the "firstborn from the dead" (Col. 1₁₈). Resurrection had begun to happen.[30]

In Peter's speeches in Acts the resurrection of Jesus is referred to in order to cancel out the negative impression his crucifixion had made on many Jews, including the disciples. Those on the way to Emmaus express the disappointment well when they say: "But we believed that he was the one to deliver Israel" (Lk. 24₂₁). But to the men at Qumran this should not have been a major difficulty. They knew how their martyred Messiah was to be vindicated in the time of resurrection. Still less was the Christian message unique in its concept of resurrection. It was not the concept but the event that gave the church the basis for a higher christology. Through a resurrection, which was itself an anticipation of the universal resurrection, Jesus had been made the Messiah, already enthroned on the right hand of God (e.g., Acts 2₃₄). The messianic character of his earthly ministry was thereby reinforced and the veil of the messianic secret was taken away. The way was also opened to a development which we mentioned earlier, where the First Coming more and more overshadowed the Second Coming.

If we add to this what was said before about the access to the Holy Spirit—another longed-for feature in the messianic expectations—we have one further point where the Christians enjoyed a higher degree of anticipation. The articles of Kuhn and Davies on this subject indicate that, although the Qumran texts speak about the Holy Spirit, they do so without the messianic precision of the New Testament, where the Spirit not only in Acts (e.g., 2₃₃) but also in Paul (e.g., 2 Cor. 3₁₇) is the Spirit of the Messiah, given to his people in the new dispensation.

Now it is time to pause and ask what we have been doing in this comparative study of the two sects. We have tried to take seriously the "episode" aspect which Edmund Wilson has emphasized. We have tried to unearth the pattern of thought within which it all actually happened as an episode, on the stage of Palestinian history. We have applied categories which were not arbitrarily chosen for apologetic or modern biographical purposes. We have tried to understand the issues as they appeared to those involved as well as to their contemporaries. And we have found that even where the claims and the tenets differed this was not a difference in ideas or in the structure of thought but that there were at some points different degrees of fulfillment, different claims as to how much of the ultimate consummation was present as a gracious and joyous anticipation of the one great event which to Christians and Essenes alike was yet to come.

Nothing has been said about what John the Baptist, Jesus, and the church might have borrowed from the Essenes. It is significant that such a question never forced itself upon us as long as we devoted ourselves to their own pattern of thought. That does not mean, however, that our approach has proved such questions to be irrelevant. We should only know that in raising them we ask questions which would have been strange and irrelevant to those originally concerned. And yet those questions must be asked—for historical reasons. In our human curiosity we want to know. The following essays will furnish such information plentifully. But it is hard to see how the authority of Christianity could depend on its "originality," i.e., on an issue which was irrelevant in the time when "Christianity" emerged out of the matrix of Judaism, not as a system of thought but as a church, a community. But one may hope that Christianity of today is spiritually and intellectually healthy enough to accept again the conditions of its birth.

It is true to say that the Scrolls add to the background of Christianity, but they add so much that we arrive at a point where the significance of similarities definitely rescues Christianity from false claims of originality in the popular sense and leads us back to a new grasp of its true foundation in the person and the events of its Messiah.

Only in this sense is it true to say that the difference between the two sects is one of messianology/christology, or that it is Jesus that makes the difference. The roots, the prophecies, the concepts were the same. But different things happened. Jesus did not come with a new doctrine about love for the sinners, but when he came he was received by sinners and rejected by the righteous. These episodes created a new doctrine and a new climate among men, once the episodes were transformed into authoritative acts and sanctions from God, i.e., once he was hailed as the Messiah risen and enthroned. The Teacher of Righteousness suffered persecution and injustice and the community held a high doctrine about its Council as the ones chosen to atone for the people (1 QS viii, 6). But in the light of the resurrection, the death of Jesus was transformd into an atoning suffering of an ultimate and cosmic significance. Thus it was the higher degree of anticipation, i.e., a relative difference, which historically gave the church its Magna Charta to apply the heavenly forgiveness already here and now, for those who accepted its Messiah. And, finally, it was this higher degree of anticipation which gave the church the possibility to spread among the Gentiles. This was not a new "idea," a universalism of modern structure. It belonged to the eschatological expectations of the Jews that when Messiah had re-established his nation then the Gentiles would come and worship with the Jews on Zion.[31] Once more it is the resurrection of Jesus which gives enough of an anticipation to warrant the church to move boyond the limitations of the very words of its Master who as the Messiah *designatus* had said: "Do not go to the Gentiles." The relative difference in anticipation led to what appears to us as an absolute difference in ideas.

# II

# The Significance of the Qumran Texts for Research Into the Beginnings of Christianity*

OSCAR CULLMANN

The French historian Ernest Renan took the position that Christianity began as a sort of Essenism, "an Essenism which succeeded on a broad scale." For its curiosity value, one might also mention the fact that E. Schuré, the author of *Les grands initiés,* held to the thesis, without proof of course, that Jesus had been initiated into the secret doctrines of the Essenes. Neither Renan or Schuré could have known anything about the Dead Sea texts. That the Essenes did have secret doctrines was known from the descriptions given by Josephus and Philo, and it is confirmed now by the Qumran manuscripts. However, that Jesus was initiated into these secret doctrines, as a member of the Essene Community, is pure and groundless speculation, for we have not the slightest hint on the subject, either in the New Testament or in Jewish writings. Whether it is permitted—on the basis of the relatedness of Essene thought, now better known, to Jesus' teaching—to conclude indirectly that Jesus was acquainted with the thinking of the sect is a question we shall deal with later.

At the outset, however, I should like to emphasize that we must distinguish between the two questions: Was Jesus an Essene? and, Was there a connection between the Essenes and the first Christians?

It has in fact always been thought, independently of the problem

* Reprinted from *Journal of Biblical Literature* 74 (1955), pp. 213-26.

of the Essenes, that primitive Christianity found its origins not in official Judaism but in some more or less esoteric offshoot; this belief does not involve a denial that primitive Christianity added something essentially new, in contrast with its Jewish origins.

In my book on the Pseudo-Clementines, Jewish-Christian writings whose oldest elements (the "Kerygmata Petrou") preserved very early material from primitive Jewish Christianity, I defended the thesis that there existed, on the edge of Judaism, a sort of Jewish Gnosticism, which, judged externally, must be considered the cradle of earliest Christianity.[1] Since this Jewish Gnosticism already shows Hellenistic influence, we must view the entire question of Hellenism vs. Judaism from a different perspective than has become habitual. In the past, as soon as Hellenistic influences could be shown in a New Testament writing, the immediate conclusion was: this must have been written very late. The Gospel of John is a case in point. Since Hellenistic elements are found in the Gospel, it was believed that a very late origin was proved. Behind this false conclusion stood a false, or at least too schematic, conception of the origin of Christianity; namely, the idea that at first Christianity was merely Jewish, and then later became Hellenistic. This basic error led to a series of further errors, such as the supposition that the so-called Gnostic heresy first sprang up late, in Hellenistic circles outside Palestine. The fact that Gnosticism, where we first encounter it in the New Testament, is closely connected with Judaism proves that this conception of Gnosticism is erroneous. There was a Jewish Gnosticism before there was a Christian Gnosticism, as there was a Jewish Hellenism before there was a Christian Hellenism.

The evolution which one generally supposes from an early narrow Judaistic Christianity to a later universalistic Hellenistic Christianity is an artificial *schema*, which does not correspond to historical reality. We shall see that both tendencies existed in the *primitive* church, and the history of primitive Christianity is the history of the interplay of these two tendencies, both of them present from the beginning in the Palestinian church.

That Palestinian Christianity could have taken over certain Hellenistic elements reaching beyond the national bounds of Judaism was known before the discovery of the new texts. Now, however, we have a clear confirmation. We knew it before, thanks to the rediscovery of the so-called Mandean texts and their publication by M. Lidzbarski in the 1920's which acquainted us with a pre-Christian baptist movement that had spread over Palestine and Syria[2] and must somehow have had an effect in the disciples of John the Baptist as well as on those of Jesus. Further, there had to be some link between early Christianity and the somewhat esoteric late Jewish Enoch literature. For the form of messianic hope, in which the expectation of the Son of Man coming on the clouds of Heaven replaces the Jewish national expectation of a Jewish Messiah, is found only on the fringe of Judaism, especially in the Enoch literature; and this form of messianic hope is the one to which the Gospels testify.

But until now, we have lacked the outer frame of reference within which it would be possible to conceive of a connection between primitive Christianity and this specially slanted sort of Judaism. Does the Essene sect, now better known, offer us this frame of reference?

At first glance there seems to be a parallel with the New Testament in the fact that the "Teacher of Righteousness" of the new texts is the object of special reverence, which seems to attribute to him near-messianic status. From Acts 5 and Josephus we learn that before Jesus men like Judas and Theudas had come forward with claims to special authority. Yet we shall see that it is precisely at this point that Christianity differs from the Jewish sects. The points of contact seem to me to lie, primarily, not in a relatedness between the Teacher of Righteousness and Jesus, nor in the way their Person and Work may have been conceived by their first disciples, but rather in their other doctrines and above all in the life and organization of the two communities, although we find differences here, too.

We shall first speak of the relatedness and the differences in life and teaching.

*The Life.* First, we point to the name. The Jewish sect called itself, among other things, the "New Covenant." In Greek this would be *kaine diatheke,* which can in turn be translated "New Testament." Then there is the designation "The Poor" which, in these texts, has become almost a proper name for the group.[3] But we also find this term in the New Testament as a name for the first Christians, namely, in Romans and Galatians, and later it was applied to the remnant of the Jerusalem congregation, the Ebionites. "Ebionites" means precisely "The Poor."

The *common meal* of the Qumran sect exhibits much similarity to the eucharistic feast of the first Christians.[4] It has a purely sacral character, and only after a two-year novitiate were new members permitted to participate. A blessing was pronounced on the bread and wine. The Essenes perhaps also had a meal without wine,[5] of which there are traces in the "breaking of bread" of the early church. In one Qumran fragment (1 QSa) we read of the presence of the Messiah during the meal.

The baths, or *baptisms,* which stand in the center of the cultic life of the Jewish sect are different from Christian baptism, as also from the baptism of John, in that they are repeated. Still, in a certain sense, they are parallel in that they served as a rite of initiation. The first admission to these baths was a sign of acceptance in the fellowship.

According to both Josephus and the new texts, the *community of goods,* regulated to the smallest detail, is typical of the Order. Here the parallel to primitive Christianity is especially tangible. Poverty is a religious ideal, in one group as in the other.[6] Yet we must also note at this point an important difference: in the Essene sect the community of goods is obligatory and organized. We read of the special office of administrator of the common fortune; whereas in the early church the community of goods was voluntary, as is clearly said in Acts. It is described as a working of the Spirit. Driven by the Spirit, one laid his possessions at the feet of the apostles. For this reason Peter called the deceit of Ananias and Sapphira a lie against the Holy Spirit. He tells them expressly that they could have kept their property, but that they must not pretend to have given everything when they secretly retained a part. This type of thing also happened in the sect's obligatory community of goods, as we see from 1 QS.

A further parallel: the groups of *twelve* apostles and seven Hellenists correspond to the organization of the sect,[7] where we hear of *twelve* plus three. Even the three priests may have their parallel in the three pillars of Gal.2₉ₜ.: James, Cephas, and John.[8]

*The Thought.* If we wish to compare the thought of the two groups, we must turn particularly to the *Gospel of John.* From the start it has been observed that more than the other New Testament writings, this Gospel belongs to an ideological atmosphere most closely related to that of the new texts.[9] The Johannine dualism of Light and Darkness, Life and Death, has its parallel in the Qumran texts. Corresponding to the Prologue of the Gospel, we have the passage in 1 QS (xi, 11) where the divine thought appears as mediator of creation. K. G. Kuhn has rightly concluded that the body of thought of the Qumran sect is, so to speak, the earth in which the Fourth Gospel plunges its roots.[10] Clearly, there will again be highly significant differences right at this point concerning the central position of Christ. All along the line we must insist on both the essential relatedness and the essential differences.

This applies as well to the teachings of Jesus as we find them in the Synoptic Gospels. There are many points of contact. The understanding of *sin* and *grace* in the new texts is not that of the Pharisees, but rather very near that of the New Testament. Actually, there are in the Rule similarities to the Sermon on the Mount.

The criticism of the Temple expressed by Jesus in the Synoptics (stated in even stronger form in John) corresponds to the Essenes' attitude toward the Jewish Temple and sacrificial worship.[11]

The differences first of all concern the attitude toward the *law.* For Jesus' freedom with regard to the law there is no counterpart in the Qumran texts. Whereas Jesus expresses clearly his claim to authority by the sharp antitheses of the Sermon on the Mount ("but I say to you"), looking beyond the law to its intention, we find nothing of the kind in the Teacher of Righteousness. On the contrary, the new texts are in fact the strongest expression of Judaism's legalistic piety. Legalism is driven to the utter limit. It is enough to compare Jesus' sayings and attitude toward the Sabbath with the Sabbath regulations of the Damascus Document (xi, 13 ff.). No greater contradiction can be imagined.

Jesus also rejected the asceticism which was so important to the Essenes. He was called a "glutton and winebibber." Nor does he have anything to do with secret doctrines. In fact, he commands his disciples to proclaim from the housetops that which he has taught them. This is the exact opposite of what was drilled into the members of the Qumran sect.

We find clear lines of relatedness to *Pauline* thought. Again it is the anti-Pharisaism of their theology which in a certain sense fits into the doctrine of justification. In the Habakkuk Commentary we note a passage relating justification to the Teacher of Righteousness in a way almost exactly equivalent to a decisive Pauline text. The well-known words of Habakkuk, "The just shall live by faith," is explained: "That means, he shall live by faith in the Teacher of Righteousness." Of course, we must point out at the same time the differences: this faith in the Teacher of Righteousness is not, as for Paul, faith in an *act of atonement* accomplished in the *death* of Christ for the forgiveness of sins. In fact, the concept of faith itself is different, containing nothing of the sense of opposition to the works of the law. The ethical or so-called paraenetic parts of Paul's epistles and other early Christian writings present the most striking parallels with analogous developments in the new texts.

Now, in what way can we *explain* the simultaneous close relationship and basic difference between the two movements? First, we should note that a movement can be affiliated with another and at the same time stand in clear opposition to it. Let us first ask whether evidences of external connection can be found. It is remarkable that the Essenes are mentioned nowhere in the New Testament although the Pharisees and the Sadducees appear very often, if only in the role of opponents. It would be false to assume therefrom that there could have been no contact between the Essenes and Jesus' first disciples. In fact, the opposite has been argued: the Essenes are not named, precisely because the first Christians were in close contact with them. Jesus and the apostles would have had no special need to combat them, since they stood so near to one another.

There is one possible way to conceive of Essene thought and practice as having found entry into the beginnings of Christianity through John the Baptist. We know from the Gospel of John that the first disciples of Jesus had previously been disciples of John the Baptist. Jesus himself seems to have first been a disciple of John. Not all the disciples of John subsequently went over to Jesus. We learn from the Synoptic Gospels that during the ministry of Jesus there still existed a group of disciples of John. Early Christian literature tells us further that after the death of Christ this baptist sect was in many ways a sort of rival of the primitive church.[12] The later Mandean writings certainly contain much old material[13] going back to this sect, which, after the death of Jesus, continued to consider John the Baptist as the true Messiah, and to refuse so to recognize Jesus (in fact, they declared him to be a false Messiah). Such ideas must have been especially current in the environment in which the Gospel of John was written, for this Gospel emphasized that John himself was not the Light, but that he came in order to testify to the true Light, which appeared in Christ. The Prologue of the Johannine Gospel combats implicitly the disciples of John the Baptist[14] and it is even possible to trace this polemical tendency throughout the whole Gospel. The disciples of John argued the supremacy of John over Jesus on the grounds that Jesus came *after* John. The Gospel answers by saying that in reality Jesus existed before the Baptist, since in the very beginning he was with God as the Logos.[15]

In spite of this argument, it is true that there existed a fellowship of disciples of John before there was a fellowship of disciples of Jesus and that, according to the Fourth Gospel, Jesus and his first disciples came from this baptist movement. The anonymous disciple in Jn. 1 is a former disciple of the Baptist. In Mt. 11₁₁ Jesus considers himself as a disciple of John. Indeed, in this passage, which is generally mistranslated, Jesus says: "The smaller (i.e., Jesus, as the disciple) is greater than he (i.e., John the Baptist) in the kingdom of heaven."[16]

Thus, if a connection between the Essenes and the disciples of John could really be established, we would have at the same time a link between the Essenes and the followers of Jesus. Such a direct connection, however, cannot be proved with certainty. John's baptism differed from theirs in that it was administered only once. Still, admission to baptism meant for the Essenes also admission into their fellowship, i.e., entrance into the life of the baptized. There is thus a parallel between John the Baptist and the Essenes, and John's baptism might have been derived from the already existent baptist movement. This may be confirmed by the fact that we find in the Mandean writings conceptions similar to those of the Qumran texts.[17] In addition, we read in the Gospel of Luke that John lived in the desert of Judah before beginning to baptize (3₂). This desert was where the Essene cloister was located, with its caves. It is impossible to think that John could have been there without coming in contact with the sect. So we must assume that, without being a member, he was influenced by them, even if he went on to found an independent messianic movement. Thus a relationship may also be seen in his asceticism.[18] The fact of John's origin in a priestly family should perhaps be mentioned too, when we think of the importance of the priests in the life of the sect.

It is difficult to say more on this question. At any rate, it may be possible in this way to explain the indirect influence of Essenism upon the beginnings of Christianity. In concluding this section, one point should be emphasized which may become important when we speak of other, perhaps more direct contacts between the Essenes and the Christians: on the one hand, there is the particular interest of the Fourth Gospel in John the Baptist and his sect; and on the other hand, there is the parallelism between its conceptions and those of the Mandeans.[19] Thus this Gospel is one possible link in the sequence: Qumran—John the Baptist—early Christianity.

With caution, we might find a further point of contact between the Jewish sect and the beginnings of Christianity. We have seen that the Essenes had a settlement in Damascus. We know also, from Paul himself, that after his conversion he remained in Damascus. Might he not have met members of the sect during his stay there? We cannot, however, answer with certainty, especially because we do not know when the Essenes came to Damascus.

It seems to me much more probable that a bridge between the Essenes and the early Christians is to be found in the Hellenists who are mentioned in the Book of Acts, and this is the particular hypothesis I shall try to establish in this article.[20] May not these Hellenists be the more direct link which we seek? They belonged to the original Palestinian church from the beginning; they are thus not a result of the Diaspora. They must have played a far greater role in the beginnings of Christianity than is immediately apparent from Acts. They were in fact the real founders of Christian missions, in that in the persecution following the death of Stephen (which they and not the Twelve suffered) they began to preach the gospel in Samaria. Universality was not introduced into Christianity first by Paul but by the Hellenists before him, of whom we know well only Stephen, who must have been an exceptional personality.

These Hellenists, like the Essenes, rejected Temple worship and for that reason were expelled from Jerusalem very early. The twelve were apparently not in agreement with their rejection of Temple worship; otherwise we could not explain how they were able to remain in Jerusalem after the outbreak of the persecution reported in Acts 8₁.

The Hellenists were soon left on the sidelines, and disappear from the Books of Acts. We find them again only in Acts 9₂₉, where we learn that Paul debated with them, and in Acts 11₂₀, where we read that the Hellenists from Cyprus and Cyrene addressed themselves to the Hellenists in Antioch.[21] The other Christian documents do not mention them, at least not directly, probably because the oldest Christian writings (besides the Johannine group) are based not on their witness but on that of the Twelve.

Generally, the "Hellenists" of Acts 6₁ are considered simply as Jews who spoke Greek, the "Hebrews" being Jews who spoke Aramaic. However, we have no evidence in any document for this meaning of the word. The Greek word from which "Hellenist" is derived *(hellenizein)* does not mean "to speak Greek" but "to live according to the Greek manner." Nor does the term indicate that they came from the Diaspora. Barnabas, who is a Cyprian, is not called a "Hellenist"; neither is Paul, nor are others. The embarrassment of the scholars who try to define the precise character of these Hellenists in Acts 6-8 may be seen in the Additional Notes of Foakes-Jackson and Kirsopp Lake, *The Beginnings of Christianity,*[22] which deals with this problem. Whatever one says, it cannot be proved that "Hebrews" refers to the language spoken by the people designated by this word. The question arises then whether these Hellenists are not Jews who differ from the official Judaism, showing tendencies, more or less esoteric, of a syncretistic origin. What other expression did the Jews have at their disposal to describe this tendency?

I have shown elsewhere[23] that the Gospel of John is particularly interested in these Hellenists and their pioneer missionary work in Samaria. In fact this Gospel even undertakes a rehabilitation of the Hellenists. I cannot repeat the whole argument here, but can only give the conclusions which seem to me very relevant for our discussion. In Jn. 4₃₈ Jesus says that not the apostles but *"others" will begin the mission to Samaria* and that the apostles will then *"enter into" the results of their work.* This corresponds exactly to the report in Acts 8. This passage tells us that the mission in Samaria was inaugurated by the Hellenists, especially by Philip, one of the Seven (who probably played the same role among the Hellenists as did the Twelve in the other part of the community). According to Acts 8₁₄, after the conversion of the Samaritans, the Twelve sent Peter and John to Samaria, who, so to speak, completed their conversion by the laying on of hands; thus they really "entered" into the work of "others." The "others" in Jn. 4₃₈ must then be these Hellenists, most of whom are anonymous. They were the true missionaries to Samaria.

Very often Luke and the Fourth Gospel report analogous traditions. Therefore it is not surprising that the Johannine Gospel also follows in this respect the Lucan tradition concerning the link between the Hellenists and Samaria, although its importance is minimized in the Book of Acts.[24]

It is certainly no accident that we find in John's Gospel a special interest in the Hellenists. We have already seen that this Gospel seems to have some connection with the sect of John the Baptist which it seeks to combat. We add now that it must have been formed from circles which, to say the least, were close to the Hellenists. Perhaps we may even dare to say more: might not the writer himself have belonged to the Hellenists within the early church?

Now we have already seen that, of all the early Christian writings, it is precisely the Gospel of John which shows the closest relationship to the Qumran texts. K. G. Kuhn came to this conclusion immediately after the first discoveries of the Dead Sea Scrolls.[25] On the other hand, we have known for a long time that the Fourth Gospel seems to be connected with other esoteric Jewish writings, such as the Odes of Solomon and rabbinical texts of a mystical character.[26]

We conclude that there is, first, a relationship between the Fourth Gospel and the Hellenists; second, a relationship between the Fourth Gospel and the Qumran sect. We still need to find an essential and characteristic point common simultaneously to the

Qumran sect, the Hellenists, and the Fourth Gospel. We have already touched on this point: the opposition to *Temple worship.* This is the main known characteristic of the Hellenists and the reason for Stephen's martyrdom. In his speech, Acts 7, he gives a summary of Israel's disobedience throughout its whole history. This disobedience culminates in the construction of the Temple, which is considered an act of the worst unfaithfulness.[27] Such an attitude provides the reason why the Hellenists had to leave Jerusalem, and why they turned to the Samaritans, who were also opposed to the Temple. As for the Essenes, we know that their attitude toward the Temple was not as favorable as that of the main body of Judaism, even if they did not go as far as the Christian Hellenists.[28] Further, we may observe that John's Gospel is more concerned with the question of the Temple than are the Synoptics. For this reason, already in the Prologue the incarnate Logos is indirectly contrasted with the "Shekina" ("glory") of God in the Temple. In the place of the Tabernacle, to which God's presence had been bound and to which v. 14 refers, steps the Person of Jesus Christ. Hence a verb is used in the Greek text which actually means "he *tabernacled* among us—and we saw his glory." The end of the first chapter (v. 51) tells us that the bond between heaven and earth is no longer limited to a holy place, such as Bethel to which there is reference (Jacob's dream), but is now in the Son of Man with angels ascending and descending upon him. This interest in the Temple is also probably the reason why John, in opposition to the Synoptics, reports the cleansing scene at the very beginning of the ministry. Here the words about destroying and rebuilding the Temple are spoken, not by false witnesses, but by Jesus himself. According to the explanation given by the Evangelist, Jesus himself, in his crucified and risen body, replaces the Temple.

The Johannine concern with the problem of worship may be shown throughout the whole Gospel. In my book, *Early Christian Worship,* I attempted to demonstrate that baptism and Eucharist are to be thought of as underlying the Johannine description of the life of Jesus. The Gospel illustrates the idea that worship in spirit and in truth should replace Temple worship. It is no accident that the saying about true worship is reported precisely in the story of the Samaritan woman. This story, in turn, contains the allusion to the Hellenists, those adversaries of Temple worship, who inaugurated the missionary work in Samaria, a country opposed for a long time to the Temple of Jerusalem.

The parallels between the Fourth Gospel and the Qumran texts concern not only the negative aspect of the problem of worship (opposition to the Temple) but also the manner in which this worship is replaced by the baptisms and the sacred meals. We must mention further the Johannine interest in the feasts of the Jewish calendar to which Christ gives new meaning. An analogous interest in the calendar may be seen in the Qumran texts.[29]

Confirmation of the connection between the Hellenists and the Gospel of John, on the one hand, and between both of these and esoteric Judaism, on the other, is provided by the fact that the name "Son of Man" (the application of which to Jesus goes back to Jesus himself, but was rapidly replaced by the name "Christ") is found in the following places: (1) in the Book of Enoch, perhaps an Essene book[30]; (2) in the last words of the Hellenist Stephen (whereas the author of Acts throughout the 28 chapters of his book never calls Jesus "Son of Man"); and (3) again in the Gospel of John, in which the title "Son of Man" is even more important than the title "Logos."[31]

The relationship between the thought of the Essenes and the Christian Hellenists and that of John's Gospel permits us to suppose that the group called "Hellenists" in the early Jerusalem church was in some way in contact with the kind of Judaism we find in the Qumran texts, as well as in the related books of Enoch, the Testaments of the Twelve Patriarchs, and the Odes of Solomon, which also belong to the Qumran pattern. I do not assert that these Hellenists were former Essenes (which is not impossible) but that they come from a kind of Judaism close to this group. It seems to me especially important that the author of the Book of Acts mentions precisely in chap. 6, which speaks of the Hellenists, the numerous "priests" who joined the church (v.7). We know that members of the Qumran sect were priests.

Why was this group of the early Christian community called "Hellenists"? I have already mentioned this difficulty of my thesis. It is much less a difficulty if we take into account that there was no other way to describe those who did not belong to official Judaism.

The name "Hellenists" was chosen because there was no other name for the representatives of what we call Hellenistic syncretism. If there is a connection: Essenes—Christian Hellenists—Fourth Gospel, we can better understand how we find, already in the New Testament, two such different forms of Christianity as those portrayed by the Synoptic and Johannine Gospels. For it is no longer possible to consider the Johannine form as later and not Palestinian, simply for the reason that it is farther from normative Judaism than the Synoptics. I repeat: both forms of Christianity existed from the beginning, because both found their roots in forms of Judaism present in Palestine. If we know the main-line Jewish form better, it is only because the other was rather esoteric in its leanings. The Hellenists were apparently the most vital and interesting part of the early Jerusalem church.

Next we may ask: Can we follow this same line beyond the early church, back into the time of Jesus himself? We can hardly suppose that there were in Palestine Hellenists, confessing Christ only *after* his death. Since they belonged to the church from the very beginning, we must assume that at least a number of them followed Jesus during his lifetime.

Can we take one more step and affirm that Jesus himself was somehow related to the Essenes? Might not the old and certainly false hypothesis that Jesus was an Essene be found to contain at least a kernel of truth, in light of the new information? Here I shall repeat the principle of interpretation which I have already mentioned: one movement may very well grow out of another and still stand in opposition to it. So it could be that, through John the Baptist, Jesus was acquainted with the Essene sect and took over from it certain elements of his thought. He shared their attitude toward the Temple. But the differences outweigh the similarities, as we have already observed in other connections. In Jesus' teaching, we do not find the legalism of the Qumran people; we do not find the role of the priesthood which was so important for them (e.g., the Teacher of Righteousness was a priest). Jesus' gospel has no asceticism and no tendency to secrecy. But this is still not the most significant point. What is decisive is what we call Jesus' self-consciousness. From what we know of the available texts, there seems to be a fundamental difference here. During his life, the Teacher of

Righteousness possessed great spiritual authority. He died, and after his death, was honored. But he died *as a prophet*. He belongs in the line of the prophets, who suffered as a *result* of their proclamation. Jesus refers to them in his plaint before Jerusalem: "Jerusalem, Jerusalem, thou that killest the prophets." But nowhere do we hear that the Teacher of Righteousness voluntarily took upon himself the mysterious role of the Suffering Servant, suffering vicariously for the sins of the world. So far we have heard nothing in the new texts of an atoning death. Nor do the Qumran Hymns, published recently by the Hebrew University, speak of an *atoning* death. Yet this is the most important aspect of Jesus' self-consciousness. That the Teacher of Righteousness also suffered death because of his priestly and prophetic activity is not the same thing, and is in no way parallel to the conscious relation to the figure of the Servant which is basic for Jesus. That *at the same time* Jesus expected to return as the Son of Man, on the clouds of Heaven (an expectation which brings him close to the Book of Enoch), and expected also to suffer as the Servant of Yahweh—that is what was new and unheard-of.

We have seen that the Fourth Gospel is in many respects related to the Qumran sect, probably by way of the Hellenists of the early church. It is understandable, therefore, that this Gospel also shows clearly the sharpest difference between the two groups, which we find in the area of christology. I believe that the tenth chapter of the Gospel has in mind such a figure as the Teacher of Righteousness when Jesus is reported as saying, "All those who have come before me are thieves and robbers . . . because they care nothing for the sheep." Verse 18 is thus especially important, as it clearly distinguishes Jesus' work from that of the martyred prophet: "No one takes my life; I lay it down of my own accord." The emphasis with which this is said makes clear that Jesus' death is being interpreted in intentional contrast to another conception.

Unavoidably, the Teacher of Righteousness has drawn attention to himself and raised the possibility of drawing parallels with Christianity. In spite, however, of all the historical and theological lines of contact, the difference remains in the Person, Teaching, and Work of Jesus, and in the role played by his death in the theological thinking of the early church. Is it not significant that Josephus and Philo can both describe the Essenes in detail without once mentioning the Teacher of Righteousness? Without the Damascus Manuscript and the Qumran texts, we would know nothing at all of such an Essene Teacher. Would it be possible to describe primitive Christianity without naming Christ? To ask the question is to have answered it. This shows that the Person of the Teacher did not possess the same significance which Jesus had in the early church, and this is to be traced to Jesus' own self-consciousness.

Thus also Pauline theology, in spite of parallels, is fundamentally different from that of the Qumran texts. One can describe the doctrine of the Essenes without a word about the death of the Teacher of Righteousness. The doctrine of Paul, on the other hand, can never be described without orienting everything around the central saving act of the expiatory death of Christ. Faith for Paul is faith in this act of atonement fulfilled by Another.

The decisive difference in christology leads us to observe a further and consequent originality of the early church. Faith in the atoning work of Christ brought the Holy Spirit into the church. Only in relation to the Holy Spirit can we understand the fellowship, worship, community of goods, and leading, which were characteristic manifestations of the Spirit. Instead of the Spirit, the Qumran movement had an organization. The way in which the community of goods was managed among them is only one example. The working of the Spirit in the early church was possible only on the basis of an intense faith in the real saving efficacy of that which Jesus accomplished for the world. Miracles of healing, speaking in tongues, i.e. the things which gave primitive Christianity its specific character and without which it would be unrecognizable, are to be understood in no other way.

It is not sufficient that the Qumran sect had a Teacher of Righteousness and wrote about the Spirit: the Teacher and the Spirit do not dominate all the thought and life of the community as Jesus and the Spirit which is given to those who believe in him dominate Christianity. This driving impulse is lacking in the Qumran sect, and that is the reason that the Essenes ceased to exist after the Jewish wars in A.D. 70,[32] whereas Christianity could survive that crisis, and from then on even more effectively spread over the world.

# III

# John the Baptist in the New Light of
# Ancient Scrolls*

W. H. BROWNLEE

John the Baptist is to the average Christian a strange but graphic figure, pictured on Sunday-school cards as a sort of semisavage, wearing only leather breeches and a coarse camel's-hair cloak thrown about him. His diet of locusts and wild honey is difficult to imagine, particularly the locusts, so that there is a common interpretation of the locusts as the beans of the locust tree. I have found this interpretation even among the Arab Christians of Palestine, where the locusts eaten by John the Baptist are identified with the beans of the carob tree, which may possibly belong to the locust family. If this were the case, why were not these locusts called pods, just as they are in the parable of the prodigal son (Lk. 15$_{16}$) where the "pods" are those containing carob beans? My friend Najib Khoury, now of Bethlehem, explained to me in Jerusalem back in 1948 that the carob withstands drought so well that even in the driest years there is at least a poor crop of them, so that Jesus' parable which portrays the availability of carob pods in a famine year is understandable. The fare of John the Baptist, however, as frequently pointed out, represents the life of the desert nomad, who does not hesitate to eat small insects, including locusts, or grasshoppers. One will note that this food represents that which grows by itself in nature, without cultivation or breeding. John the Baptist may have felt that by living with nature in the raw he was living close to God. This may represent a repudiation of civilization as corrupting.[1]

* Reprinted from *Interpretation*, 9 (1955), pp. 71-90. This essay has been brought up to date by considerable revision by the Author.

The scene of John's ministry was in the Wilderness of Judea, generally defined as the stretch of hot desolate hills along the west bank of the Dead Sea. According to the ancient boundary lines of the twelve tribes, Judaea (the territory of Judah) would extend only a little north of the Dead Sea; but since similar terrain continues beyond that point, the Gospel writer (Mt. $3_1$) may have used the term loosely to include some of the desolate region farther north. In fact the old tribal boundaries were now obsolete and all the territory governed by Pilot (Lk. $3_1$) was called Judaea. What was John doing there? One readily recalls the explanation found in all four Gospels that he was fulfilling Is. $40_3$; and Jn. $1_{23}$ quotes John himself as saying: "I am the voice of one crying in the wilderness, 'Make straight way of the Lord,' as the prophet Isaiah said."

Now, in the territory most strictly defined as the Wilderness of Judaea are a series of caves from which have come the Dead Sea Scrolls, more accurately called the Qumran Scrolls after the name of the wady, or ravine, cutting through that section of cliff. Here some of the Essenes lived in tents and caves; and here they had community buildings where they went for study, worship, bathing, eating, and fellowship one with the other. Why were they out in the wilderness? The answer is found in their own Manual of Discipline brought to light by the discovery of these now famous scrolls:

They will separate themselves from the midst of the habitation of perverse men to go to the wilderness to clear there the way of the Lord, as it is written:
"In the wilderness clear the way of the Lord;[2]
Level in the desert a highway for our God."
That means studying the Law which He commanded through Moses, so as to do according to all that was revealed time after time and according to that which the prophets revealed through His Holy Spirit (1 QS viii, 13-16).

This clearing, or preparing, of the way of the Lord was the preparation of the Messianic Age. The idea was that if they were good enough God would honor them by sending them a Messiah (or Messiahs) who, like Moses (cf. Deut. $18_{18}$), would make his appearance in the wilderness in order to lead his people into the promised land (cf. Mt. $24_{26}$) of the Messianic Kingdom. This particular stretch of wilderness was chosen, rather than the Wilderness

of Sinai, because Is. $40_3$ used words for wilderness which sometimes designated the basin of the Dead Sea (*arabah*), or even more
specifically a district west of this lake (*midbar* as in Josh. $15_{61}$
and II Chron. $26_{10}$). Here would the Lord's glory be revealed in
the work of the Messiah(s). The study and practice of the Law and
the Prophets would bring in this glad day.

John must have been familiar with Essene thoughts regarding the
coming of the Messianic Age. He too believed that the way was to
be prepared in the wilderness and that the Messiah would make his
appearance there (Jn. $1_{33}$). He may even have been reared by Essenes,
for Luke represents John as having gone out into the desert as a
mere boy (Lk. $1_{80}$). How did he live out there? Who took care of
him? How could he receive there proper training for his prophetic
mission? One prominent American scholar has branded this detail
as "intrinsically improbable" and serving "largely to fill a blank
period in earlier accounts of his life."[3] Now, the ancient Jewish
historian Josephus describes the principal group of Essenes thus:
"Marriage they disdain, but they adopt other men's children, while
yet pliable and docile, and regard them as their kin and mould them
in accordance with their own principles."[4]

In view of John's thorough acquaintance with Essene thought, it
is not at all improbable that he spent his childhood in the wilderness, being brought up by the Essenes. What it was that led his
parents to send him there we do not know. It may be that they
themselves, though not Essenes, were sympathetic with them.[5] Or it
may be that they died of old age (Lk. $1_7$) and he was taken by the
Essenes to rear after the death of his parents. Moreover, this life
with the Essenes does fill a very important blank in the life of John
the Baptist. It need not be regarded as merely fanciful or imaginary,
for it explains in a marvelous way the teaching of John the Baptist.
Any critic who is skeptical of the nativity story can of course allow
for the possibility of its embodying true historical traditions, such
as the fact that John was the child of his parents in old age and
that he grew up in the desert.

Now, John was not satisfied with the way the Essenes were seeking
to fulfill Is. $40_3$. They were preparing only themselves for the
Messiah's coming, not the nation. His attention was caught by the
reference to the "voice crying in the wilderness." As he understood

the passage, the Essenes should become a voice calling the nation to repentance. We do not know by what propaganda means the Essenes were able to attract new members to their monastic communities. They too believed in the importance of repentance, however, and called themselves the "penitents of Israel." Still they believed in complete separation from society, not allowing outsiders to attend their meetings, and keeping much of their teaching secret. To join their group required a period of indoctrination and two years' probation. John felt that this was not being a "voice." The day came when he turned his back upon them and went out alone to become that voice. He did not forsake the wilderness, but he found places in the wilderness where he could meet people and preach to them the necessity of preparing for the impending messianic judgment. One of his centers of activity was "Bethany beyond the Jordan" (Jn. 1$_{28}$). This was a trading post at an important ford of the river. All was desert there except for a ribbon of green along the very edge of the Jordan. Here travelers came and went. and at the festival seasons when people went up to Jerusalem, he would encounter great crowds. However, he quickly gained a great reputation as a prophet, so that people in throngs sought him out, to hear firsthand his proclamation of the imminent kingdom of God.. Later he removed to "Aenon near Salim" (Jn. 3$_{23}$), which W. F. Albright locates in the semi-arid region southeast of Shechem, at springs near the head waters of Wadi Farah.[6] This may represent an attempt to awaken the Samaritans to the need of repentance.

One issue strongly debated among scholars is where John got his ideas for baptism. Does it represent a pagan influence, borrowed from some Oriental mystery cult? Was it original with John? Or was it an adaptation of some previous Jewish rite? We will be safer to assume the last position, for originality usually starts with ideas which are not entirely new, and John was not one to borrow directly from the Gentile world. Some have suggested that John adapted proselyte baptism as practiced in the synogogue. Proselyte baptism seems to have been introduced to wash away the defilement believed to cling to one who had not previously been a Jew, a defilement which had befallen him through failure to observe the Jewish ceremonial law. It thus marked his turning from paganism to the service of the true God, and his introduction into the community of

God's people. The originality of John would be in his insistence that this rite be applied, not only to proselytes, but to persons who were born Jews. If so, this would imply that the whole nation was apostate and sinful and if it was to become the people of God it must enter the society of God's people through repentance and baptism. This is an idea so radical that some scholars have shied away from such a position, regarding this to be too extreme a view to attribute to John the Baptist. Yet John uses some rather severe language in the Gospel accounts (Mt. 3₇, Lk. 3₇): "You brood of vipers! Who warned you to flee from the wrath to come? Bear fruit that befits repentance, and do not presume to say to yourselves, 'We have Abraham as our father'; for I tell you, God is able from these stones to raise up children to Abraham." Being a descendant of Abraham, according to the flesh, is here not enough. One must have the character of Abraham if one is to be counted among God's people.

Now, this severe indictment of Jewish society as utterly corrupt and as outside the pale of God's people is precisely characteristic of the Essenes. In one of the hymns from Qumran (1 QH v, 27 f.), the enemies of the sect are branded as "sea serpents," "dust crawlers," and "serpents that cannot be charmed." The Qumran folk regarded all those outside their communities as utterly defiled and as belonging to the realm of Belial, or Satan; whereas they with their religious strictness and frequent ablutions were the true Israel. They could not worship at the Temple for it was in the hands of corrupt priests; but they had priests of their own who conducted their worship. Their only sacrifices were the lustral ones, which alone according to the law were legitimately performed away from the sanctuary. The sacrifice for the cleansing of a leper was among these (Lev. 14₁₋₉; 14₄₈₋₅₃); but the most common was the sacrifice of the red heifer (Num. 19). The ashes of the heifer were used for the preparation of a purifying water for the removal of uncleanness. It was also a sin offering. Since this heifer was slain "outside the camp," it was especially suited to the needs of the Essene community in its self-exclusion from the Temple. However, the blood of the heifer was sprinkled in the direction of the sanctuary, "toward the front of the tent of meeting." The Holy Water prepared with the ashes was called "water for impurity"; and this water is mentioned more than once in the newly discovered Essene Manual of Discipline. Josephus had written this puzzling description of the Essenes: "When they send what they have dedicated to God into the temple, they do not offer sacrifices, because they have more pure lustrations of their own; on which account they are excluded from the common court of the temple, but offer their sacrifices themselves."[7]

Joseph M. Baumgarten has noted that the sacrifices of the Essenes seem to be equated with the "more pure lustrations."[8] He therefore posits a rather free use on the part of Josephus in his employing of the verb "offer sacrifices," taking it to mean simply "worship." However, when we keep in mind the lustral sacrifices which were performed away from the Temple, Josephus' description of them as "lustration" is readily explained. The Essenes regarded their lustrations as "more pure," because the law had specified (Num. 19₉) that only a "man who is clean" should gather up the ashes of the heifer; and, in their belief, the only ceremonially clean men were members of their order.

Now, a reading of Numbers 19 reveals that this "water for impurity" was intended for frequent use. It was not the initiatory rite, introducing one into the society of God's people. The Essenes doubtless used it frequently. This, however, was not their only ritual washing. The Manual mentions others, including washing in seas and rivers. There was probably also an initial bath taken by one who was admitted to the community after two years' probation. Concerning this rite the Manual seems to speak when it warns that the unrepentant may not participate: "These may not enter into water to be permitted to touch the Purity of the holy men, for they will not be cleansed unless they have turned from their wickedness, for uncleanness clings to all transgressors of his word" (v, 13 f.). Though this is negatively stated, it may well imply that for the penitent the entrance into this society of "holy men" was by "entering into water."

Among the marvelous discoveries at Khirbet Qumran are a number of well-constructed cisterns. Some of them were outside the sacred compound, below the terrace, whereas others were inside. These were fed by an aqueduct which conducted the rain water from the hills above the terrace to the cisterns of the holy community. The sect's fondness for ritual ablution, as shown by its own literature, suggests that at least some of these cisterns were utilized for ritual washings. The construction of one principal indoor cistern is very suggestive. There are fourteen steps leading down into the pool. One notes that this is a multiple of the sacred number seven. The steps are further subdivided into smaller groups, so that if the sectaries had desired to perform certain prayers, say at the seventh or the tenth step, they could have determined by a single glance the number of the step upon which they were standing. Near the top, the stairs were railed off into four passage ways. This may have served to guide those going down into the water. Thus it would have been possible for two rows to proceed down the outside and to return up the center, the divisions near the head of the stairs marking the course they should take. The point we make here is the admirable suitability of especially this cistern for ritual lustration; but one must not forget that other cisterns elsewhere in Palestine (as R. de Vaux reminds me) were similarly constructed without any implied liturgical use. It is the nature of the society, rather than the distinctiveness of the cisterns themselves, which makes it appear probable that at least a few of them may have served as bathing pools (i.e., as piscinas).

Baths were taken regularly by the Essenes, according to our ancient historians. Yet one's full admission into the community was probably marked by a bath which marked him off henceforth as belonging to the "holy men." Anyone joining the true Israel had to come that way. This would be an exact parallel to John's extreme demand that everyone, not simply proselytes from the Gentile world, receive baptism. John's originality would be the great stress upon the once-for-all baptism of the initiatory rite and in extending a public invitation for all to repent and to be baptized. John's baptism was also an administered rite, not a self-ablution. Yet even Pharisees had many different ritual lustrations, so that it would probably be a mistake to suppose that baptism represented the only lustration practiced by the disciples of John.

What was the value of John's baptismal rite? Aside from the information in the Gospels, we have a brief statement by Josephus: "For John was a pious man, and he was bidding the Jews who practiced virtue and exercised righteousness toward each other and piety toward God, to come together for baptism. For thus it seemed to him, would baptismal ablution be acceptable, if it were used not to beg off from sins committed, but for the purification of the body when the soul had previously been cleansed by righteous conduct" (*Ant.* 18, 5, 2).

This does not appear to be in full harmony with Mk. 1₄, which states that John preached "a baptism of repentance for the remission of sins." The inconsistency is to be accounted for, in part, by Josephus' attempt to portray John in the best possible light. By denying that John's baptism was intended "to beg off from sins," he probably implies the interpretation that the fulfillment of the moral conditions for cleansing is what does bring remission of sins, not baptism per se. Moreover, in the Gospel repentance is stressed as quite essential; and it must have fruits that befit repentance. The evangelical word "repent" was avoided by Josephus, but amendment of life is involved in his reference to the previous cleansing of the soul.

On the other hand, unless it be in the vague reference of Jn. 3₂₅,[9] the Gospels say nothing about John's baptism being for the purification of the flesh on the part of one whose soul had been previously purged from sin; but precisely this is what the Essenes taught with regard to the validity of their lustral rites. An important passage of the Manual reads (iii, 3-9):

> He cannot be *justified* while he conceals his stubbornness of heart
>     and regards darkness as ways of light.
> While in iniquity, he cannot be *reckoned perfect,*
> he cannot purify himself by atonement,
>     nor cleanse himself with water-for-impurity,
>     nor sanctify himself with seas or rivers,
>     nor cleanse himself with any lustral water!

Unclean! Unclean! shall he be as long as he rejects God's laws so as not to be instructed by the community of His counsel. For it is through the spirit of God's true counsel . . . all his iniquities will be atoned . . . and through a holy spirit disposed toward Unity in His truth that he will be cleansed of all his iniquities, and through an upright and humble spirit that his sin will be atoned, and through the submission of his soul to all God's ordinances that his *flesh will be cleansed* by the sprinkling of water-for-impurity and by the sanctification of himself with purifying (or rippling?) water.

In summarizing this passage of the Manual one could easily reduce the moral conditions required for baptismal efficacy to sincere repentance and amendment of one's ways, in full harmony with the representation of John's baptism in the Gospels; or he could justify the language of Josephus, that the efficacy was for those "who practiced virtue, etc.," and that purification of the soul must precede the cleansing of the body. The thought of forgiveness in the above is constantly near the surface. Notice near the beginning the references to being "justified" and "reckoned perfect." The continuation of the above passage expressly mentions forgiveness for those who order their lives according to God's ways: "Then will he procure pardon before God through agreeable atonements; and this will become for him a covenant of eternal Communion." These lustral washings and sacrifices are by no means merely initiatory rites. Yet the moral qualities required for their efficacy as regards remission of sins are precisely the same as those John held necessary for baptism and divine forgiveness, and they testify to the important background of John's thought.

The greatest interest attaches to John's messianic expectation. What was it? Who is the one whom he calls "mightier than I"? Carl Kraeling is doubtless right in finding here a reference to the Messiah; for God would not naturally be referred to in this way, but rather as the Almighty. Yet this would be the might of God conferred upon his Messiah, for we find that "Mighty God" is one of the theophorous components of the messianic king in Is. 9₆: "and his name will be called Wonderful, Counselor, Mighty God, Everlasting Father, Prince of Peace." Those acquainted with the practice of the theophorous names in antiquity know that they did not deify the bearers, but expressed an aspect, or aspects, of the deity intended to be expressed through the lives of those thus named. Hence the Messiah is to be called "Mighty God," because the might of God is to be revealed in his life. Another possible translation is "Mighty Hero." The Septuagint, interestingly, compresses the whole messianic title of Is. 9₁₄ (9₆) to "Angel of Great Counsel." The avoidance of the word "God" in the translation was occasioned by the desire of holding to a supernatural Messiah without compromising monotheistic faith. One of the hymns of the Qumran Community refers to the Messiah as "a Wonderful Counselor with his (or His) might."[10] The antecedent of "his" is uncertain, but it is clear that the royal Messiah is to be mightier than ordinary mortals.

The Mighty One, when he comes, says John, "will baptize you

with the Holy Spirit and with fire" (Mt. 3₁₁-₁₂ par.). This is in a context of judgment by fire: "His winnowing fork is in his hand, to clear his threshing floor, and to gather the wheat into his granary, but the chaff he will burn with unquenchable fire." It has been suggested that the baptism with fire in John is related to Zoroastrian religion. Carl Kraeling explains this point thus:

> In Persian eschatology, the mountains which are made of metal melt at the end of the world, and the molten metal pours over the earth like a river. All men pass into this river of molten metal and in so doing are either purified or destroyed. Since in Persian thought this conception, already presupposed in the Gathas, is part of a well-coordinated system of eschatology, it is entirely possible that we have here the ultimate source of all these realistic interpretations of the function of fire in the final judgment, and thus also the source of Daniel's river of fire (Dan. 7₁₀) and its variant, the fiery breath of the Messiah.[11]

When Kraeling wrote it was purely hypothesis which would link this Persian thought with the ideas of Judaism. Since then the Manual of Discipline has been published with an important dualistic passage explaining the origin of evil in the world through God's creation of the angels of light and of darkness, a passage which is permeated with Zoroastrian ideas. Moreover, a passage from one of the Qumran hymns actually depicts for us the eschatological river of fire:

> And the bonds of death surrounded so that there was no escape,
> and the torrents of Belial overflowed all their banks.
> The fire consumes all beings who draw from it,
> causing to disappear from their rivers every tree, both green and withered;
> and it lashes with whirlwinds of flame
> until there is no longer any creature who drinks there.
> It consumes the foundations of asphalt and the base of the earth;
> the foundations of the mountains are the prey of burning,
> and it consumes even as far as the Great Abyss
> and the torrents of Belial break into Abaddon. . . . (1 QH iii, 28ff.).[12]

The finding of this passage in an ancient Jewish document of Palestine makes it seem quite reasonable to suppose that the baptism of fire of which John spoke may have been in the torrents of hell so vividly described here. Here, moreover, we see the justification of critical hypotheses.

But what of the baptism with the Holy Spirit of which John

spoke? Are we to delete it as secondary, treat it as a separate saying, or interpret it in connection with the baptism with fire? Mark, it will be noted, mentions only the baptism with the Spirit, so that this could represent one form of statement employed by John upon some occasions, and the baptism with fire could have been used by John in other contexts. In that case the combining of the two statements, as they are found in Matthew and Luke, could represent a conflation, with the reference to the Spirit secondary in that context, but not thereby foreign to the teaching of John. We would then interpret the baptism with the Spirit with reference to those who sincerely accepted John's baptism and reserve the baptism with fire for those who either refused or underwent hypocritically John's rite. At any rate, the Qumran literature leads us to believe that John preached a baptism with the Spirit which would be beneficial in character; for it mentions "a man" upon whom "God will sprinkle . . . the Spirit of Truth as purifying water," (1 QS iv, 21). Here the sprinkling with the Spirit is compared to a sprinkling with water, which is precisely analogous with the comparison we get in Mk. 1₈! The identity of the "man" involved has been a subject of dispute, whether a prophet-messiah or "each one" of the Essene society.[13] In either case the idea of a beneficent baptism of the Spirit is evident. It may be that this was expected to come in connection with the sect's lustral rites; for the gift of the Spirit is associated with a sprinkling of clean water in Ezek. 36₂₅f.; and in the messianic prophecy of the Testament of Levi 18₇ such a prospect is held out: "And the spirit of understanding and sanctification shall rest upon him in the water."[14] Certainty is not possible here; but we know Jesus' baptism with the Spirit was in connection with water baptism, and this appears to be the promise held out by Peter at Pentecost (Acts 2₃₈).

The parallel in the Scrolls is not complete, however, without a reference to the Messiah himself baptizing others with the Spirit; but texts pointing in that direction are uncertain. First of all there is the messianic reading of Is. 52₁₄f. in the complete Isaiah scroll from Qumran: "Just as many were astonished at thee, So have I anointed his visage more than any man, and his form than the sons of men, So shall he sprinkle many nations because of himself, and kings shall shut their mouths. . . ."

Here there seems to be the picture of an anointing which qualifies the Lord's Servant to sprinkle others.[15] That the Messiah is to impart the knowledge of the Holy Spirit to the righteous remnant, identified with the sect, has been inferred from the Damascus Document: "Yet in all of them He raised Him up men called by name, In order to leave a remnant to the earth, And to fill the face of the earth with their seed. And through His Messiah He shall make them know His holy spirit, And he is true, and in the true interpretation of his name are their names: But them He hated He made to go astray" (ii, 12f.).[16]

The issue is important, since all four Gospels represent John as teaching a messianic baptism with the Spirit; but unfortunately the text of the Damascus Document has been misread, and it is also partly corrupt. Y. Yadin has argued persuasively for the reading: "And He made them know—through the hand of His anointed (ones) with the Holy Spirit, and (through) His seers of truth—their exact names." This refers to the work of the Old Testament prophets, and not at all to any messiah(s)![17] Therefore we are left with only Is. 52₁₅ as a possible support of the Messiah's role in giving the Spirit. The issue at present remains in doubt.

In Essene expectation (at least at first) there was the expectancy of three great eschatological figures who would inaugurate the Messianic age: a prophetic forerunner, an anointed priest, and an anointed king. This is the commonly accepted interpretation of 1 QS ix, 11: "until the coming of a prophet and anointed ones of Aaron and Israel." The recently published column from an appendix to the Manual of Discipline mentions an "anointed one of Israel" in association with a "priest," and it is assumed that the priest is the "anointed one of Aaron," although the latter title is unattested. This interpretation is in accord with the recently published blessings of the society, also apparently once attached to the Manual of Discipline; for in them "the Prince of the Congregation" is clearly a royal Messiah with all the requisites of Is. 11, and there is a fragmentary benediction pronounced upon a priest whose role seems no less messianic.[18] It appears probable that the "prophet" came to be identified with the Teacher of Righteousness who had already come and that the future expectancy thus narrowed itself to that of the two Messiahs of Aaron and Israel.[19]

In the Damascus Document there are repeated references to "the messiah of Aaron and Israel." According to several scholars, the text should be emended to read "the messiahs of Aaron and Israel," in harmony with the Manual.[20] That would be very risky, however; for the singular reading may possibly represent a further narrowing of the expectancy from two Messiahs to one, a priest-king. There are many differences between the Manual of Discipline and the Damascus Document, of which this may well be another. A similar unification has occurred in the extant text of the Testaments of the Twelve Patriarchs, where this may be the result of Christian editing. The Damascus Document did not pass through Christian hands, however, and if its scribes were Qaraite Jews, as seems probable, it appears less likely that they would have altered the plural to the singular.[21] Thus we must reckon with the probability that in some Essene (or Covenanter) circles there was already a tendency toward a unified messianic expectation, prior to the time of John the Baptist and the ministry of Christ.

The messianic expectation of the Essenes would, in that case, tally in a remarkable way with the expectation of John the Baptist as recorded in the Gospel According to John. Higher critics have generally dealt severely with this Gospel's portrayal of John the Baptist, supposing the account there given to have been largely created out of thin air for a polemical purpose. There is undoubtedly a polemical purpose in the Gospel, designed to prove that Jesus, not John the Baptist, was the expected messianic "light" which was to come into the world. Wherever such a purpose exists, the critical theory is that one should discount its testimony *as compared with* other sources from which the polemical element is absent. This is sound criticism, to be sure, but it often fails to take into serious account not only the fragmentariness of our knowledge but also the possibility that the party engaging in the polemics might be telling the truth. Not always is it necessary to misrepresent the truth in order to uphold one's cause in debate, thank God! In fact the polemics would be all the more powerful if the arguments employed were founded upon historical fact. Now, the Fourth Gospel portrays both John and Jesus quite differently from the Synoptic Gospels and the differences lie in a special theological and apologetical approach. Are we to see here different, but legitimate interpretations of these men or mere theological creations with little or no connection with the historical figures? One of the most revolutionary results of the Scroll studies is that the language and ideas in the Fourth Gospel have profound connections with Essene thought as represented in the Manual of Discipline, so that one may *almost* say that in John's portrayal of Jesus we have the Essene Christ. That being so, the same would be expected with regard to the Baptist.

In the Baptist's witness as recorded in the Fourth Gospel ($1_{19\text{-}22}$) he denies that he is himself the Prophet, Elijah, or the Messiah; he affirms that he is only the "voice" referred to in Is. $40_3$. That the son of Zechariah should have been considered at all as a messianic candidate is to be explained by the expectancy of the priestly Messiah; whereas his denial that he is either the Prophet or Elijah is in accord with the probable Essene belief that this figure (the Prophet and Elijah presumed to be the same) had already come in the person of the Teacher of Righteousness. Here we have an important divergence from the Synoptic Gospels, where John is interpreted as Elijah—not only by the Evangelists' use of Malachi (Mk. $1_2$; Lk. $1_{17, 76}$; Mal. $3_1$; $4_{5t}$.), but also by the very words of Jesus himself (Mt. $11_{14}$; Mk. $9_{13}$; Lk. $7_{26t}$.). It is noteworthy, however, that even in the Synoptic Gospels John nowhere claims himself to be Elijah.

Is the Fourth Gospel truly representative, then, of the Baptist's own estimation of his ministry? The answer of critical scholarship seems to be "No." At least the difference in the Fourth Gospel is to be explained by its anti-Baptist polemics whereby John is demoted from being Elijah to a mere "voice" and "witness" to Jesus. However, in case of rivalry between Christian and baptist movements, it would have been wiser procedure not to demote John, but to give him as high a place as possible next to the Christ. It would have been to the advantage of Christian apologetics to use John as Elijah and to inject thereby a note of conciliation. Moreover, if Jesus had really taught that John was Elijah, would any Gospel writer have put within John's mouth a speech contradicting it unless he had been sure of his historical grounds? Either the Fourth Evangelist wrote sufficiently early that he did not know the Synoptic Gospels or he had an independent line of tradition which he valued more highly than the Synoptics in this matter. In either case his testimony as to John's own conception of his ministry is to be given serious consideration. John's ministry is well explained as that of a "voice," not in any vague sense that adheres to Is. 40₃ itself, but in the dynamic sense that here was a neglected function which the Essenes had not been performing as they sought to prepare the Lord's way in the wilderness. John's own deliberate assumption of this role, set forth only in Jn. 1₂₃, well explains how John, brought up in an Essene environment, came to break with it and to launch his own independent program. We do not know what henceforth his estimate of the Teacher of Righteousness was. It may be that he distinguished between the Prophet and Elijah, identifying the former with the renowned Essene teacher and the latter with the coming Messiah. Or, again, it may be that in departing from the Essenes he no longer accorded their master any important role. In any case, it is clear that we have represented in the rival positions of the Synoptic and Fourth Gospels one view in which the Prophet Elijah was expected to precede the Messiah and another in which he was not.[22] The Baptist, according to John's Gospel, adopted the latter view; and, as we shall see, this testimony is worthy of credence.

The most difficult saying of all ascribed to John is: "After me comes a man who ranks before me, for he was before me." This saying, given in two slightly different forms (Jn. 1₁₅, ₃₀), is in agreement with the Logos doctrine of the Fourth Evangelist's prologue. Hence it is discredited as a theological intrusion of the Fourth Evangelist. Yet before making this easy assumption we should first inquire as to what evidence there is that the Baptist could not have used this language. Our first approach should be to interpret the saying as it might possibly have been meant by the Baptist, and not according to the Logos terminology of the Evangelist; for it is apparent that the Evangelist has had sufficient regard for the matter of anachronism as never to have imposed this term upon the lips of either Jesus or John the Baptist. When Jesus speaks of his pre-existence, it is rather as the Son of Man or the Son of God, never as the Word.[23] The Son of Man never occurs at all in John's Epistles. It is surely a historical sense on John's part which accounts for this difference in terminology. Since the interpretation of the Messiah as the Logos seems to be original with the Evangelist, this would be the wrong approach for the interpretation of the Baptist's saying. One may think of the coming Son of Man, of whom it was easy to infer pre-existence from the pictures given in 1 Enoch. There he is pictured as one who will destroy the wicked with the word of his mouth (62₂); and this is further elaborated in 4 Ezra 13₁₀f.: ". . . but I saw only how he sent out of his mouth as it were a fiery stream, and fell upon the assault of the multitude which was prepared to fight, and burned them all up, so that suddenly nothing more was to be seen of the innumerable multitude save only dust of ashes and smell of smoke."

This fiery stream from the mouth of the Son of Man reminds us of the river of fire in which it would seem that John (as described in the Synoptic Gospels) believed the unrepentant would be baptized. Can it be that the Baptist who expected the Messiah to baptize with fire had in mind the Son of Man? In the case of 4 Ezra, we have a knotty problem as to dating, but R. H. Charles thinks the interpretation of the Son of Man is earlier than A.D. 70, and H. Gressman believes that back of the picture given there are very old traditional elements.

Another strong possibility is that the Baptist had in mind Elijah as the Messiah. Mal. 4₄₋₅ seems to interpret the Prophet like Moses (Deut. 18₁₅) as Elijah *redivivus*, and an examination of the Elijah legends leads one to note many striking resemblances between their careers, most notably in the revelation each received at Horeb and in the mysterious end to their lives in Transjordan. Mal. 4₄₋₅ also seems to interpret Elijah as the "Messenger of the Covenant" of Mal. 3₁, a verse where some of the language echoes Is. 40₃, so that it is easy to see why Jesus son of Sirach interpreted Elijah as the Servant of the Lord (as Joachim Jeremias has observed) for Elijah in Sir. 48₁₀ has as his eschatological mission the Servant's task "to raise up the tribes of Jacob" (cf. Is. 49₆).²⁴ Now Elijah, as Sirach notes, brought down fire from heaven three times (48₃; cf. 2 Kings 1₁₀, ₁₂; 1 Kings 18₃₈); and judgment by fire is to be a prominent part of his eschatological mission according to Mal. 3₂₋₃. It is clear therefore that in Sirach, and possibly in Malachi, the expected Messiah is to be Elijah in the role of the Servant of the Lord and that his judgment will be one of fire.

What was the Essene point of view here? Their sectarian literature as so far read and interpreted presents us with no clear references to Elijah or the Son of Man. It is possible that the Essenes who resided near Damascus thought that the Messiah would be their great leader, the Teacher of Righteousness *redivivus*—an interpretation first proposed by S. Schechter and recently championed by A. Dupont-Sommer; but this is uncertain. It is also possible that the Covenanters of Qumran, with their anticipation of two Messiahs, expected their teacher to return as the Priestly Messiah; but as yet we have no clear proof of this. From the manuscript fragments found in the Qumran Caves, it is certain that the Essenes possessed most of the Book of Enoch, but unfortunately there is no indication that the parables in which the Son of Man figures was known to them. J. T. Milik does not think that their absence among the identifiable fragments is accidental. Several manuscripts of the Wisdom of Sirach are represented also among the as yet unpublished texts.[25] Since this book offers no serious problems as to unity of authorship, we may assume that the Essenes were familiar with its portrayal of Elijah, and that John may have been influenced by it. In any case, the hypothesis which identifies Elijah with the Messiah in John's expectancy reasonably explains the divergent data of the four Gospels: (1) the messianic judgment of fire mentioned in the Synoptics, (2) the Baptist's avowed belief in the Messiah's preexistence according to the Johannine Gospel, and (3) his denial that he himself is Elijah as reported in the Fourth Gospel. The Synoptic interpretation of John himself as Elijah cannot be taken as evidence as to John's own understanding of his mission; hence we find no reason here for impugning the testimony of the Fourth Evangelist.

Another saying of John recorded in the Fourth Gospel is, "Behold the Lamb of God who bears away the sin of the world" ($1_{29}$). This saying is generally regarded by critics as unauthentic; for it seems impossible at first to harmonize this picture of the sacrificial lamb with that of one coming with a judgment of fire; but Rev. 11, a passage whose presence in a Christian document can only be explained as appropriated and adapted from an older Jewish work, presents us with the picture of two martyred prophets, namely, Moses and Elijah *redivivus*,[26] and for a period before their martyrdom "fire pours from their mouth and consumes their foes." In the old Jewish source, these prophets were two Messiahs, for they are explained as "the two olive trees and the two lampstands" of Zech. 4, and therefore as the "two anointed ones" of Zech. $4_{14}$. By means of this passage two contending explanations of the Prophet of Deut. 18₁₅ were joined, by allowing for both Moses (Rev. 11₅, ₆ᵦ; cf. Num. 16₃₅; Ex. 7₁₇, ₁₉) and Elijah (Rev. 11₅, ₆ₐ; cf. 2 Kings 1₁₀; 1 Kings 17₁) who are presented as persons essentially alike. This expectation of the return of Moses and Elijah lies back of the transfiguration experience of Jesus, but when they appear they bear witness rather to *his* suffering and resurrection, thus correcting the notion that it is they who must become martyrs. When it comes to Elijah's suffering, we have a reference in Mk. 9₁₃, which is highly significant: "But I tell you that Elijah has come, and they did to him whatever they pleased, as it is written of him." The only natural interpretation of this passage is that John the Baptist's martyrdom is in fulfillment of prophecy regarding a suffering Elijah. Where is such prophecy found? It may be that reference is made to a lost apocalypse.[27] In any case, this statement must ultimately rest upon an equation of Elijah with the Suffering Servant through interpreting Malachi after the manner of Sir. 48₁₀, as discussed above. It is noteworthy that Mk. 9₁₂ ᵢ. presents us with the martyrdom of both the Son of Man and Elijah in fulfillment of prophecy related to the Servant.[28] Thus again we see two different interpretations of the Suffering Servant loosely joined, by making a place for each of them in John and Jesus. These interpretations are probably older than the Gospel in which they are found, therefore, and are available to explain John's statements as to a pre-existent Messiah who is expected to suffer!

That John should have said, "Behold the Lamb of God who bears away the sin of the world," is not so impossible as it once seemed; for the Suffering Servant motif is one of wide application among the Qumran Covenanters. It was applied to the community as a whole, to a special group of twelve or fifteen men who actually (or ideally) headed the society, to the Teacher of Righteousness, and probably also to the Messiahs of Aaron and Israel. In the third column of the Hymns we are presented with a "pregnant one" whose birth pangs are coming upon her and who is about to give birth to the "Wonderful Counselor," quite certainly the Davidic Messiah of Is. 9₆. The "pregnant one" is surely the community as a whole with whom the author of the hymn identifies himself as its corporate head, and the birth pangs which issue in this wonderful birth are sufferings of the persecuted sect. The womb of this corporate mother is referred to as her "refining furnace." From this it appears certain that the pathway to messiahship was one of suffering.[29] Once one became the royal Messiah, however, there seems to have been no place for suffering. Messianic judgment would then be in place, if we infer aright from the blessing invoked upon the "Prince of the Congregation": "Destroy the earth with thy scepter, And with the breath of thy lips slay the wicked" (I QSb, v, 24).

Naturally the messianic candidate would remain unrecognized by his fellows until his spiritual endowment to become the Messiah; and this may well be referred to in an obscure, but probably messianic hymn studied by John V. Chamberlain[30]. "But a holy branch shoots forth, as a planting of sacred truth; In not being esteemed, and in not being known, is the seal of its secret" (1 QH viii, 10f.).

This as a characterization of the Messiah would be precisely in line with Is. 53$_{2-3}$, and also with the Baptist's teaching in Jn. 1$_{26, 33}$. The difficulty is one of ascertaining for sure whether the "branch" is corporate or messianic. In favor of the latter position is the use of the same word for "branch" employed in Is. 11$_1$, and also in the same immediate context the same word for "stump." In any case, it is evident from other passages that the suffering of the one destined to be the Davidic Messiah is in connection with the suffering of the corporate Servant of the Lord, and that therefore he would not at first be distinguishable from the community itself. But once his refining became complete he would be endowed with authority and power through his anointing with the Spirit. All this fits remarkably the teaching of John the Baptist as related in the Fourth Gospel, except that nothing is said of suffering as a purgation; and, as the Evangelist presents it, one would suppose that John's reference to the Lamb of God relates to the later crucifixion of Jesus. This difference may be explained as a Christian adaptation, or as evidence that John the Baptist modified the Essene messianic expectation, placing the prophetic ministry of fire before martyrdom, precisely as in Rev. 11. Here we must necessarily remain uncertain; but in either case, there are important Essene conceptions in John's messianic expectation.

In the composite picture of John the Baptist given above, one can see how essential all the sources are for a true understanding of him. From Josephus one would never suspect the messianic teaching of John recorded in the Gospels. In making his works appealing to a non-Jewish audience, Josephus omits all references to messianism. Similarly he does not present us with the messianic expectation of the Essenes or of the Pharisees. On the other hand, what Josephus says of the purificatory character of John's baptism is important supplemental information, which we are able to bring into harmony with the Gospel representations by means of the Essene Manual of Discipline. Almost every detail of the Baptist's teaching in both the Synoptic and the Fourth Gospels has points of contact with Essene belief, so that we are led not to place the Gospels in conflict and to choose between them, but to see them as fragmentary bits of information which are essentially supplemental in character. In order to explain the messianic judgment by fire and the Messiah's preexistence, it will be recalled, the Qumran Scrolls were not adequate. We had to consult material more strongly apocalyptic.

The most astonishing result of all is the validation of the Fourth Gospel as an authentic source concerning the Baptist. Concerning this, Bo Reicke, an outstanding Swedish scholar, now teaching at Basel University in Switzerland, has already written. In an important study which he prepared in Swedish, he strongly endorsed my previous views, expressed in the *Biblical Archaeologist*, September, 1950; but he went into the subject much more thoroughly.[31] Already in December, 1948, in a paper presented at the American Schools of Oriental Research program in connection with the national Society of Biblical Literature and Exegesis meeting in New York, I expressed myself guardedly, to the effect that time would probably validate "some such conclusion as that of Graetz" that it was John the Essene who proclaimed the coming Messianic Age in the wilderness. That position taken when the study of the Scrolls had only started, when the Manual of Discipline had been scanned but not translated, has been fully vindicated by the later studies of both Bo Reicke and myself and is not an unimportant item in the revolutionary "new look" of New Testament criticism.

In conclusion it must be stressed that the Qumran Scrolls do not disprove the validity of literary and historical criticism, for they confirm the reasonableness of some views previously reached by scholars. Moreover, they simply provide us with new data from which to construct our critical theories, the data which bring disparate bits of information into a composite picture in a way previously impossible. Not all contradictions will be, or can be, eliminated from our documents of the New Testament, as for example whether John was or was not Elijah. It is to be noted that the picture of John the Baptist as I have painted him finds all the Gospels wanting when it comes to accurate and full perspective regarding him; and the picture of him given here is indeed a critical reconstruction in itself! Biography in the sense of giving a complete, well-balanced portrait of a character was not a concern in antiquity. None of the Gospels attempts this for either John or Jesus; we have rather selections from a mass of data for given purposes, as the Fourth Evangelist confesses unashamedly regarding Jesus (Jn. 20$_{30}$ $_f$.; 21$_{25}$); and the same was true regarding John the Baptist.

In connecting John with the Essenes in his youth, there has been no intention of locating him specifically at Qumran, although this possibility cannot be excluded. The Manual of Discipline allows for society units of only ten men, of whom one must be a priest. John may have been connected with some such small unit residing elsewhere. As a priest he would have been qualified to teach and so perhaps he rose to leadership in his group; and when he received his call to be a prophet, his own cell group may have followed him. All this is sheer speculation about which we have no definite opinion. Of this alone we may be sure, that John was already in the Wilderness when called to become the "Voice," and that his life in the Wilderness since early youth involved some Essene associations.

It needs also to be stated that we have not entered into the question of John's relation to Jesus. On this question we are dependent upon the Gospel records alone, with all the possibilities of contradiction and harmony; but in the light of the present study we must not assume contradiction too readily. Nothing in the Qumran Scrolls can shed any light on this question; for, though the scrolls are a very important background for the interpretation of the Gospels, they can only attest the presence of certain beliefs in the milieu of John the Baptist which we cannot reasonably deny to him; they cannot attest Gospel events per se.

# IV

# The Two Messiahs of Aaron and Israel*

KARL GEORG KUHN

In the first published manuscripts from Qumran there was only one passage which spoke of the Messiah: "And they (the members of the Qumran Community) shall be ruled (or: judged) by the first laws with which the men of the community began to be disciplined until the coming of a Prophet and the anointed ones (*meshihe*) of Aaron and Israel" (1 QS ix, 10-11).[1]

It was most remarkable that the text had the unequivocally legible plural "the anointed ones." The different attempts to avoid this plural by plain emendation[2] could not find convincing support. Apparently the Qumran sect held a view which could not be reduced to the usual concept of "the Messiah."[3]

That this understanding is the correct one is now made clear in a more recently published text. Its two columns were first considered as the lost beginning of the Manual, but later they were rightly recognized as an independent text and given the name *Serek ha-edah*, "Order of the Congregation." (1 QSa).[4]

Both columns of 1 QSa depict the eschatological congregation of the people of Israel, and the way it was to be built and organized, according to Essene expectation. The title of the writing reads correspondingly: "This is the Order for the entire Congregation of Israel in the last days" (i, 1).

It is a vision of the eschatological Israel. The end of column ii depicts the communal meal of this eschatological Israel as an exact

* Reprinted with some revisions from *New Testament Studies* 1 (1954/55), pp. 168-80.

counterpart to the communal meal of the Essenes, as we find it described in 1 QS vi, 4-6.[5] The two meals are referred to with the very same terminology, "Preparation of the table (for eating) and of the wine for drinking." 1 QSa ii unfortunately contains several lacunae. Yet, for the most part, the context makes it easy to fill in the gaps. In the following, my insertions are given in square brackets.[6] In 1 QSa ii, 18 ff. we read (again with nearly identical expressions as in 1 QS vi, 4-6): "No one [is allowed to touch] the first part[7] of the bread or [of the wine] before the priest. For [he] blesses[8] the first part of the bread and of the wine [and touches] the bread before them."

This passage with its vision of the eschatological Israel and of the heavenly banquet continues—and now without any parallel in 1 QS vi—by referring to a Messiah: "And there[after shall] the Messiah of Israel reach for the bread, [and then (only) shall the whole congregation say the benedi]ction e[ach according to] his rank."[9]

The "Messiah of Israel" is unequivocally singular here. This title is not found in the Old Testament where the king is always called "the Messiah of Yahweh;" it is found three times in the Targum, but not related to "the Priest."[10] Thus we have good reasons for believing that it refers to one of the two Messiahs, of whom 1 QS ix spoke as "the Messiahs of Aaron and Israel." The Messiah of Israel stands here second in rank in relation to the priest. In such a context the reference to "the priest" takes on significance. It does not refer to just any priest, but to the presiding priest or the high priest. Used in this restricted sense, "the priest" is a frequent Old Testament designation for the high priest. So we find that when directions concerning sin-offerings are given in Lev. 4, the beginning of each passage ($4_{3-12, 13}$ ff.) uses the full title of the high priest, "the Anointed Priest" (ha-kohen ha-mashiah), the continuation of the passage ($4_{3, 5, 16}$) has only the succinct term "the priest." From this we may conclude that "the priest" of 1 QSa ii, 18 ff., likewise stands for the high priest, whose full title is "the Anointed Priest." We should conclude further that this priest, whose rank is above that of the "Messiah of Israel," is precisely the "Messiah of Aaron" mentioned in the formula "the two Messiahs of Aaron and Israel."

Thus 1 QSa envisages the eschatological Israel as having two Messiahs at its head, the "Messiah of Aaron," who is the high priest, and the "Messiah of Israel." The Messiah of Aaron stands above the Messiah of Israel: the Messiah of Israel ranks only second, "after him."

This finds confirmation in the immediately preceding section, 1 QSa ii, 12-17. Here, too, the text contains several lacunae, which, however, can be filled in with a fair degree of certainty, owing both to the context and to analogous passages elsewhere. In any case, the meaning of the section as a whole is clear. The order of ranks within the Congregation of Israel is given here, and the Messiah of Israel appears even here as second. "And then [comes the Messi]ah of Israel and before him are seated[11] the heads [of the tribes, each] according to his place of rank" (ii, 14-15).

In line 12 we read about a Messiah. Of him it is said that he is "the head of the entire Congregation of Israel and [before him are seated the sons] of Aaron, the priests." As the context clearly shows that this Messiah stands above the Messiah of Israel, he must be the Messiah of Aaron, the priestly Anointed One, as is also shown by the fact that he stands above the priests. Consequently we can fill in the lacuna in front of "the Messiah" in line 12 and read "the Anointed Priest" (ha-kohen ha-mashiah), that is, the full title of the high priest, as we found it in Lev. 4; and, just as in Lev. 4, the full title here given is followed in line 17 by the shorter term "the priest."

The following translation of 1 QSa ii, 12-17, is based on my reading of the manuscript itself.[12] Barthélemy's edition differs here and there from mine, but only in one instance is the difference of major importance for the interpretation.[13] The text shows with exactitude how strict the order of rank was within the community. In the following translation this is pointed out by the partitions.

I. (a) "[And the Priest], the Anointed One, shall come with them, [for he is] the head of the entire Congregation of Israel; (b) [and before him shall sit the sons] of Aaron, the priests; (c) and the [conveners] of the assembly (?), the honored men,[14] they shall sit [before him, each] according to his place of rank.

II. (a) "And then [shall come the Messi]ah of Israel; (b) and befor him shall sit the heads [of the tribes, each] according to his place of honor, according to [their . . .] in their 'camps' and their march formations[15]; (c) and all heads [of the houses of the Congrega]tion, together with the wi[se men of Israel] shall sit before them, each according to his proper place of rank."

The entire passage shows us with complete certainty the concept of two Messiahs: (1) the Messiah of Aaron, the high priest and head of the entire Congregation of Israel, and (2) the Messiah of Israel, the political leader, subordinate and second in rank to the former.[16]

## II

It is exactly this concept that is found in the *Testaments of the Twelve Patriarchs*. The understanding of the messianic concept in Test. XII Patr. had for a long time been misdirected by the theory of R. H. Charles[17] that the statements concerning a Messiah from the tribe of Levi and a Messiah from the tribe of Judah, both of which are found side by side in Test. XII Patr. were two competing concepts. Charles was of the opinion that the original text of the Test. XII Patr. expressed only the expectation of the Messiah of Levi. Under the powerful influence of the priestly dynasty of the Hasmoneans and especially of John Hyrcanus, this concept should have canceled out the otherwise current Jewish concept of the Messiah of Judah, the Davidic Messiah. Consequently, Charles thought it possible to find allusions in the original text to John Hyrcanus. But when Hyrcanus broke with the Pharisees, the idea of the Messiah of Levi should have given place again to the usual concept of the Messiah of Judah which could be seen in additions (from the first century B.C.) to the original text of the Test. XII Patr.

Yet, the Test. XII Patr. have no allusions to John Hyrcanus, nor are the Messiah of Levi and the Messiah of Judah mutually competing concepts. Much rather, the Test. XII Patr. show, with complete unanimity, the expectation of two Messiahs, one a high priest from the tribe of Levi and one royal from the tribe of Judah. The priestly Messiah receives the highest place, the royal Messiah ranks second.[18]

So we see, side by side in Test. Rub. 6[7-12] the Anointed High Priest of Levi[19] and the Eternal King of Judah. Levi has the highest rank, while Judah is subordinated to him. Especially interesting is the fact that it is the high priest title, already familiar to us from

Lev. 4 which appears here in the same Greek translation as the Septuagint used in Lev. 4₅, ₁₆, 6₁₅, cf. 4₃. In Test. Levi 17₂, ₃ the high priest of Levi is called the Anointed One (*ho chriomenos* = *hamashiah*).[20]

According to Test. Sim. 7₂, God will cause a high priest to arise from Levi and a King from Judah.[21] It is from these that the salvation of God will come upon Israel (Test. Sim. 7₁; likewise Test. Levi 2₁₁; Dan 5₁₀; Gad 8₁; Jos. 19₁₁).

Test. Levi 18₂₋₁₄ praises the high priest Messiah of the Last Days, the New Priest in a hymn. This is practically paralleled in Test. Judah 24 by the hymn in praise of the royal Messiah of Judah. That the worldly kingship belongs to Judah is stated in Test. Judah 12₄; 15₂₋₃; 17₃, ₅₋₆, 22₂₋₃; it is most clearly stated in 21₂₋₅: "To me (Judah) God has given the kingship, to him (Levi) the priesthood; and the kingship he has subordinated to the priesthood." The same is said in Text. Iss. 5₇. The subordination is also stressed in Test. Judah 25₁₋₂; Napht. 5₃₋₅. If we add Test. Sim. 5₅₋₆; Levi 8₁₄; Dan 5₄, ₇; Napht. 6₆; 8₂, in all of which we find Levi's priesthood and Judah's kingship, we have named all of the messianic passages of the Test. XII Patr.[22] All of them exhibit, with complete unanimity, the concept of the priestly Messiah of Levi and the political and royal Messiah of Judah, the latter ranking after the former.

Thus, information about this very form of messianic expectations was available before it was found in the Qumran texts. Had not Charles been so influential in this matter, the additional evidence of the Scrolls were hardly necessary. On the other hand, it is even now more obvious that the Test. XII Patr. belong to the cycle of Essene writings. To be sure, this is not the only point where the Test. XII Patr. and the Qumran texts agree. In manner of speech and in matters of concepts they are closely related.[24]

### III

It is only from this more secure basis that we can rightly understand the messianic expectations of the Damascus Document (CD) and find their proper relation to parallel concepts. In an article of 1950 I showed, on grounds of similarity in language and thought, that CD belongs to the same Palestinian-Jewish sect as the Qumran texts, i.e., to the Essene circles.[25] The discovery of the CD fragments in the Qumran caves in 1952 gave the confirmation.[26] CD speaks of the "coming of the Messiah of Aaron and Israel" no less than three times (xii, 23; xiv, 19; xix, 10), while CD xx, 1, speaks of the future appearance of the "Messiah from Aaron and from Israel." The terminology is undoubtedly the same as that of the Qumran formula. This makes the singular form "Messiah" the more remarkable. As the plural meaning of the formula has been definitely confirmed by the evidence from 1 QSa, the singular form can be understood only as a secondary correction by a medieval copyist of the CD.[27] Apart from the Essene texts, the entire Jewish tradition knows, after all, only of the concept of "the Messiah"—in singular. Thus the medieval Jewish copyists did not know what to do with the plural construction "the Messiahs." By dropping the plural ending they brought the text into conformity with the universally held concept. They did exactly what we found some modern scholars doing when interpreting 1 QS ix, 11. That the formula in CD was originally in plural is, however, confirmed by the other two places in CD where the word "Messiah" occurs (ii, 12 and vi, 1).

In vi, 1, the given text violates basic rules of syntax—a genitive cannot be attached to a noun with suffix. With the evidence from Qumran, it becomes obvious that this was another instance where the copyists met and disposed of a plural form, "the Messiahs."[28] Now we can read the passage as follows: "For they 'spoke rebellion' against the commandments of God, given by the hand of Moses and also by the hand of the holy *anointed ones,* and prophesied falsehood so as to cause Israel to turn away from following God."

That "the holy anointed ones" are the Old Testament prophets is made clear when the verb "to prophesy" follows. The expression "Moses and the holy anointed ones" is the twofold description of the Old Testament revelation, a terminology which in the form "Moses and the prophets" is familiar to the reader of the New Testament (Lk. 16₂₉, ₃₁, 24₂₇; Acts 26₂₂; cf. Mt. 5₁₇).

Also in CD ii, 12, an original plural has become a singular. The copyists understood it to read "and he made known to them his holy spirit by the hand of his Messiah," but the correct understanding, which in this case does not require any textual change, must be ". . . by the hand of his anointed ones." This plural interpretation can be substantiated by a parallel from 1 QM xi, 7, where, in a hymn in praise of God, we read: "You have made known to us the times of the war of your hands, through the hand of your anointed ones, who had prophetically foreseen the moments of (your divine) testimonies." Here the plural is the only possible reading. It is also certain that the reference is to the Old Testament prophets. Column xi of 1 QM is a survey of the Old Testament scheme of redemption. These are the redemptive acts of God: (a) "through the hand of your servant David" (xi, 2); (b) "and likewise through the hand of our kings" (xi, 3); (c) "and through the hand of your anointed ones" (xi, 7).

Thus we arrive at the conclusion that all instances where the word *mashiah* occurs in the CD, it originally had a plural form, sometimes used as a noun (Messiah) and sometimes as an adjective (anointed).

## IV

The concept of the two Messiahs, a priestly and a political one, is actually not as strange as it first appears to be. The entire structure of postexilic Israel shows the side-by-side position of the priestly hierarchy and a worldly political leadership. This structure is given already in the juxtaposition of the priests and the "princes" as worldly leaders, found in Ezekiel (44-46). In Zech. 4₁₄ (*ca.* 520 B.C.) we see, side by side, the Aaronite Joshua, the high priest, and the Davidic Zerubbabel, the worldly leader of the Israelite community, as "the two anointed ones." In the final stage of development, more than 500 years later, during the second Jewish insurrection against the Romans (A.D. 132-135), the same juxtaposition occurs. The high priest Eleazar stands side by side with the political messianic leader of the uprising,[29] Simon ben Kosba (bar Kokba).[30] Here, however, contrary to the Essene order of precedence, the political head has the first place, while the high priest ranks second.

A special position in this respect was taken by the Hasmoneans. They were, after all, a priestly family. Judas Maccabeus and his brothers were the leaders of the Maccabean revolt and by this their family achieved the rank of high priesthood. Judas himself did not attain the office of high priest,[31] but Jonathan certainly did (1 Macc. 12₃, ₆) and from the time of Simon on, the office of the high priest became, by official decision of the people in 141 B.C., an hereditary right of the Hasmonean family (1 Macc. 14₄₁₋₄₆).[32] From the days of the Maccabean revolt on, the Hasmoneans were, *de facto*, also the political and military leaders of the nation. This is expressed in the fact that Simon, besides holding the office of the high priest, had the title of "Generalissimus" and Governor of the Jews.[33] Aristobulus I (104-103 B.C.) even assumed the title of king.[34] Yet, even with the Hasmoneans there is a distinction, even a separation— *de iure*, at least—between the high priesthood and the political government. To be sure, there is no second-individual besides the Hasmonean high priest, but as the bearer of the political power we find "the people of the Jews." Thus, already in the time of Judas Maccabeus, the emissaries who were sent to Rome in order to conclude a treaty, speak of themselves as representing (1) Judas Maccabeus and his brother; and (2) the people of the Jews (1 Macc. 8₂₀). This is still more clearly expressed in the case of Jonathan: the treaty with the Romans is renewed in the name of "Jonathan, the High Priest, and the Jewish Nation" (1 Macc. 12₃). The treaty with the Spartans is made in the name of "Jonathan, the High Priest, and the Council of the Nation" (1 Macc. 12₆). This division of the high priestly and political leadership (in which the political leadership is in the hands of the Jewish people or its Council) is expressed most clearly by the official titles on the coins of John Hyrcanus: "Johanan, the High Priest, and the Congregation of the Jews."[35]

Aristobulus, in spite of his having adopted the title "king," retained on his coins—at least on those intended for intra-Jewish use—this official division between the priestly and the political power: "Jehuda, the High Priest, and the Congregation of the Jews.[36] Even Alexander (103-76 B.C.) retains on his coins the fiction of this division of powers: "Jehonathan, the High Priest, and the Congregation of the Jews,"[37] although he also issued bilingual coins with the inscription, "Jehonathan the King [Hebrew]/King Alexander [Greek]."[38]

Thus we find the distinction between the high priestly and the political office to be an integral part of Jewish tradition. When the actual politico-military leadership was in the hands of the Hasmoneans, it could still be understood as entrusted to them by the people.[39] Yet Jewish tradition did not allow the Hasmoneans as a priestly family (from the tribe of Levi) to become kings. The title befitted only a son of David (from the tribe of Judah) as messianic king. By assuming the title "king" (from the time of Aristobulus I on), the Hasmoneans adapted themselves to their Hellenistic environment. Thereby they placed themselves in opposition to Jewish tradition. Alexander Jannaeus was the first one to set himself so entirely over and against this tradition that he even engraved his royal title on his coins. Such a usurpation of the royal title by men who, because of their priesthood, could never claim it, was nothing short of a sacrilege to pious Jews. Their protest is voiced in the Psalms of Solomon: "Thou, Lord, has chosen David for a king over Israel, and has sworn concerning his seed that his kingdom should never cease before thee. Yet because of our sins, sinners have arisen against us, men have placed themselves against us and driven us out, men to whom this promise was not made. They have taken (it) for themselves, set the kingship up in the place of their high rank,[40] caused the Throne of David to be deserted through the insolence (of this) changing of things" (174-6); this passage dates from the time shortly before 63 B.C.[41]

The resistance of the Jewish people against this usurpation of royal prerogatives also comes to the fore in the proceedings before Pompey in Damascus in 63 B.C. Here we meet the two Hasmonean brothers Aristobulus II and Hyrcanus II quarreling about which of them was to become the ruler, but there appears also a delegation of the Jewish people, deposing both: "The people were opposed to both, as they did not want to be ruled by a king. For, they said, they had a custom, inherited from their fathers, to obey the priests of the God they worshipped. Yet, these (Aristobulus and Hyrcanus), although they were descendants of priests, were attempting to bring the people under a different sort of rule (namely, the kingship) and so to make them slaves" (Josephus, Ant. 14, 3, 2; § 41).

The arrangement which Pompey made, once Jerusalem had been conquered, corresponded to this. He confirmed Hyrcanus' status of high priest, but denied him the title of a king.[42] To the Jewish people this meant the preservation of their basic principle of a separation between the priestly sacral leadership and the political leadership, of which the nation itself considered itself to be the bearer.

Once more the same pattern is witnessed to by the records of history. When, after the death of Herod the Great in 4 B.C., his sons in Rome were waiting for Caesar Augustus' decision concerning the succession to the throne, there appeared a strong delegation of "the people of the Jews," who denied the claims of the Herodians and requested, instead, the autonomy of the people, governed by their own laws alone (Josephus, Ant. 17, 11, 102; Bell. 2, 6,1-2, where we find the revealing formulation "emissaries . . . for the autonomy of the people").

It is, finally, worth noting that in the official titles of the Hasmoneans the bearer of the high priestly office is named first, and then only the bearer of the political power ("the community of the Jews"). Even with the Hasmoneans this is a witness to a political structure as it had been since the Maccabean revolt. As for the order of precedence, it completely agrees with the Essene concept of the two Messiahs, the Messiahs of Israel being second to the Messiah of Aaron. Yet, with the Essenes this was not a description of a present historical reality, but an ideal description of the eschatological Israel of the Age to Come.

## V

It is from the New Testament that most of us are familiar with the title "Messiah" or its Greek equivalent "Christ." What is the significant connection between the New Testament and the distinct form of messianic expectation of the Essenes? Let us return to the basic formula which gave our study its point of departure: ". . . until the coming of a Prophet and the (two) Messiahs of Aaron and Israel" (1 QS ix, 11). The expectation of a prophet in the last days is related, without any doubt, to the promise in Deut. 18$_{15}$: "God will raise up for you a prophet like me (Moses)." This expectation of the new prophetic lawgiver of the Age to Come is found also in Test. Benj. 9$_2$,[43] and in 1 Macc. 4$_{46}$ and 14$_{41}$.

Thus 1 QS ix, 11, actually speaks of three different heroes of redemption, who were to stand side by side in the Eschaton: (1) the new prophetic lawgiver, (2) the "Messiah of Aaron," the new high priest out of the tribe of Levi, and (3) the "Messiah of Israel," the new king out of the tribe of Judah.

The juxtaposition of a new prophet and the messianic king can be seen in the question of whether John the Baptist (Jn. 1$_{20f.}$) or Jesus (Mk. 8$_{28}$ par.; Jn. 7$_{40f.}$) were one or the other of these two figures.[44] On the other hand, the New Testament does not know of an expectation of two Messiahs. The New Testament, to be sure, speaks often enough of Jesus as the new prophet (Lk. 7$_{16}$, Jn. 7$_{52}$, 9$_{17}$, Acts 3$_{22}$, 7$_{37}$). It speaks of his messianic kingship (by giving him the title "Christ"), and in the Epistle to the Hebrews his high priestly office is dealt with at length. Yet nowhere in the New Testament is there a claim that the expectation of the two Messiahs finds its fulfillment in the person of Jesus. The title "Messiah" appears in the New Testament in singular, and is a reference to the Davidic type of a royal Messiah. The New Testament presupposes the messianic expectation of the average Jew, not the special two-Messiah concept of the Essenes.

Yet, the later church concept of the convergence of the three offices—prophet, priest, and king—in the person of Jesus is prefigured in a remarkable way by the Essene juxtaposition of the three: the eschatological Prophet, the Messiah of Aaron, and the Messiah of Israel.[45] In this connection, the statements of Eusebius (*Hist. Eccl.* 1, 3) are important when he says that these three offices of Christ as "the Anointed One" are foreshadowed (1) in Aaron, the high priestly "Anointed One," mentioned in Lev. 4; (2) in the successor to Moses' political-military leadership, Joshua, and the "anointed kings"; and finally (3) in the "anointed" prophets. These three functions, says Eusebius, are now united in the person of Jesus Christ.[46]

# V

# The Lord's Supper and the Communal Meal at Qumran*

KARL GEORG KUHN

The identity of the Qumran sect and the Essenes, described by Josephus and Philo, has now been accepted in principle.[1] There are still some divergencies in the opinions of scholars whether this is a complete identity or a relative one, whether the Qumran sect constitutes only a special group of the Essenes of Josephus or a group closely related to them.[2] Since we, in the following, are concerned with the daily cult meal of the community, on the basis of its descriptions in the Qumran texts, Josephus' description of this daily cult meal will be brought in only for purposes of comparison; and for our study it is of little consequence whether one considers the identity absolute or relative. Our argument will remain valid even if the term "the cult meal of Qumran" is substituted for the term "the cult meal of the Essenes." Let us, however, state briefly that the Qumran texts and Josephus' description of the Essenes agree in all principal features, and especially in the important features which distinguish this community from the rest of Judaism. Both sources describe a definite, strictly organized, "monastic" community, where membership was for life, and where property was owned communally. It existed in Palestine for *ca.* 250 years—from the second century B.C. up to the great conquest of A.D. 66-70. The Qumran texts, as well as Josephus, agree that this Order had, as its peculiar

* This translation is a substantially revised and enlarged edition of Professor Kuhn's article, "Über den ursprünglichen Sinn des Abendmahles und sein Verhältnis zu den Gemeinschaftsmahlen der Sektenschrift," *Evangelische Theologie* 10 (1950/51), pp. 508-27.

features, the constantly repeated bath of immersion and the daily communal meal of the community. Admission into the Order was preceded by a novitiate, consisting of two stages: after the completion of the first stage, the novice could take part in the baths of immersion, but only after the second stage could he share in the cult meals. He pledged himself, by an oath of initiation, to unconditional obedience to the Order, and secrecy with regard to its teachings and writings. To these points should be added the many agreements concerning minute yet most significant characteristics, which will become clear as we compare Josephus' report on the cult meal with its description in the Qumran texts.

Josephus' presentation of the sect's theology shows, beside many similarities, some differences from the Qumran texts. This is due to the literary style of Josephus: his presentation is disfigured in the case of the Essenes, exactly as in the case of the Pharisees and the Sadducees, by his adjustment to the taste of his Roman readers. Other differences concern relatively unimportant information. So, for instance, according to the Qumran texts, the two stages of the novitiate are of one year each, while according to Josephus the first stage is of one year and the second is of two years. This may be purely an error on Josephus' part.

We must also keep in mind that Josephus describes to us the Order in the last stage of its existence, somewhere in the years A.D. 50-70, while the Qumran texts were composed 100 or even 150 years earlier. Thus certain differences between the Qumran texts and Josephus could be accounted for by the development of the Order within this period.

This may apply, also, to the name of the Order. The name "Essenes," known only to Josephus and Philo, is not found in the Qumran texts. Here the Order is called "The Congregation of God," "The Covenant of God," "The People of the Truth," "The Sons of Light," "The People of God's Lot," etc. It is possible that the name "Essene" came to be used only in the first century A.D., and that only as a description used by outsiders (in Greek, *essenoi* or *essaioi* = Aramaic *hasayya*, "the Pious"), as is often the case with such groups.

Let us now compare Josephus' information about the Essene cult meal and the corresponding information found in the Manual of Discipline (1 QS). At the same time, we shall be aware of the New

Testament accounts of the Lord's Supper. Secondly, we will bring into the picture the second account of the cult meal at Qumran, found in a fragment similar to the Manual and called, according to its first line, *Serek ha-edah* (1 QSa). This text is particularly significant for comparison with the New Testament. Thirdly, attention will be drawn to the cult meal described in the Jewish-Hellenistic legend, *Joseph and Aseneth*. Finally, in what constitutes the main section of our study, we will address ourselves to the question of the origin of the Lord's Supper as it presents itself in the light of our new material.

(1) Josephus' report on the Essene cult meal is as follows (*Bell.* 2, 8, 5):

After the purification, they assemble in a special room which none of the uninitiated is permitted to enter; pure now themselves, they repair to the refectory, as to some sacred shrine. When they have seated themselves in silence, the baker serves the loaves in order, and the cook sets before each one plate with a single course. Before the meal, the priest gives the blessing, and it is unlawful to partake before the prayer. The meal ended, he offers a further prayer; thus at the beginning and at the close they do homage to God as the bountiful giver of life.

Beside this description we place the report on the community meal of the Qumran Community, found in 1 QS vi, 1-6:

In these (regulations) they shall walk in all their sojournings:[3] Everyone, finding himself together with his fellow,[4] the lesser shall hear the greater,[5] with regard to the work[6] and the mammon. And in common[7] they shall eat[8] and in common they shall pray and in common they shall take counsel. And at every place where there are ten men[9] of the Council of the community there shall also be a priest,[10] and each is to sit before him[11] according to his own rank and in this way[12] are they to ask for counsel with regard to every matter. And when the table is prepared for eating or wine[13] for drinking, the priest shall first raise his hand so that the first portion[14] of the bread and of the wine be blessed.

The best way to analyze the agreements and differences between these two descriptions of the meal is to give a running commentary on the text of Josephus:

*After this purification:* by *purification* is meant the daily baths of immersion of the Essenes, which, according to Josephus, always precede the meal. The Qumran texts also describe the bath of immersion as "sanctification" (1 QS iii, 4, 9). The usual technical term for it in the Qumran texts is *tohorah*, "purification" (1 QS v, 13; vi, 16 and *passim;* likewise CD ix, 21, 23).

To be sure, no passage in the Qumran texts has yet been found where it says expressly, as in Josephus, that the meal is always to be preceded by the bath. Yet this could have been the practice, since the Order originated with a group who severed their relations with the Jerusalem Temple and went out into the wilderness, and in the Jerusalem Temple the priests had to take a ritual bath before and after each cult action. In the evening, their daily offices being concluded, the priests gathered—after a final bath—in a special room in the Temple set aside for them; and here they partook of the priestly meal. This consisted of "holy things," i.e., those pieces of the offerings which were set apart for the priests. Once separated from the Temple, the Essenes discontinued the sacrificial cult, but continued to lead their lives in acordance with priestly purity. They continued daily baths and sacral meals.[15] Removed from the Temple, these practices were given a deeper religious significance— and this was decisive for the development that was to come. Thus the baths had for the Essenes, over and above their old meaning (to secure cultic purity), the sacramental function of mediating in the divine forgiveness of sins (1 QS iii, 3ff.). In place of the sacrificial cultus of the Temple, which was no longer possible for them by reason of their distance from it, the baths, and apparently also the communal meal, took on a new meaning, mediating salvation from God. Thus the Old Testament concept of sacrifice is applied to the baths and even to the mission of the community as such in 1 QS iii, 3-13, and viii, 5ff. This is also reflected in Josephus' report, when he says that Essenes go into their refectory "as to some sacred shrine."

. . . *in a special room:* This dining hall for the common meals has been uncovered during the excavations of Khirbet Qumran. Even the dishes were found, all piled up in a corner, next to the hall.

. . . *which none of the uninitiated is permitted to enter:* This corresponds to the directions in 1 QS, according to which the novices were never allowed to take part in the cult meal. Members of the Order, under censure for some transgression, were also excluded for the period of their punishment. It follows as a matter of course that no outsider could take part in the cult meal.

*When they have seated themselves in silence:* According to Josephus, the silence during the Essene meals is based on the regulation that they may only speak in due order: they speak in turn (in order, *en taxei*), each making way for the other. This corresponds exactly to the prescription in 1 QS vi, 10: "No man shall interrupt the speech of the other before his brother has finished speaking. Nor shall he speak out of his rank."

This provision throws interesting light on the Johannine description of Jesus' last meal with his disciples. In the Gospel of John, the "Beloved Disciple" is always described as standing in rank above Peter. Thus, in Jn. 13$_{24}$ it is not Peter who asks the Lord who the traitor is—he cannot take it upon himself to speak—but Peter gives a sign to the Beloved Disciple, who has a more honored seat than himself, that he, the Beloved Disciple, should ask the question. This is now understandable in the light of this provision in the Qumran texts. In the Gospel of John the last meal of Jesus with his disciples is apparently described in the style of the communal meal of the Essenes.

We may also compare the silence at mealtime and the permission to speak only in accordance with one's rank, with Hippolytus' description of the Christian Agape (Hippolytus, *Apostolic Tradition*, chap. 50; *Didascalia et Const. Apost.*, ed. Funk, II, pp. 113f.): "Those who are invited to the Agape must partake of it in silence, without arguing (*cum silentio, non contendentes verbis*); they are to speak only when addressed by the bishop."

*. . . and the baker serves the loaves in order:* The serving of the bread according to rank corresponds to the provision in 1 QS vi, 4 (quoted above): ". . . each is to sit before him (i.e., the presiding priest) according to his rank."

*Before the meal, the priest gives the blessing:* It is one of the most significant agreements between Josephus and the Qumran texts that it has to be a priest who presides over the meal and thus, as the one highest in rank, gives the blessing at the beginning of the meal. This corresponds to what was mentioned already about the priestly structure of the Essene Community and the derivation of its cult meal from the priestly meals at the Jerusalem Temple.

*. . . and it is unlawful to partake before the prayer:* This corresponds to the prescription in 1 QS vi, 5, already cited: the priest shall be the first to touch the food. The negative form of the prescription

is not found only in Josephus, but also in 1 QSa ii, 18f.: "No one is to reach for the bread and wine before the priest, as he blesses the first portion of the bread and the wine."

*The meal ended, he offers a further prayer:* Nothing is said about this closing prayer in the passage cited from 1 QS. Yet one is tempted to ask whether the priest's benedictions over the bread and the wine, which in 1 QS vi are placed immediately beside each other, were, in reality, not divided into the prayer before and after the meal. This was the common practice at all other Jewish meals.[16] It is, however, only by the help of a passage in 1 QSa that this question can be properly assessed.[17]

Let us conclude at this point that we have found general agreement between Josephus and 1 QS vi, in that all of the meals of the Order were held in common, and that they had the character of the cult meal of the community. This is shown by 1 QS, where it considers the eating and the prayers as parallel features, and the character of the meal as an official manifestation of the community. The stipulation that at least ten men have to be present (the required minimum for a Jewish service—women do not count) also points to the cultic character of the meal, as does Josephus' information about the requirement that the meal be preceded by baths of purification. To this should be added Josephus' emphatic expression about the cult meal, "as some awful mystery."

(2) Let us now turn to the other Qumran text which deals with the cult meal, viz., the two columns of the *Serek ha-edah* (1 QSa).[18] It shows how this Essene group visualized the Congregation of Israel in the time of consummation, a picture which coincides with the forms and institutions already manifested in the community at Qumran. Thus the cult meal, as celebrated in the community, has its proper place in the picture of the eschatological Israel.[19] To the eschatological hope of the Essene Community belonged the expectation of two messianic saviors, "the two Messiahs of Aaron and Israel." The Messiah of Aaron, of the tribe of Levi, the eschatological high priest, is the spiritual head of the entire people. The Messiah of Israel, of the tribe of Judah, is the political leader of the people. In rank he is subordinated to the Messiah of Aaron.[20] For this reason, the Messiah of Aaron, the eschatological high priest, appears in the 1 QSa description as the priest who presides over the

cult meal, just as we saw a priest having that function in 1 QS vi. In 1 QSa, however, the Messiah of Israel also is brought into the picture of the cult meal. In accordance with his rank, he is to be the second to touch the bread and wine. It is only after this that the congregation can approach the food.

At the actual meals of the Essenes there was, to be sure, no one who could represent the Messiah of Israel. He is not to come until the time of the final consummation, so there is nothing that would correspond to him in the description of the communal meal as the Essenes actually celebrated it (1 QS vi).

The text of 1 QSa ii, 17-22, reads as follows:[21]

... and when they gather to the table of the community and to the drinking of the wine and when the table of the community is made ready and the wine has been mixed for drinking, then no one is to touch the first portion[22] of the bread and the wine before the priest. For it is he who blesses the first portion of the bread and of the wine and who touches as the first the bread. Then may the Messiah of Israel touch the bread and then (only) may (those who belong to) the congregation say the blessing, each according to his rank. And in accordance with this rubric they shall act at each meal, when (at least) ten men are gathered (for it).

It is immediately apparent that this description of the cult meal completely agrees with that of 1 QS vi, 1-6 (except for the peculiar feature of the eschatological Messiah of Israel), even to the extent of verbal identity in the terminology. Thus both texts present the same liturgical rubric. In both we find the term "preparation of the table and of the drinking of the wine" (peculiar to 1 QSa, however, is the expression "table of the community"); here, too, we find the distinctive expression for wine, *tirosh;* here, too, it is the presiding priest who touches and blesses the bread and the wine first, and only after that do the other members touch the food, and that strictly in the order of their rank. Here, too, is stipulated the necessity of having at least ten men present for the valid observance of the cult meal.[23]

In addition to what we saw in 1 QS vi, we now learn that the priestly blessings of the bread and the wine both take place at the beginning of the meal, the one immediately after the other. Thus "the blessings of the bread and the wine" do not refer to the usual Jewish custom, by which the blessing "over the bread" was given at the beginning of the meal, while blessing at the end of the meal was said "over the wine." The priestly blessing of the bread *and* the wine at the beginning of the meal points to a rite which is peculiar to this cult meal. No blessing at the end of the meal is even mentioned here. It is, however, clear that the Essene meal could not have ended without such a benediction. The requirement of an opening and closing benediction at each meal belongs to the established old Jewish *halaka*.[24] Josephus, on the other hand, mentions such a blessing, but says nothing about a priestly blessing of the wine at the beginning of the meal. The explanation can only be, in my opinion, that the liturgical rubrics of the Qumran texts contain only what was peculiar to their cult meal, but that the common Jewish rite of the opening and closing prayer is a matter of course, and just taken for granted. Josephus refers to what was in accordance with Jewish tradition. He has nothing to say about the special rite of the Essenes, because this special rite belonged to the *disciplina arcana*, the "secrets," known only to the members of the Order, and not to be communicated to outsiders.

This difference between the Qumran texts and Josephus may at first appear slight, but it proves to be highly significant for our knowledge of the origin of the Christian Eucharist. In comparing the Essene cult meal and the Eucharistic traditions, we must first make a clear distinction between (a) the oldest form of the Lord's Supper, the meal of the Jerusalem church and (b) the form and structure of the last meal of Jesus with his disciples according to New Testament accounts of its institution.

As for the first, the similarity between the oldest form of the Lord's Supper and the Essene cult meal lies in its being celebrated by the first Christians daily, communally, and as a complete meal of a cultic character. This similarity was true only in respect to the oldest, Palestinian form of the Lord's Supper. It disappears very soon in the further development of the church, especially when Christian congregations spread into the Hellenistic-Roman environment. Soon the Lord's Supper was observed only once a week, on Sunday, or on the Sabbath day, and a little later it ceased to be celebrated as a complete meal. It became the Eucharist with bread and wine. It is exactly with reference to the old Palestinian form of the Lord's Supper as a common meal that the similarity between the meal-prayers in the *Didache* (9-10) and the Essene cult meal according to the Qumran texts is significant. Just as the blessings of the bread and the wine at the cult meal of the Qumran texts stood at the beginning of the meal, so it is also in Did. 9. While it is admittedly a remarkable fact that the Didache has the blessing over the cup before the blessing over the bread, the decisive similarity lies in the fact that both stand at the beginning of the meal.[25]

Very remarkable, also, are the similarities found in the New Testament accounts of Jesus' last meal with his disciples. For the time being, we leave without consideration what is the peculiar and unique feature in these accounts, namely, the fact that Jesus adds explanatory words of his own to the blessing over the bread and the wine. Yet the ritual framework of the meal is that Jesus gives the blessings over the bread and the wine.

In Mk. 14 22-24 (and in the parallel in Mt. 26 26-28) we find the two blessings over the bread and the wine immediately following one another. Paul, on the other hand, says in 1 Cor. 11 23-35—although even with him the forms follow immediately one after the other—that Jesus said the blessing over the cup after the meal (so also Lk. 22 20). According to the Pauline and Lucan text, then, the blessing over the bread was at the beginning and that over the wine at the end of the meal; that is to say, they corresponded to the common Jewish custom. Consequently, P. Billerbeck[26] and Joachim Jeremias[27] have interpreted the Marcan and Matthean account in accordance with the Pauline Text, claiming that the entire meal took its course between Jesus' words over the bread and those over the cup. Jeremias expressly says: "The fact, therefore, that the Words of institution over the bread and the wine occur together in both Matthew and Mark must not lead to the conclusion that they were said the one immediately after the other. Rather, this reflects the development of the Christian Liturgy of the Eucharist."[28] It is quite possible that the Marcan and Matthean texts reflect the later rite of the church, where, because the meal had been removed, the bread and the wine of the Eucharist were placed one immediately after the other. Yet the very early date of the Marcan text of the words of institution, maintained by Jeremias (A.D. 40–50) makes this rather unlikely. At that time, as we can see from 1 Cor. 11, the Lord's Supper was certainly still a complete meal. It is more likely that the immediate sequence of the blessings over the bread and the wine in Mark and Matthew reflects not a later Christian usage, but on the contrary, an earlier pre-Christian usage, namely, that of the Essene cult meal, as we have met it in the Qumran texts. When the Pauline and Lucan texts divide the words of the blessing by using the phrase "after the meal," it is to be understood as an interpretation in accordance with common Jewish usage. This interpretation came in due to the fact that the distinctive character of the older liturgical formula in Mark (and Matthew) was no longer understood.[29]

The relation between the Marcan and the Pauline text in their description of Jesus' last meal would then be quite similar to the relationship of the formulae of the Qumran texts to the text of Josephus in his description of the cult meal of the Essenes, the Qumran formula, and Mark reporting the peculiar usage of the "sect," while for Josephus and Paul the common Jewish custom has to provide the framework.

(3) Neither of the two Qumran passages we have considered so far has given us any information about the religious (or perhaps even the sacramental) significance which the Essenes attributed to their cult meal. Nor can we expect it, actually, from rubrics, as both these passages are. There is, however, a text which gives such an interpretation of the significance of a Jewish cult meal—and we have to find out whether or not this meal is that peculiar to the Essenes or refers to a meal of a similar nature. The text we have in mind is the Egyptian-Jewish legend, *Joseph and Aseneth.*[30] G. D. Kilpatrick has recently drawn attention to the parallels in this text which have a bearing on the Christian Eucharist.[31] But Kilpatrick overlooks the connection between the passages in *Joseph and Aseneth* and the Essene cult meal, primarily as these meals are seen in the Qumran texts. And exactly this connection is decisive for an understanding of the passages in *Joseph and Aseneth.*

*Joseph and Aseneth* is a novelistic story, built on Gen. 41₄₅. It describes how Joseph meets Aseneth in Egypt. She is the daughter of the Egyptian priest Pentephres. We are told about her conversion from paganism to Judaism and her marriage to Joseph.[32] The story is obviously Jewish and in all probability it stems from the Jewish community in Egypt. It has even been argued that the original was in Hebrew, the Greek text being a translation. That is, however, very unlikely.[33] It is difficult to say anything exact about the time of its origin.[34] No clear Christian interpolations and revisions of the text are demonstrable and they are unlikely when one considers the structure and character of this writing.

In this text we find five instances where the distinctive mark of the pious Jew is that he "eats the blessed bread of life and drinks the blessed cup of immortality."[35] It is certainly wrong to take for granted that these instances refer to the Christian Eucharist and that they are therefore Christian interpolations.

Even if one thinks in terms of a Christian revision of the text, the Jewish character of the original is beyond doubt,[36] and the references to a cult meal must belong to the original, since they form an integral part of the narrative.[37] Thus they must be originally Jewish, and have to be interpreted accordingly.[38] Christian interpolations and revisions of such Jewish writings look quite different. We may refer, for example, to the Christian interpolations in the *Testaments of the Twelve Patriarchs.* Furthermore, the complete absence of any christology in *Joseph and Aseneth* is another fact which speaks against its having undergone Christian revision or interpolation. At this point, it is helpful to refer to the Test. XII Patr. where most of the interpolations are distinctively christological, as is also the case in the Christian revisions in the *Ascension of Isaiah.*

The five passages from *Joseph and Aseneth* mentioned are:

". . . a god-fearing man who . . . eats the blessed bread of life and drinks the blessed cup of immortality. . ." (8$_5$).

Joseph prays to God for Aseneth, that she may be blessed, ". . . and let her eat your bread of life and drink of your cup of blessing. . ." (8$_9$).

Archangel Michael says to Aseneth: "From today on you will be created anew, and you shall eat the blessed bread of life and drink the cup filled with immortality. . ." (15$_5$).

Archangel Michael blesses Aseneth after her miraculous partaking of a heavenly honeycomb: "Behold, you have eaten the bread of life and drunk the cup of immortality. . ." (16$_6$).

Aseneth says to Joseph. "Today the angel came to me and gave me the bread of life and I ate and I drank the blessed cup" (19$_5$).[39]

The similarity between these five passages shows that the expression "to eat the blesed bread of life and to drink the blessed cup of immortality" is a technical formula, especially since the narrative itself does not require such an expression. Aseneth never receives any bread to eat or cup to drink; she receives a heavenly honeycomb. Thus the formula is not a natural outgrowth of the events described in the story, but an independent and established ritual formula for a cult meal in which the "pious" and "god-fearing" Jew participates. When we recognize the striking similarity between this formula and the formulations in the Qumran texts, a connection between the two must be postulated. Thus Riessler was on the right track when he claimed an Essene origin for *Joseph and Aseneth,* and he referred especially to the passages just quoted and the cult meal of the Essenes.[40] Riessler, however, sees this connection as a more immediate one than, in my estimation, can be substantiated. According to Josephus and the Qumran texts, only men had a part in the cult meal of the Essenes. Now Aseneth receives the holy meal. For this reason, *Joseph and Aseneth* can hardly be referring to the cult meal of the Palestinian Essenes, but that of the Egyptian Therapeutae, described in Philo's *On the Contemplative Life* (8). According to this document, women also took part in those meals. These Egyptian Therapeutae had their settlement at the Mareotic Sea. Though they did not belong to the Essenes proper, and were an Order by themselves, they certainly had a close relationship to the Essenes. They were an Egyptian offshoot of the Palestinian Order of the Essenes; in this way their cult meal, and thereby also the meal in *Joseph and Aseneth*, is related to that of the Essenes.

The meal in *Joseph and Aseneth* reveals its deeper significance by the use of the interpreting genitive constructions "the bread of life" and "the cup of immortality."[41] The eating of the blessed bread and the drinking of the blessed cup mediates immortality and eternal life, and consequently the meal has a sacramental character. The terminology reminds us of Jn. 6, with its discourse on "the bread of life," especially the passage in $6_{51e-58}$: in the bread of the Eucharist the "flesh" of Jesus is partaken of, and in the cup his "blood" is drunk, and thereby one receives everlasting life. In Jn. $6_{58}$ it is clearly stated: "He who eats this bread will live for ever." We are also immediately reminded of Ignatius' *Epistle to the Ephesians* ($20_2$), where the Eucharist is "a medicine of immortality."

Yet, in spite of these close parallels, comparison is burdened with two great difficulties. First, there is the uncertain date of *Joseph and Aseneth*. Nevertheless, the passages we have cited from it are certainly not later than the passages from the Johannine Gospel and Ignatius. We found them to be at least contemporary with them, if not earlier.

Secondly, we are not allowed to ascribe the sacramental interpretation, which is expressed clearly in *Joseph and Aseneth*, to the cult meal of the Essenes. A sacramental understanding could have been given to the meal by the Therapeutae, when they appropriated the practice of the Essenes in Palestine. The Egyptian-Jewish group responsible for *Joseph and Aseneth* was probably influenced by their Hellenistic environment, when they understood the cult meal as "food of immortality." This influence could even have been that of Hellenistic Christianity. Since the theory of Christian interpolation must be renounced, there is no possibility of distinguishing between Jewish and Christian material by means of literary criticism. But an ideological influence is quite possible to the effect that pagan, or even Christian, Hellenism made its impact upon the Therapeutae.

In any case, great caution is advisable in transferring the sacramental understanding of the meal in *Joseph and Aseneth* to the meal of the Essenes at Qumran, since nothing of the sort is found in the Qumran texts themselves.

Nevertheless, it is obvious from the central position of the cult meal of the Essenes that they must have attributed to it a deep religious significance, perhaps even a sacramental one. We do know from the Qumran texts that the bath of immersion, which was, beside the cult meal, a cult act peculiar to the sect, did have actual sacramental significance for the community, mediating the divine forgiveness of sins.[42]

(4) Before we conclude this part of our investigation, devoted to the new comparative material for the origin of the Christian Eucharist, let us also emphasize the difference between the cult meal found in sectarian Judaism and the Eucharist of the Christian church, a difference which exists in spite of all parallels mentioned. The Eucharist is from the very first the "Lord's Supper," the meal of the Lord Jesus Christ. Thereby it is decisively Christian, and from this fact stems its substantial difference from all cult meals of sectarian Judaism.

To be sure, there were already at an early time different interpretations as to how the person of Christ was related to the meal. The original Palestinian church understood the meal as a continuation of the "meal fellowship" with their Master, from the time when he was yet among them here on earth; but now they had the additional certainty that this Jesus, having risen, was exalted into heaven, from whence he was soon to come as the Son of Man, to judge the world and save the congregation of his elect ones. Here the meal of the Lord is consequently one of eschatological joy, expressed in the expressive prayer *maranatha*—"Our Lord, Come!" Already, in the first decades of the Christian church, we find that the Lord's Supper is increasingly understood as mediating the salvation brought forth by the death of Jesus: by taking part in the meal, the believer acquires the forgiveness of sins, which Jesus wrought when he gave himself "a ransom for many," a motif which is present already in the words of Jesus during his last meal with his disciples.[43]

Whether the church understood the meal in this or that way, the person of the historical Jesus and his redemptive role is of central significance for the religious meaning of the meal. In the Qumran texts we find no trace of such a ultimately redemptive significance of an historical person.[44] Thus the person of Jesus and his redemptive significance, i.e., the christology, is the decisively new fact of Christianity. This becomes especially clear in comparison with Essene Judaism, as it is now known through the Qumran material, no matter how great the similarities and even the dependence of Christianity upon the Judaism of the Qumran texts may be and actually is.

With the new material from Qumran the questions about the origin and the earliest development of the Christian Eucharist are raised anew, and an old discussion enters into a new phase. The literature on the subject is immense, and the views held by different scholars vary widely. Nevertheless, these diverse views can be roughly systematized if one recognizes the two extreme poles. On the one side are those scholars who take their point of departure in the sacramental understanding of the Eucharist as Paul (especially 1 Cor. 10 and 11) knows it, from the churches in the Hellenistic world: Partaking of the bread and the wine, the believer shares in the body and blood of Christ, and he becomes thereby incorporated into the Body of Christ. According to this school of thought, this was the original meaning of the Eucharist, and the account of the institution as found in Mk. 14₂₂-₂₄ par. is consequently an etiological cult legend which originated in the Hellenistic churches. First, by such a legend the purely sacramental meal was given the character of an act instituted by the Lord while still on earth. Furthermore, the fact that it had been instituted at the *Passover*, the night before Jesus' execution, becomes a mere historization of the legend, due to the development of the synoptic tradition.

Bultmann may be taken as the foremost representative of this opinion in modern scholarship.

On the other side, we find the scholars who start with the Gospel passages and subject them to historical criticism, in order to find the facts about the last meal and its character. Today the leading representative of this view is Joachim Jeremias. In his view, the account of the institution in Mk. 14$_{22-24}$ par. is a very old piece of tradition, which certainly stems from the primitive Palestinian church. While the framework of the account, which shows Jesus' last meal to be the Passover before his death, is secondary to the account proper, nevertheless, Jesus' last meal was the Passover, which he ate with his disciples on the eve of his death. This fact is substantiated by an analysis of the account proper. Consequently, the institution must be understood and interpreted in the framework of such a Jewish Passover meal, and the words of institution may be taken as a twin parable, in which Jesus, by using the bread and the wine, gives his disciples a sure promise of their sharing in the redemptive effect of his death as a ransom for many.

Two questions are especially pertinent to a discussion of these two diametrically opposite views: (1) Is the account of the institution in Mark a later product of the Hellenistic Christianity, or does it stem directly from the tradition of the primitive Palestinian church? Or we may, with Jeremias, pursue this question one step further and ask: Do the words of institution go back to the historical Jesus himself? (2) Was Jesus' last meal a Passover meal or was it not?

The material from Qumran adds new aspects to this discussion, with regard to both Bultmann's and Jeremias' positions. In order to demonstrate how, we have to go, even if only in the briefest possible manner, into the whole problem of the origin and development of the Eucharist.[45]

(1) A substantial agreement has, in my judgment, been reached with regard to the actual account of the institution in Mk. 14$_{22-24}$ as an independent *cult formula*.[46] Its transmission was subject to the laws peculiar to liturgical traditions. The variant forms in which the words of institution are transmitted (Mk. 14$_{22-24}$; 1 Cor. 11$_{23-25}$; Lk. 22$_{19-20}$)[47] are not a result of literary dependence, but witness to forms of the liturgical text in which the writers knew it in their own church.

The Pauline text (1 Cor. 11) is naturally the oldest from a literary point of view. A critical analysis of the tradition makes, however, the Marcan form the oldest one available to us,[48] and, in comparison, the Pauline text has the marks of secondary changes and late accretion. This is especially true of the twice-repeated additional "do this in remembrance of me."[49] In the Lucan form, we find even more signs of a later liturgical development.

(2) A linguistic analysis of the Marcan formula reveals a high degree of Aramaic or general Semitic manner of expression and form, and compels us to conclude a Palestinian origin.[50] However, two expressions in the Marcan text must be excepted from such an Aramic derivation: "While they were eating" is an editorial connection made by Mark[51] and "of the covenant" as a genitive to "my blood" is an impossible construction in any Semitic language.[52] The latter is an interpretive comment added to the Greek text. Thereby the "covenantal blood" of the death of Jesus is seen as the foundation of the "New Covenant," the term used expressly in the Pauline and Lucan texts.[53] The old covenant at Sinai, with its "covenantal blood" (Ex. 23₈), is now annulled and exceeded by its new counterpart in God's plan of salvation. Such an understanding of the Last Supper within the framework of sacred history, the covenants being the focal points, belongs to a distinctively later stage in the history of the Eucharist. It is peculiar to Hellenistic-Jewish Christianity.

Bultmann[54] takes not only the words "of the covenant" but also the following "shed for many" to be a later addition. In doing so, he achieves a completely balanced structure of the two sayings, over the bread and over the wine. This, however, cannot be done. While "of the covenant" is possible only in the Greek text, the apposition "shed for many" has the distinctive marks of a Semitism. If one disposed of this apposition as a later interpretive comment, one would have to assume two stages in the process of accretion: (1) the addition of "shed for many" already to the Aramic text; and (2) a later additional accretion of "of the covenant" in a Greek setting. Furthermore, the appositions are of a different type even as to their content: "shed for many" points to Jesus' death as an atonement through substitute; "of the covenant" makes Jesus' death the foundation of a new covenant in sacred history, exceeding and transcending the old. The fact that the two sayings of Jesus were different in form, the second phrase containing the apposition "shed for many," is no argument against this phrase's being original to the formula. A dissimilarity, as that in the Marcan formula, implies a heightening of the emphasis in what is the climax of the sentence, a phenomenon familiar to the student of form criticism.[55] Thus the words "shed for many" constitute the climax of the whole saying: the death of Jesus is an atonement through substitute.[56]

One thing seems to me certain—and here I differ from many scholars, especially from Bultmann: the pre-Marcan cult formula, which our analysis has helped us to discern, could not have originated in the Hellenistic-Christian church as a result of the understanding of the Supper as a sacramental incorporation into the Body of Christ. The entire structure of the cult formula presupposes Jewish meal customs. This seems to me to speak against its possible Hellenistic origin even more strongly than the various Semitisms which Jeremias has pointed out. It is worthy of notice that the formula does not presuppose the special Jewish Passover, but the Jewish meal in general. The Marcan "taking bread he blessed, broke and gave to them" corresponds exactly to the Jewish usage: the *pater familias* takes bread, pronounces over it the benediction, and distributes it, piecemeal, to those present at the table (cf. also Acts 27₃₅). Furthermore, the immediate sequence of the blessings over the bread and the wine, as well as other traits which we shall yet discuss, betray a special affinity to the peculiar practices of the Essene cult meal, as they are now found in the texts from Qumran. Such a form is no longer possible in the Hellenistic Christianity. Had the cult formula arisen first in a Hellenistic setting, under the influence of Hellenistic mystery religions, it would have had a different character, without as specific Jewish features.

(3) The originally independent cult formula (Mk. 14₂₂₋₂₄) has been placed by the Synoptics within the framework of a Passover meal, which is at the same time the last meal of Jesus. To this framework belongs the account of the preparation of the passover (Mk. 14₁₂₋₁₆ par.), but this section does actually not belong to the original tradition.[57] Nevertheless, the eschatological double pronouncement of Jesus regarding his eating and drinking (Lk. 22₁₅₋₁₈—the last part being found, also, in Mk. 14₂₅) clearly refers to the Passover.[58]

Jeremias has shown that, while Mark has kept the older linguistic form, Luke has preserved the original doublet form.[59] Luke could not have developed the eschatological doublets in 22₁₅₋₁₈ from Mk. 14₂₅. If so, he had to expand Mk. 14₂₅ (=Lk. 22₁₈) by (a) making up its counterpart

(22₁₆) and (b) creating the introductions to Jesus' word in vv. 15 and 17.[60] Consequently, since Lk. 22₁₅₋₁₈ is not deducible from Mk. 14₂₅, Luke draws here on his special source.[61] For this reason the original longer text of Luke[62] contains two traditions of different origin. Each of them has a doublet saying of Jesus at his last meal (not to eat—not to drink: this is my body—this is the cup of the new covenant). In this way we get a picture of the Last Supper, with four acts,[63] but the doublets of Lk. 22₁₅₋₁₈ and Lk. 22₁₉₋₂₀ are actually competing traditions of different origin. The first of these traditions clearly presupposes a Passover meal; the second does not.

(4) When we make this distinction between the two traditions now combined in Luke and state that the second (the words of institutions proper with their parallel in the Marcan cult formula) does not presuppose a Passover setting, we part company with Jeremias' arguments, which we have followed so far. He gives four reasons for his view that the cult formula itself reflects a Passover setting:[64]

(a) The last meal took place during the night. This is suggested by the cult formula only since the phrase "as they were eating" connects the formula with the synoptic context. While Jeremias recognizes this phrase as editorial, he deduces the "night-aspect" of the meal from the phrase "in the night when he was betrayed" in 1 Cor. 11₂₃. This expression belongs to Paul's introduction to the cult formula, not to the formula itself. It is doubtful whether Paul gives—or even intends to give—in this introduction historical and biographical information; he may rather refer to the literary context of the formula in the Passion narrative as it was known to him. In Paul's missionary preaching there was already a place for a Passion narrative, with a chronological sequence of events. Thus the Pauline reference to the "night" has more significance for the literary history of the tradition than for the actual history of the event.

(b) Jesus and his disciples drink wine at their last meal (Mk. 14₂₃). This, according to Jeremias (op. cit., p. 27 f.), indicates a Passover setting. Yet, even if wine was not usual at the ordinary Jewish meal, the passages from the Qumran texts, which we have dealt with at length, show that both bread and wine were integral parts of the daily communal meal of this Jewish sect in Palestine. Thus the use of wine refers not necessarily to a Passover, but may be indication of a communal meal similar to the cult meal of the Essene Community.

(c) As a further argument for a Passover setting of the cult formula, Jeremias points to the fact that Jesus and his disciples were drinking red wine, the type prescribed for the Passover meal. The use of red wine at the Passover meal is, however, only the teaching of a single rabbi from the fourth century A.D., preserved in the Jerusalem Talmud[65]; it is not a prevailing *halaka*. Furthermore, the wine in Palestine was usually red wine. Thus when we are told that wine was served at the last meal, it is most probable that this was red wine, but this does not necessarily make it a Passover meal. On the other hand, Jeremias' argument for red wine is not beyond doubt. It rests upon his interpretation where the red color is the point of comparison between the wine and Jesus' blood. This is, however, a rather questionable interpretation (see p. 93).

(*d*) The fact that Jesus relates his interpretive words to the elements of the meal is, to Jeremias, an especially strong point in favor of a Passover setting: "interpreting the elements of the meal is a fixed part of the Passover ritual" (*op. cit.*, p. 31). But the interpretation of the different courses of the Passover meal is, according to the Passover *haggada*, expressly restricted to those elements which make the Passover meal different from other meals. When, e.g., the Mazzoth is referred to as "the bread of affliction" (Deut. 16s) ,[66] this reference explains the peculiar usage of unleavened bread, contrary to all other meals. The bread as such is not interpreted. It would be out of keeping with the Passover ritual to give similar explanatory statements with reference to the courses which occur also at ordinary meals. The blessing of the bread and the thanksgiving with the wine are such ordinary features. The explanatory words of Jesus can, therefore, not be understood as a natural part of a Passover meal. That would require a comment on the unleavened character of the bread, not on the bread as such.

Thus the only point of comparison between the Jewish Passover meal and the words of institution that remains is one of formal structure. Both include interpretive statements, even if the character and the meaning of the interpretation differ. This purely formal similarity does not make an argument for a Passover setting, especially since such explanatory statements can be found, although only rarely, in Jewish literature without reference to the Passover meal.[67]

Thus the cult formula contains no reference to a Passover setting.[68] On the contrary, there are several features which speak against such a setting when the traditional Passover meal is taken into account:

(*a*) Jesus shares his last meal only with the Twelve, i.e., a community of men. The Passover meal, on the other hand, is definitely a family meal. The questions of the children form an integral part of the ritual. Even if children were not always present, e.g., at a Passover meal celebrated by pilgrims in Jerusalem, women certainly were. Granted the Passover character of the meal, where are the women mentioned in Mk. 1540, 161? An explanation is lacking.

(*b*) Why is it that the only ones present are the Twelve, the closed and narrow group, the ones he had chosen himself? This was not a characteristic of the usual meals with Jesus,[69] nor would a Passover meal call for such a restricted arrangement.

(c) In keeping with the family character of the Passover meal, the *pater familias* presides. Yet, Jesus is not portrayed as such, but rather as a leader and master of the Twelve.

(d) At a Jewish meal, as well as at the Passover meal, it is certainly customary for the *pater familias* to give the opening blessing over the bread, but someone else, usually the guest of honor, is called upon to give the closing benediction over the "cup of blessing."[70] Yet, according to the accounts of the institution, Jesus pronounces as a matter of course both benedictions. Furthermore, as we have seen above, the oldest form of the tradition—the Marcan form, in contrast to the Pauline—has the two blessings side by side at the beginning of the meal, still another feature which does not corroborate the Passover setting.

Yet, it is exactly these features, peculiar to Jesus' last meal in the Marcan account and unexplainable by Passover customs, that find their parallels in the Essene cult meal described in the texts from Qumran. Here we learn that: only men take part in the meals; only those of the inner circle, the full members of the Order, take part in the meal; he who presides at the Essene meal is not characterized as a *pater familias*, but as the properly appointed leader of the community[71]; and, finally, at the Essene meal the leader of the community pronounces both the blessings over the bread and the wine; and both are given together at the beginning of the meal.

Thus, while the most original tradition (the Marcan form) contains no specific indication of a Passover setting, it has several features which are unexplainable by such a setting, and these very features correspond to the structure of the Essene cult meal.

This is not to say that we encounter in Jesus, and more specifically in the Last Supper, some kind of Essenism. We are confronted with a new and original phenomenon, but a phenomenon where forms and praxis are often analogous to those of the Essenes. The "monastic" structure of the Qumran community is not that of Jesus and his disciples, not even in matters of the meals. It is only at the Last Supper that we find the exclusive practice of a meal limited to Jesus and the Twelve. Apart from this, Jesus always exercised great freedom regarding his meal companions, quite contrary to the Essene principles. The priestly character of the meals and the community of the Essenes has no parallel in the New Testament.

Furthermore, Jesus and his disciples did not constitute an esoteric community, separated from the world and closely guarding their secret doctrines, as was essential to the very constitution of the Essenes. Such a seclusion would be contrary to the total character of Jesus' message, his good news about the imminent kingdom of God, with salvation available to all and everyone. It would also contradict his sending forth of the disciples to preach this message (Mk.3₁₄ₑ.; 6₇.₃₀). The subsequent development of the apostolic work and of the world-wide mission, with the fundamental obligation of Christ's church to preach the gospel to all the world, all this could not have followed had the beginning been an esoteric community of disciples, with closely guarded secret teachings concerning the way of salvation, as was the case with the Essenes.

Sayings with quite an esoteric ring are admittedly found in the Synoptic Gospels. Such a passage is the one found in Mark 4, where the reason for Jesus' use of parables is stated: "Only to you (my disciples) has been given the secret of the kingdom of God. For those outside everything is in parables, in order that seeing they may see and yet not perceive, and hearing they may hear and yet not understand, lest they should attain God's forgiveness by their conversion." This is very much in accord with Essene theology, but it does not fit well into the over-all picture of Jesus' preaching, the good news addressed to every man, the tax collectors and the sinners, the blind and the lame, those from the highways and the hedges (Lk. 14₂₁ₑₑ.). Mark's way of answering the question why Jesus used parables is rather an indication that in the primitive church there were groups who understood and interpreted Jesus and his message in accordance with principles similar to those of the Essenes, and it adds nothing to our insight into the actual character of Jesus' preaching.

All this leads us to an important methodological consideration. Our comparative study of the Essene meal and the Last Supper has no direct bearing on what the last meal actually was, historically speaking. It only gives information about how this meal is described in the formula of institution. This formula, in its most original form, describes the Last Supper not as a Passover meal but as a communal meal, the forms of which correspond to those of the cult meal of the Essenes.

(5) After having spoken of the New Testament accounts of the Last Supper in the context of the Passion narratives, we now have to turn to the practices of the primitive church in Palestine. It has already been stated (p. 72) that it is important to make this distinction. According to Acts 2₄₂,₄₆, meal celebrations took place daily. The first Christians always ate together, just as did the Essenes. Such a daily communal meal cannot be explained by an early Christian understanding of the words of institution as a bequest of such a daily meal; the Marcan account has no traces of a bequest of a future regular repetition of the meal. This aspect is found only in the Pauline formula, which contains the additional clause "do this in remembrance of me." The old Palestinian formula did not yet contain such a bequest and consequently it could not provide the basis of daily celebrations; nor was such an implication intended. The daily celebrations of the primitive church in Palestine were rather a continuation of meal fellowship with the historical Jesus, as it is portrayed in the stories of Jesus feeding the multitudes (Mk. 6₃₅ₜₜ.; 8₁ₜₜ. ₚₐᵣᵣ.; cf. the meal at Emmaus, Lk. 24₃₀ₜₜ.).[72] On the other hand, these celebrations find their pre-Christian and Palestinian analogy in Judaism in the daily cult meal of the Essenes.

Just as was the case with the Gospel material, so it is true about the parallels which we find between the life of the Palestinian church and the Essene Community that such an analogy does not make Christianity into a branch of Essenism, granted only certain modifications. The analogy of the meals is no more conclusive than, e.g., that of the community of goods, practiced by both groups. In Palestinian Christianity, Jesus of Nazareth and the redemptive significance of his person is the creative element. Therefore, the differences are just as important as the analogies. There is once more the pronounced lay character of the church, and the fact related to this fundamental difference, that women belonged to the church as a matter of course. In the attitudes toward the Temple we find another difference. Acts 2₄₆ states that "they were every day in the Temple" and their participation in the Temple cult is witnessed by Acts 21₂₄,₂₆. The Essenes, on the other hand, stayed aloof from the Temple and its cult. Important is that the message of the church was openly addressed to all, while that of the Essenes was strictly esoteric. Furthermore, the Christian message was centered in what was new and peculiar to the church, its christology, and the message was the call to repentance, addressed to all in view of the fact that the End was about to come, through the impending return of Jesus, the Son of Man, who was now enthroned on the right hand of God.

The abiding significance of the Qumran texts for the New Testament is that they show to what extent the primitive church, however conscious of its integrity and newness, drew upon the Essenes in matters of practices and cult, organization and constitution. The daily meals of the Essene Community are certainly analogous to the daily meals of the Jerusalem church. As we saw, such a practice was not based upon the original formula in the Marcan account, but existed independently. The theological meaning of this daily meal was not the remembrance of Jesus' death, but rather the eschatological expectation of the *Parousia,* the return of the Lord: the risen Jesus, now enthroned in heaven, would soon return to judge the world and save his church. The faithful will eat and drink with him at his table in a renewed and transfigured world. Therefore, the daily meal of the primitive church is a joyful act, the eschatological exultation, in view of the redemption close at hand; this attitude finds its concise expression in the *maranatha* (1 Cor. 16$_{22}$, Did. 10; cf. "Come, Lord Jesus," Rev. 22$_{20}$), a cry which echoed through their daily meals.

(6) From this primitive form of the meal of the church, let us return now once more to the Marcan account of the last meal of Jesus, and to those words of Jesus which are the heart of the matter: "This is my body . . . This is my blood shed for the 'totality' *(Gesamtheit)*."[73] We have shown above that the account as well as these words of Jesus stem from the Palestinian tradition.[74] Yet, as it is not the basis of the Palestinian celebration of that meal, its creative milieu *(Sitz im Leben)* was not the cult of the Palestinian church. Consequently, the tradition preserved in Mark was not from the beginning a "cult formula," but became such later on. Originally it was simply one of the Sayings *(logia)* of Jesus, contained in the tradition of the church, confined to a specific situation, which required its doublet form. Its setting was Jesus' last meal with his disciples. This setting was, however, originally not considered as

having any connection with the daily cult meal of the church.

Nor did this double logion originally refer to a sacramental communion with the Lord, mediated through bread and wine. Such an interpretation—rather, reinterpretation—belongs first to the Hellenistic church. Its original meaning lies in its concluding phrase, which is its climax, ". . . shed for the totality."[75] Jeremias (*op. cit.*, p. 145) rightly understands the doublet form of the logion as a double parable of Jesus, similar in form to parabolic acts of the Old Testament prophets (Ezek. 4$_{1-17}$; Jer. 19$_{10ff.}$): in distributing bread and wine, Jesus interprets his death as the substitutionary atonement for all.

If we stick to this original meaning of Jesus' words, they cannot be called "words of institution." Such they became at a later stage, when incorporated in the cult formula. Originally they were only the words by which Jesus explained the twin parable.

The Hellenistic church took over the practice of the meal from the Palestinian church. With the entire treasury of the Sayings of Jesus it also received the twin parable from his last meal. 1 Cor. 11 gives us a clue to what happened. The double logion became associated with the cult meal of the church, and the tradition preserved in Mk. 14$_{22-24}$ takes on the function of a cult formula. Theologically the meal undergoes a considerable change. While it had originally a tone of exultation in expectation of the eschatological banquet, it now becomes a remembrance of the atoning death of Jesus: "as often as you eat . . . you proclaim the Lord's death." In this change of emphasis, Jesus' explanatory words take on the role and the significance of "words of institution."

A close study of the Pauline text indicates, however, that these two Palestinian traditions—the daily meal practice and the account of the last meal—were not woven together just by adding the one to the other. The cult formula is not applied to the whole meal, but to an act which we may call the Eucharist proper, celebrated with bread and wine.[76] This distinction between the meal and the Eucharist is also found in the Didache, where first the meal is described (9-10$_5$), followed by an introduction to the Eucharist, while the Eucharist itself and the words pertaining to it are omitted, since they were to be kept secret (*disciplina arcana*).[77] Later on, the Eucharist, as the cult proper, becomes detached from the congregational meal and attached to the principal morning service. The celebration of the evening meal continues for a while separately as the "Agape." In Hippolytus' *Apostolic Tradition* (chaps. 49 ff.), the Agape is still called *cena dominica*, "the Lord's Supper."

Yet, it remains an open question when the meal and Eucharist were welded into that unity which 1 Cor. 11 portrays. Paul is not responsible for the combination; he has "received" it as tradition (1 Cor. 11₂₃), and, furthermore, Paul can give still another meaning to the Eucharist: ". . . participation in the body of Christ; as the bread is one, so we, the many, are one body" (1 Cor. 10₁₆f.). The partaking of bread and wine in the Eucharist gives the church its sacramental union as the body of Christ. Such an interpretation, in the line of Hellenistic sacramental thought, indicates a later stage of development. Yet, it is already a part of the tradition that was passed on to Paul, as was the cult formula itself. As early as A.D. 40-50 i.e., within fifteen years after the death of Jesus, the account of the Last Supper had become a cult formula, which in its turn opened up new ways of interpretation.

Consequently, there is nothing astonishing in that Mark considered this account as a formula of institution when he incorporated it in his Gospel. He just knew it as such, as Paul had already done. For this reason we have a perfect right to characterize Mk. 14₂₂₋₂₄ par. as an independent cult formula and to deal with this synoptic tradition according to the laws governing the development of liturgical texts (cf. p. 73). It is only the more valuable that Mark did preserve such an ancient form of this cult formula that it allows us to pursue our inquiry even further back into a time when the text had not yet become a formula. But how far back does the Marcan text actually lead us? We have been able to assert that we have here a Palestinian tradition. In early Palestinian Christianity it was not related to the daily meals. Consequently, it did not develop out of liturgical practice, nor does it originally serve as the rationale for any cult practice.

It is, therefore, rather safe to conclude that this tradition is not a later creation of the Palestinian church. We are forced back to the proximity, rather, of Jesus' last meal as it actually took place.

(7) We have pointed to the fact that Mark does not describe the last meal with Jesus as a Passover meal, but as a cult meal, similar

to that of the Essenes. But where, when, and whence comes the tradition of its Passover character?

The only dependable source for the Passover setting of the meal, we found to be the first part of the Lucan text, with its renunciation of the lamb and the wine (22₁₅₋₁₈).[78] This passage, with its eschatology and its Semitic character does certainly not come from Hellenistic Christianity. The Semitic character of the original form of this passage remains clear in spite of Luke's effort to polish what he may have received in the form of a rough-translation Greek,[79] and points to the Palistinian church as its background.

We are apparently confronted with two different traditions concerning the last meal, both of which have a Palestinian origin, and both in the form of doublet sayings of Jesus. On the one side, we have the Marcan formula, where the death of Jesus is interpreted in terms of a substitutionary atonement, without any reference to the *Parousia*. It is not eschatological, nor is it a Passover meal. It is a cult meal similar to that of the Essenes. On the other hand, there is the Lucan tradition of a Passover meal, where Jesus gives voice to the eschatological expectation of the imminent kingdom of God (22₁₅₋₁₈). In this tradition there is, however, no interpretation of Jesus' death. The fact that Jesus speaks of himself here simply as "I"—without messianic titles or claims and without reference to the Son of Man—adds to our impression that both these traditions are ancient and dependable.

In Mark we found no indication of a rationale for any liturgical practice in the Palestinian church. We may ask: what about Lk. 22₁₅₋₁₈ in this respect? In the earlier edition of this article, I gave this answer: "Jewish-Christian usage gives no basis for a later interpretation of the last meal of Jesus as a Jewish Passover meal." I believe that today a different answer can and must be given.

In 1953, B. Lohse published his impressive study of the Passover celebrated by the so-called Quartadecimans (who celebrated Easter the 14th of Nisan).[80] His study of the sect's calendar and theology gives us dependable information on the age and origin of their Passover observance. Their Passover was celebrated on the same day and at the same hour as that of the Jews. This Christian Passover was one of fasting. The Jewish Passover was one of joyous recognition of the deliverance out of Egypt and of the future de-

liverance through the Messiah. In fact, fasting was strictly forbidden in Judaism during the month of Nisan (*op. cit.*, p. 139).
While the Jews were celebrating, Christians fasted and mourned
on their behalf. This fasting during the hours of the Jewish
Passover was not in remembrance of Jesus' death, but was a
vicarious fasting and prayer on behalf of the Jews, the "strayed
brethren of God's People." As the Jews, during their celebration,
spoke of the coming of the Messiah on the day of the Passover, so
was the Christian Passover with fasting bound up with the expectation of Jesus' *Parousia* on the Day of Passover. At three o'clock in
the morning of the 15th of Nisan, the Jewish Passover being ended,
the sect broke its fast with the celebration of the Lord's Supper,
in the form of an Agape meal combined with the Eucharist. This
observance of the Jewish Passover by fasting goes back to Palestinian
Christianity. According to Lohse, it is nothing short of the Passover
celebration of the Jerusalem church.

Thus it is a "noncelebration," a counterobservance, and not a
commemoration of the death of Jesus, which gives the original
meaning to this rite. The rationale for the Passover fasting was
that Jesus had told his disciples during his celebration of the Passover, prior to his death, that henceforth he would no more eat of
the lamb and drink of the wine until it would be celebrated anew
in the Kingdom of God. This is now an exact parallel to the tradition contained in Lk. 22₁₅₋₁₈: "I have earnestly desired to eat this
paschal lamb with you before I suffer. For I tell you that I shall not
eat it until the fulfilment in the kingdom of God. And he took the
cup, said the benediction and said: Take it and divide it among
yourselves. For I tell you that from now on I shall not drink any
more of the fruit of the vine until the Kingdom of God comes."[81]

We may conclude that this Lucan tradition is the basis for a
practice of fasting during the Jewish Passover. It may be considered
as the etiological cult legend of the Passover fasting of the Jerusalem
church.[82]

The Passover setting is woven into the very texture of the passage,
and we find no original connection with the celebration of the
Lord's Supper, this being due to the fact that the Passover was
celebrated once a year, while the Lord's Supper was the daily meal
of the Jerusalem church. On the other hand, the Lucan account is

closely related to the practice of fasting during the Passover of the Jews. It contains even the words of Jesus upon which this practice is based. Consequently, Lk. 22₁₅₋₁₈ is a creation of the Jerusalem church, the "words of institution" for their Passover fasting. The Jews had rejected Jesus the Messiah, and they were wrong in their continued celebration of the Passover. In vain, they expected another Messiah. The Christians fasted and interceded for them, that they might turn back from their mistake. The Christians celebrated *their* cult meal in the early morning, when the Jewish Passover had come to an end. Thus there could be no confusion between this Christian meal, with its eschatological joy and expectation of the *Parousia* of Jesus, and the Jewish Passover meal, with *its* messianic expectation. Furthermore, Jesus had given clear orders not to celebrate the Passover during the interim between his death and the *Parousia*.

The picture of Jesus' last meal as a Passover meal is, therefore, organically connected with the observance of fasting at Passover in the Jerusalem church. This means that at a very early stage, a few years after the death of Jesus, the Jerusalem church had two different traditions about the last meal. This is not so surprising as it might seem. The same is certainly true about other primitive traditions in the Gospels. From the point of view of method, it must be emphasized, however, that the analysis of these traditions does not allow a definite conclusion about the actual procedure and character of the last meal. We can only say that the tradition of the Passover setting of the last meal is, in all probability, a creation of the Jerusalem church, while the Marcan tradition is not. The Marcan formula comes much closer to what actually happened at the last meal of Jesus. In any case, the least acceptable of all methods would be to harmonize the two traditions and to "restore" our picture of the last meal by combining them.

(8) The material which has now become available through the findings of the Qumran texts has led us to reconsider the vast and entangled problem of the sacred meal practices of the church. We have had to face the nature of the cult formula in its most original form. The Pauline form of the Eucharist proved to be from a later stage of the tradition, influenced by a type of Hellenistic sacramentalism akin to the ideas of mystery religions. Furthermore, we

were led to challenge the view expressed, e.g., by Jeremias, that the cult formula in its Marcan form, the most original available to us, required a Passover setting.

If the cult formula is freed from its Passover context, the parallelism to the practice of the communal meal of the Essenes becomes far more significant, especially since we could list quite a few concrete and striking similarities between the two (p. 73); and, regardless of the formula proper, the similarities between the communal meals at Qumran and the daily meals of the Jerusalem church become more relevant to the whole picture.

The interpretive words of Jesus in the Marcan account should, consequently, have a meaning which would not be dependent upon the Passover setting. The point of comparison of the twin parable would be the distribution, rather than "the elements." The very term "elements" sounds alien in this connection when seen in a Jewish context, and seems to have crept into the discussion about the Lord's Supper from the theological debates of later, and more Western, sorts. If the distribution is what matters, the meaning of the meal, the act itself as well as the interpretive words of Jesus, would be: Even as all present at the meal partake of the bread and the wine, so will they all share in the atonement of his death, of his body to be given and his blood to be shed. If this was the original meaning of a parabolic saying and act, and if it intended to promise the disciples that they all were to share in the vicarious atonement which his death would bring forth, then these words not only are possible but quite plausible as actually spoken by Jesus.

The comparative material would sharpen our vision for the specific christological character of this cult formula (see p. 78). At the same time they give to the meal situation as such valid and extensive Palestinian parallels, in the light of which the arguments for a Hellenistic origin lose much of their weight.

# VI

# New Light on Temptation, Sin, and Flesh in the New Testament*

KARL GEORG KUHN

The reason for this study was a rather accidental one, an attempt to interpret the words of Jesus to his disciples in Gethsemane: "Watch ye and pray, lest ye enter into temptation. The spirit is willing, but the flesh is weak" (Mk. 14₃₈). The key words of this saying, "temptation, spirit, flesh" *(peirasmos, pneuma, sarx)*, led immediately into the wider complex of New Testament theology. It became obvious that, in the light of the Qumran texts, this whole complex could now be approached afresh and with more accuracy.

The saying of Jesus in Mk. 14₃₈ has this meaning: to fall into *peirasmos*[1] is the risk which faces the disciples. In order to avoid it, they have to "watch and pray." He who does not accept this discipline of vigilance and prayer gives in to the "weakness of the flesh" and falls thus into *peirasmos*. However, the disciples have a "willing spirit" which actually should discipline the "weak flesh," and thus prevent the danger of *peirasmos*.

If one asks for the meaning of the concept *peirasmos* in this line of thought, he is well advised to start from the New Testament use of the word and not from the special case of the temptation of Jesus. The special use has to be interpreted in the light of the general usage.[2]

The originator of the *peirasmos* in Mk. 14₃₈ is apparently not God, since it is through the weak flesh that one falls into *peirasmos*. God does not tempt as he did when he "tested" Abraham's obedi-

* Translated with some revisions from *Zeitschrift für Theologie und Kirche* 49 (1952), pp. 200-222.

94

ence by requesting the Sacrifice of Isaac (Gen. $22_1$ LXX *epeirasen;* Heb. $11_{17}$). It is rather the devil who "tempts." Even if that is not directly stated in our text, it is the general view in the New Testament, e.g., in Paul: "that Satan tempt you not" (1 Cor. $7_5$); and "lest by some means the tempter have tempted you" (1 Thess. $3_5$). Also in Mk. $4_3$, the devil is called "the Tempter." Likewise is the devil the originator of *peirasmos* in Lk. $8_{13}$ (cf. "diabolos" $8_{12}$) and in Rev. $2_{10}$. When, on the other hand, James ($1_{2.12}$) says that we should be happy when we fall into divers temptations, the suggestion that God might be the originator of *peirasmos* is expressly refuted in the very same context ($1_{13}$): contrary to what was the case with Abraham when God tested the obedience of faith, it is man's own lust that brings him into *peirasmos,* and *peirasmos* means that we fall into sin if we give in to our lust. This is very close to the Gethsemane saying, where it is the "weak flesh" through which one comes into *peirasmos,* that is, into sinful acts. 1 Tim. $6_9$ (cf. also $3_7$) contains the same connection between *peirasmos,* the snare of the devil, and lust.

When does this *peirasmos* through Satan come about? Is it a constant and present occurrence or does it belong to the end of time? Here arises the question of the eschatological character of the *peirasmos.* Once in the New Testament *peirasmos* is understood plainly within the framework of apocalyptic thought as a feature of the last days: "Because you (in this time) have kept my word (i.e., commandment) in patience, I also will keep you from the hour of *peirasmos,* which shall come upon all the world, to try *(peirasai)* them that dwell upon the earth" (Rev. $3_{10}$). Here *peirasmos* is the great decisive struggle in the last days, the fight of Satan against God, into which he drags the whole world on his side, but which is ended with the victory of God and the annihilation of Satan. If and how the petition of the Lord's Prayer, "And lead us not into *peirasmos,*" is related to this concept is a question which we must leave open at this point.[3] Elsewhere in the New Testament *peirasmos* certainly does not have this eschatological connotation, but refers to the constant danger of the faithful in the world here and now. So in Paul, 1 Thess. $3_5$, 1 Cor. $7_5$, Gal. $6_1$; the last-named passage particularly shows that *peirasmos* means to "fall into sin" (cf. "transgression" in the preceding phrase). Likewise in 1 Cor. $10_{13}$

*peirasmos* is the constant danger for the believer to fall ("lest he fall" in v. 12, which in the context of vv. 6-11 means to fall into divers sins).

The endeavor of Satan in such *peirasmos* is always to bring the believer to fall away from his faith. In 1 Thess. 3₅ the *peirasmos* of the Thessalonians would nullify the work of Paul, who had brought them into the faith. In Gal. 4₁₄ the "weakness of the flesh" in which Paul had preached the gospel to the Galatians, i.e., his unimpressive, pitiful way of appearance or, even more concretely, his illness might have been the *peirasmos* that made the Galatians reject Paul, and with him Christ. *Peirasmos,* by definition, applies only to the believer. The unbelievers, who stand outside, are not in the state of *peirasmos.* Satan already has them in his power. In the interpretation of the parable of the sower in Lk. 8₁₃, *peirasmos* strikes those "who for awhile believe," and means their falling off again. Again in the letter to the Hebrews the situation of the believers in the world is of "those subject to *peirasmos*" (2₁₈, 4₁₅). Likewise in 1 Pet. 1₆: "for a while, if need be, now you may have to suffer manifold *peirasmoi.*" In the same letter (4₁₂ff.) *peirasmos* strikes the "house of God" as seduction away from faith, and it comes in the form of persecution and through the fact that the believer must suffer injustice in the world. Here too the means of defense are "to be sober and watch" (1 Pet. 5₈), for "the devil, as a roaring lion, walketh about, seeking whom he may devour." *Peirasmos* is just that: the constant danger that Satan may devour the believer. Therefore, one must watch constantly, like a soldier at his post (1 Thess. 5₆ff.). One must "watch and be sober," and arm oneself with the armor of faith, love, and hope. Only with such armor can one withstand the "attacks of the devil" (Eph. 6₁₁). The exhortation in 1 Cor. 16₁₃, which through its abrupt position in the context shows itself to be a formal phrase of paraenetic[4] tradition, has the same meaning: "watch ye, stand fast in the faith, be courageous and strong." It is the attitude of a brave soldier of God in battle with the devil.

Thus the concept *peirasmos* has its roots in the imagery of a state of war between two powers in the world, that of God and that of Satan, in which the believer, as God's soldier, is constantly exposed to the attacks of the devil and must therefore be watchful and armed at his post. Paul's concept of the powers in Rom. 6 is to be understood in this same way, as the either/or of the rule of God or of the power of sin. Therefore, the believer should put his limbs in God's service as "weapons of righteousness" and not as "weapons of injustice" in the service of sin. One can only be the *doulos* ("slave," "servant") of the one or of the other. There is no neutral position in this battle between the two powers in the world. The same basic thought—the state of war between two powers—determined the teaching of Jesus. Jesus sees his work within the general framework of the struggle between God and Satan in the world and for the world. It is he who enters "in the house of the mighty" to plunder, after he has bound the mighty one (Mk. 3₂₇); his work breaks Satan's power and establishes that of God (Lk. 11₂₀).[5]

Only in this context can the thought of Jas. 1₂,₁₂ be understood: rejoice when you are exposed to divers *peirasmoi*. This is the pride of the experienced soldier, who has been tried in many wars and now deservedly receives the reward of the wreath of victory: "for when he is tried he shall receive the crown of life."

Thus we have here come upon a concept which can be found throughout the New Testament. The exhortations related to this concept show the marks of set formulae of a paraenetic tradition. The question is: where does this tradition, which evidently determines the thoughts of the primitive church, arise?

Today, after having found the Hebrew texts at Qumran, we can give a clear answer to this problem. With these manuscripts we have before us the writings of a Palestinian Jewish sect from the first century B.C.[6] Here the religious ideas and the way of thinking are considerably and characteristically different from that form of Judaism which we, up to this time, considered to be *the* form of Palestinian Judaism at the time of Christ. They are the writings of the Essenes; this cannot be doubted any longer.[7] Here we find the entire set of concepts described above: the two powers, the state of war, and the *peirasmos* of the believer. The eschatological structure of this thinking is fully developed as the main idea of the whole theology of the sect. This is most clearly shown in the basic doctrinal passage in 1 QS iii, 13-iv, 26.

The situation of man in the world is determined, according to this presentation, by his belonging *either* to the "sons of light," "sons of righteousness," "people of truth" *or* to the "sons of darkness," "people of perversion," "people of deceit," and "hosts of Belial." This allegiance is determined by primeval divine pre-destination.

> From the God of knowledge comes everything that is and shall be.[8] And *before* their (men's) existence he has determined all their reflections and thoughts. And *during* their existence . . . all their deeds are irrevocably fulfilled . . . (God) has assigned two spirits to him, through which (or: in which) he wanders until the season of His visitation. These are the spirits of truth and of perversion. From the source of light (issue) the generations of truth and from the source of darkness the generations of perversion (1 QS iii, 15-16, 18-19).[9]

The origin of this idea of predestination must be understood in the light of comparative religion. As it is expressed here, it is foreign to Jewish thinking as we know it in the Old Testament. An influence of the concepts of the older Parsiism is obvious.[10] There, too, we find in the beginning the dualism of the two original spirits of good and evil (Yasna 30, 3 ff.), as a result of which all mankind is divided into the two opposing groups of "followers of Asha" and "comrades of Drug," i.e., "the people of truth" and "the people of lies." This dualism rests on a primeval *choice*. The determination of these two original spirits as good and evil comes from the fact that they themselves made the original choice. In the same way the determination of men as belonging to one of the two inimical groups is due to the fact that each individual has made the choice between Asha and Drug, truth and lie, well-doing and evil-doing. According to this choice of theirs, they then must act accordingly. Their ultimate fate is determined thereby: a state of either glorification or damnation and annihilation.

While in the Iranian way of thinking the determination of man as good or evil is decided by his own choice, our passage from the Qumran texts gives a somewhat different picture. The dualism which was taken over from Iranian religion, and which there had presupposed an original choice, is here connected with the Jewish, monotheistic concept of God from the Old Testament, that is, with the idea of creation. "God created the two spirits of light and dark-ness" (1 QS iii, 25). Not man through his original choice, but God has decided the allegiance of each man to one or the other side *before his existence,* and, as a result of this, has established his deeds and his end irrevocably.

Out of this combination of the dualism with the monotheistic idea of creation of the Old Testament, the following problem, of course, arises immediately: How can God, on the one hand, create evil and predestine man to do evil and then, on the other hand, because of these predestined deeds, which are unavoidably ungodly and evil, judge and damn mankind? But the writing of the sect does not reflect on this problem at all. In the purely dualistic scheme of Parsiism the problem does not exist. In that case everyone, first the two original spirits and then each man, has made a choice in the beginning; his deeds are according to this choice, and according to it he will also eventually be condemned and annihilated. The unsolved problem arises first when this Jewish sect puts the divine predetermination in the place of the determination of man by his own choice. And since the Christian church adopted this basic concept—the juxtaposition of dualism and the monotheistic idea of creation—this unsolved problem has been woven into the very fabric of Christian theology, a fact which has had far-reaching effect through the centuries.

According to the Qumran texts, then, each man is placed in the ranks of one of the two powers, of light or darkness, truth or perversion, God or Satan, in accordance with his predestined lot. He stands either under the dominion of the one or under the dominion of the other, and his deeds are proof and expression of his subjection, as they are, at the same time, the execution and realization of the dominion of one or the other power: "In the hand of the Prince of Lights[11] lies the dominion of (or: over) all the sons of righteousness, who walk in the ways of light, and in the hand of the Angel of darkness lies all dominion of (or: over) the sons of perversion, who (in accordance with this) walk in the ways of darkness" (1 QS iii, 20-21).

It is decisive for our study, which takes the word *peirasmos* as its point of departure, to see how this sect understands the situation of its members, the sons of light, within the framework of its anthropology. The world is for them the "land of Belial," of Satan, or, as he is called in the preceding passage, "the Angel of darkness." The situation of the believer in the world is that of being "enticed," of being attacked by the Angel of darkness, who leads astray into error and sin; this is brought about mainly by persecution and affliction: "All 'going astray' of the sons of righteousness and all their sins and their failures and their transgressions occur through the Angel of darkness and under his dominion . . . and all their afflictions and their seasons of distress under the dominion of his hostility[12]; and all the spirits of his lot[13] strive to trip the sons of light. The God of Israel, however, and the Angel of his truth help all the sons of light,[14] and he created the spirits of light and darkness and on them has he based all action" (1 QS iii, 22-25).

The text then gives a logical application of this dualistic structure of power in detailed lists of the *deeds* of the two sorts of men. The pattern is strictly that of "The Two Ways": on the one hand, the ways of light; on the other hand, the ways of darkness, the works of the spirit of perversion.[15]

What then follows is another passage of utmost importance for our matter, a passage which clarifies the eschatological character of the state of war: "God has given them (the two spirits of truth and of perversion and accordingly the two parts of mankind, the sons of light and of darkness) equal power until the last days. And he has put eternal enmity between their divisions . . . for they shall not walk together. And God, in the mysteries of his understanding and in his glorious wisdom, *has set a limit to the duration of perversion,* and (when this limit has expired) will eternally annihilate it at the time of his visitation" (1 QS iv, 16-19).

The situation of the believer in the world is, therefore, that of the soldier of God, who is at war with Satan and with his army on earth, the sons of darkness; he is constantly attacked by temptations to sin, by need, and by affliction. Therefore, it is demanded of him "not to retreat before any fright or anxiety or test . . . under the rule of Belial" (i, 17ff.). The "military" structure of the congregation as that of an army in battle position against the world is described in detail in 1 QM, the "rules of war,"[16] which gives a close-up picture of the battle of the sons of light against the sons of darkness. Here are formations, size, and divisions of the army of the sons of light, the armor of the various types of troops, the tactics for attack and following through as well as for defense; in addition, there are the speeches to be made at various junctures of battle, and hymns to be sung.

"Watching and praying" is an essential means of help in the "soldier life" of the sons of light. This is substantiated by many passages of 1 QM as far as the "praying" is concerned. "Watching" is not expressly mentioned in the texts which are so far at our disposal, but it is an exercise which is constantly demanded of the community, e.g.: "And everywhere, where there are ten men,[17] there must always be one who studies the Law constantly, night and day . . . and the members[18] shall watch in the community one third of all the nights of the year[19] for the reading of scripture and for the search for justice and for thanksgiving[20] in the community"[21] (1 QS vi, 6-8).

Now, we can hardly proceed any further in our study before we have discussed more thoroughly the meaning and significance of the concept of "flesh."

Rabbinical Judaism describes man with the stereotyped formula "flesh and blood"—and always with the double expression.[22] Thereby man is marked by his limitations as a creature, in contrast to God's infinite omnipotence. In the Qumran texts man is called "flesh"—with the single expression. The pious hereby denotes his unworthiness to praise God: "Who is such great flesh and what is such a great image of clay, that it could glorify the wonders (of God)?" (1 QH iv, 29). Even if we still feel here the Old Testament way of speaking, where man is contrasted, as the frail, withering "flesh," to the "spirit of Yahweh," which alone is worthy of trust (Gen. 6₃, Is. 31₃, *et al.*), nevertheless, there is a great difference from the anthropology of the Old Testament. In the Qumran texts the word "flesh" is contrasted not only to the spirit of *God* but to the "spirit of truth," which the believer possesses, in accordance with his predestination. Therefore, man as "flesh" is unworthy of God and prone to do evil, or rather, prone to succumb to the Evil One, while the spirit of the pious, as the "spirit of truth," places him in the battlefront on God's side against the Evil One. Thus "flesh" becomes a contrast to the "spirit" which rules the pious man and determines his good actions, and dwells within him; consequently "flesh" becomes the area of weakness through the natural inclinations of man; it becomes almost synonymous with evil.

A few examples may suffice at this point. The War Scroll (1 QM) gives the inscriptions on the various field-standards which lead the divisions of the army of the sons of light. In these inscriptions the religious ideas of the battle are expressed. The inscription on the standard of one group of a hundred men reads: "The fist of war falls from God on all *flesh of evil*" (iv, 3).

Exactly the same expression is found in 1 QS xi, 9. Here the "company of the *flesh of evil*"[23] is synonymous with the "man(kind) of perversion" and "those who walk in darkness," all characterizations of the human existence. In using the pronoun "I" even the believer counts himself as belonging to this "company of the flesh of evil," since he is a man, and as such, in the context of the passage, he commits sin. The passage runs as follows: "To those whom God has chosen he has given them (viz., the aforementioned gifts of salvation: knowledge, righteousness, strength and glory) as an eternal possession, and allows them as heirs of the lot of the holy ones, and he has associated their assembly with the sons of heaven[24] for a gathering of the community ... *But I* belong to the mankind of perversion and to the *company of the flesh of evil*. My transgressions, my wickedness, my sin together with the rottenness of my heart (mark me as belonging) to the company of worms[25] and to those who walk in darkness" (1 QS xi, 7-10).

Most important for the New Testament is the "I"-style of this saying. We have in this text the same "I" as in Rom. 7; it is the same "I" not only in regard to style, but especially in regard to theological connotations: "I" is here, just as in Rom. 7, not meant individually or biographically; it is gnomic, descriptive of human existence. The "I" in this Qumran passage, as in Rom. 7, signifies the existence of mankind, which is flesh. Man is flesh because and inasmuch as he sins and thereby stands under ungodly power. One may compare the sentence in the Qumran text, "I belong to the company of the flesh of evil" with Rom. 7₁₄, "I am *fleshly* (and that means:), sold, under sin." Likewise Rom. 7₂₄: "I ... miserable man! Who will rescue me out of this body which is bound to succumb to death (because of sin!)."

This "I"-style is found with identical theological meaning not only in the quoted Qumran passage, but also frequently in the Qumran Hymns (1 QH). Here we find in one instance how the poet, after having praised the fullness of salvation, which has been promised him as a member of the community of God's salvation, goes on to say: "But I, an image of clay, what am I? Kneaded with water, what am I worth? And what strength have I? For I stand in the domain of evil, and with the miserable is my lot" (iii, 23-25).

This "I"-style of the Qumran Hymns is evidently connected with the "I"-style of the Old Testament psalms and, from the point of view of form, this genre is here developed further. In the Qumran texts, however, the "I"-sayings appear within the framework of the dualistic power-idea, and are, therefore, essentially different from the Old Testament. In the Qumran setting, the "I" represents the human existence as "flesh" in the sense of man's belonging to the sphere of the power of the ungodly. Because of this completely new accent and meaning of the "I" sayings, it is the Qumran texts rather than the Old Testament psalms which offer the true and immediate parallel to the "I"-sayings of Rom. 7.

The "company of the flesh of evil," to which the believer counts himself as "I," stands in the Qumran texts in antithesis to the "elect of God," the "heirs of the lot of the holy ones." Nevertheless, the believer belongs exactly *to* this group of those "elected by God." This is clear from a sentence taken from the same context as the ones just quoted: "My eyes see wisdom, which is hidden from men, (and) knowledge and prudent purpose, which (are hidden) from the children of man (and) a source of righteousness and a basin of strength together with the spring of glory (which are hidden) from the company of flesh" (1 QS xi, 6-7).

The believer therefore belongs to both groups: inasmuch as he is man, that is, inasmuch as he sins, he is *"flesh of sin"*; inasmuch as he is "the elect of God" (by strength of the "spirit of truth" which dwells in him and determines his deeds according to predestination) he belongs to the "eternal community," to the "army of the holy ones,"[26] and thereby he stands in battle *against* the "company of deceit, the congregation of uselessness."[27] This dialectical way of understanding the situation of man has certainly far-reaching significance for the interpretation of Rom. 7 and 8.

From the same context we also find a text which can help us to determine the meaning of "flesh": "And if I totter, God's mercies are my help forever; and if I stumble through a *sin of the flesh,* nevertheless, my right stands on the righteousness of God[28] eternally" (1 QS xi, 11-12). To be sure, the expression "sin of the flesh" here does not yet have the narrower meaning of sexual sin, but means sin in general. Sin is brought about through "flesh" as that which qualifies human existence as much.[29]

It is only when we have taken the entire anthropology of the Qumran sect into account that we can understand its theology. Not only the above-discussed concept of *peirasmos* as the situation of the believer in the world, but the whole framework within which it stands, the "two-power" system, "sin" as a characteristic as well as an effect of the ungodly powers in the world and "flesh" as the sphere of this ungodly power, becomes understandable, in regard to its origin as well as in regard to a more exact interpretation.

We see now how the pattern of the two powers, which is highly developed in the New Testament, belongs to the Jewish Palestinian tradition found at Qumran. That means that it does not come from Hellenism or from Gnosticism, a fact with great bearing on Pauline studies, and especially on our understanding of Rom. 6 and 7, where the concept of two powers determines the entire logic. Here Paul does not speak about "God and the devil" but rather about "God and Sin," whereby Sin is the power controlling the world and mankind. But Sin is not distinguished from concrete sin, sins in plural, but both are always included in the one. As a *power* it brings about concrete sin, and vice versa: by the fact that man sins concretely he comes under this power. That is why Paul, in the same context, can use "servant of uncleanness and unlawfulness" (Rom. 6₁₉) and "servant of sin" (16ff.) interchangeably. To be a servant of these powers means "to bear fruit," that is, to do deeds accordingly, either sins or good deeds (20-22). This insoluble connection between "power" and "fruit" proves the analogy with the Qumran sect. Further, in Gal. 5₁₆-₂₃, "flesh" and "spirit" are in battle against each other, and that is shown, on the one hand, by the "works of the flesh" and, on the other, by the "fruits of the spirit," which are enumerated in antithetical catalogues.[30]

This is just as clear in Rom. 6₁₂ff., where the dominion of the one or other power consists in the fact that man puts his limbs at its disposal (i.e., in action) either as "weapons of righteousness" or as "weapons of unrighteousness." "Righteousness" is used here not in the specifically Pauline sense; the contrasting pair points rather to the Jewish terminology: "right action"/"evildoing." This agrees completely with the pattern and terminology of the Qumran texts, where the "sons of light" or "of righteousness," and, on the other hand, the "sons of darkness," or "of unrighteousness," or "of perversion" are interchangeable, and where the term "weapons of light" means exactly the same as "weapons of righteousness." As in Rom. 13₁₂, these *weapons* can be contrasted to the *works* of darkness.[31]

Paul's use of the concept "flesh" shows equally great similarity to the concepts we have found expressed in the Qumran texts. When

Paul says in Rom. 7₁₄: "I am carnal, sold under sin," the character-istic of human existence as "flesh" is interpreted through its being controlled by sin as a power. This is in content as well as in expres-sion[32] the same as the saying of the pious man (quoted, p. 102): "I belong to the company of the flesh of evil. My sins (marks me as belonging) . . . to the company of worms and to those who walk in darkness." Paul says in Rom. 7₁₇₋₂₀: "that which determines my acts (*against* my will, which is directed toward good!) is the sin which dwells in me." And he interprets this "in me" as "i.e., in my flesh." The Qumran texts speak in the same way of "flesh" equal to "sin" as the ungodly realm of power, in contrast to the "spirit of truth" in the believer, which wills good and determines well-doing. Paul speaks in Rom. 7₂₅ of the antithesis of "flesh," through which man is enslaved to the "law of sin," as against the "mind," through which man is the servant of the "law of God." Flesh and mind are in battle with one another (7₂₃). The same thing is said in Gal. 5₁₇ of "flesh" and "spirit," and in 1 QS iv, 23, we read: "Until now (that is, as long as the end is not here) the spirits of truth and of perversion battle within the heart of man."

Here the words from the Gethsemane passage comes into focus again, since they witness to this very same opposition within man: "The spirit is willing, but the flesh is weak" (Mk. 14₃₈ ₚₐᵣ.). The analogy to the terminology of the Qumran texts is even stronger than in Paul. Whereas Paul in Rom. 7 equates "mind," "inward man," and "to will the good," in Mark/Matthew it is a question of the "spirit" which the believer has. It is, as is often said in 1 QS, "his spirit," the spirit of the believer.[33] And as "the willing spirit" in Mark/Matthew reminds us of the expression of Ps. 51₁₄, "may the spirit of willingness support me," so also the Qumran texts show acquaintance with the terminology of Ps. 51 in using the phrase "a broken spirit (v. 19: 1 QS viii, 3 and xi, 1).

When Paul speaks of the "spirit" he is, to be sure, also speaking of the "dwelling in you" (Rom. 8₉), but with him the emphasis is not on its being the willing spirit of the believer. He is anxious to stress that it is the spirit of *God*, and that means the spirit of Christ, "Christ in you" (Rom. 8₉₋₁₀).[34] With Paul, the "spirit" has a christo-logical motivation; its manifestation as well as its effect is rooted in the historical act of salvation of Jesus Christ, the eschatological

Saviour. Such thoughts are completely absent from the Qumran texts. And this is connected with another, more important *difference*: for Paul the spirit is not something which the believer has according to a preordained order—Paul's intense concern with predestination notwithstanding—but rather that which he receives in Baptism as the Gift of God when he accepts the Gospel of Christ in faith. The Qumran texts are deterministic in a less dialectic way: Those who belong to the redeemed community are by the strength of predestination the people of the "spirit of truth," and their deeds are irrevocably in correspondence with this.[35] (And if they sin, that is really only an "irregular straying"[36] from the predestined structure of their existence, caused by the "flesh" which is theirs or, in other words, through the attack of Satan.) With Paul, on the other hand, even though in many aspects he shares his anthropology with the Qumran texts, *this determinism is broken through* by the completely different train of thought of concepts like the gospel of Jesus Christ—"proclamation" (*kerygma*)—"faith." Through the proclamation of the gospel of salvation in Jesus Christ, man is called out of his distance from God and his enmity with God, out of his previous existence as a "son of darkness," and in accepting the gospel in faith he becomes a *new* man, a "son of light." Thus "spirit" is for Paul no longer a static, predestined *habitus,* but the divine gift of grace of an existence which is taken hold of in faith, and is given in baptism. This is man's proper existence. Paul interprets "spirit" existentially.[37] If these two characteristics—on the one hand, the christological and, on the other hand, the existential interpretations —are the things that are essentially new in Paul, we find nevertheless that the over-all anthropological pattern inside which Paul affirms what is new with Jesus Christ is that of the Qumran texts. This analogy is found in both terms and concepts, as was particularly clear in the concept "flesh."

To be sure, the concept "flesh" has many more shades of meaning in the writings of Paul than it would seem according to that which has been said here, especially about Rom. 7. Paul can use "flesh" in a completely "neutral" sense. But even this use of language is shared with the Qumran Texts. Paul uses "flesh" simply in the sense of "body" (e.g., 1 Cor. 7:28; 2 Cor. 12:7; Gal. 4:13; Phil. 1:24, *et al.*)[38] Likewise 1 QS iii, 9 reads: "His flesh shall not become clean" (cf. 1 QS iv, 21). And when Paul describes the Jews as "my kinsmen according to the flesh" (Rom. 9₃, cf. 11₁₄) and speaks of Abraham as his "forefather according to the flesh" (Rom. 4₁), this has its parallel in CD vii, 1; viii, 6; xix, 9.

The expression "the body of flesh," which is found twice in the New Testament (Col. 1₂₂, 2₁₁), is particularly important in this connection. 1 QpHab ix, 2, now gives us a literal parallel. It is said there of the "wicked priest" (the adversary of the "Teacher of Righteousness"): "And they did dreadful things to him in the way of evil illnesses and performed acts of vengeance against his body of flesh."[39] This expression is found also in Sirach 23₁₈, where it is said with reference to masturbation: "He who is a fornicator on his body of flesh will not stop until the fire is burnt out." The Greek text to the last chapters of Enoch also offers the same expression.[40] There the souls of the faithful among the dead are addressed: "Do not be sad, that . . . God was not friendly[41] to your body of flesh; for your days were (after all) days of sinners and men accursed on the earth." One might add as a fourth passage Enoch 16₁. Here the giants are spoken of, who, according to Gen. 6₄, were conceived between fallen heavenly spirits and "flesh," i.e., earthly women. After the death of the giants the spirits left the "body of their flesh."[42] These passages indicate that "the body of flesh" is a quite "neutral" expression for the bodiliness of man, and is common in Judaism. Thus it is also applied to the Christians in Col. 2₁₁. Their baptism is there described as "putting off the body of flesh," since it is the "act of dying with Christ." In Col. 1₂₂ the deed of reconciliation of Christ on the cross is called an act of salvation "on his body of flesh through death." It is significant that it is in Colossians we find this specific expression, which proves to be a *terminus technicus* of Judaism.

Of greater importance is, however, the fact that Paul shares not only this general, "neutral" sense of "flesh" with the Qumran texts, but above all the theologically loaded use which we analyzed above. Both in Paul and at Qumran, the "neutral" use of "flesh" is completely embedded and overshadowed by the loaded meaning. "Flesh" is the sphere, the realm where ungodliness and sin have effective power. Thus Bultmann's very precise and correct statement about the Pauline formula "in the flesh" is exactly as valid for the concept of "flesh" in the Qumran texts: "A phrase which can be explained neither from the Old Testament nor from the Greek usage.

This formula, which shows that according to Paul a man's nature is not determined by what he may be as to substance (in the way the Old Testament says that man is flesh), nor by what qualities he may have (as the Greeks' thinking would put it), but that his nature is determined by the sphere within which he moves, the sphere which marks out the horizon or the possibilities of what he does and experiences."[43]

Just as in the case of "sin" and "flesh," it is now possible to draw the connecting lines for the concept of *peirasmos* in the New Testament; it has the same structure in the New Testament as in the Qumran texts. It has its roots in the idea of the two *powers* which are at war with one another in the world, God and Satan, light and darkness, the right action and the doing of evil. *Peirasmos* describes the situation of the believer in this battle as that of being constantly attacked by Satan, being at all times exposed to his assaults and having to hold one's own against him. To be *attacked* in this way means to be constantly exposed to the satanic temptation to sin, and thereby to fall away from faith. In this predicament the weak spot which Satan attacks is either the "flesh," which is "weak," or "one's own greed," through which one is brought to sin. But the believer must *stand fast* against all this, well armed with the spiritual armor, as the "sober" and "watchful" soldier of God. And just as in the texts of the Qumran sect, so in the New Testament it is mainly "tribulation and persecution" which make the attack acute. Thus in Lk. 8₁₃ "the time of *peirasmos*" corresponds to the "tribulation and persecution" (*thlipsis e diogmos*) in Mk. 4₁₇ and Mt. 13₂₁.

Just as it says in 1 QS iii, 24, that God *helps* the pious man that he may not succumb,[44] so also 2 Pet. 2₉: "The Lord knows how to deliver the godly out of *peirasmos*." Paul speaks in the same way in 1 Cor. 10₁₃: He who in the face of the terrible example of vv. 6-11 comprehends the heavy earnestness of the exhortation of v. 12, "Therefore let any one who thinks that he stands take heed lest he fall," could easily lose his courage. But, says v. 13, be comforted; the weight of the attack will not rise above that degree of power of resistance which is attainable by man: "God is faithful—he helps—he will not suffer you to be tempted above that you are able." "With the *peirasmos*" he creates also the way out, "the ability to endure." How is "with the *peirasmos*" to be understood? The translation "together with the tribulation" seems the most likely. Just as he has sent the tribulation itself, God also creates the possibility to escape, the ability to withstand. That would imply that God is the originator of the *peirasmos*. This, however, would contradict not only the general idea of *peirasmos*, but also the context of this passage. *Peirasmos* refers to the constant danger to the believer, that he may *fall*, i.e., sin, just as the generation in the wilderness, according to the examples of vv. 6-11, fell into divers sins and was therefore annihilated by God's judgment. It is out of the question that God was the cause of this sin. Therefore, *peirasmos* in v. 13, as the temptation to sin, cannot have God as its originator. The preceding sentence, "God will not suffer you to be tempted above that you are able," points in the same direction. Therefore, it is to be assumed that "with the *peirasmos*" is to be understood in a purely temporal sense, "at the same time as," in the moment of the critical situation, during the attack of Satan, God also gives the believer the necessary power to withstand, so that he does not fall, but endures.

The sixth petition of the Lord's Prayer, "lead us not into *peiras-mos*," could suggest that God is the originator of *peirasmos*. But it can hardly refer to God, who tests our faith and obedience, as in Gen. 22₁, Ex. 16₄ (and some few other passages of the Old Testament). If that were the case, the plea would be a positive one: "Lead us into it" or "Test our faith." The plea to be spared from *peirasmos* makes sense only if *peirasmos* in this passage too refers to the satanic attack, as the temptation to sin and the danger of falling. Then the meaning of the plea is: "Let us not come into the attack, into the danger of falling,"[45] in which case the seventh plea, included in Mt. 6₁₃, correctly interprets the sense, by formulating positively what is said negatively in the sixth petition: "but tear us out of the power of Satan."[46]

A more difficult question here is that of the eschatological character of this *peirasmos*. Does Jesus refer to the great end of the fight of Satan against God in the last days, the apocalyptic battle at the end, of which Rev. 3₁₀ speaks? Or does he mean the Now of the believers in the world as a situation of attack, as do the other passages of the New Testament? Or—this would be the third possibility—are these alternatives not to the point? Can the Now and the Then be differentiated and separated in this way, or must they be seen together and as aspects of one and the same situation?

In the presentation of the Qumran pattern of thought (see p. 99) the Now is understood as the state of war between "Belial and the people of *his* lot" and God and *his* "elect," who are God's warriors in this world, which is the domain of Belial. This battle will come to an end with God's victory and the annihilation of all evil at the point in time which is foreseen in God's counsel. That is then the "time of dominion for all people of his (God's) lot and of eternal ruin for all that belongs to the lot of Belial" (1 QM i, 5). Up until that time the battle wavers back and forth: "(God) has put them (the two inimical groups of warriors) in equality until the time of the judgment and the new creation"[47] (1 QS iv, 25). But the Now and the Then cannot be so distinguished, that the believers have to stand firm *now* in the battle in the world and prove themselves— left more or less to their own devices—whereas *then* it will be essential that God act and destroy Satan. Rather, God already now interferes constantly with the battle; he *helps* the pious (1 QS iii, 24) and takes care that they do not succumb to the attacks of Satan and his people. To be sure, the community is saturated with the certainty that if it is victorious over Satan and sin, if it withstands the temptations, this is not in the least due to its own achievement, but exclusively to God's deed and miraculous power:

"But I am dust and ashes./What do I plan—except you purposed it,/And what do I think—except you willed it,/And what strength do I unfold—except you make me stand firm,/And how can I be successful— except you make me so,/And what can I say—except you open my mouth,/ And how can I speak and give answer—except you have taught me./You are the Lord of Gods,/and the king of the honored,/ and the lord of every spirit,/And the ruler in all action./Nothing can be done without you,/And nothing can be known without your will,/There is nothing beside you,/And nothing approaches you in strength,/Nothing has meaning compared with thy glory,/And thy strength surpasses all value" (1 QH x, 5-10).

Thus the Now and the Then, the life of the pious here in this world and the apocalyptic end, are not at all separated from each other, in terms of the weight of the divine interference. The Now develops into the Then continuously. In this sense the sect knows itself to be an eschatological company of warriors, the People of God of the last days.[48]

The teaching of Jesus displays the same basic structure. He sees his situation as a state of war: "I came to bring not peace but the sword" (Mt. 10$_{34}$); "Who is not with me, he is against me" (Mt. 12$_{30}$; Lk. 11$_{23}$). And indeed it is the war of God against Satan, in which he is God's warrior. By his works, especially by casting out demons and by healing the sick, he attacks the dominion of Satan, breaking into his house, binding him and stealing his armaments: "Or else how can one enter into a strong man's house, and rob weapons, unless he first binds the strong man? Then we can plunder his house" (Mt. 12$_{29}$). It is a question of the kingdom, the domain of God; *it is coming.* He teaches us to pray, that it may come. But even here this final moment, the Then of the coming of the kingdom of God, cannot be separated from the Now of the battle against the kingdom of Satan. Inasmuch as Jesus breaks the power of Satan with his word and with his deeds, the kingdom of God is actually made manifest: "When I with the finger of God cast out demons, then the kingdom of God is there with you" (Lk. 11$_{20}$ par.). God's domain is enacted now as a kingdom in the process of manifesting itself. The Now and Then, the breaking into Satan's domain, the victory over him in the word and works of Jesus here and now, and the final victory of the coming kingdom of God, are different aspects of the same continuing act.[49] The kingdom of God is a concept neither of the apocalyptic future nor of a static present—and certainly not of an evolutionary development—but a dynamic eschatological concept, just as *peirasmos* as the attack of Satan is *always* an eschatological concept. When Jesus teaches us to pray: "Lead us not into *peirasmos,*" no distinction can be made between the Now of the believer in the world and the Then of the final battle to come. Both belong together as one act. It can be said, however, that the entire teaching of Jesus is dominated by the thought of pressing time. The thunderstorm is on its way (Lk. 12$_{54}$), the battle is about to turn into its final stages. "I saw how Satan was thrown out of heaven like a bolt of lightning" (Lk. 10$_{18}$).[50] The final battle may stand in the foreground when the sixth petition of the Lord's Prayer speaks of *peirasmos,* and yet the complex view of the final *peirasmos* and the *peirasmos* here and now as one and the same act is not thereby jeopardized.

We may now have enough of a background for the understanding of the story about the temptation of Jesus. The point of departure must be the genuine and concrete concept of the *peirasmos*: The situation of the believer in the world is that of *peirasmos*, and in this framework stands the concept of the "tribulation of Jesus" as it is spoken of in the Epistle to the Hebrews 2₁₇₋₁₈. Jesus had to be "made like his brethren" and was, therefore, during his life on earth subject to *peirasmos*, just as they were. In this christology the emphasis lies on his having become man. Since Jesus was exposed to temptation as a man just as are his brethren, he is now able to help them when they are attacked. The difference is that Jesus passed this test of an attacked existence. The *peirasmos* did not seduce into sin. He was "tempted in every respect just as we," but "without sin," without letting the temptation reach its goal of bringing him to sin. The same thought, which corresponds to the actual meaning of *peirasmos*, is found in the "testament" (Lk. 22₂₈ff.): "You (disciples) are those who have held by me in my *peirasmoi* (i.e., in my life on earth, the scene of *peirasmoi*), and therefore I leave you (now at the end of my life) the kingdom by will. . . ."⁵¹

When the Marcan account of the temptation of Jesus (1₁₂₋₁₃) limits this exposure to *peirasmos* to forty days, it is due to an intentional limitation. That which can truly be said of Jesus' entire life on earth is here changed into a vignette, picturing in the style of myth the "forty days" before his mission begins. Furthermore, it is also said that "he was together with the wild animals; and the angels served him." However one may care to interpret it in detail, this is a statement as to his heavenly dignity and includes implicitly the thought that he survived the temptation victoriously. Thus this story of Mark has epitomized the whole redeeming work of Jesus, his existence as man in the temptation, his victorious withstanding, and his heavenly dignity, all in this mythical period of "forty days."

In the temptation story of Mt. 4₃₋₁₀ and Lk. 4₃₋₁₂, the triple argument with the devil has obscured the original significance of the term *peirasmos*. Now there is only a dispute in rabbinical style, where Jesus defeats the devil with the proper quotations from the Scriptures. This dialogue takes place at the end of the forty days (which are simply taken over from Mark). The concept of temptation as the structure of life in this world has been transformed into legend.

It is different with the story of the *peirasmos* of Jesus in Gethsemane.[52] Here the original, loaded sense of *peirasmos* is fully retained. Jesus warns the disciples to "watch and pray"; for by so doing one can escape the *peirasmos*. He himself watched and prayed in Gethsemane. His *peirasmos* was the attack of the devil with the threatening horrors of the "tribulation and persecution" on his way toward suffering and death. But the devil was not able to tear him away from the fulfillment of his redemptive work. Jesus survived this temptation victoriously through his watching and praying, and thus gave the disciples and the church the example for the proper fighting off of *peirasmos*.

# VII

## "Peace Among Men of God's Good Pleasure" Lk. 2₁₄*

ERNEST VOGT, S.J.

Most scholars agree, rightly, that the Greek word *eudokias* stands for the Hebrew word *rason* (good pleasure[1]) and refers not to the good will of men, but either to the will of God conferring grace on those he has chosen or to the pleasure of God delighting in and approving of the goodness in men's lives.[2]

Until now there had been no known text in which this Hebrew term for God's good pleasure was used to designate men as Lk. 2₁₄ does. However, C. H. Hunzinger has pointed out that the phrase "sons of his good pleasure" occurs in the Qumran Hymns (1 QH iv, 32 f.).[3] It is now found also in 1 QH xi, 9.

The Hymns and the Manual of Discipline found in the Qumran area show the deeply religious sentiment of the community which possessed these books and lived in the Judean desert in the time of Christ .Their teaching and pious way of life certainly could have had an influence outside the community, and prepared for the message of the gospel. There is no reason why sincere Israelites like the Bethlehem shepherds, Simeon, Zechariah, John the Baptist, his diciples, and Christ's future apostles could not have been acquainted with them and have held them in high esteem. The ideas and religious language of these texts, therefore, may well cast light on the language of the Gospels.

The meaning of the term *bene resono* should especially be determined from its context. 1 QH iv, 30-38: "For I know that

---

* Translated with some revisions from *Biblica* 34 (1953), pp. 427-29.

righteousness does not belong to man, nor does the perfection of the way belong to a son of man.[4] To the Most High God belong all works of righteousness, but the way of man is firm only by the spirit of divine impulse (*beruah yeser el*). It is for God to make perfect the way of the sons of men, that they may recognize all his works (he performed) by his mighty power and the abundance of his mercies (that he poured) over all the sons of his good pleasure (*bene resono*) . . . But I said in my sins: I have become an outcast from your covenant. But recalling the strength of your hand and the riches of your mercy, I rose and I stood myself upright . . . because I relied on your graces and on the riches of your mercy; for you will wash away guilt and purify man from sin by your justice, and it is not because of man . . . that you do (so), for you created the just and the wicked (. . .).'' And in 1 QH xi, 7-10, we read: "I know that truth is (in) your mouth, and righteousness in your hand, and all knowledge in your thought, and all power in your strength, and all glory is with you. In your anger are all judgments of affliction (*naega*), and in your goodness is abundance of forgiveness.[5] And your mercy is for all the sons of your good pleasure (*bene resoneka*), for you taught them the secret of your truth and you gave them insight in your wonderful mysteries."[6]

In these texts "the sons of His good pleasure" are the men in the community. In the Manual of Discipline they are called: the sons of light (i, 9; ii, 16; iii, 131, 24 ff.)—the sons of justice (iii, 20, 22)—the sons of truth (iv, 5ff.)—the sons of the eternal assembly (ii, 25)—the men of holiness (viii, 17, 20; ix, 8)—the men of the covenant (vi, 19)—the men of God's destiny (*goral el*, ii, 2)—the chosen of the way (ix, 17ff.)—the chosen of men (xi, 16)—the chosen of the Time (ix, 14), i.e., the time of the future fulfillment (iii, 18)—the chosen of God's good pleasure (*behire rason*, viii, 6). In view of the difference between "men of God's good pleasure" (Lk. 214) and "sons of God's good pleasure" (Qumran Hymns) it may be noted that "sons" and "men" are interchangeable, for "the sons of the truth" are also called "the men of the truth" (1 QpHab vii, 10), and "the men of the covenant" are the same as "the sons of the covenant" (1 QM xvii, 8).

The word *rason* in 1 QH iv, 33, and xi, 9, refers to God's will as electing and predestining rather than to the Divine Pleasure; for the entire passage stresses the active power of God and the insufficiency of man. The same meaning is clear in the modifier "the elect of his good pleasure" (1 QS viii, 6). The identical idea appears in

1 QH x, 5-7: "I, however, am dust and ashes, and what can I propose for myself, if you are unwilling, and what can I think up without your good pleasure (been resoneka)? How shall I put forth strength, if you have not put me upright, and how shall I turn out to be wise, if you have not predestined (this) for me?"

The same doctrine is set forth in 1 QS iii, 15-17, concerning God's creating and predestining will: "From the God of knowledge (comes) all that is and all that will be, and before they come to be, he has settled all their thoughts, and when they come to be, they fulfill their task to (give) their testimonies in accordance with the plan of his glory, and in his hand the judgments of all things cannot be changed."

We find the same view again in 1 QS iv, 15-26, where the two kinds of men are described, the sons of light and the sons of darkness. Whom God has chosen, at "the appointed time of judgment," "he will purify (him) with a holy spirit from all crimes of wickedness, and sprinkle over him the spirit of truth, like a lustral water, (washing from him) all defilement of lying, teaching the upright the knowledge of the Most High, and the wisdom of the sons of heaven, instructing the morally perfect. For he has chosen these for a covenant never to end . . . For he knows the outcomes of their works (that is, of the two kinds) for all times (. . .) and he assigns them to the sons of man that they may know good (. . . , and he) bestows destinies on each living being in accord with the pattern of his spirit . . ."

The final hymn of the Manual (1 QS xi, 7-17) speaks of predestination and divine grace: "Those whom God has chosen he has made an eternal inheritance and has assigned to them the destiny of the saints and associated their group with the sons of heaven . . . But I belong with the men of wickedness . . . Truly the way of a man does not belong to him and no one can fix his own steps, for judgment belongs to God and from his hand (comes) the perfection of the way. And through his knowledge all things are made, and whatever is, he determined (it) by his plan and without him nothing comes to be. And even if I totter, the graces of God are my salvation for ever; and if I slip into a failing of the flesh my judgment will be in God's righteousness which will remain for ever. . . . In his mercy he drew me near and by his graces he will bring about my judgment; by his faithful righteousness he (will) justify me and by his abundant goodness he will purify all my faults and by his righteousness he will cleanse me from the uncleanness of man and from the sin of the sons of man ... Strengthen in righteousness all the deeds (of your servant), and fulfill for the son of your handmaid what it has pleased you to grant (*rasita*) to the chosen of men, to stand before your face for ever. For without you no way is perfect and without your good pleasure nothing comes to be. ..."

In the Manual "God's good pleasure" at times certainly signifies also the will of God that must be done (1 QS v, 1, 10; ix, 13 ff., 23), be loved (ix, 24), and be searched after (v, 9). Good action is like a sacrifice that is pleasing to God (*kenidbat minhat rason*, ix, 5; cf. ix, 24); the good man "pleases just like a sweet expiation before God" (iii, 11).

However, the attributive phrase "the sons of his good pleasure" designates first of all those whom the Divine Will has chosen, the ones "chosen of (his) good pleasure." To them he will give "eternal peace" (ii, 24), "bountiful peace" (iv, 7), when the "times of peace" (iii, 15) shall come.

From these documents that are almost contemporaneous with the Gospel, it is clear that modern critics very rightly prefer in Lk. 2₁₄ not the commonest reading of codices, the tripartite "Gloria in excelsis Deo—et in terra pax—in hominibus bona voluntas," but the reading of far fewer but more ancient codices and the Latin Vulgate, composed of two parts: "Gloria in excelsis Deo—et in terra pax hominibus bonae voluntatis."

But the Qumran texts do more than lend decisive support to this reading. They also indicate that "God's good pleasure" here refers more naturally to the will of God to confer grace on those he has chosen, than to God's delighting in and approving of the goodness in men's lives. Thus neither "good will toward men" nor "peace among men with whom he is pleased" is an accurate translation, but rather "peace among men of God's good pleasure," i.e., his chosen ones.

# VIII

# The Sermon on the Mount and the Qumran Texts*

KURT SCHUBERT

The Babylonian Talmud contains a tradition which at first sight seems to refute what Mt. 5₁₇ gives as a word of Jesus: "Think not that I am come to destroy the law, or the prophets; I am not come to destroy, but to fulfill." It reads:[1]

Come and give ear. The Gillajonim[2] and the books of the heretics may not be saved from a fire, but they should burn where they are, together with all the namings of the Name of God that are therein . . . Rabbi Josse said: "On weekdays, let them cut out the namings of the Name of God that are therein, and put them into a Geniza, and burn the rest." Rabbi Tarfon said: "May I bury my sons, if in the case that they come into my hands, I not burn them together with all the namings of the Name of God that are therein. Even if one is being pursued with intent to kill, or a snake to be after one, let such a one flee rather into an idolatrous house, before he enter into one of their houses, for these people indeed know (God or Holy Writ), and deny in spite of this, but the others do not know (them), and deny for this reason." Rabbi Ishmael said: "This we conclude by proceeding from that which is easier to that which is more difficult. In order to make peace between a man and his wife, the Torah saith: My (i.e., God's) name, that is written in holiness, shall be washed away with the water of curses (cf. Num. 5₂₃). How much more doth this apply to those who cause strife, enmity, and dissent between the Israelites and their Father in Heaven[3] . . . Rabbi Meir calls it (i.e., the Gospel) pages of sin; Rabbi Johanan calls it pages of wickedness. Imma Shalom, the wife of Rabbi Eliezer, was the sister of Rabbi Gamaliel. In her neighborhood there dwelt a Jewish Christian,[4] who was known for his integrity. They wanted to amuse themselves at his expense. Therefore she brought to him a golden

* Translated from *Theologische Quartalschrift* 135 (1955), pp. 320-37.

lamp, and came before him with it, and said to him: "I want to have my share in the treasures of my father's house."[5] Thereupon he said to them, "Divide amongst yourselves." Thereupon he replied (i.e., Rabbi Gamaliel, who had obviously accompanied his sister): "For us it is written, that when there is a son, the daughter shall inherit nothing."[6] Then he (i.e., the Jewish Christian) answered them: "Since that day, when ye were driven from your land, the Law of Moses has been taken from you, and ye received in its place the Gospel,[7] in which it is written: Son and daughter shall inherit equally."[8] On the following day he (i.e., Rabbi Gamaliel) came again to him, and brought him a Libyan ass, and said to him: "Now I have studied the Gospel through, and it is written therein: *Think not that I have come to take away from the Torah of Moses, but*[9] *in order to add to the Torah of Moses have I come;* and therein it is written, when there is a son, the daughter shall inherit nothing."

From many details it is clear that the whole passage cited deals with Jewish Christians and Jewish Christianity. The Jewish Christians, according to the passage cited, had a tradition differing from the rabbinical, according to which sons and daughters were to have equal rights in the inheritance; further, in a Gospel of the Jewish Christians, it is supposed to have been said that Jesus came to add to the Torah of Moses, to make its requirements more difficult. The former is not of interest to our purpose here, but the latter point will be examined more closely.

First of all it must be quite clear that it is entirely possible that the passage cited is a special Jewish Christian tradition which distorts the original meaning of this saying of Jesus, and that its correct wording is to be sought, not in the Talmud, but in Mt. 5₁₇. The reading offered in the Talmud contradicts the whole tenor of the teachings of Jesus. At this point we shall only point to Mt. 11₃₀: "For my yoke *is* easy, and my burden light."[10] The view that Jesus demanded fulfillment of the Mosaic Law is a peculiarity of the Jewish Christians. Furthermore, it is possible that the talmudic tradition has distorted, deliberately or accidentally, its Jewish Christian source. We shall now show in detail that this suspicion is entirely probable.

H. J. Schoeps, who is the best contemporary guide for a study of Jewish Christianity, believes that the Jewish Christian text and interpretation of Mt. 5₁₇ is "taken up in the Talmud as well, and there it has been distorted for polemical reasons."[11] On the other hand, according to Jewish Christian christology, and following Mt. 5₁₇, the Mosaic Law is not supposed to have been abrogated. Schoeps refers to a Jewish Christian statement in the Pseudo-Clementine literature: "What he abolished did not belong to the Law" (Hom. 3₅₁).[12] The Jewish Christian Ebionites, then, looked upon Jesus throughout as having affirmed the Law of Moses.[13] Schoeps' opinion that the talmudic form of the text preserved the word of Jesus, which it knew, in a distorted form gains in likelihood when one views it within the framework of Jesus' entire teaching—the Sermon on the Mount in particular.

The key to the religious and historical understanding of broad parts of the Sermon on the Mount, and with it, of Mt. 5₁₇ as well, seems to me to be given in Mt. 5₄₃f., where we read: "You have heard that it has been said, 'You shall love your neighbor, and hate your enemy.' But I say unto you 'Love your enemies. . . .'" Who were these listeners, who had heard that they should hate their enemies? Nowhere in the entire Jewish tradition, and still less in the Old Testament, is there any trace of a command to hate one's enemies.[14] Probably, however, such a concept is to be found in the writings of the Qumran sect, which is associated by the majority of investigators, and with good reason, with the Essene movement.[15] There we read: "(It is the duty of members of the sect) to love everyone, whom he (God) has elected, and to hate everyone, whom he has rejected" (1 QS i, 4); ". . . to hate all sons of darkness, each one according to his sinfulness in the revenge of God" (i, 10); ". . . and the Levites curse all men of Belial's lot, lift their voices and speak 'Cursed art thou'" (ii, 4); "(The duty) of the elect of God's pleasure is to redeem the earth and to repay the wicked" (viii, 6f.); "these are the rules for the wise man in these times, for his love as for his hatred, (which is) an eternal hatred toward all men of destruction in the spirit of the mystery" (ix, 21f.). From 1 QS and from 1 QpHab it is evident that this hatred for enemies, in the conception of the sect, had an eschatological character; 1 QS ii, 5-9; viii, 6f., 10f.; ix, 23; but especially 1 QpHab v, 3-5: "The explanation is this, that God will not exterminate his people by the hand of the Gentiles but that he through the hand of his elect will hold judgment upon all Gentiles; and when all these are chastised, all the wicked from among his own people will have to pay the price."[16]

For the Essene group, a tightening of the Mosaic Law is demonstrable. This was fostered by the expectation of a near eschatological consummation, an expectation which was also the prime agent for the formation of the sect of Qumran. Above all, the regulations for purity, sexual and otherwise, were so far expanded that the sect approached in large measure a monastic ideal, and in its order-settlements actually attained it. We shall treat their sharpening of the Sabbath law later. In transforming the law of hatred for the enemy into the commandment to love him, Jesus was aiming at a very specific point of his auditors' eschatology. He wanted, to a certain degree, to soften it.[17] It is apparently in this sense that Mt. 5:17 has to be understood. If the Mosaic Law, in Essene circles, was made distinctly stricter, in order to hasten the End of Days, then here too Jesus brought relief for his followers. The Law is certainly not abolished through the words of Jesus. But the interpretations of the Law which Jesus communicated to his followers in the Sermon on the Mount point to the essential ethical core of the Law, and not to a sharpening of accidental externalities.[18] By the inversion of the commandment of hatred toward enemies into the commandment to love them, as well as by the elimination of the emphasis on the incidental provisions of the Law, Jesus showed that the eschatological event was not dependent upon only the exercise of human will, and that man was not the instrument of revenge.[19]

The assumption that Mt. 5:17 and 5:43f. are to be understood within the framework of Jesus' encounter with Essene concepts gains in credibility when we consider that the Sermon on the Mount seems in many places to refer to Essene practices and that Jesus himself in conversations with Pharisees, at times presumes that they are acquainted with Essene regulations.[20] Accordingly, the dissemination of Essene thought in the time of Jesus seems to have been more extensive than was commonly supposed before the publication of the Qumran texts. It is possible that Essene or "Essenizing" conventicles existed all over Palestine. If we consider the fact that the cemetery of Khirbet Qumran alone contains more than a thousand graves,[21] that there was an Essene Gate[22] in Jerusalem, and that the settlement of Khirbet Qumran was probably by no means the only Essene settlement,[23] then it is easy to visualize the widespread distribution of Essene thought in the age of Jesus.

The very first of the beatitudes (Mt. 5:3) indicates a conscious awareness of Essene thought and an intention of Jesus to make clear his stand against their sect. Basically Jesus takes a positive attitude toward them, since it was just these Essenes whose lives were determined by a strict religious attitude. Much has already been written about the question of who "the poor in spirit" may have been, to whom Jesus promised nothing less than the "kingdom of heaven," the participation in the kingdom of God. *Strack-Billerbeck* express the widespread opinion that it probably means the so-called *am ha-ares*, the vast group of little and despised people.[24] This opinion will now have to be abandoned. The term "poor" *(ptochoi)* in Mt. 5₃ and Lk. 6₂₀ by no means presumes that the destitute are called blessed. The Hebrew equivalent to the Matthean addition "in spirit" had the word *ruah*, which does not mean only "spirit," but also "will," "agreement." Thus it is by no means sure that the usual rendition of the passage "poor in spirit" is correct. It can just as well mean "poor in will, poor in inward agreement, voluntarily poor." This seems to hit on the real sense of the passage. Jesus called those blessed to whom worldly goods were nothing. In so doing he aligned himself with one of the basic tenets of the Essenes, to which 1 QS and Josephus jointly testify.[25] In 1 QpHab xii, 3, 6, 10, the members of the sect call themselves *ebionim*, "poor ones."[26] In the apocryphal hymns as well, a member of the sect describes himself as *ebyon*, "a poor one."[27] This name seems, then, to have been one of the numerous expressions used by the Essene Community to describe itself. Probably the Essenes took this name because they practiced full community of goods in their settlements and because contempt for money was one of their chief principles.[28] Accordingly, on the basis of the introductory words of the Sermon on the Mount alone, it does not seem improbable that Jesus' audience consisted of people who might have been familiar with Essene teaching.

In the course of the Sermon on the Mount Jesus again dealt with Essene concepts.[29] In Mt. 5₁₂ we find Jesus' words of comfort to his listeners: "Rejoice and be glad, for your reward is great in heaven, for so have they persecuted the prophets before you." This passage may mean that the followers of Jesus, as prophets of the kingdom of God[30]—as was earlier the case with certain similar "prophets" within the Essene Community—now had to reckon once more with severe persecution; or it may merely mean that the prophets of earlier epochs were persecuted; or it may mean both conjointly. Both interpretations can easily be understood in the framework of Essene ideas. Josephus has reported that certain of the Essenes were gifted with the gift of prophecy.[31] That the members of the sect believed that they possessed supernatural knowledge is most clearly seen in the psalmlike prayer which ends 1 QS. There we read (xi, 5-7): "Out of the source of his (i.e., God's) justice arise the norms of the light in my heart. From the secrets of his miraculous power mine eye saw the eternal Being (or: the ground of being of the world), a knowledge (or: salvation?), which is hidden from him who seeks knowledge,[32] and wise insight, which is greater than that of the sons of men, namely the origin of justice and the concentration of strength together with the place of (God's) Glory.[33] Among mortals God gave it (i.e., this knowledge) to those whom he elected, for their eternal possession, and let them participate in the lot of the holy ones, and with the sons of heaven[34] he combined their assembly, thereby forming the council of the community." Here it is clearly stated that the members of the sect, as the only mortals who will be saved, are the recipients of supernatural insight, *gnosis*. This separates them from the mass of the sons of men and gives them a share in the community of the sons of heaven.

A further corroboration for the assumption that all or at least large groups of the Essenes regarded themselves as "prophets" is to be found in the first part of the *Ascension of Isaiah*, the so-called *Martyrdom of Isaiah*. It was early recognized that this is a corpus peculiar to the Essenes.[85] Recently Dr. David Flusser has devoted himself intensely to Mart. Is., and has come to suspect (and the suspicion cannot be dismissed offhand) that the name "Isaiah" in this text can only be understood as a pseudonym for the Teacher of Righteousness, familiar to us from 1 QpHab and CD.[86] In Mart. Is. his followers are in fact called "prophets": All put on sackcloth, all were prophets (2:10); Bechirah, however, perceived and saw the place where Isaiah was, and the prophets who were with him (3:1); to the prophets who were with him, he said before being sawn asunder ... (5:13).[87] Since the arguments brought forward by Flusser make it seem quite probable that this document belongs to the Qumran literature, we may draw the conclusion that the members of the sect, or at least certain of the members, regarded themselves as prophets; no longer prophets in the sense of Old Testament prophecy, but as heralds of the kingdom of God, members of which they already are, in a certain sense, because they are no more mere "sons of men" but are already reckoned to the "sons of heaven."

We hear of persecution of the members of the sect not only in Mart. Isa. but also in 1 QpHab, 1 QH, and CD. Thus it is quite possible that listeners to the Sermon on the Mount may have understood Jesus' words in a similar sense.

If, however, Christ's listeners themselves are not meant by the prophets mentioned in Mt. 5₁₂, also the more traditional interpretation fits in well within the framework of the particular Essene tradition. The idea of persecution of prophets grew as a result of the religious persecutions under Antiochus IV and the persecution of the members of the sect by the mundane Hasmonean high priestly kings. Consequently, a martyrdom of Isaiah, of which the Old Testament knows nothing, was invented. The only biblical basis for this tenet is offered in 2 Kings 21₁₆: "Manasseh shed innocent blood very much, till he had filled Jerusalem from one end to another." Josephus (*Ant.* 10, 3, 1) paraphrases this passage: "Manasseh went so far in his contempt for God that he had all of the just among the Hebrews put to death, sparing not even the seers." In the Talmud (Yebamoth 49b) it is explicitly said that Isaiah was killed. Thus it appears, at first glance, that the tradition found in Mart. Is. was also independently known in pharisaic-rabbinic Judaism, but closer investigation seems to refute such an assumption. The very general report of Josephus should cause us no astonishment, since he was relatively well informed about the Essene movement. Therefore, it is entirely conceivable that his information about the martyred prophet is taken from Essene sources. As for the talmudic text, it falls into a short baraitha, under the superscription of Simon ben Azai (*ca.* A. D., 130-160), and into a detailed explanation suspended by Rabba (bar Nahmani), who died in Babylonia about A.D. 330. It simply and clearly relates that Ben Azai found a genealogical scroll which said, among other things, that Manasseh had killed Isaiah. The person of Ben Azai himself gives us the best help toward an understanding of what this genealogical scroll may have meant. He is reported to have pursued Gnostic studies (Hag. 14b). I have tried to show elsewhere[38] how Jewish Gnosticism had its origin in certain tenets of the Qumran sect. Thus it is quite possible that the genealogical scroll in question fell into Ben Azai's hands as he was searching for Gnostic literature. The interpretation which Rabba gave the short report is interesting. The arguments of Manasseh's accusation of Isaiah are those found as the words of Bechirah in Asc. Is. 3ₛᵣ. Rabba can report, also in agreement with Asc. Is., that Isaiah was sawn asunder, even if he does paraphrase the story a bit, saying that Isaiah is said first to have been swallowed by a cedar.[39]

Herewith, it also becomes probable in the light of the Qumran literature, that the tradition of Manasseh's persecution of Isaiah and of his martyrdom was originally peculiar to the Essenes. From the allusion in Mt. 5₁₂ it is, in my opinion, evident that Jesus was dealing with people conversant with this special tradition. Consequently, it does not seem improbable that the words, "the prophets who are/were before you" are in general to be interpreted as referring to Jesus' listeners at the Sermon on the Mount, also having reference to the Essene tradition of the persecution of important prophets.[40]

With regard to the reference to the disciples as the light of the world (Mt. 5₁₄₋₁₆) a parallel can be found in 1 QS (as well as elsewhere), where we read: "All the sons of justice tread in the ways of light" (iii, 20).

Parallels for Mt. 5₂₀ can be found in the ideas of the Qumran sect. Jesus demands that the righteousness (*sedakah*) of his listeners must exceed that of the scribes and Pharisees, for otherwise they will not enter the Kingdom of Heaven. Judging from the context given in v. 19, the original meaning of the passage seems to be that one must be more scrupulous with the Law, i.e., more ascetic and pious—as far as the spirit if not the letter of the Law is concerned—than the Pharisees. Opposition to the Pharisees, particularly to their interpretation of the Law, is likewise already familiar from the Qumran literature.[41]

In Mt. 5₂₁ and 5₃₃ the speech of Jesus begins with the words: "You have heard that it was said to the men of old . . ." The description of past generations as "of old" or "of the beginning" (*archaioi*) has its parallel in CD, in which we find mention of *reshonim,* "the earlier ones, who have gone into the covenant" (4₁₀); "and God was mindful of his covenent with the earlier ones" (8₄).

As a possible parallel to the words in Mt. 5₂₂ about him who is angry with his brother, we can take the strictly regulated community life of the Qumran sect. Consequently, the word "brother" in this passage refers not to a natural brother nor to our fellow men in general, but to a brother in the religious community. 1 QS often witnesses to the love which a person must show toward his brother in this sense. As an example let us cite vi, 1: "Let no man bring something against his brother before the Many if he have not already admonished him before witnesses," cf. Mt. 18₁₅ff.

In Mt. 5₂₈ the provision of Ex. 20₁₄ against adultery is sharpened in the spirit of the Essene ideal of self-denial: "But I say unto you, that whosoever looketh upon a woman to lust after her hath committed adultery with her already in his heart." Let us present only a few of the passages which help us recognize the fully complementary relationship. In 1 QS i, 6, we read: "Stubbornness of a sinful heart and eyes of unchastity," and in iv, 10, we hear of "a spirit of wantonness." Even clearer parallels are to be found in 1 QpHab v, 7: ". . . those who do not lust after their eyes," and in CD, e.g., 3₃: "Thoughts of sinful lusts and eyes of wantonness," and 7₂ff.: "Whoredom by taking two wives during their lifetime." The last passage is evidently directed at divorce, which was allowed under rabbinic law. Jesus too came to the same topic in connection with his presentation of an ideal of sexual morality very similar to that of the Essenes (Mt. 5₃₁f.). Jesus' controversy with the Pharisees, described in Mt. 19₃₋₉, belongs in the same context. In order to bring scriptural proof for the indissolubility of marriage, Jesus here cites Gen. 1₂₇, as does the author of CD, in direct connection with the quotation given above: "The basic principle of Creation is 'Male and female created he them'" (7₃). In Mt. 19₈ "hardness of heart," "stubbornness," is given as the reason for the impure lust which leads to divorce. The passage from 1 QS cited above offers us an interesting parallel to this (i, 6).

The radical rejection of oaths in Mt. 5₃₃₋₃₇ also has a parallel in Essenism. Josephus reports the Essenes' refusal to swear an oath: "Their word once given means more to them than an oath. They refrain from swearing, for they hold it worse than perjury. They say that a man who is not believed unless he call upon the divinity is already condemned in advance.[42] We may also refer to CD 19₁, where we read, "It is forbidden to swear by God's name El, and by God's name Adonai."[43]

The extraordinary statement in Mt. 5₃₈f. about not resisting evil, but turning the other cheek, has an interesting parallel in 1 QS x, 17f:

"I will not repay a man with evil, I will follow the man of power with good, for God has judgment over all life, and he repays each according to his works."[44] In contrast to the attitude of hatred toward enemies discussed above, which had an eschatological character, here it is just a case of personal forgiveness of "men of power." Just as Jesus rejected eschatological hatred, he went further in his condemnation of hatred toward personal enemies than did the Qumran sect. I believe that it is not by chance alone that Mt. 5₃₉ offers a parallel only to the first part of the passage from 1 QS and not to the second; for from the second part it is evident that the Essenes did not strike back *because* they relied on God's judgment.

Outside of Mt. 5 we find only occasional Essene parallels.[45] Mt. 6₂₄ reminds us strongly of the sect's negative attitude toward money, which is so apparent in all its texts. Only two examples will be given. In 1 QS x, 19, we read: "I desire not the gold of unrighteousness," and in CD 9₂₁: "They rolled in the paths of whoredom and in wicked gold." According to 1 QS, too, it is impossible to serve God aright if one has one's desires directed toward the earning of money. Out of this conviction grew the Essene ideal of community of goods.[46]

It is not only in the Sermon on the Mount that Jesus shows himself versed in Essene rules. As a matter of fact, he also assumes his opponents among the Pharisees to be familiar with them. Mt. 12₉₋₁₄, Mk. 3₁₋₆, Lk. 6₆₋₁₁, are the clearest examples. In the Matthean form of the story of the cure of a man with a withered hand on the Sabbath, Jesus reproaches the Pharisees, saying that they have no right to criticize the healing, as they all would take a sheep which had fallen into a pit on the Sabbath out of it again without scruple (Mt. 12₁₁). In CD (13₂₃f.) such a procedure is actually forbidden: "If it (the animal) fall into a pit, it may not be drawn out on the Sabbath."

The Sabbath rules in the Qumran sect were markedly stricter than those of Pharisees, as Josephus also informs us (*Bell.* 2, 8, 9). A provision found in CD 13₂₆f. indicates that Jesus' cure of the man with the withered hand was forbidden not only by the Pharisees, but much more so by the Essenes: "A living man who falls into a water-pit or a pond on the Sabbath may not be drawn out with a ladder, nor with a rope, nor with any other device." Not even the Pharisees were this strict, for in the Mishnah Yoma 8, 6 (83a) we read: "Every question of danger to life takes precedence over the Sabbath." The anger of the Pharisees was roused solely by the fact that the withered hand did not indicate danger of death.

Thus Jesus by no means followed Essene thought in all and every particular, but on the contrary he sometimes taught and acted in diametrical opposition to it. He is also distinguished from the Essenes by the fact that he decisively rejected all excessive features, such as eschatological hatred or the anxious pedantry in the observance of the Law (which also grew out of the eschatology of the sect). Whenever the meaning of a rule had been perverted into its opposite by the Essenes' eschatological yearning, as in the case of the tightening of the Sabbath regulations, Jesus' words and deeds provided the sharpest rejection.

In the light of such an encounter between Jesus and Essene thought, as we have seen it, it also becomes quite likely that Shabbath 116b—the extensive quotation with which we started this essay—reproduces the meaning of Jesus' words, Mt. 5₁₇, in a distorted form. It therefore seems improper to depend on the Talmud passage for an interpretation of this difficult saying of Jesus.

# IX

# The Dead Sea Manual of Discipline and the Jerusalem Church of Acts*

SHERMAN E. JOHNSON

As soon as the Manual of Discipline from Qumran was published, scholars immediately recognized its significance for New Testament studies. Parallels are to be observed between 1 QS and the teaching of Jesus and Paul, the special material in Matthew, and the Johannine literature, but by far the most interesting contacts are with the first few chapters of Acts.[1]

One should first note that the author of Luke-Acts is unique among New Testament writers in his interest in, and information about, John the Baptist and his disciples. It also appears that he is in closer touch with the Jewish sectarian background of Christianity than any other New Testament author. Many critics have noted that Luke omits most of the traditions of Jesus' controversies with the Pharisees, particularly those mentioned in Mk. 7₁₋₂₃. The usual explanation is partly correct: he writes for Gentile Christians and at a time when the Law is no longer a serious problem for the church. But this does not accord completely with his obvious interest in the Jewish origins of the new Way. Therefore, something more must be said. Luke sees the development out of Judaism toward the Gentile mission through the eyes of the Jerusalem church, about which he has considerable information. This church settled the

* Reprinted from *Zeitschr. f. d. alttest. Wissensch.* 66 (1954), pp. 106-20.

problem of the Law in its own way, which was different from that of Paul as disclosed by the Epistles. Therefore, his view of Jesus' ministry and of Paul's place in the development of the Gentile mission is slightly distorted.

Luke apparently supposed that Jesus had made no such sweeping criticism of the purity laws as Mk. 7 indicates. On the other hand, he thought that Paul at least tacitly accepted the compromise on the Law set forth in Acts 15. An irenic historian, interested in celebrating the triumphant missionary expansion of Christianity, might easily come to this conclusion. Both the conservative Jewish Christians and radicals such as Paul no doubt acted conscientiously and from premises which they considered unassailable. The former appealed to the fact that Jesus had lived within the framework of the Law and never repudiated it; therefore, they kept the Law with the modifications Jesus himself had made and were not inclined to go further. The latter may well have realized that Jesus did and said some things that logically canceled the purity laws; and these were, after all, the basis of separation between Jew and Gentile. When Christianity moved into the Gentile world, they realized the implications of Jesus' teaching and acted upon them. Particularly was this true when uncircumcised Gentiles showed signs of possessing the Spirit. The author of Acts sympathized with this development but also with the position of the Jerusalem church. Hence he tells the story of Christianity in Jerusalem and the more liberal Antioch but omits the controversial section Mk. 7₁₋₂₃ when he writes his Gospel.

The Jerusalem church, as we see it in Acts, is in several ways reminiscent of the Qumran sect.

1. The church is founded on an experience of the Spirit, and all who repent are baptized and receive the Spirit. Peter is quoted as saying: "Repent, and let each of you be baptized in the name of Jesus Christ for remission of your sins, and you will receive the gift of the Holy Spirit" (Acts 2₃₈). The Judean covenant sect believes that it possesses counsels of the Spirit which lead to eternal blessedness (1 QS iv, 6) and that a holy spirit cleanses man from sin, sprinkling upon him a spirit of truth like purifying water (iv, 21). These words suggest those Old Testament passages which speak of a spiritual sprinkling or cleansing (e.g., Mic. 7₁₈₋₂₀, Is. 1₁₆₋₂₀, Jer.

$4_{14}$, Ezek. $36_{25-27}$, $47_{1-12}$) and which are often thought to have been the background for the early Christian theology of baptism.[2] At the same time, the Qumran sect has a water baptism. Only those who have bound themselves by oath to separate themselves from the wicked (v, 10-11) may enter the water and touch the pure things of the holy men, for repentance must precede baptism and communal life (v, 13). The baptism of spirit, repentance, and water baptism are therefore closely connected. This is parallel to Josephus' statement that the rite of John the Baptist was for the purification of the body, the soul already having been cleansed by acts of righteousness, a passage which at one time was thought to be no more than rationalistic explanation of a cultic act.[3] It appears, then, that for the Qumran sectaries, for John, and for the early Christians baptism was a final rite of purification and initiation which was permitted only after thoroughgoing repentance.[4] The proof-text referring to John's work, Is. $40_3$, found in all three Synoptics, occurs also in 1 QS viii, 14. The Manual of Discipline, however, connects the text with the work of the sect in studying the Torah.[5]

The Book of Acts takes it for granted that those who are baptized receive the Spirit. Not only so, but the Spirit is attested by outward manifestations, such as the speaking with tongues. There is no parallel to this in the Qumran Scrolls or in the stories of John's activity. Phenomena of the Spirit are a distinguishing mark of the Christian community, and the Gospels trace them back to the baptism of Jesus himself.

2. The Jerusalem church and the Qumran sect led lives of communal sharing. Initiates of both groups brought their possessions into the common store (Acts $2_{44f.}$, $4_{34-37}$; 1 QS i, 12, vi, 16-20). Acts follows up this tradition with the story of the miraculous deaths of Ananias and Sapphira for "lying to the Holy Spirit" by pretending to have given all their goods when they actually withheld a portion. It is explained that giving away one's possessions was not obligatory (Acts $5_4$) and perhaps no regular rule demanded such sacrifice. Or is Peter's statement meant to imply that only entrance into the inner circle involved the giving up of possessions? In this case, Ananias and Sapphira were free to use their property and go back to private ownership up to the moment of their final vows; but now they have taken the vow fraudulently. It is noteworthy that the Manual of

Discipline provides punishments for a member who lies about his wealth (vi, 25).[6]

3. Closely connected with communal ownership is holy poverty. Paul's collection was for the poor among the saints in Jerusalem (Rom. 15₂₅; cf. 1 Cor. 16₁ and 2 Cor. 9₁). Acts connects this collection, or some other, with a famine in the time of Claudius.[7] Yet the famine may have done no more than aggravate an already existing condition, and Christianity in Jerusalem no doubt had its holy poor. Jesus' call to the rich man to sell all his goods and give to the poor (Mk. 10₂₁) must have been taken by some individuals as a rule to be followed if at all possible. Certainly Luke, more than any other evangelist, idealizes the pious poor who wait for the consolation of Israel. The parents of John the Baptist, and particularly the old saints Simeon and Anna, may be portrayed in accordance with this religious ideal. The Beatitudes and Woes, and indeed all the peculiarities of Luke's Sermon on the Plain (especially 6₃₈), fit in with it. The rich men of the Gospel are mostly fools (Lk. 12₁₆₋₂₂, 16₁₉₋₃₁), and it may not be without significance that Luke includes the parable of the lost coin (*drachma*, 15₈₋₁₀: a drachma is a day's wages for poor people). Lk. 14₃₃ contains the saying that no one who does not give up everything he possesses is fit to be Jesus' disciple. It is possible that Luke heightens this element in Jesus' teaching; if so, it may be due to the influence of the Jerusalem church.[8]

Our earliest source for knowledge of the Jerusalem church is Galatians. The three who, about the year 46, were recognized as pillars of that community (Gal. 2₉), and who urged Paul to remember the poor, were James the brother of the Lord, Cephas, and John. The tradition connects all of these with the ideal of poverty. Peter is the interlocutor who in Mark says, "See, we have left everything and followed you" (Mk. 10₂₈). In the story of the lame man at the Beautiful Gate, Peter and John are the actors, and Peter says: "I have no silver and gold, but what I have I give you" (Acts 3₆). But it is James who appears particularly as the prototype of the holy man. The late and legendary account of his martyrdom in Hegesippus pictures him as a Nazirite who wore only linen garments and had knees calloused like those of a camel (Eusebius, *Hist. eccl.* 2, 23, 5f.). In one respect he is very different from the baptists, for he does not bathe at all.

The New Testament Epistle of James may claim him as its patron and author. Here the rich are the oppressors and it is the poor who are pious. E. Lohmeyer may be correct in assigning many passages in the Gospels to a group of Christians who led a quietistic existence, kept aloof from political and public activity, and expected the coming of the Son of Man.[9] Whether or not they are—as Lohmeyer thinks—Galileans is not a matter of great importance. The point is that some of their traits are found in the Gospels, particularly Luke, the Epistle of James, and in the parts of Acts which describe the Jerusalem church. The tradition may preserve correctly some of the characteristics of James and of the community in which he was a leader. In all probability there is some connection between the Jerusalem church and the later Ebionites of Palestine.[10] We must, however, recognize that in the Manual of Discipline the emphasis is upon communal life and not on poverty as such. "The poor" is not a technical term in this literature. The feeling of the Qumran sect toward its persecutors is, however, comparable to that of the pious poor of the canonical psalms (1 QS ix, 21 f.).[11]

Perhaps, as in later times, Jews moved to Jerusalem to spend the remainder of their lives in religious exercises. When their money ran out they subsisted on offerings from pious friends in the farming regions of Palestine or the Diaspora, perhaps even on alms from visitors. There may have been such persons among the Jerusalem Christians. Thus the poverty of the church would be in part a permanent sociological condition, not due merely to an enthusiastic experiment in religious communism. The great famine of A.D. 46 would of course have aggravated their misery and provided added reason for Paul to make his collection for the poor saints of Jerusalem. On this assumption the Jerusalem church, particularly in its attitude toward wealth, would be somewhat different from other Christian churches.

4. The Judean covenant community was ruled by an inner group of twelve laymen and three priests (1 QS viii, 1). The final redactor of Acts thinks of the Jerusalem church as ruled by "the apostles and elders" (e.g., 15₆, 22f.), and other churches ordinarily have councils of elders. But in some of the earlier chapters of Acts it is the Twelve who rule (e.g., 6₂), and according to one tradition it was

found necessary to complete the number of twelve by the choice of Matthias (1₁₅₋₂₆).

The motivation of the Matthias story has never been quite clear. Certainly there is no evidence that a college of twelve was for any length of time a feature of church organization.[12] The passage in Acts suggests only that a twelfth man was needed as a witness (perhaps an official witness, v. 22) of the Resurrection. But this is simply the general point of view of Luke-Acts, namely, that the Christian mission is a witness to Jesus' deeds and teachings and his resurrection.[13] A more likely supposition is that the Twelve are the community's council for the coming Messianic Age, when they will sit on thrones judging the twelve tribes of Israel (Lk. 22₂₉₋₃₀ = Mt. 19₂₈). A similar thought may lie behind the institution of a council of twelve in 1 QS viii. After all, they rule over a community of apocalyptic expectation.

James the brother of the Lord, however, presents a special problem. Two points should be noted: (1) Galatians speaks of three pillars of the church, James, Cephas, and John. This reminds one of the three priests of the Manual of Discipline, although there is no reason whatever to think that the Jerusalem pillars were members of the old Aaronic priesthood. (2) Acts gives the impression that James did not immediately become a pillar of the church. This is probably so, even though it has sometimes been suggested that in a few of the early traditions Peter, John, and the apostles have taken the place of James.[14] Cephas is mentioned in Galatians as the one whom Paul consulted on his first visit to Jerusalem (Gal. 1₁₈), though he later saw James as well (1₁₉). But on the next visit James is named first, then Cephas and John. It is only after certain emissaries from James come to Antioch that Cephas ceases to eat with the Gentiles (2₁₂). By this time the position of headship has apparently passed to James, and the evidence of Acts, which mentions him in 15₁₃ and 21₁₈, seems to bear this out. James, the new leader, appears to be a stricter Jew than Peter.

5. Acts tells us that a large number of priests submitted to the new faith (6₇). It might be fanciful to suggest that members of the covenant sect joined the Christian church but both groups must have had much appeal for pious priests who disapproved of the activities of Sadducean priestly leaders. Both were communities that looked for the true restoration of Israel in the coming age. Mem-

bers of the Jewish priesthood did not, so far as we know, have by virtue of their priesthood any place in the Jerusalem church comparable to that which they enjoyed in the covenant sect (1 QS ii, 20; v, 29; vi, 3, etc.).

One interesting question may be raised concerning the priesthood of the covenant sect. The Damascus Document (CD iv, 2 f.), referring to Ezek. 44$_{15}$, explains that "the priests" are "the repentant of Israel who went forth out of the land of Judah," while "the sons of Zadok" are "the elect of Israel called by that name, who hold office in the end of the days." This may mean that they are the loyal members of the old priesthood, but it is conceivable that the priesthood of the sect was not derived from the old priestly families.[15] Can it be that the three pillars of the Jerusalem church were priests in the Zadokite sense and that such a priesthood existed for a brief time? The suggestion may be fantastic, but it nevertheless springs to mind. Incidentally, there is a tradition in Jn. 1$_{40}$ that Peter and his brother Andrew were originally disciples of John the Baptist and therefore perhaps members of a Jewish sectarian group.

6. Professor Cadbury has called to my attention the use of the word *plethos* in Acts. Usually this means simply "crowd," but in 6$_{2, 5}$, 16$_{12, 30}$, and perhaps in 4$_{32}$ it refers to the assembly of Christians, much as *ha-rabbim*, "the Many," is used in 1 QS.[16] In Acts 6$_5$ it might in fact be translated "majority." The passages in question probably represent both Judean and Hellenistic-Antiochian sources of Acts.

7. It is difficult to know whether there is a significant parallel between the communal meals of the Judean covenanters and the "breaking of bread" in Acts. The covenanting sectaries were required to eat, bless, and take counsel communally (1 QS vi, 2-3), and a priest must bless the bread and wine before the meal begins (vi, 4-6). The description in Acts 2$_{42-47}$ gives a similar impression, except for the priestly blessing, although nothing is said about wine (cf. also Lk. 24$_{30, 35}$ and Did. 9$_{1-4}$, where the cup is mentioned).[17]

8. Another possible connection between the groups is in the realm of biblical interpretation. According to Acts, at a later time Paul came upon certain "disciples" who knew only the baptism of John (Acts 18$_{25}$, 19$_{1-4}$). Some may have been disciples of John, though it is said of Apollos, at any rate, that he was "instructed in the way of the Lord." Apollos is described as powerful in the Scrip-

tures. The Judean covenanters put great emphasis on biblical interpretation as a regular part of the group life, and the Manual of
Discipline furnishes several examples of their method.[18] We have
already mentioned the proof-text Is. 40₃. 1 QS viii, 7-8 uses Is. 28₁₆
with reference to the council of the community:

> This is the tried wall, the costly corner bulwark,
> Whose foundations shall not be shaken asunder,
> Nor dislodged from their place!

The speeches in Acts do not contain this famous passage; the stone
of Acts 4₁₁ is the rejected one which becomes the cornerstone (Ps.
118₂₂). But in 1 Pet. 2₄f. the priestly race of Christians is built up as
stones into a spiritual house, the chief cornerstone, elect and
precious, being Christ. It may be more than coincidence that the
rich Christian midrashic material on stones and cornerstones (found
also in Mt. 16₁₈ with reference to Peter) runs parallel to the tradition of the covenanting sect.

The peroration of Stephen's speech denounces "you who are stiff-
necked and uncircumcised in heart and ears" (Acts 7₅₁). This is a
possible reminiscence of Deut. 10₁₆ and perhaps other Old Testament passages. 1 QS v, 5 speaks of "the uncircumcision of desire and
the stiff neck" (cf. ii, 13; iii, 3; iv, 11). Furthermore, the passage in
Amos (5₂₅-₂₇) quoted by Stephen as a condemnation of Israel's idolatry is the same that CD vii, 14 f. interprets allegorically. Amos 9₁₁,
"I will raise up the tabernacle of David that is fallen," is quoted
in CD vii, 11 ff., as fulfilled by the covenant sect. For Stephen's
speech (Acts 7₄₄-₅₀) and the Epistle to the Hebrews, the Tabernacle,
not the Temple, is the true institution, and James' speech in Acts
15₁₆ uses the Amos 9₁₁ passage with reference to the admission of
Gentiles. The habit of finding in Scripture references to recent
events and persons—particularly frequent in the early chapters of
Acts—is shared by the Manual of Discipline, the Habakkuk midrash,
and the Damascus Document.

## II

In both the Book of Acts and the Manual of Discipline the existing Temple cultus is repudiated. But Acts shows that there were
two divergent developments in the Jerusalem church. The very first
chapters of Acts show the disciples frequenting the Temple (2₄₆,

$3_{1.11}$) and there is no indication of hostility toward the sacrificial system. This may of course be nothing more than conjecture on Luke's part, and the picture artistically parallels that of John the Baptist's father Zechariah, Mary and Joseph, and old saints Simeon and Anna, and Jesus himself. On the other hand, both Acts and the later tradition in Hegesippus give the impression that James continued to be a loyal supporter of the Temple cultus. According to Acts, James is among those who urged Paul to take a temporary Nazirite vow and enter the Temple ($21_{18-26}$).

With Stephen the situation is very different. The speech attributed to him repudiates the Temple and its worship more sweepingly than does any other part of the New Testament. The Manual of Discipline by itself does not prove that the members of the sect participated in the Temple sacrifices or refrained from them. The Damascus Document, which in all probability comes from the same group, denounces the contemporary cultus. When the Manual of Discipline uses sacrificial language it does so metaphorically. Aaron is not only to enact laws but to offer up an agreeable odor (viii, 9). When the Torah of the new community is established in Israel, it will be "for divine favor of the land more than flesh of whole burnt offerings and than fats of sacrifice, while an offering of lips is accounted as a fragrant offering of righteousness and perfection of way as an acceptable freewill oblation" (ix, 4-6).

This is not very far, after all, from the "spiritual sacrifices" of 1 Pet. $2_5$ and the sacrifices of praise and sharing in Heb. $13_{15f}$. According to Hebrews, all past sacrifices have been superseded by Christ's self-offering. The fourth book of the Sibylline Oracles praises a group of men who repudiate all temples and altars ($4_{28}$) and avoid murder, bartering for dishonest gain, and adultery ($4_{31-33}$). They love the Mighty God and bless him before eating and drinking ($4_{24-26}$). Toward the end of the oracle the author bids men to repent, to turn away from swords, killing and violence, and to wash their bodies in ever-running rivers ($4_{64-65}$). This group has sometimes been identified as Christians, yet there is nothing in the oracle that demands this. There may be some connection between them and the disciples of John the Baptist in Ephesus. The fourth Sibylline oracle probably comes from the Maeander valley, and groups of Jewish baptists were to be found there.[19] J. B. Lightfoot went so far as to ascribe the oracle to the Essenes and to identify their doctrine with the heresy of Colossae.[20] Certainly 1 QS x, 1-8, like Jubilees and CD vi, 18; xvi, 2, teaches the absolute sanctity of times and seasons, a doctrine combated in Col. 2₁₆.

But there the similarity ends, for the Damascus Document shows that the covenanters believed in the regular Old Testament sacrifices, despite the metaphorical use of sacrificial language in the Manual of Discipline. The allegorical interpretation of Amos in CD vii, 11 ff. denounces the apostasy of the older Israel, but Siccuth, Chiun, and the Star are identified with good things, not bad. Siccuth is "the tabernacle of David that is fallen" and will be raised up again (Amos 9₁₁); Chiun stands for the books of the prophets whom Israel despised. Israel's privileges have simply passed to the new priestly sect.

Thus Stephen and his followers, in contrast to the party of James, represent a more liberal movement in the Palestinian church. The covenanting sect had developed a homiletic tradition according to which the true keeping of Torah was a valid equivalent to animal sacrifice, but sacrifice was not excluded. Now a group of Old Testament passages, and the traditional midrash on them, was developed by Stephen's party into a polemic against the old cultus. This could have happened among certain Jewish baptist groups as well as among Christians, though it does lead one to ask whether the fourth book of the Sibylline Oracles is not, after all, Christian.

Evidently Stephen's influence was far-reaching. His followers may have been responsible for much of the dissemination and development of non-Pauline Gentile Christianity. Possibly they had a hand in the collection of some of the synoptic materials and the traditions preserved in the Book of Acts.

The Epistle to the Hebrews is a further development of some of their characteristic ideas. So also, as B. W. Bacon recognized, is the Fourth Gospel.[21] According to John, neither in Jerusalem nor on Mount Gerizim is the place where the Father is to be worshiped: the temples are superseded by the new worship in spirit and in truth.

### III

Several scholars have recognized similarities between the teaching of the Dead Sea Scrolls and the special material of the *Gospel of*

*Matthew.* W. D. Davies refers to the ideas of perfection and esoteric wisdom.[22] W. H. Brownlee has called attention to the regulations for dealing with offending brothers in Mt. 18₁₅₋₂₀, which recall 1 QS v, 26-vi, 1 and are also paralleled in the Pauline Epistles (2 Cor. 13₁; 1 Cor. 5₃₋₅). In the Manual of Discipline a man must reprove his fellow before witnesses prior to bringing an accusation in the presence of the Many. According to the judgment of the majority a divinely guided decision is reached.[23]

Other parallels can be added. As we have seen, there is a contact in the realm of biblical interpretation; the rock midrash is applied to Peter in Mt. 16₁₈. The Manual of Discipline speaks of a period appointed by God during which wrongdoing can exist (1 QS iv, 18-20). The Gadarene demoniacs ask Jesus if he has come to torment them before the (appointed) time—this is a touch added by Matthew (8₂₉).

The most important point, however, has to do with law. The Gospel concludes with an injunction of the Risen Christ to make disciples of all nations, baptize them, and teach them to observe all that he has commanded (28₁₉f.). As in the Manual of Discipline, the keeping of a special tradition of commandments is essential. Most of the law of the new community is traced to the historic Jesus. The church has no "father" but God, no teacher or rabbi but Christ, for all are brothers (23₈₋₁₀).[24] Those passages in Mt. 23 which are not paralleled in Luke heighten the polemic against the Pharisees to the bitterest point reached in the synoptic tradition (e.g., 23₁₅), and Jesus' teachings are given in more exact legal language than elsewhere (e.g., 23₁₆₋₂₂). In fact, it is in Matthew's special material that we most clearly find the early church legislating, and Peter is here the example of the ideal rabbi. When we read the sayings on binding and loosing (16₁₉, 18₁₈) we can understand why Matthew contains such modifications as the exception clause in the divorce law (5₃₂, 19₉). 1 QS viii, 9, speaks frankly of enacting laws which are to be in force until the coming of the future age (1 QS ix, 10f; cf. the saying in Mt. 19₂₈ = Luke 22₂₉f. regarding the Twelve as judges of Israel).[25]

There are, to be sure, differences between Matthew and the Book of Acts, but the differences are between Matthew and the Stephen-Antiochian tradition, not the Jerusalem material centering in Peter. In contrast to the favorable treatment of Samaria given in Acts and the Fourth Gospel, Matthew contains a purported saying of Jesus forbidding a Samaritan mission (10₅). And we must remember that, even in Acts, this radical departure is not approved until Peter and John, two of the pillars, come to Samaria and by the laying on of hands call forth the reception of the Holy Spirit (8₁₄₋₁₈).[26]

## IV

Many years ago, Frederick A. Schilling suggested that when Paul went from Jerusalem to Damascus, armed with letters, to root out the early Christians, it was partly because their presence in Damascus suggested some sympathy with the covenanting or Zadokite sect. They had, in fact, migrated to a home of Jewish heresy.[27] The identity of the "Damascus" sect with that of Khirbet Qumran is increasingly accepted, and recent archaeological investigations make more plausible the suggestion that this is an Essene group.[28] I. Rabinowitz has recently argued that Damascus is only a symbolic word and that the covenanters did not live in that city.[29] However this may be, there were enough similarities between Christians and the covenanters that they may often have shared the same fortunes. There can be no doubt that members of both groups were often bitterly opposed to the Pharisees, though there are apparent exceptions, as in the case of James. The attitude of the Pharisees appears to vary. Probably they were well disposed toward James.[30] There is some evidence that, at least at times, they had a certain admiration for the Essenes.[31] It seems reasonable to suppose that, as in all instances where religious parties are in close contact, the degree of friendship and enmity varies among individuals and from time to time.

May it not be that all of the living religious influences in first-century Judaism sprang out of the restoration of Jewish law and piety which occurred in the early Maccabean period?[32] The time of Antiochus Epiphanes marks the most severe religious crisis in the history of postexilic Judaism. Up to this time various religious traditions—prophetic, priestly, legal, and wisdom—were carried on side by side perhaps without much conflict or depth of zeal. The Wisdom of Yeshua ben Sira attacked the Hellenizing movement, but Ben Sira still lives in the peaceful, ordered atmosphere of the older wisdom literature. The persecution changed all this. What resulted was not only a war of independence but a holy war; and not only a war but a resurgence of faith, as the Book of Daniel and all the other writings of the period indicate. After the crisis passed there was a new alignment of religious parties. Hellenism and assimilation were largely repudiated, and brotherhoods were formed to keep the Law more strictly.

Pharisaism was one outgrowth of this movement. The Pharisees came to assume responsibility for social direction and the adaptation of the Law to new conditions; they also carried on some of the best features of the wisdom tradition. By the beginning of our era, while Pharisaism included intimate groups of associates, it had some of the psychology of a majority movement and was the principal bearer of Jewish culture. The Sadducees may have had conservative traditions of their own—at least they rejected Pharisaic innovations —but culturally and spiritually they were to a large degree descendants of the Hellenizers.

Alongside the two larger parties were the sects. They took no general responsibility for the national life, only for the direction of their membership. They protested alike against the wickedness of the priesthood and the rulings of the Pharisees. There are, to be sure, some similarities between the Pharisees and the sectarian groups, but for the latter "wisdom" and knowledge of God are their own esoteric traditions, not the broader Jewish culture.

The Christian church as portrayed in Acts and the special material of Matthew has some sectarian features. Some of the parallels with the Manual of Discipline may be significant—particularly communal sharing, church discipline, and biblical interpretation. Certain others may be shared by first-century Judaism generally. In its understanding of its own purpose in the world, the church apparently oscillated between the tendency to be a closely knit sect, with strict laws of its own, and the drive to preach a gospel to all Judaism and ultimately to the whole world. The church ruled by James and Stephen's movement went in different directions. Peter stands between the two and is a symbol of this oscillation. The relatively late writings, Matthew and Luke-Acts, recognize both as parts of the church and attempt to include the message of both.

It seems clear, however, that the followers of the new Way after the Resurrection were a more closely knit group, with a firmer discipline and organization, than the disciples of Jesus had been during his ministry. This was not only because of the Resurrection but partly because they patterned their organization on the only models they knew.

Jerusalem probably contained conventicles of sectaries who were separated geographically from their religious centers. Suppose, for example, that some adherents of the Qumran sect lived there, temporarily or permanently. It would have been difficult for them to carry on all the practices of their agricultural brethren of the Jordan valley. They would no doubt have learned and taught the precepts of their sect and maintained their purity so far as possible. They might have kept the special food laws if their fellows on the farms sent agricultural produce in to them. One can imagine them frequenting the Temple precincts but taking no part in the sacrifices.[33] Members of such groups may from time to time have joined the Christian church, with resultant influence on the life of their new fellowship.

There remains an important question which cannot be fully discussed here. Is the Jerusalem church as portrayed in Acts a peculiar and one-sided development of Jesus' movement or does it reflect Jesus' interests quite accurately? Certainly Jerusalem seems to be unique among Christian communities, and Paul and the followers of Stephen, though they respected it highly and could not ignore it, had to assert a certain independence of it. In another place I hope to deal with this famous problem,[34] and here I can only record my opinion that Jesus' teaching is public, not esoteric; not an elaborate law directed toward the formation of a perfectionist sect but a gospel freely offered to the whole Jewish community; accepting the Law in principle and making stringent demands but allowing broad freedom to the conscience of the individual. The teaching of Paul, rather than that of the Jerusalem church, appears to be the logical development of the work of Jesus.

# X

# The Constitution of the Primitive Church in the Light of Jewish Documents*

BO REICKE

This essay on the constitution of the primitive church is not a study in biblical theology or in the New Testament concept of the church. We are rather focusing on the historical problem of the structure of the earliest Christian community. Naturally, theory can never really be separated from practice, but our emphasis is on practical relationships, while theological views are largely to be left unconsidered. We take our point of departure in asserting the "complexity" of constitutional structure in primitive Christianity; and for the support of this assertion we shall make reference to analogous Oriental material. In such a context we will turn to Qumran texts of a similar character.

## I

It is not only the apologists for different ecclesiastical interests—Episcopalians, Presbyterians, and Congregationalists—who have reached widely different conclusions in dealing with matters of constitution in the primitive church: this is true also of those who have approached the New Testament and the primitive church as scholars and historians. Thus the outstanding British church historians, who collaborated in the volume *The Apostolic Ministry*, claim, on the basis of painstaking investigations, that the bishop's office must be considered as the original and basic office of the

* Translated from *Theologische Zeitschrift* 10 (1954), pp. 95-113.

church.[1] In contrast, W. Michaelis has recently made the presbyter central and the prototype, without wasting many words on the episcopate.[2] A way of thinking which savors strongly of Congregationalism can be found in E. Schweizer's book on *The Life of the Lord in the Church and in Its Ministries*, where he reaches the conclusion that in the New Testament there are neither offices nor clergy, but simply functions of service, for which the congregation as a whole is responsible.[3] Here we see reputable scholars defending radically opposed theories about the constitution of the primitive church. In fact, we have represented here the three basic patterns listed by Aristotle in his *Politics*, i.e., monarchy (characteristic of episcopal organization), oligarchy (presbyterian organization), and democracy (congregational organization).[4]

What is the reason behind these differences of opinion? Are scholars letting their personal inclinations influence them? This may in part be true.

It must be noted, however, that political interests may not be assumed as motivations. It is generally recognized that specifically religious categories are implied, and that New Testament concepts of the church may not be equated with the forms and tendencies of secular society. If we speak of "monarchy," "oligarchy," or "democracy" in connection with the constitution of the church, then we use, for pedagogic reasons, certain political concepts familiar to the educated man. Thereby, however, we certainly do not intimate a dependence of church constitution upon manifestations and ideals of secular society.

On the other hand, it is certainly partly to be reckoned with that the personal religious orientation of scholars consciously or unconsciously influences their conclusions in this connection. Modern Christianity is, after all, badly divided on the question of church order, and episcopal, presbyterian, and congregational forms of organization are competing with one another all over the world. Consequently, the theologian can hardly avoid approaching the material with certain subjective preconceptions.

Nevertheless, we should like to maintain that the objective, historical circumstances themselves contribute substantially to the differences which generally arise in the study of church order in the primitive church. In fact, it seems that objective arguments for each of the constitutional ideas to be considered, for the monarchic as well as for the oligarchic and democratic forms, can be found in the New Testament.

A predominantly monarchic administration is found in the congregations of the pastoral Epistles, where Timothy and Titus obviously play the most prominent role, not, however, without the support of elders and others. In the church in Jerusalem, too, certain tendencies to monarchy can be discovered, as Peter, and after him James the Lord's brother, at times appear as spokesmen and leader of this congregation. Peter is indeed, in the first chapters of Acts, the real spokesman for the congregation in Jerusalem. At the Apostolic Council (A.D. 49, Acts 15), James won a more authoritative position, and he later appears in the last chapters of Acts as the actual leader of the Jerusalem church. According to the traditions preserved by Josephus and Eusebius, he remained "high priest" or "caliph" of the Jewish Christians until his death in about A.D. 64.

In essence, however, the Jerusalem community was dominated by an oligarchic system. According to the first chapters of Acts, the first church was in fact administered jointly by all of the apostles. The eleven apostles, later restored to twelve by a special election, formed a "college," which was responsible in general for the affairs of the congregation. Gradually the seven "Hellenists" (Acts 6)—who themselves probably formed another college, in the fashion of the septemvirate of the Jewish synagogue—and in addition to them a special class of "elders" also took part in the administration (Acts $11_{30}$, $15_{2-22}$). In the first of these two passages, the elders appear as the only representatives of the congregation, the apostles not even being mentioned.

In spite of the importance of the apostles and the presbyters, it nevertheless becomes apparent from time to time that the congregation as a whole had, judicially speaking, a decisive role to play. This is the case in Acts $1_{15-25}$, the incident of the election of a new apostle after the defection of Judas Iscariot. It is true that the election takes place at Peter's behest and that the apostles propose two men, between which the divine lot is to choose. Yet it is emphasized that a considerable number of the Christians in Jerusalem were present, viz., one hundred and twenty people (v. $15$). This number is not without significance in constitutional law. According to the Jewish concept, a town congregation must have one hundred and twenty persons in order to elect members to the Sanhedrin.[5] Obviously Luke specially mentioned the number of people present at the election because he wanted to show that the election of the new apostle was legally correct. By so doing he (or his source) has in the last analysis ascribed considerable importance to the congregation in weighty matters. On the other hand, the congregation had no direct part in the election. Nevertheless, its presence alone was an important legal point, and if less than sixscore persons of the congregation had been in attendance the election would not have been valid in law. The fundamental importance of the congregation can be seen from Acts 15:22. Here, after the leading apostles of the Jerusalem church have carried on momentous negotiations to decide whether the Mosaic Law also binds Gentile Christians (Acts 15:6-21), a decision is reached, which v. 22 presents as a resolution of "the apostles and the elders, with the whole church." Clearly only the presence of the congregation gave legal validity to the resolution, although the members of the congregation did not take part in the discussion and did not vote in the decision.

Thus, in spite of the great authority of the leading apostles, on the basis of which Peter and James won an almost monarchic position, and in spite of the practical importance of the apostolic college and the presbyters, the great body of the members of the congregation played an important legal and administrative part in the mother congregation of Christianity.

In fact, it looks as though the Jerusalem church had a mixed or "complex" constitution, where inclinations toward monarchy, oligarchy, and democracy were present together, without being mutually exclusive or even in conflict. Certain circumstances seem to indicate that the situation was no different in other Christian communities. In the apostolic Epistles the authors can speak to their readers with great authority, but they address themselves to the elders or leaders of the congregation and to the great body of believers without distinction, as though both had decisive authority in all questions.

## II

Thus we come close to the views reached by the Swedish exegete O. Linton in his well-known dissertation on *The Problem of the*

*Primitive Church.*[6] Linton points out that, according to Greek and modern concepts, a body competent to pass resolutions consists of individuals who are treated as equals. If there is in addition an advisory circle with greater authority than the full assembly, then this is also conceived as an assembly of equal individuals, and the higher authority of the advisory body or college consists only in the right to make recommendations, which may then be accepted or rejected by the congregation as a whole. According to Linton, however, we cannot think of early Christian organization as such an arrangement. Primitive Christianity can only be understood in its Oriental context and in the light of procedures peculiar to the East and strange to us, as, e.g., that of a nonegalitarian, legislative assembly.

In order to demonstrate the existence of such an unequal, hierarchic assembly with legislative power, Linton cites first of all the above-mentioned passage (Acts 15$_{22}$) where the decision reached at the Apostolic Council is represented as the resolution of "the apostles and the elders, with the whole church." The apostles and the elders did not stand over against the congregation, but there was rather a single congregation, unequally constituted. No special *collegia* were set up over against the assembly: the whole formed an organically structured unity. There were, in fact, specially honored persons, as the elders were. But their honor did not consist in being elected to a committee, but rather in the fact that within the congregational assembly they were given the places of honor and their words were highly regarded. In this connection Linton finds reason to believe that the unequally structured, legislative assembly was identical with the worshiping congregation, the cult group, the people of God. This explains why in primitive Christianity the local congregation could identify itself with the church as a whole and why it liked to conceive of its resolutions as the expression of the Will of God.

The second example of this conception of ecclesiastical administration offered by Linton is 1 Cor. 5$_{3-5}$. Here Paul says that, despite his absence, he has resolved together with the Corinthian church to excommunicate a certain sinner. Indeed, the spirits of those addressed (i.e., the Corinthians) and of the apostle have come together in the name of the Lord, through the power of Jesus, in order to make this resolution. Thus it is thought that the Lord himself co-operated, and the resolution is made in his power by means of common discussion by the apostle and the congregation in a gathering which was only spiritual and not physical. In so doing the apostle assumes the initiative and exercises an almost monarchic authority, but the resolution has no legal force without the agreement of the congregation. The apostle already knows in the spirit that he can count on their approval.

The organic unity of the church, which existed in spite of inequalities, presupposed that in cases of a difference of opinion the opposition would always loyally give in. No developed opposition parties would have been thinkable inside the church; rather, when serious and lasting differences of opinion arose, the opposition would always have withdrawn from the community. Voting would not have been held. The term regularly encountered by elections, "to elect by raising the hand," is interpreted by Linton as an expression for acclamation. The majority group would never have been thought solely responsible for a decision, but the community as a whole would have taken over the responsibility as an organic unity, a hierarchic totality. This system of organization is alleged to have been practicable because of the patriarchal authority of the leaders and because of the common awareness of community, both factors which had their natural preconditions in the Orient.

We should like to agree in principle with these arguments of Linton's. The New Testament texts really give the impression that the primitive church had an organically "hierarchic" constitution. In particular, Acts seems to presuppose such a complex social order as something quite natural. Even if much is idealized in Acts, the treatment is rather dependable on the whole, since Luke was not trying to make propaganda for a particular constitutional system.

It also seems to be quite correct to consider this nonegalitarian, hierarchic, and yet organically unified assembly of a patriarchal nature as a specifically Oriental phenomenon. Yet Linton had no proofs for the existence of such a constitutional form in the Orient. He only made the programmatic reference to Eastern collectivism as the proper background for our understanding of primitive Christian constitution and law.

This gap we should like to fill in with a few observations from

Jewish texts which have the character of "constitutions" or "church orders," viz., the Manual of Discipline from Qumran (1 QS) and the Damascus Documents (CD). These two documents are not only examples of Oriental conditions, but also belong, geographically and chronologically, to the immediate milieu of the early church.[7]

In the *Qumran Community* there is a definite order of rank (1 QS i, 10). One must love all the Children of Light, but each according to his position in the community. Thus the congregation is divided into classes. At the head stand the priests, and then come the Levites, and last "Israel," or the entire community (i, 18, 21f., etc.). These several classes constitute a unified body which considers itself, like the Christian church, a new covenant (i, 8, 16, etc.). At the annual Covenant Feast the order of the ranks is most clearly expressed (ii, 19-25). According to this passage, the priests come first, followed by Levites, and after them come the people in groups of "thousands," "hundreds," "fifties," and "tens." Within each group everyone has his particular rank. Notwithstanding all this, it is made quite clear that it is just this hierarchic order which preserves unity, love, and justice. This unity, maintained by means of minute prescriptions concerning ranks, is often emphasized. The very word "union" or "unity" is even chosen as a technical term for the community. In v, 20, we learn that the members of the sect shall "constitute a unity" in order and administration. The individual member is responsible before the "Sons of Zadok," i.e., the leading priests, but also before the entire community (v, 2-3). This is a basic principle throughout the document. Sometimes the priests appear as the deciding authority; sometimes it is the entire assembly that counts; and there is no decisive distinction between the two.

When a man is initiated into full membership of the sect he must pledge himself by oath to the Law. This takes place before the assembly of the faithful, but the Law is to be especially interpreted by the Sons of Zadok (v, 8f.). The moral quality of the novice is investigated by the priests in part, and in part by the assembly (v, 21f.). This refers hardly to two parallel investigations, but rather to the fact that the priests carried out the initial investigation and transmitted their findings to the congregation for detailed consideration. According to the results of the investigation, the novice was given his place and rank (v, 23).

The great body of the faithful is divided into smaller groups. Even there their rank is strictly kept, although in these small groups the members work, eat, and pray together (vi, 2f.). If a group consists of a minimum of ten people, then one of them must be a priest (vi, 3f.). He has to recite the grace before and after the common meal (vi, 4-6).[8] He always has the highest rank in the group, and the others follow him in their proper order. Still, the group decides as a whole questions of every sort, with the reservation that when a question is discussed the men may speak only in the exact order of their rank (vi, 4).

At the plenary session the order of rank is to be followed consistently (vi, 8-10). The first places are occupied by the priests, the second by the "elders"—who hereby show themselves to be identical with the so-called "Levites"—then follow the entire assembly of members, divided up into classes. All judicial and administrative matters are dealt with within this order. Everyone has the right to speak out, when his class has its turn (vi, 10f.).

The negotiations are under the direction of a "superintendent" or "moderator" (*mebaqqer*), who gives the floor to each in his turn (vi, 11f.). This *mebaqqer* is also mentioned in CD, where he has been associated, by some scholars, with the Christian bishop.[9] In the Qumran Manual, taken by itself, the *mebaqqer* is not significant enough to justify such a comparison. On the other hand, he is not only supposed to preside at the plenary session, but is the actual head of the community and is in special care of the novices (vi, 14f.). Thus he is certainly more than a presiding officer, chosen for each occasion.

Final decision about the acceptance of a novice is reached by the assembly after common deliberations (vi, 16). After the novice has passed through a trial year, the priests first express their opinion of his knowledge and his behavior; when their report is positive, then he is considered to belong to the community, but merely "on principle" (vi, 18-20). Only after a second trial year, when he has passed a second test, this time before the entire assembly, is he regarded as a full member of the community. Now may he enjoy first the sacramental drink of the initiates, then definitely give his possessions over to the community, and exercise his right to vote in the common administration and jurisdiction (vi, 20-23).

These are regulations which have their parallels in primitive Christianity. The surrender of his property by the novice reminds us obviously of the communion of goods in the Jerusalem church, as described in Acts 2₄₄ff., 4₃₂, 5₁-₁₁. On the other hand, there are marked differences between the conditions in the Qumran Community and the New Testament. In the New Testament we hear nothing of novices, of a trial period, of the division of all the faithful into different classes, of a common life and common work for all the brothers, etc. Such features are confined to later Christian monasticism. It is, no doubt, important that the Qumran texts have given us new material for the prehistory of Christian monasticism. In this way the attempts to trace the monastic movement, in part at least, back to Jewish influences, gain new weight. Such attempts were earlier based on the writings of Josephus and other writers, where the Essenes are described as a sort of Jewish monastic organization. In view of the treatment of the novices, communal ownership, and other such details, the Qumran Scrolls must be closely associated with the Essene movement. The disciplinary injunctions of 1 QS vi, 24-vii, 25 remind us of the Essenes and at the same time of monasticism. Yet, we are now interested only in the relationship of the Qumran authorities to the community at large, and we have already seen that their Manual takes for granted just such a hierarchic and yet unified community as may well have characterized the primitive church.

But this text has further information, which is particularly instructive for a comparison with Christianity. There is to be a "council" in the community, consisting of twelve men and three priests (viii, 1). This looks like an analogue to the college of the twelve apostles of Jesus. It is, however, not clear from the text whether the three priests are inside or outside the circle of twelve. Perhaps the inclusion of the three priests is to be preferred, because it enables one to see in the expression "priest" an especial mark of honor and to avoid the rather improbable result that the other twelve were laymen. If  the three priests can be included in the circle of twelve, then we are reminded of the fact that Peter and the two sons of Zebedee, or later Peter, John, and James the Lord's brother constituted a distinct group within the circle of twelve. This is still just a possibility; and it cannot be maintained with any certainty that those three priests represent an analogy to the most intimate disciples of Jesus. On the other hand, the number twelve for the members of the Council of the Qumran Community is certainly significant. It is true that with Jesus, as probably with the Qumran Community, the number twelve is intended to correspond to the number of the tribes of Israel. In addition, the Jewish synagogue may have had colleges of twelve men. Thus we cannot say that Jesus is directly dependent on the Qumran sect in this matter. Still, it is valuable from a historical point of view to find here a partial analogy to the twelve apostles of the church. In the primitive Christian community the Twelve constituted just such a council as our passage from the Qumran text indicates.

It is also worth noting that the Council of the Twelve is given a theological significance as an instrument of salvation, and this in a way which reminds us of the concepts of the apostles as the pillars of the church (viii, 5-10). The Council of the community (in the above mentioned connection this must mean the twelve men with the three priests) is "an eternal planting, a holy dwelling for Israel, a foundation for the Holy of Holies for Aaron." Further, the members of the Council are called, among other things, "tried walls" and a "valuable cornerstone," and are finally called "the foundation of the congregation." There is proof, then, that the occupants of the highest office in the Qumran Community were thought of, like the apostles of the church, as those who bear the entire community. We may compare with passages in the New Testament, such as Mt. 16₁₈, where Peter is addressed as the foundation "rock" of the church, or Gal. 2₉, 1 Tim. 3₁₅, Rev. 21₁₄, where "pillars" and "foundations" are mentioned in connection with the apostles. At Qumran the members of the Council are to work especially for divine reconciliation (viii, 6, 10); when Paul calls the apostolic office "the ministry of reconciliation" (2 Cor. 5₁₈), he is expressing a very similar idea. It is obvious that the members of the Council at Qumran have a theological significance which reminds us of the apostolic ministry of the church.

In spite of the almost superhuman authority of the highest officers, the possibility is never considered that administrative or judicial matters might be decided without the community's taking part. On the contrary, the regulations concerning the Council are followed by provisions, according to which the assembly is responsible for deciding on the readmission of excommunicated members and similar matters (viii, 17-ix, 2). This whole section deals in part with common members of the community and in part with especially holy individuals (a sort of *homines religiosi*). Both classes are expected to take part in the common sessions of the general assembly. Each has the right to speak out in the sessions.

And still it is not as though all members had the same authority. A democracy according to the Greek pattern is out of the question here. It has several times been emphasized that the order of rank of those allowed to vote must be preserved exactly. That this is not merely an empty form can be seen from this provision found at the end of the Manual: "Only the sons of Aaron (the priests) may administer justice and property, and in accordance with their recommendation the resolution will be formed concerning each class of members of the community" (ix, 7).

Thus the Qumran Community was a strictly hierarchic, non-egalitarian body. In spite of the sharp divisions between the ranks, which were maintained with what seems to us pedantry, the sect formed a firmly knit unity—assuming that everything functioned more or less as the Manual prescribes. There were regular, parliamentary sessions of the community, at which each had the right to voice his opinion. But it was expected without question that the priests and the prominent men would be able to put across their view. If it is not entirely proper to speak of a patriarchal order here, since priests and not *patres familias* play the first role, yet the Qumran structure is similar to it. We find here an organic mixture of oligarchy and democracy, which substantiates Linton's picture of primitive church order, with its alleged Oriental influence.

In the *Damascus Community* there is a similar ranking of the members, with the exception that here provision is made also for a special class of strangers. At the annual appraisement, according to CD, the different classes come forward in the following order: first, the priests; second, the Levites; third, Israel (the laymen); and fourth, the strangers (xiv, 3-6). This was also the order at their sessions and deliberations.

Because of the last-mentioned provision, it may be assumed that the Damascus community also had plenary sessions, at which all could take part in the discussion, but only through observance of the prescribed order of rank. But that is about all. Otherwise there is no indication in CD of the fundamental role of the assembly, which is so prevalent in 1 QS. On the contrary, the officials are far more prominent in CD, and it is expressly stated that every group of ten must give its priestly leader unconditional obedience (xiii, 3).

In the Damascus community the "superintendent," or *mebaqqer,* is the most important official. We mentioned that he is referred to briefly in 1 QS, but in CD he occupies a considerable part of the text. Here his functions are rather elaborate. He is supposed to receive all reports concerning violations of the Law (ix, 17-22), as well as all claims of a more private nature (xiv, 11f.). The priestly leaders of the groups of ten are obliged to appeal to him, if, e.g., the law concerning leprosy in a particular case is unclear to them in its application (xiii, 6). But he plays the role not only of a judicial authority but also that of a preacher and pastor (xiii, 7-10). He is to instruct the community about the acts of God, and tell his people of the events of the past. He must have mercy upon them, like a father for his children, like a shepherd for his flock, and he shall loose the bonds of the prisoner. The *mebaqqer* plays an important part in the initiation of novices (xiii, 11-12; xv, 7ff., 11), and in this capacity his right of decision is much more clearly stated in CD than in 1 QS. Thus great demands are made of him. This is especially true of the *mebaqqer* who is in charge of all the community centers or camps. In order to fulfill what is required of him, such a *mebaqqer* must be a man in his best years, that is, according to CD xiv, 9, between thirty and fifty.

Under the *mebaqqer* are not only the priests but also a special council of ten "judges." This council is chosen by the assembly, and consists of four priests or Levites and six laymen, all learned in the Scriptures and between twenty-five and sixty years old (x, 4-10). In addition to their judicial responsibilities, these judges have to assist the *mebaqqer* in the distribution of alms for the poor (xiv, 12-16).

This *mebaqqer,* who may be the "curator" of the Essenes mentioned by Josephus,[10] has been compared with the Christian bishop.[11] There is, however, little reason to assume that the church got its episcopal office from the Essenes and their *mebaqqer.* On the other hand, it can be said that perhaps the development of the episcopacy has a Jewish parallel in the growth of the *mebaqqer* to an office with almost monarchic authority, granted that CD represents a later stage in the development of this particular religious community than does 1 QS. For many reasons this seems to be the most natural assumption—in view of, e.g., the class of "strangers" found only in CD. Furthermore, compared with the Qumran Community the Damascus group is doubtless an institution of the Dispersion. Here circumstances led to a concentration of authority in the hands of the *mebaqqer*, while in Qumran the authority remained largely with the general assembly. Nevertheless, it is a question only of degree, since the *mebaqqer* and an assembly are found in both texts. Such a gradual development toward monarchy as CD indicates over against 1 QS has often been suggested in connection with the Christian episcopate. If this theory is correct, then the texts we have dealt with are instructive for the understanding of the episcopate—not as though the development which they describe could have influenced the growth of Christianity, but because they may offer an interesting analogy.[12]

Thus the development of the ministry of the church toward monarchy is to be understood in the light of conditions provided by the Oriental milieu of the primitive church. Once more Linton's suggestion of an Oriental background for a proper understanding of the primitive Christian constitution can be confirmed. At this point, it is not a question of taking over a specific office or particular functions, but rather an example of similar types of internal development.

Albeit the Qumran Manual shows a predominantly oligarchic and at the same time democratic order and the Damascus Documents a predominantly monarchic one, the former is not lacking in monarchic features nor the latter in oligarchic-democratic ones. The *mebaqqer*, the leading men, and the community as a whole all play a certain part in both texts. If CD shows a certain development when compared with 1 QS, still both texts stood in close relationship to each other. Their relative incongruity does not testify to a revolution or to an influx of new elements but rather to an elasticity which allows the given order to develop itself, according to need, in different directions.

The two Jewish documents which we have dealt with in this

essay, and which are close to primitive Christianity in terms of both geography and time, indicate a constitutional structure which is, in a very specific sense, "complex." Monarchic, oligarchic, and democratic tendencies exist side by side without open contention. In spite of the drastically unequal importance of the members, the community forms an organic unity. This was clearly the case in the primitive church as well, although the hierarchic stratification of the various members is much more strongly expressed in our Jewish documents. He who wants to appeal to the New Testament in matters of contemporary church order may take notice of the fact that, in a Jewish movement slightly older than Christianity or contemporary with it, monarchic, oligarchic, and democratic tendencies could work together in organic unity. And yet its members were not nearly so closely united as the brothers in Christ were soon to feel themselves.

# XI

# Paul and the Dead Sea Scrolls: Flesh and Spirit

W. D. DAVIES

Modern scholarship has sought to approach Paul along certain well-marked avenues, those of the Old Testament, of Hellenism, of Hellenistic Judaism, Apocalyptic, and more recently, Rabbinic Judaism.[1] In varying degrees each avenue has contributed to the understanding of the Apostle. Nevertheless, because of signs which could not easily be ignored, each has also pointed beyond itself. The recognition has grown that the first-century milieu against which we are to place Paul was variegated and, above all, complex. In particular has it become clear that the traditional convenient dichotomy between Judaism and Hellenism was largely false. In the fusions of the first century the boundaries between these are now seen to have been very fluid. This has emerged as much from the work of those who set Paul primarily over against the Hellenistic world, as from that of those who have emphasized his affinities with Judaism[2]; and it has been indubitably confirmed by archaeologists.[3] Thus the discovery of the Dead Sea Scrolls has occurred at a time when the multiple intricacy of the background of Paul is becoming increasingly evident. Have they merely added to this intricacy, as they inevitably must by adding another item to the sectarian scene in the first century, or do they also open a new avenue, and perhaps a more excellent one, than those that have previously been available, for the approach to Paul?

Before we begin the examination of the Scrolls from this point of view, it is well to recall that they have also appeared when what we may call the foreground of Paulinism has come to be far better recognized and understood. The old view of Paul as a solitary colossus who dominated the early church, even while he was not understood by it, has given place to the awareness that the Apostle was rooted in the life of the early church with which he shared a common faith. Paulinism is no longer regarded as "an isolated entity without connection with the past or influence in the future."[4] It is no longer studied as a watertight compartment but far more in relation to the rest of primitive Christianity. And this same primitive Christianity, to judge from the many points of contact that have been discovered between it and the Scrolls, now appears, even before the advent of Paul, to have been deeply open to sectarian influences such as we can study in the Scrolls.[5] Thus there are those who claim that John the Baptist, who can hardly have failed to have been aware of the Qumran sect, was profoundly influenced by it, so that the stream of Christian tradition would from the first be colored by its ideas.[6] Some have urged that the priests who joined the church, as recorded in Acts 6₇ are to be connected with Qumran,[7] some that this was true of the Hellenists of Acts 6,[8] while others hold the same of the Hebrew Christians.[9] Each of these views implies that Paulinism, if it was rooted in the early church, could not but have been indirectly, to some extent at least, influenced by the sectarians. But it has further been suggested that Paul would have been quite directly under sectarian influences at Damascus (a city always hospitable to dissentients), because at one stage the sect had actually been stationed there and because it is not unlikely that there were sectarians living in the city at the time of Paul's conversion.[10] But just as we cannot stay with Dr. Teicher's thesis,[11] that Paul is actually represented by the wicked priest in the Scrolls, so we cannot examine these different views. It will not be our concern to pin down any one point through which the influence of the sectarians reached Paul. This could at best produce only conjectural results. Rather, it will be our aim to begin by inquiring whether the Apostle shares a common reservoir of terminology with the sect. Even though the scholarly sifting of the Scrolls is still incomplete, this can be assessed fairly accurately on the comparatively solid ground offered by a comparison of the Pauline Epistles and the pertinent literary remains of the sect. But particular words and phrases do not in themselves prove very much (as so often in the political sphere, East and West have recently, painfully discovered when they use the same terms, for example, "freedom," "democracy" and "liberty"). We, therefore, have to go on further to ask whether the conceptual world of the sect or, as Schweitzer would put it,[12] whether the "sets of ideas" in the Scrolls are allied to, and illumine, those of Paul.

Apart from a number of words and phrases[13] which recall similar ones in the Pauline Epistles, at several specific points the Scrolls have been thought to have a bearing upon Paulinism. Anticipations of the doctrine of justification by faith have been discovered in them,[14] and much light on the Pauline terminology about "mysteries" and "wisdom" and "knowledge" of God now revealed in Christ.[15] The exegetical methods of Paul have been claimed to recall those of the sect.[16] Space forbids the examination of all these points here. We shall, therefore, confine ourselves to one field where sectarian affinities or influences have been detected in Paul—his understanding of the "flesh" and of the "Spirit."

## I

In many traditional Pauline studies the point which has been most emphasized as suggesting Hellenistic influences is Paul's concept of the flesh. In an examination of this, published in 1948, I pointed out that there is no need to turn to Hellenistic sources for its elucidation, but that the Pauline idea of the flesh seemed to be "adequately explained as an accentuation of the ethical connotation that the term already had in certain late documents in the Old Testament."[17] One thing appeared clear, that Rabbinic Judaism offered no parallel to this accentuation nor had we a parallel in any other Judaistic milieu then known to us. Perhaps I then dismissed the rabbinic sources too categorically.

There is a passage in Mishnah Aboth 2[7] where the term "flesh" (*basar*) may have an ethical nuance. It reads: "[Hillel] used to say: the more flesh the more worms; the more possessions the more care; the more women the more witchcrafts; the more bondwomen the more lewdness; the more bondmen the more thieving; the more study of the Law the more life; the more schooling the more wisdom; the more counsel the more understanding; the more righteousness the more peace . . ." Israelstam's comment on the term "flesh" here is too trite.[18] He takes it quite literally to refer to obesity. But the context gives to "flesh" here a possibly ethical connotation. The collocation of "flesh" and "worms" re-emerges in Sotah 5a: "R. Johanan said: The word for man indicates dust, blood and gall; the word for flesh indicates shame, stench and worm. Some declare that [instead of "stench" we should have the word] Sheol, since its initial letter corresponds."

A passage in the Targum of Jerusalem on Gen. 40s might also perhaps be taken to imply that the flesh is prone to sin: "Joseph left the mercy above, and the mercy beneath, and the mercy which accompanied him from his father's house, and put his confidence in the chief butler: he trusted in the flesh and the flesh he tasted of, even the cup of death. Neither did he remember the scripture where it is written expressly, Cursed shall be the man who trusteth in the flesh, and setteth the flesh as his confidence. Blessed shall be the man who trusteth in the Name of the Word of the Lord and whose confidence is the Word of the Lord. Therefore the chief butler did not remember Joseph, but forgot him, until the time of the end came that he should be released."[19] Jastrow,[20] it should be noted, takes "flesh" here to refer to "a mortal." But at least it has the connotation of untrustworthiness. In view of the above, therefore, an accentuation on the ethical connotation of "flesh" should not, perhaps, altogether be denied to Rabbinic Judaism.

Nevertheless, the examples we have quoted are not numerous nor entirely unambiguous. Certainly they do not compare in cogency to what we find in the Scrolls from Qumran, where the term "flesh" appears in several contexts which suggest a close parallel to Pauline usage, i.e., where the ethical connotation of the term is as evident as in Paul.[21]

In the Qumran texts there are passages where the term "flesh" signifies merely a physical entity without moral connotation, as in 1 QS ix, 4, "The flesh of whole burnt offerings"; CD vii, 1 ("The kin of his flesh"); viii, 6.[22] Other passages point to the "flesh" as designating the frailty and mortality of man:

"What flesh is like this
And what is a vessel of clay to exalt thy wondrous deeds?" (1 QpHab
    iv, 29.)[23]

There are other sections where the meaning of "flesh" is ambiguous. What, for example, is its meaning in the following passage from 1 QS iii, 6ff., the most pertinent words of which are underlined: "But in a spirit of true counsel for the ways of a man all his iniquities will be atoned, so that he will look at the light of life, and in a holy spirit he will be united in his truth; and he will be cleansed from all his iniquities; and in an upright and humble spirit his sin will be atoned, *and in the submission of his soul to all the statutes of God his flesh will be cleansed,* that he may be sprinkled with water for impurity and sanctify himself with water of cleanness?" (Burrows' translation).

Kuhn takes "flesh" here to have a merely physical meaning. But in the preceding verses (iii, 4, 5), the person who has refused to enter God's covenant (ii, 26) is regarded not only as having refused instruction (iii, 1) and practiced dishonesty (iii, 2), so that acceptance of him into the community is defiling (iii, 3), and not only as having a darkened mind, but also as being so corrupted that no atonement or baptismal rite can cleanse him. In iii, 6 ff., it is only the spirit that can avail to make him clean. Before any water rite can cleanse his "flesh," that flesh must previously have been "cleansed" by submission to the statutes of God. Is there not here the thought that the flesh has been involved in rebellion? The implication is that the flesh is polluted in such a way that it requires moral purification: the same verb is used for cleansing iniquities, which are here parallel to "flesh," as for cleansing the flesh. The verb is thus used in Ps. 51₄, 9, which is often echoed in the Scrolls.[24]

Similarly in 1 QS iv, 20, Kuhn finds a purely physical meaning for "flesh." The passage reads: "And then God will refine in his truth all the deeds of a man and will purify for himself the frame of man, consuming every Spirit of error in his flesh, and cleansing him with a holy spirit from all wicked deeds" (Burrows). The peculiar problems presented by the Hebrew of this passage do not concern us.[25] The significant point is that the flesh is the seat of evil spirits and can be purged only by God's truth. The term is at least ambiguous in this context.

In other passages, however, as Kuhn has so persuasively indicated, the association of the flesh with evil becomes so close that it seems to denote the morally lower nature of man. Thus in 1 QS xi, 12, we read: "As for me, if I slip, the steadfast love of God is my salvation forever; and if I stumble in the iniquity of the flesh my vindication in the righteousness of God will stand to eternity" (Burrows). "Flesh" is here used somewhat absolutely; the reference is not to what we normally understand by "sins of the flesh." Nor is it clear whether "flesh" has reference here to mankind which is, as a whole, in iniquity or to the psalmist's own flesh as such, in which case we should, however, expect "my flesh." In 1 QS xi, 7, the phrase "the company of flesh" (Burrows) seems to be used simply of "mankind," because it is parallel to "the sons of man" in line 6. But even here the implication is that mankind, the company of flesh, outside the Covenant is in ignorance and unrighteousness. In 1 QS xi, 9, the "company of erring flesh" is parallel to "wicked humanity." In 1 QM "erring flesh" denotes the "sons of darkness." The phrase "The Hundred of God, a hand of war against all erring flesh" is placed on one of the standards of the sons of light.[26] The point might be made that if the term "flesh" bore in itself the connotation of evil it would not be necessary, as here, to qualify it by the addition "of error" or "of wickedness." The same phenomenon, however, of a term being qualified by that which it already designates is met with elsewhere.[27] Moreover, this difficulty is here offset by the simple fact that "the company of flesh" is equivalent to "the company of erring flesh," and probably to "the company of flesh and those who walk in darkness" (see 1 QS xi, 6-10). It seems clear that to belong to the flesh is to belong to that sphere where the spirit of perversion, the angel of darkness, rules.[28] Kuhn asserts that "('flesh') becomes almost synonymous with evil."[28]

Nevertheless, as Kuhn rightly insists,[29] it is not a Hellenistic view of the "flesh" that we encounter here. The author of the psalm in 1 QS xi can, here and now, while physically he is in the flesh, yet belong to the "chosen of God," the "sons of heaven," to the "lot of the holy ones." If, as is likely, we are to understand by these terms in lines 6ff. angelic or celestial beings with whom the sect shares its worship,[30] so that, while still on earth, its members participate in a heavenly comunity, it is clear that existence in the flesh does not in itself, as in Hellenistic thought, suggest or signify perversion. Similarly, as we have seen, the flesh can be "cleansed" and "purified" (1 QS iii, 6ff.; iv, 20). In Hellenistic thought it is not the purification of the flesh that is desired but escape from it, because the "flesh" is conceived there not only as the sphere where evil dwells but as itself constituting evil.[31]

When we turn to Paul we find that the term "flesh" is used in two broad ways as in the Scrolls—with and without a moral connotation. Where the moral connotation is present we find the Pauline use of the word very similar to that in the Scrolls. The evidence for this has been given by Kuhn and need not be repeated here; a glance at the passages listed in the second group below would confirm his conclusions. Let it suffice here to compare the sentence quoted above from Kuhn with some definitions made by J. A. T. Robinson: "Flesh represents mere man, man in contrast with God—hence man in his weakness and mortality" . . . "Flesh stands for man, in the solidarity of creation, in his distance from God" . . . "One could describe the situation by saying that flesh as neutral is man living in the world, flesh as sinful is man living for the world."[32]

But identity of terminology, we wrote above, does not mean very much. It is more important to ask whether the sets of ideas within which the term "flesh" is used are identical or similar. At this point it will be well to tabulate the incidence of the term "flesh" in its various broad meanings in Paul:

The incidence of the term "flesh" (*sarx*) in the Pauline Epistles: (1) Places where "flesh" has a physical connotation: Rom. 1₃; 2₂₈; 3₂₀; 4₁; 9₃, ₅, ₈; 1 Cor. 1₂₆, ₂₉; 5₅; 6₁₆; 7₂₈; 10₁₈; 15₃₉, ₅₀; 2 Cor. 4₁₁; 7₅; 12₇; Gal. 1₁₆; 2₁₆, ₂₀; 3₃; 4₁₃, ₁₄, ₂₃, ₂₉; 6₁₂, ₁₃; Eph. 2₁₁, ₁₄; 5₂₉, ₃₁; 6₅, ₁₂; Phil. 1₂₂, ₂₄; 3₃, ₄; Col. 1 22, 24; 2₁, ₅, ₂₃; 3₂₂; Philem. 16. (2) Places where "flesh" has a moral connotation: Rom. 6₁₉; 7₅, ₁₈, ₂₅; 8₃, ₄, ₅, ₆, ₇, ₈, ₉, ₁₂, ₁₃; 2 Cor. 1₁₇; 5₁₆; 7₁; 10₂, ₃; 11₁₈; Gal. 5₁₃, ₁₆, ₁₇, ₁₉, ₂₄; 6₈; Eph. 2₃; Col. 2₁₁, ₁₃, ₁₈.

These listings prompt two comments. First, it is noteworthy that the term "flesh" with a moral connotation occurs far less frequently in the Pauline Epistles than discussions of Pauline theology would lead us to expect. Secondly, almost all the instances where Paul uses "flesh" with that connotation occur in three types of material: (*a*) in Rom. 7 and 8, where Paul is concerned with the individual experience of sin; (*b*) in the polemic portions of Colossians; and (*c*) in the paraenetic section in Galatians. Let us look more closely at these.

In Rom. 7 and 8 Paul deals with the problem of sin not metaphysically or theologically but experientially: he uses the term "flesh" in describing his personal struggle with his lower nature, as it were. Where Paul is concerned to speculate on the origin of sin on a large scale in Rom. 1, 2, and 5, and not to enlarge upon its working in his own life, the term "flesh" does not occur with a moral connotation. He there deals with sin in terms of idolatry and of the Fall, without having recourse to the nature of the "flesh" at all.[33] The mere fact that in Rom. 1, 2, and 5 Paul is concerned with the universal and corporate aspects of sin and in Rom. 7 with its more personal aspects does not in itself sufficiently account for the emphasis on "flesh" in the latter section and its neglect in the former, if his understanding of "flesh" was an *essential* element in his approach to the problem of evil. It seems that his concept of the flesh has perhaps *not* been integrated into the main structure of his thought: is there a kind of hiatus between his experiential awareness of the flesh as his lower nature and his theoretical understanding of sin?

But the same phenomenon confronts us in the Scrolls. Those passages in which *basar* ("flesh") has a moral connotation occur mainly (and, if we follow Kuhn, exclusively) in those sections where the personal experience of sin is being described, namely, in the psalms.[34] Where the Scrolls present a system of belief the term is notably absent. Thus in 1 QS iii, 13-iv, 26, there is only one reference to "flesh" which, as we saw, Kuhn treats as having no moral connotation. Elsewhere in the Scrolls the term is not particularly significant for our purpose. Thus, as in Paul, so in the Scrolls the concept of the "flesh," as having moral connotation, seems to stand outside the fundamental theology of the sect, and emerges fully only where the more directly experiential aspects of life are described. When we encounter the theology of the sect as such, we find not a treatment of "flesh" in its relation to sin but a dualism, derived, according to Dupont-Sommer[35] and Kuhn,[36] from Iranian sources. While, therefore, the use of the term "flesh" in Paul recalls its use by the sect, it does not necessarily follow that there is any fundamental similarity between Paul's thought on sin and that of the sect. In itself it merely proves that Paul's conceptual milieu coincides at this one point with that of the sect. The "sets of ideas" with which Paul associates the term are not the same as those with which the sect seems to associate it.

If what we have written above be valid, we find the term "flesh" used by Paul in connection with the Fall and idolatry, ideas which belong to the main stream of Judaism: the sectarian term "flesh" coexists with what would seem to be ultimately Iranian concepts which have been yoked to Jewish monotheism. It is tempting to suggest that it is the Hellenization both of Judaism and of Zoroastrian currents in Palestine that accounts for this phenomenon. I have elsewhere pointed out that in Rom. 7 what we have is a description of Paul's struggles with his Evil Impulse. Throughout he uses rabbinic concepts, *except* where he locates the Evil Impulse in the flesh. A lengthy quotation may be permitted[37]: "We saw that the Evil Impulse was located generally in the heart, whereas Paul clearly regards the 'flesh' as the base of operations for sin. The question is inevitable whether, had Paul been describing the conflict with his Evil Impulse, he too would not have spoken of 'the heart' rather than 'the flesh'? It has been suggested that the Apostle regarded the 'flesh' as the seat of sin because he was thinking more particularly of sins in the 'flesh' in a restricted sense; but that the sins of the flesh included for Paul not merely sexual sins but also such things as pride is clear from Gal. 5. The probable explanation, however, of why Paul used 'flesh' is not far to seek. There was no scientific fixity or accuracy about the use of psychological and anthropological terms in his day and the Old Testament use of 'flesh' would naturally and suitably suggest itself to him. In addition to this the location of the Impulse in the heart, while dominant in Rabbinic thought, must not be too hard pressed. The Evil Impulse had a long start over the Good Impulse in man, and some passages suggest that it had gained dominion over the whole 248 members of the human body: it would not be difficult then for Paul to envisage sin as invading all his members and having its base in all his flesh."

In the light of the Scrolls, however, we now see that Paul had predecessors; there was much precedence for the accentuation of the moral connotation of the Old Testament term "flesh"; and we may recognize that it may have been Hellenistic influences in Palestine that supplied the impetus for this. And this same impetus may have affected the "Zoroastrianism" of the sect. The source criticism of 1 QS, and the other sectarian documents, has not been much attempted as yet, but it may well be that the section iii, 13ff., reflects an earlier "uncontaminated" stage in the history of the sect before Hellenistic influences had deeply colored its thought, while the psalms reflect a later stage when this had taken place. It is tempting to see in the Pauline and the sectarian "flesh" a common term which emerged into significance in a Hellenized Rabbinic Judaism and a Hellenized Zoroastrian Judaism, respectively. This common term does not necessarily point to identity of thought but merely to a common background where Hellenistic forces were at work, nor is it inconsistent to claim this while at the same time holding that neither in Paul nor in the Scrolls is "flesh" a totally Hellenistic concept.

Do the other passages where Paul uses "flesh" with an ethical connotation justify us in going further than this? Let us next look at Col. 2₁₁₋₂₃:

> In him also you were circumcised with a circumcision made without hands, by putting off the body of flesh in the circumcision of Christ; and you were buried with him in baptism, in which you were also raised with him through faith in the working of God, who raised him from the dead. And you, who were dead in trespasses and the uncircumcision of your flesh, God made alive together with him, having forgiven us all our trespasses, having canceled the bond which stood against us with its legal demands; this he set aside, nailing it to the cross. He disarmed the principalities and powers and made a public example of them, triumphing over them in him.
> Therefore let no one pass judgment on you in questions of food and drink or with regard to a festival or a new moon or a sabbath. These are only a shadow of what is to come; but the substance belongs to Christ. Let no one disqualify you, insisting on self-abasement and worship of angels, taking his stand on visions, puffed up without reason by his sensuous mind, and not holding fast to the Head, from whom the whole body, nourished and knit together through its joints and ligaments, grows with a growth that is from God.
> If with Christ you died to the elemental spirits of the universe, why do you live as if you still belonged to the world? Why do you submit to regulations, "Do not handle, Do not taste, Do not touch" (referring to things which all perish as they are used), according to human precepts and doctrines? These have indeed an appearance of wisdom in promoting rigor of devotion and self-abasement and severity to the body, but they are of no value in checking the indulgence of the flesh (RSV).

Recently this whole section has been understood to reflect the presence of Qumran sectarian influences. The "heresy" confronting Paul at Colossae may have had Stoic undertones.[38] Nevertheless, its predominantly Jewish character is indicated clearly by the references to "principalities and powers" and to "the rudiments of the world" (RSV: "elemental spirits of the universe"); to the observance of rules on meat and drink, holy days, the new moon and Sabbath days, the worshiping of angels. But it has always been difficult to gauge the exact nature of the forces at work, and scholars have hitherto had to be contented with vague references to Jewish Gnosticism.[39]

The Scrolls, however, present what seem to be specific points of contact with the Colossian heresy. The exact phrase "the body of the flesh," a highly puzzling one, has appeared in the Habakkuk Commentary on 2₇, ₈: "(7) *Will they not suddenly arise, those who torment you; will they not awake, those who torture you? Then you will be booty for them. (8) Because you have plundered many nations, all the remainder of peoples will plunder you.* This means the priest who rebelled . . . his scourge with judgments of wickedness; and horrors of sore diseases they wrought in him, and vengeance in his body of flesh." Here the phrase "body of flesh" means the physical body and there is an exact parallel in Col. 1₂₂, while in Col. 2₁₁ the phrase is made to refer to man's lower nature which the Christian has put off in Christian "circumcision."⁴⁰ But more important are the echoes of the Scrolls in other matters. There is the same emphasis on calendrical niceties, although it must be noted that this would not be a peculiarity of our sect. Passages such as CD iii, 13-16; 1 QS i, 14; x, 1-9, point to a calendar different from that of official Judaism, a solar one. (The phrase which appears in Gal. 4₁₀ recalls exactly 1 QS i, 14.) The specific reference in Col. 2₁₆ to the Sabbath comports with the many regulations of the Sabbath in CD x, 14-xi, 18; so too the distinctions between meats and drinks find an echo in CD vi, 18. Thus the asceticism condemned in Col. 2₂₀ff. could well be illustrated by the life of the sectarians. But, finally, behind all these particular points, stand the references to wisdom and knowledge in the Epistle and the warning in Col. 2₈, "Beware lest any man spoil you through philosophy and vain deceit, after the tradition of men, after the rudiments of the world and not after Christ." The claim of the sect to a special wisdom or knowledge needs no emphasis; it is writ large over the Scrolls.⁴¹ Moreover, this "knowledge" is bound up not only with the observance of Sabbaths, Festivals, etc., but also with an understanding of the world which recalls much in Colossians. In 1 QS iii, 13ff., we read of the spirit of truth and the spirit of error: the former is the prince of lights, the latter the angel of darkness, and there are destroying angels under his dominion. The spirit of truth is also called the angel of truth. The angelology of the Scrolls may indeed illumine for us the reference to the worship of angels in Col. 2₁₈, and the "intruding into those things which he hath not seen" may be aimed at the kind of thing referred to in 1 QM x, 1of., where the people of the Covenant are said to be those who hear the voice of the venerated One and see the holy angels and who hear ineffable things. The most frequent term for the supreme force of evil in the Scrolls is Belial, who is the angel of darkness.[42] In Colossians the terms used of the forces of evil ranged against Christians (and the Law itself is included among these forces, Col. 2₁₄) are "the power of darkness" (1₁₃), "principalities," "powers" (2₁₅), "thrones" (1₁₆), "the rudiments of the world" (1₂₀), and, in a more individual vein, "the old man." The correspondence in terminology, it must be conceded, is not here very exact and, by itself, could not be taken to point to influences of the Qumran type as certainly as some have so unhesitatingly held. Nevertheless, along with the other factors mentioned above, it would seem that the forces of evil in Colossians may be the same as those referred to in the Scrolls. This is particularly reinforced when we turn to Ephesians, which is at least deutero-Pauline, and where the correspondence with the Scrolls is perhaps more close. There too we meet principalities and powers, might and dominion, "and every name that is named"; "the prince of the power of the air"; "the spirit that now worketh in the children of disobedience"—this last especially being reminiscent of the Scrolls (1 QS iii, 13ff.).[43]

Assuming then that Paul confronts belief in the kind of "evil forces" which emerge in the Scrolls, are we to conclude from Colossians (and Ephesians) that he himself accepts their reality? Does he take them seriously? Do they constitute an important element in his thought or is Paul merely using his "opponents'" terms without really giving credence to them? To judge from Colossians and Ephesians alone it might be argued that he is merely using the terms. This was the view, for example, of Lightfoot,[44] and C. H. Dodd[45] urges the same. On the other hand, Paul refers to these same powers in Galatians, Romans and 1 Corinthians, where the argument seems to demand the belief in their reality.[46] The question, perhaps, cannot be fully decided. Nevertheless, it may be said that it was the necessity to fight against the significance attached to such powers among Christians not untouched by the conceptual climate of the sectarians that led Paul to deal with them, and thereby to formulate some of his most profound assertions on the all-sufficiency and supremacy of Christ. For our present purpose, which is the examination of the term "flesh" in the Scrolls and in Paul, what is noteworthy is that it is precisely where Paul has most clearly to combat what seem to be influences of the Qumran type of idea that there emerges in his epistles the use of the term "flesh" with a moral connotation. Polemic against sectarian ideology seems to call forth his use of the term: he comes to speak the language of his opponents (Col. 2₁₁. 1₃. 1₈). He can express himself otherwise, as, for example, in Col. 3₅, we read: "Mortify, therefore, your members which are upon the earth," where we should expect him perhaps to say simply, "Mortify therefore your flesh." The obvious fluidity, however, with which Paul can use language, a fluidity which is the despair of his expositors, makes the particular incidence of the term "flesh" in his epistles even more significant. It is sectarian contexts that seem to be evocative of it. The occurrence of "flesh" in 2 Corinthians, in which there are traces of what can be claimed to be Qumran terminology, confirms this[47] (See especially 2 Cor. 6₁₄ᶠ.: "Be ye not unequally yoked together with unbelievers: for what fellowship hath righteousness with unrighteousness? and what communion hath light with darkness? And what concord hath Christ with Belial? or what part hath he that believeth with an infidel?")

There remains to consider in connection with the term "flesh" the paraenetic section in Gal. 5₁₃₋₂₁, which reads:

For you were called to freedom, brethren; only do not use your freedom as an opportunity for the flesh, but through love be servants of one another. For the whole law is fulfilled in one word, "You shall love your neighbor as yourself." But if you bite and devour one another take heed that you are not consumed by one another.

But I say, walk by the Spirit, and do not gratify the desires of the flesh. For the desires of the flesh are against the Spirit, and the desires of the Spirit are against the flesh; for these are opposed to each other, to prevent you from doing what you would. But if you are led by the Spirit you are not under the law. Now the works of the flesh are plain: immorality, impurity, licentiousness, idolatry, sorcery, enmity, strife, jealousy, anger, selfishness, dissension, party spirit, envy, drunkenness, carousing and the like. I warn you, as I warned you before, that those who do such things shall not inherit the kingdom of God (RSV).

This list recalls other similar ones in the New Testament such as that in Mk. 7₂₀ᶠᶠ., which runs: "And he said, That which cometh out of the man, that defileth the man. For from within, out of the heart of men, proceed evil thoughts, adulteries, fornications, murders, thefts, covetousness, wickedness, deceit, lasciviousness, an evil eye, blasphemy, pride, foolishness: All these evil things come from within, and defile the man" (AV). The items that are the same in both passages are adultery, fornication, lasciviousness, murders. The Galatian list is more directed, however, at those evils which create disunity—hatred, variance, emulations, wrath, strife, seditions, heresies, envying; it also slightly emphasizes more the specifically religious ills, idolatry, witchcraft, although the Marcan list also includes the "evil eye" and "blasphemy." Moreover, we are equally reminded of lists of vices found in the Qumran material: "But to the spirit of error belong greediness, slackness of hands in the service of righteousness, wickedness and falsehood, pride and haughtiness, lying and deceit, cruelty and great impiety, quickness to anger, and abundance of folly and proud jealousy, abominable works in a spirit of fornication and ways of defilement in the service of uncleanness and a blasphemous tongue, blindness of eyes and dullness of ears, stiffness of neck and hardness of heart, walking in all the ways of darkness and evil cunning" (1 QS iv, 9-11). The list in Galatians, despite its points of similarity—anger, folly, jealousy, fornication, uncleanness, blasphemy—is more directed against "heretical" tendencies to disunity. The Qumran list concentrates on the immoral tendencies within the community.

Lists drawn from Hellenic sources[48] have rightly been compared with those in Galatians and Mark, and any direct relation between the Pauline and the Qumran material cannot be assumed. But it should be recalled that the paraenetic sections of the Pauline Epistles have previously been connected with Jewish sources. D. Daube in particular traced the imperatival participle which often appears in these sections to rabbinic usage. There is, therefore, considerable justification for a readiness to see the same paraenetic tradition behind Paul and the sect, especially since the imperatival participle is emerging in the Scrolls.[49] Moreover, the combination of "doctrine" and "paraenesis" which emerges in the Pauline Epistles is precisely what we find in the Qumran tradition: the "form" of the paraenesis and its setting would appear to be much the same in Paul and the Scrolls.[50] In addition, we have previously indicated the possibility that influences similar to those found in the Scrolls appear among the Galatian "judaizers."[51] At least we can claim in the light of all this that it is not impossible that Paul was drawing upon a didactic tradition within Judaism which is represented for us in one of its forms in the Scrolls.

But at this point we must again halt. The vices in Mark are described as coming "from within, out of the heart of man," there being no specific reference to the flesh. In the Scrolls the vices are those of the "spirit of error." The term for error is used elsewhere in the Scrolls in connection with the "flesh," but it should be noted that the ethical dualism of the sect is expressed in terms of two spirits whereas in Paul it is expressed in terms of the antithesis of flesh and spirit. Nowhere is the "flesh" in the Scrolls equated with the spirit of error, rather is it the sphere where this works. The parallelism between Paul and the Scrolls at this point, therefore, is loose. The terms used by the sect and its literary conventions reappear in Paul but the fact that Paul thinks of a dualism of flesh and spirit still further confirms what we have previously noted, that the influence of the sect on Paul cannot be regarded as in any way determinative: Paul shares its terminology at certain points but not its doctrinal formulations. This will further appear as we turn to the doctrine of the Spirit. Does Paul's understanding of the Spirit reveal points of contact with that of the Scrolls?

## II

Fortunately the Scrolls are fairly rich in their use of the term "spirit." The fundamental treatment of it occurs in a section which is remarkably well constructed and apparently a self-contained unit.[52] The section is 1 QS iii, 13-iv, 26, and its substance may be set forth in the following tabulated form:

*THE GOD OF KNOWLEDGE*

(Source of all that is or will be)

The designs[53] of all things

(These and all things are unchangeable)

Man created for dominion over all

| *SPIRIT OF TRUTH* | SPIRIT OF ERROR |
|---|---|
| (from abode of light | (from source of darkness |
| =Prince of Lights | =Angel of darkness) |
| =Angel of Truth) | |

Both shine in the heart of man

| *Counsels of Spirit of Truth* | *[Counsels] of Spirit of Error* |
|---|---|
| Spirit of humility | Greediness |
| Slowness to anger | Slackness of hands in service of |
| Great compassion |    righteousness |
| Eternal goodness | Wickedness |
| Understanding | Falsehood |
| Insight | Pride |

| [Counsels of Spirit of Truth] | [Counsels of Spirit of Error] |
|---|---|
| Mighty wisdom | Haughtiness |
| Leaning on works & love of God | Lying |
| Spirit of knowledge in acts | Deceit |
| Zeal for right judgements | Cruelty |
| Holy thought | Impiety |
| Sustained purpose | Quickness to anger |
| Love for sons of truth | Abundance of folly |
| Purity | Proud jealousy |
| Abhorrence of idols | Fornication |
| Walking with humility | Uncleanness |
| Prudence | Stiffness of neck |
| Concealing the truth of | Blasphemous tongue |
| the mysteries | Hardness of heart |
| | Blindness of eye |
| *Rewards for Sons of Truth* | Walking in darkness |
| | Deafness of ears |
| Healing | Walking in cunning |
| Peace | |
| Length of Days | *Punishments for Sons of Error* |
| Seed | |
| Eternal Blessings | Afflictions by destroying angels |
| Everlasting Joy | Eternal perdition in fury of |
| Life of Eternity | God's vengeance |
| Crown of Glory | Eternal trembling |
| Raiment of Majesty | Destroying Disgrace in dark places |
| in Eternal Light | Sorrowful mourning |
| | Bitter calamity |
| | Dark disasters |
| | No Remnant |
| | No Escape |

All men share in both: both spirits are at enmity

But

*A PERIOD OF RUIN FOR ERROR IS SET BY GOD*

Truth of the world will emerge
Man purified of evil spirit: sprinkled with spirit of truth
Given wisdom and knowledge of God and Sons of Heaven
The new comes.

In the above table there is described a sharp dualism between two spirits. These spirits are both the creation of God, but (and it is important to notice this) they are regarded as a kind of permanent element in every man, since creation, until the "End" decreed by God. On the other hand, that they are not merely inherent properties of man, as such, emerges clearly from the use of the term "angel" to describe the two spirits: this preserves the "otherness" of the two spirits even when they appear to be merely immanent.[54] Nevertheless, the emphasis in the Scrolls is not on the invasive, transcendent character of the two spirits, but on their enduring presence and persistence until the End: they suggest not an *inrush* of specially given energy but, if we may so express it, two constant *currents* of good and evil forces in conflict.

But, it will be asked, is not the coming of the Spirit a mark of the End in the Scrolls? There is one passage where it is declared that at the End "*the truth of the world*" will emerge victorious. But the meaning of the phrase "the truth of the world" is difficult to assess. Some have found here a personification of the Messiah as truth,[55] but in view of the sect's expectation of two Messiahs this is hardly tenable. Probably it is best to take the phrase here to be a kind of synonym for the spirit of truth. At the End, this will appear and will be "sprinkled upon man." The whole passage reads:

> But God in the mysteries of his understanding and in his glorious wisdom has ordained a period for the ruin of error, and in the appointed time of punishment he will destroy it forever. And then shall come out forever the truth of the world, for it has wallowed in the ways of wickedness in the dominion of error until the appointed time of judgment which has been decreed. And then God will refine in his truth all the deeds of a man, and will purify for himself the frame of man, consuming every spirit of error hidden in his flesh, and cleansing him with a holy spirit from all wicked deeds. And he will sprinkle upon him a spirit of truth, like water for impurity, to make the upright perceive the knowledge of the Most High and the wisdom of the sons of heaven, to instruct those whose conduct is blameless . . . (1QS iv, 18ff.; Burrows).

Here the spirit's function at the end of time is not merely a negative one, one of purification. It is positive: "to make the upright perceive the knowledge of the Most High, etc. . . ." Nevertheless, the reference to the Spirit here somehow lacks that connotation of empowering energy which we associate with the eschatological gift of the Spirit in both the Old Testament and the New. Moreover, it must be doubly emphasized that it is only here that the spirit is ascribed a strictly eschatological significance at all in the Scrolls. This is particularly noteworthy in the literary remains of a sect which was steeped in the interpretation of Scriptures that made the Spirit a sign of the End, and which apparently regarded itself as living in the period preceding the End. Nor does the "charismatic" character of the sect make the absence of a markedly eschatological interpretation of the Spirit more understandable; on the contrary, it is precisely such *charismatic* groups that we should expect to emphasize the eschatological role of the Spirit.[56]

So far, then, the Scrolls reveal two spirits who are constantly opposed to each other, until the good spirit prevails at the End. But this same spirit, which can be regarded, along with its rival evil spirit, as a kind of permanent possession of man since his creation, is also deemed to have expressed itself in certain particular persons. There were special manifestations of it through Aaron and Moses, just as, on the other hand, there were special manifestations of the spirit of perversity. Thus the two spirits, which are from one point of view abiding elements in man's constitution, as it were, are also conceived as occasionally invasive. The pertinent passage is CD v, 16ff.: "For also in ancient times God visited their deeds and his anger was kindled against their practices, 'for it is a people of no understanding.' 'They are a nation void of counsel, inasmuch as there is no understanding in them.' For in ancient times Moses and Aaron arose by the hand of the Prince of Lights and Belial raised Jannes and his brother by his evil device, when Israel was delivered for the first time . . ." (Rabin's translation).

The Prince of Lights, it will be recalled, is the spirit of truth, and Belial the most frequent term employed for the spirit of error. The spirits here are deemed to have been especially given at particular times. The same concept appears in CD iv, 13ff., perhaps: "And during all those years shall Belial be let loose upon Israel as He spoke by the hand of the prophet Isaiah son of Amoz, saying: 'Fear, and the pit, and the snare are upon thee, O inhabitant of the land.' Its explanation: the three nets of Belial, about which Levi son of Jacob said that he 'catches in them the heart (or 'the house') of Israel' and has made them appear to them as three kinds of unrighteousness . . ." (Rabin). The term "Belial" is virtually defined in what follows it: what is meant is that the spirit of error would express itself in three ways—whoredom, wealth, conveying uncleanness to the sanctuary; and it could express itself, at a particular point, in such a way that it could be said to be "let loose." In a similar way the same spirit of error, which we repeat, could be understood from one point of view as being a permanent ingredient of man's constitution, can be deemed to depart from a man, although we should not think of this departure probably as complete, because the spirit of error is in man till the End. This appears from CD xvi, 4: "And on the day that a man imposes upon himself by oath to return to the Law of Moses, the angel Mastema will depart from behind him, if he carries out his words. For this reason Abraham 'was saved' on the day when he acquired knowledge" (Rabin).

Further, just as Moses was regarded as having been given the spirit, so too the spirit was the source of prophecy, as it is elsewhere in Judaism.[57] Thus in 1 QS viii 14ff., we read: "When these things came to pass for the community in Israel, by these regulations, they shall be separated from the midst of the session of the men of error to go to the wilderness to prepare there the way of the Lord; 'upon the wilderness prepare the way of the Lord, make straight in the desert a highway for our God.' This is the study of the law, as he commanded through Moses, to do according to all that has been revealed from time to time, and as the prophets revealed by his Holy Spirit" (Burrows). The awareness of the spirit of truth as a specially given energy emerges again in a much-discussed passage in CD ii, 9ff.: "And He knows (or: knew) the years of their existence and the number (or: set times) and exact epochs of all them that come into being in eternity (or: in the worlds) 'and past events,' even unto that which will befall in the epochs of all the years of eternity (or: the world). And in all of them He raised for Himself 'men called by name,' in order to leave (?) a remnant' for the land and to fill the face of the universe of their seed, and to make (or: be made) known to them by the hand of His anointed ones His holy Spirit and shew them (or: demonstration of) truth . . ." (Rabin). Thus Rabin takes the Hebrew word for "His anointed one(s)" to be a plural (with a defective writing in the text, a feature which is found elsewhere: MSHYHW instead of MSHYHYW) and interprets it as referring to "the prophets."[58] Burrows[59] reads it as a singular and simply translates "And through his anointed one he shall make them know his Holy Spirit and a revelation of truth," and interprets it as referring to Zadok. Teicher claims this to be a reference to Christ, since in his view the Scrolls are Jewish-Christian documents.[60]

This last reference to Teicher's thesis reopens the question of the relation of the Messiah to the spirit in the Scrolls. If we reject the strictly messianic reference in 1 QS iv, 20, and in CD ii, 9ff., then in no case in the Scrolls is the spirit specifically connected with the Messiah(s), although in 1 QS iv, 20f., it is connected with the End. The problem of the relation of the spirit to the Messianic Age emerges with peculiar force in 1 QS ix, 3ff., which Burrows renders thus: "When these things come to pass in Israel according to all these regulations, *for a foundation of a holy spirit,* for eternal truth, for a ransom for the guilt of transgression and sinful faithlessness . . . at that time the men of the community shall be set apart, a house of holiness for Aaron, to be united as a holy of holies and a house of community for Israel, those who conduct themselves blamelessly. . . . They shall not depart from any counsel of the law, walking in all the stubbornness of their hearts; *but they shall judge by the first judgments by which the men of the community began to be disciplined, until there shall come a prophet and the Messiahs of Aaron and Israel.*"

Brownlee renders the first of the phrases we have put in italics by "for an institution of a holy spirit," but tentatively suggests also "for an institution of spiritual holiness." One thing alone is clear. The period "when these things happen" is to be distinguished from the Messianic Age: when the two Messiahs have come, they shall presumably bring new judgments with them, which are to be sharply distinguished from the judgments, i.e., the laws, prevailing in the pre-Messianic Age. There are two possibilities. *Either* the community in the days immediately preceding the End is to be in possession of the Holy Spirit, on the grounds of its fulfillment of the Law in the right way *or* the strict discipline of the sect becomes a foundation on which, when the Messianic Age has come, the Holy Spirit will be given. The first possibility goes with the translation "institution" and means that the "holy spirit" is preparatory to the End and not strictly necessarily a mark of it. The second possibility goes with the translation "foundation" and conceives the Spirit as a future sign of the End. This last, it must be conceded, involves a somewhat tortuous understanding of the text.[61] Moreover, the context suggests that the life of the sect before the Messianic Age is throughout in view as in 1 QS viii, 5 ff., and it is possible that all that is meant by "holy spirit" here is "a spirit of holiness," the emphasis being on "holiness," not on "spirit"—i.e., "spirit here refers primarily to disposition or character, as it often does in the Scrolls (see 1 QS iv, 3; viii, 3; ix, 14 ff.; ix, 22; xi, 2).

It would in any case be too precarious to see in 1 QS ix, 3ff., anything that would seriously cause us to modify what we wrote above, that the Scrolls do not *emphasize* the spirit as a sign of the End.[62]

Before we turn to Paul himself there is one further possibility to be noted, namely, that the term "spirit" in the Scrolls came to mean what we would refer to as "the self," this under the influence of Persian ideas about the *daēna*. This is suggested by Schweizer.[63] Not all his evidence for this is equally convincing.

Thus in 1 QS vii, 18: "If a man's spirit wavers from the institution of the community, so that he becomes a traitor to the truth and walks in the stubbornness of his heart . . ."—as in 1 QS vii, 23: "If any man is in the Council of the community for ten full years and his spirit turns back so that he becomes a traitor to the Community . . ." (Burrows)—"spirit" may refer merely to "disposition," although Schweizer's claim that it refers to "man's total existence, particularly that of man facing God, i.e., man as religious being" is probable.

More doubtful is the use of 1 QS viii, 12, in this connection. The whole passage reads: "When these men have been prepared in the foundations of the community for two years with blameless conduct, they shall be separated in holiness in the midst of the Council of the men of the community; and when anything which has been hidden from Israel is found by the man who is searching, it shall not be hidden from these men out of fear of an apostate spirit" (Burrows). The phrase "out of fear of an apostate spirit" may merely anticipate a situation where a member of the community might be led not to communicate new truths (of Scripture) to them—truths revealed particularly to him—when he was afraid that, by his words, he would appear heretical. It is not difficult to imagine how stifling and prohibitive could be the inquisitorial atmosphere of the sect.[64]

More convincing is Schweizer's reference to 1 QH viii, 5: "Thou hast cast for man an eternal lot/With the spirits of knowledge/to praise Thy name together in joyful song/And to recount thy wonders in the presence of all thy works . . ." Here the "spirits of knowledge" are the members of the community.

At obvious points the use of the term *ruah* in the Scrolls will have recalled that of *pneuma* in the Pauline Epistles. In both the terms are found respectively to express disposition or temperament[65]; to denote the self[66]; to indicate the origin of prophecy.[67] Moreover, the marked communal emphasis of the Spirit in Paul finds its counterpart in the Scrolls.[68] The limitation of the use of the term *ruah* to human and moral realities, without reference to the created order, is largely the case with Paul and the Scrolls.[69] The long-standing discussion as to whether Paul was the first to "ethicize" the Spirit can now be regarded, in the light of the Scrolls, as closed.[70]

Over a large area, therefore, the sectarian documents and the Pauline Epistles reflect a common understanding of the concept of "Spirit" (*ruah/pneuma*).

Furthermore, before we seek to assess the degree to which they shared a common milieu, it is fair to observe that Paul, who lived in a community which believed that the Messiah had come, could not but differ radically in his understanding of the "Spirit," in emphasis, at least, from the sectarians who still awaited their Messiahs. Complete identity in this, as in other things, it would be unreasonable to expect for this reason. Perhaps the real relation between Paul and the sectarian influences that may have been upon him can be clarified by asking a simple question: Had Paul been much influenced by the kind of thought on the spirit revealed to us in the Scrolls, would he have developed his "doctrine" of the Spirit as he did? To ask this question is at once to be made aware of the points at which Paul differs from the sectarians.

Here again the incidence of Paul's use of the term *pneuma* is instructive. The frequency with which it occurs in various senses is as follows:[71] of the spirit of man (22 instances); of the spirit as opposed to flesh (6); of the spirit of God (Holy Spirit: 72); of the spirit as opposed to the Law and the letter (4); of the spirit denoting a quality or disposition (13); of the spirit of Christ (8); of the spirit of evil or of the world (2).

There would, perhaps, be differences in the interpretation of some of the passages in the categories submitted above, but the lists are at least sufficiently accurate to supply a broad picture of the Pauline emphasis.

The predominance of references to the Spirit of God, or the Holy Spirit as the Spirit of God, and the paucity of references to the spirit of evil is clear. There are only two examples of the use of *pneuma* specifically as an evil force[72]: 1 Cor. $2_{12}$ and Eph. $2_2$. As for 1 Cor. $2_{12}$, the whole passage concerned is 1 Cor. $2_{6-16}$. The Jewish affinities of the opponents of Paul in the Corinthian church have been recently urged particularly by Dupont.[73] They are made more than ever probable by the parallelisms which the above passage, as others also, offer to the Scrolls. The "mystery" revealed to Christians ($2_{10}$), which is hidden from this world and was not recognized by the powers of this world ($2_6$),[74] recalls the "mysteries" revealed to the sect and hidden from the "men of the pit" (1 QS ix, 17, 22) and also recalls the expectations of a fullness of knowledge at the End anticipated by the sect. Paul virtually claims that this is already his "in Christ." The "wisdom" spoken by Paul among the "perfect" echoes the wisdom cherished by the sectarians who regarded themselves as "perfect." In the light of all this, perhaps we should expect the Pauline use of *pneuma* to suggest further the conceptual milieu of the Scrolls.

But here caution is right. The term "holy spirit," as we have seen, occurs frequently in the Scrolls, but there is no direct parallel in them either to the term "the spirit of God" or "the spirit from God," or to the phrase "the spirit of the world." Is it, then, the same opposition between two spirits that we find in 1 QS iii, 13ff., and in Paul in 1 Cor. 2? The meaning of the phrase, "the spirit of the world," which might be taken, at first glance, to correspond to "the spirit of perversity" in the Scrolls, is difficult to assess. Does it refer to "a system of organized evil, with its own principles and its own laws" (cf. Eph. $2_2$, $6_{11}$, which, we have already suggested, recall the Scrolls), or is it a somewhat colorless phrase meaning merely "the spirit of human wisdom," with no suprasensible undertones such as we find in Eph. $2_2$?[75] But even if we connect "the spirit of the world" with Eph. $2_2$, we still have no exact terminological parallel with the "spirit of error" in the Scrolls. Moreover, difficult as it is to define "the spirit of the world" in 1 Cor. $2_{12}$, it is equally clear what Paul means by the Spirit of God, because he himself defines it for us as "the Spirit (which comes) from God"; its divine origin is emphasized. It will at once be recalled that, although God is the creator of both the spirit of truth and of error in the Scrolls, in 1 QS iii, 19ff., the source of the spirit of truth is defined as being "in the abode of light." It is not said to be "from God," although made by God. So too the spirit of error is derived from "a source of darkness."[26] The parallelisms between the two spirits mentioned by Paul and those opposed in the Scrolls cannot, therefore, be too closely pressed in 1 Cor. 2.

There is a more likely parallel in Eph. $2_{1-2}$. As we previously suggested, it is not difficult to see here, as elsewhere in Ephesians, the reflection of a conceptual climate like that revealed in the Scrolls. The spirit "that is now at work in the sons of disobedience" is reminiscent of the "spirit of error" in 1 QS iii, 13ff., by whom is "the straying of all the sons of unrighteousness." It is noteworthy that in 1 QS iii the "spirit of error" is not called "a prince" or "a power," but "an angel." The term "prince" is reserved for the "spirit of truth" who is called both "angel" and "prince of lights." However, too much should not be made of this because the "spirit of error" has a dominion over its minions, the evil spirits, so that by implication it too is a prince.[77] The author of Ephesians, it seems not unlikely, combated ideas such as emerge in the Scrolls and used these very ideas in the service of the gospel.

But apart from these two passages—and the one in Ephesians alone offers anything like a close parallel—Paul does not mention the spirit of evil. He is primarily concerned with another spirit— the Spirit from God; indeed he is almost exclusively so concerned. The evidence need not here be repeated that Paul is aware of himself as living in the community of the Spirit, in the New Israel, the people of the End, called into being by Christ.[78]

Whereas in the Scrolls the eschatological significance of the Spirit is not emphasized, for Paul the Spirit is the sign of the End *par excellence*. The difference can perhaps best be expressed by saying that, whereas in the Scrolls the "spirit of truth," already and constantly at work in men, would again find expression in a renewed "sprinkling" at the End, in Paul we find a dynamic sense of the "newness" of the gift of the Spirit. This is not to deny that Paul would regard the Spirit, which had been poured forth in Christ, as the same Spirit that was previously at work in prophecy and in other ways in the Old Testament. But his emphasis is not on the continuity of the Spirit in the Old and New Dispensations, real as this was for him, but on the new creation which the coming of the Spirit in Christ had inaugurated.[79]

This is illustrated in two ways. First, in the relation which the Spirit in Paul bears to the Law. One of the most striking aspects of the Scrolls is the coincidence in them of a "legalistic" and a "charismatic" piety.[80] The obedience to the Law demanded in the sectarian sources is even sharper than in Rabbinic Judaism.[81] But at the same time there is found, especially in the Hymns, an awareness of the need of God's justifying help which surpasses anything known to us in pre-Christian Judaism. The community is aware of itself as under "the Law" and yet as a "household of the spirit"; it reveals no sense of an *essential* incompatibility or *essential* tension between life under "the Law" and life under "the Spirit." On the other hand, Paul sets "the Law," as we are often reminded, in radical opposition to "the Spirit." To judge from the table given on pp. 171f. this opposition occurs far less frequently in Paul than treatments of his theology would lead us to suppose. Nevertheless, that Paul did set life under "the Law" over against life "in the Spirit" is clear. To this there is no parallel in the Scrolls. The chief pertinent passage is 2 Cor. 3₄₋₉. Paul here asserts that a New Covenant has come into being of which he is a minister. The terms of this New Covenant are written not on tablets of stone or in letters of ink; terms written in and on such media "kill." Sectarian influences, such as we are here concerned with, as we saw, may well have been active in the Corinthian church, and it is not impossible that Paul in 2 Cor. 3 is casting a side glance at our sectarians or at Jerusalem Christians[82]; the true New Covenant, Paul may be implying, has no *written* code. Nevertheless, the contrast drawn by Paul is with the Covenant at the Exodus and it is to the Israelites, in a general way, that he explicitly refers.[83] It is, therefore, precarious to find polemic against the Covenanters here. What is noteworthy is that, whereas the concept of the Spirit in the Scrolls has been domiciled within a "legalistic" community, it refuses to be so neatly domiciled in Paul. There are, indeed, passages in Paul where the Law itself seems to be regarded as one of the hostile forces, which belongs to the "spirit of error" (see p. 168).

But, secondly, the difference between Paul and the Scrolls emerges in a point related to the first one made. We claimed that Spirit and Law are antithetical in Paul. But, as we have written elsewhere, this antithesis is transcended in Paul through the Christifying of the Spirit, so that the Spirit itself becomes both gift and demand: Paul almost equates the Spirit with the Christ and so, in part at least, resolves the tension between Law and Gospel.[84] On the other hand, as we saw above, there is no very close relation in the Scrolls between the Messiahs expected and the Spirit. This is not to be pressed, because, on the basis of Scripture, the sect would naturally expect the Messianic Age to be an age of the Spirit. Nevertheless, in the Scrolls the connection between the Messiahs and the

Spirit is not explicitly made, whereas for Paul the Lord, if not identified with, is at least equivalent to the Spirit.[85]

Are we to conclude from all the above, therefore, that Paul, while he used the term "spirit" much as did the sectarians, nevertheless, shows no marked parallelism and, certainly, no dependence on them in the essentials of his "doctrine" of the Spirit? This would seem to be the case. The Spirit in Paul is far more understandable in terms of the Old Testament expectation than in those of the Scrolls.[86]

Thus our discussion of "flesh" and "spirit" in Paul has led to the same conclusion. The Scrolls and the Pauline Epistles share these terms, but it is not their sectarian connotation that is determinative of Pauline usage. As the Epistles themselves[87] would lead us to expect, Paul stands in the essentials of his thought on these matters more in the main stream of Old Testament and Rabbinic Judaism than in that of the sect. There is no reason to suppose that in other aspects of his thought the case would be different. But this does not mean that the Scrolls have no significance for the understanding of Paul, because, as we have seen, they do supply an added clue to the connotation of terms that he used.

# XII

## The Qumran Scrolls and the
## Johannine Gospel and Epistles[*]

RAYMOND E. BROWN, S.S.

In comparative studies of the Qumran' Scrolls and the New Testament[1] much interest has been focused upon the Johannine literature. Once the dating of the Qumran material can be considered reasonably sure, on the basis of comparative paleography and archaeological excavations, the possibility of an interrelationship between the Qumran literature and St. John's writings[2] should be taken into account.[3]

Such a discussion can follow varied lines. The method of "historical" identifications within the Scrolls has already been employed, but not with much success. Dupont-Sommer's first book[4] on the Scrolls painted a very suggestive portrait of the Teacher of Righteousness (the great hero of Qumran)—a just man, nay "divine," who, having been persecuted and put to death by the wicked priest, came back to life and founded a church. The volatile French press immediately interpreted this as a proof that there was a Christ before our Jesus, and that the latter was nothing but a pale image of the former.[5] While recognizing the value of the many original observations of Dupont-Sommer, a good number of scholars[6] have rejected the theory of the Teacher's death and resurrection (which are dependent on his interpretation of a very obscure text, 1 QpHab xi, 4-7); and under closer examination, many of the similarities between the Qumran Teacher and Jesus Christ have been found wanting.

* Reprinted from *Catholic Biblical Quarterly* 17 (1955), pp. 403-19, 559-74.

Another example of "historical" identification is that of J. Teicher,[7] who claims that the community described in the Qumran Scrolls is that of the Ebionites, the second century Jewish-Christian group, who were destroyed by Diocletian. For Teicher the wicked priest and the Teacher are Paul and Christ. Despite interesting similarities between the Scrolls and Ebionite literature (which may well indicate that some of the Qumran ideas were adopted by the Ebionites), the excavations at Khirbet Qumran eliminate Teicher's hypothesis by showing that the Qumran Community was destroyed in A.D. 70. Today the majority of writers recognize the Qumran Community to be Essene,[8] although perhaps not in exactly the same stage of development as the Essenes described by Josephus and Philo. At any rate, in view of our very incomplete knowledge of the history of the Qumran Community, an attempt to build a theory of Qumran-Christian relationship on identifications of characters within the Scrolls seems unwise.

However, if we establish relationships on the basis of terminology and ideology, which this article hopes to do, we are on much more solid ground. There is enough of Qumran literature to determine certain aspects of the sectarians' thought and its phrasing, aspects which we may compare to similar points in the Johannine literature. Even here we should note the wise cautions that Fr. Coppens offers.[9] Similarities in thought and terminology between two such groups of documents could be expected because they are mutually dependent on the Old Testament and the Pseudepigrapha, and because they are dealing with roughly the same religious subject matter. Therefore, to establish interdependence, we must concentrate on similarities which are *peculiar* to the two.

## Modified Dualism

The outstanding resemblance between the Scrolls and the New Testament seems to be the modified dualism which is prevalent in both. By dualism we mean the doctrine that the universe is under the dominion of two opposing principles, one good and the other evil. Modified dualism adds the corrective that these principles are not uncreated, but are both dependent on God the Creator.

In the Old Testament there is really no predominant dualism.[10] True, there are evil spirits, such as the tempter of Gen. 3, and evil men whose ways are opposed to those of good man (Ps. 1). But it does not emphasize any theory that the world is divided into two great camps locked in eternal struggle. In their very practical outlook, the Hebrew Scriptures are more interested in the individual man's struggle to follow the Law and live righteously. In the Qumran literature we find a new outlook. All men are aligned in two opposing forces, the one of light and truth, the other of darkness and perversion, with each faction ruled by a spirit or prince. While much of this ideology is phrased in a quasi-biblical language, the guiding inspiration of the dualism is clearly extrabiblical.

In a series of brilliant articles, K. G. Kuhn of Heidelberg seems to have successfully identified this source as Iranian Zoroastrianism.[11] In its primitive form,[12] the Zoroastrian religion taught a dualism where the forces of good and evil, led by Ahura Mazda and Angra Mainyu, respectively, are in combat. As Kuhn stresses, this dualism is not physical (i.e., an opposition between matter and spirit); it is an *ethical* struggle between truth and deceit, light and darkness. And it is *eschatological*, for the ultimate triumph of Ahura Mazda is definitely envisaged.[13] In comparing the dualism of Qumran with early Zoroastrianism, Kuhn has found a great deal of similarity; for in the former the ethical, eschatological trend predominates too. In fact, there are interesting points of resemblance between passages of the Gathas and the Scrolls.[14] One great difference separates them: in Zoroastrianism the good and evil spirits are coexistent, independent, uncreated forces; in Qumran thought, as will be seen, they are both created by God. The imported dualism of Qumran has come into contact with the Old Testament theology of God the Creator, and is subservient to that great truth.

Zoroastrian influence on Qumran is not at all difficult to postulate if we realize that many Jews remained in Mesopotamia after the Captivity, and lived side by side with Iranians. Such proximity may well have influenced Jewish thought, especially in those elements which were compatible with the Hebrew religion.[15] From time to time Babylonian Jews returned to Palestine (witness Esdras in the late fifth century); and undoubtedly the formation of the Maccabean free state in the second century drew many more. It seems to have been just at the end of the Maccabean wars that the Qumran Community came into existence. If the founders of the community were of Babylonian Jewry, or in contact with it, the strain of Zoroastrian influence need not astound us.

When we turn to the Johannine writings, we find there also a modified dualism. Once again there is talk of forces of light and truth struggling with forces of darkness and perversion. There are hints of this elsewhere in the New Testament, especially in St. Paul; but nowhere does it reach the intensity of St. John's works. To account for this, many suggestions have been made. The fact that the Fourth Gospel was so popular with the Gnostics gave rise among the critics to the hypothesis of a Gnostic background. However, the discovery of the Gnostic codices at Chenoboskion in Upper Egypt in 1945[16] has considerably enlightened us on the true nature of this heresy. As W. F. Albright remarks, "We now know that the Church Fathers did not appreciably exaggerate their accounts of Gnosticism, and that the gap between Christianity and any form of second-century Gnosticism was tremendous. The efforts of recent historians of religion to picture a Gnosticism which resembled the Gospel of John more closely than anything known from Patristic tradition have been nullified . . ."[17] And besides, as Kuhn points out, the dualism of Gnosticism is a physical one; the dualism of John is ethical and eschatological, like that of Qumran.[18] Both streams may have had their very ancient sources in Zoroastrian dualism, but into Gnosticism have poured the muddy tributaries of pagan Greek philosophy and Judeo-Christian heresy; and in the end Gnosticism flows far away indeed from the Evangelist's "living waters."[19]

Now a new attempt has been made to identify the source of the modified dualism of St. John. Kuhn, Albright, Reicke, Brownlee, Braun, and Mowry see in the ideology and terminology of Qumran the Jewish background of Johannine thought and phrasing. A careful comparison of the two literatures on various points connected with this modified dualism will enable the reader to review some of the evidence for such a theory.

*(a) Creation.* Qumran states unequivocally the biblical doctrine of creation: "From the God of knowledge exists all that is and will be" (1 QS iii, 15). "And by his knowledge everything has been brought into being. And everything that is, he established by his purpose; and apart from him, nothing is done" (xi, 11).[20] We get a very similar statement in the Prologue of St. John, "All things

were made through him, and without him was made nothing that has been made."[21]

The Qumran literature goes on to state specifically that the two spirits, or leaders, of the forces of good and evil were created: "He created the spirits of light and darkness . . ." (1 QS iii, 25). For John, as we shall see, the problem does not arise; and so there is no similar statement. If the Zoroastrian background of Qumran dualism is correct, the specific statement of the creation of the two spirits may have been intended as a corrective. Miss Mowry suggests the possibility of a similar apologetic motive in John.[22] Perhaps the position of his universal statement of creation at the very beginning of his Gospel was directed against the idea of an uncreated evil spirit. Yet John is never specific on the creation of such a spirit, and he never returns with emphasis to the theme of the universality of creation.[23]

(b) *The Two Spirits.* The world, according to Qumran, is divided under two created leaders, one of whom God hates, while loving the other. The good spirit is called variously "the spirit of truth, the prince of lights, the angel of His truth, the holy spirit."[24] The evil spirit is called "the spirit of perversion, the angel of darkness, the angel of destruction."[25] Most often the name "Belial" is applied to him. This evil spirit seems to have subordinate spirits in his forces too, for the spirits of Belial are mentioned (CD 14$_5$).

In any case the names applied to the two principal spirits are clearly of a personal nature. As personal entities outside of man, they help or hinder man: "the God of Israel and his angel of truth have helped all the sons of light" (1 QS iii, 24-25; 1 QM xiii, 10). "And it is because of the angel of darkness that all the sons of righteousness go astray" (1 QS iii, 21-22). Yet they also conduct their struggle within man: "Until now the spirits of truth and perversion strive within man's heart (iv, 23-24).[26] Consequently, in many instances, one gets the definite impression that the spirits are being spoken of impersonally as ways of acting.[27] The two aspects are not necessarily contradictory: it is natural to shift from speaking of two personal spirits exercising a dominion over man to speaking of two spirits of acting by which man shows his respective adherence to their dominion.

In St. John we have both pairs of terms which Qumran uses interchangeably: light and darkness, truth and perversion. However, in his theology there is a difference between the leader of the forces of light and the Spirit of Truth; and so for the present we shall concentrate on only the light and darkness antinomy. For St. John, "God is light, and in him is no darkness" (1 Jn. 1₅). With the Son of God, Jesus Christ, light has come into the world,[28] so that Christ can call himself "the light of the world" (Jn. 9₅). Thus in the Fourth Gospel there is no created spirit of light such as we find in the Qumran literature—the leader of the forces of light is the uncreated Word himself.

John often speaks of the darkness, and he mentions an evil spirit —the devil or Satan.[29] Yet nowhere does he characterize Satan in the exact terminology of Qumran as the leader, spirit, or angel of the forces of darkness. (St. Luke with his mention of the "power of darkness" and St. Paul's Belial are terminologically closer to Qumran on this point than John is.)[30] Perhaps we may see a similarity to the Qumran literature in the struggle which John paints between Christ and "the prince of this world."[31]

In summary we may say that there is a similar general outlook in John and in the Qumran literature on the forces of light and darkness, each with its personal leader. Yet in John, Christ as the light of the world is a significant development over Qumran's created angel of light. There is difference too in the terminology for the leader of darkness.

*(c) The Struggle.* In the Qumran literature we are told that between the two spirits there is undying enmity and bitter conflict— a struggle which, until the last age, is waged on equal terms.[32] Clearly, however, the evil spirit is equal only by the sufferance of God,[33] and at the end God will intervene and crush him: "Now God through the mysteries of his understanding and through his glorious wisdom has appointed a period for the existence of wrongdoing; but at the season of visitation, he will destroy it forever; and then the truth of the world will appear forever" (1 QS iv, 18-19). Apparently, this divine intervention will be seen in a great battle where, thanks to God and his angels, the sons of light will be victorious. 1 QM gives a detailed plan for the organization of the forces, for standards, signals, and weapons of battle. The punishment of the wicked, after their defeat, will be severe, and their

sufferings are graphically described in apocalyptic language: multitude of plagues, eternal ruin, everlasting terror, destruction in the fire of the dark regions, calamities of darkness.[34] The end result will be that "wickedness will disappear before justice as darkness before light."[35]

In this whole picture of the struggle it is noteworthy that the writers always seem to be living in the period of trial, when Belial is still loose and waging war on equal terms. 1 QM, with all its minute details, is still a description of a future battle.

When we turn to St. John, we find there also a struggle between light and darkness, but a struggle which is passing through its climax and where victory is already decided. Christ has brought light into the world; darkness has tried to overcome this light, but "the darkness has not overcome the light" (Jn. 1₅ RSV). As a result the darkness is now going into decline, "the darkness has passed away (is passing away: RSV) and the true light is now shining" (1 Jn. 2₈).[36] John also phrases the victorious aspect of the conflict in terms of Christ's casting out the prince of this world (Jn. 12₃₁), so that the Saviour can cry out, "But take courage, I have overcome the world" (16₃₃). The victory, as we know, has not reached its culmination; only the second coming of Christ can establish the conclusive triumph of light. The Apocalypse (Rev.) presents the ultimate battle between the forces of good and evil. However, it must be admitted that even in this work we have no real parallel to the detailed accounts of 1 QM.

Once again, in summary, we see a similarity of thought between the two groups of writings on the conflict, and both are sure of the ultimate success of light. Yet here, as before, Christ makes a tremendous difference in John's outlook. For Qumran victory is still in the future; for John light is already triumphant.[37]

*(d) Man's Role.* Fr. Coppens has said that the Qumran Community gives no evidence of deep abstract religious speculations.[38] This seems particularly true in the problem of predestination and free will—a problem at the root of the domination of man by the spirits of light and darkness. As is inevitable when two trends of thought meet and are harmonized, difficulties occur which did not exist before the union. From the Old Testament there came to Qumran the basically simple Hebrew notions of morality, involving

the obviously free behavior of man and his consequent reward or punishment. From outside, presumably from Zoroastrianism, came the idea of two spirits dominating the human race, so that man acts according to one or the other: this is a concept which, when developed logically, would lead to a deterministic predestination. The sectarians never seem to have defined the conflict between these two notions, or to have attempted a speculative solution of it. Throughout their works are statements which favor one or the other view; but to me it does not seem accurate to classify them definitely on either side as if they had passed a reflex judgment on the problem. It was only later, when Jewish thought came into closer and closer contact with Hellenic and Hellenistic philosophies, that the full depth of the problem was realized and discussed; twenty centuries afterwards it is still a mystery.

Grossouw says of man's role according to Qumran theology: "The so-baffling difference in the conduct of good people and bad people is reduced here to the influence of 'the spirit of truth' and 'the spirit of perversion or deceit.' "[39] And of these spirits he says: "On the other hand, their mastery over man's moral actions seems to be absolute, the consequence of which would be that these actions are determined and no longer free."[40] Certainly there are many statements in the Qumran literature which can be so interpreted. 1 QS iii, 15 ff., states: "From the God of knowledge exists all that is and will be. Before they existed, he established all the design of them. And after they exist, according to their ordinances (in accordance with his glorious purpose), they fulfill their task; and nothing can be changed . . . Now, he created man for dominion over the world and assigned him two spirits by which to walk until the season of his visitation." Again in iv, 15, we find, "In these (two spirits) are the families of all mankind; and in their divisions do all their hosts receive an inheritance according to their societies and in their ways do they walk." And finally iv, 24, adds: "Until now the spirits of truth and perversion strive within man's heart; they walk in wisdom and folly; and according as man's inheritance is in truth and righteousness, so he hates evil; but in so far as his heritage is in the portion of perversity and wickedness in him, so he abominates truth."

Thus man would seem to be placed under one or the other spirit and to behave accordingly. In fact, the two spirits are so in control that they can be said to raise up men for their work: "For aforetime rose Moses and Aaron through the prince of the Lights. But Belial raised Jochanneh and his brother with his evil device . . ." (CD 7₁₉).[41] In the case of the sons of light, there seems to be a special divine predilection whereby they are chosen by God almost independently of their works. "For God has chosen them for an eternal covenant" (1 QS iv, 22). In fact they may be called "the ones chosen according to God's good pleasure."[42]

Such texts certainly seem to favor determinism. When we peruse some other statements, however, we find observations which appear to demand freedom of the will. Throughout 1 QS the importance of virtuous works is emphasized, and even the men of the community are blamed for succumbing to temptation and committing bad deeds. In general, the evil are punished precisely because they have rejected the will of God and have done *their own will*. "Because they did their own will and kept not the commandment of their Maker" (CD 3₇ and 4₉₋₁₀). A heinous sin is the refusal to accept the sectarians' interpretation of the Torah, and this refusal is spoken of as deliberate.[43] A very clear passage is 1 QS v, 11, where the wicked are said to have committed both "unknown sins" and "deliberate sins."[44] And finally we might note the strong emphasis of the Qumran texts on repentance, and the possibilities of reform offered to recalcitrant sectarians. All these ideas can scarcely be harmonized with a hopeless determinism.[45]

In St. John no such conflict of ideas exists. Of course there is a very orthodox statement of God's predilection: "You have not chosen me, but I have chosen you" (Jn. 15₁₆).[46] There is no hint, however, of anyone's being determined to evil without choice. Rather the culpable deliberateness of man's adherence to darkness is emphasized: "The light has come into the world, yet men have loved the darkness rather than the light, for their works were evil. For everyone who does evil hates the light, and does not come to the light, that his deeds may not be exposed" (Jn. 3₁₉₋₂₀). In view of this obstinate refusal, Christ tries to persuade men to come to the light before it is too late. "Yet a little while the light is among you. Walk while you have the light, that darkness may not overtake you. He who walks in darkness does not know where he goes" (Jn. 12₃₅).[47]

We might note that this idea of walking in light and darkness is very similar to the two ways in which men are to walk according to the Qumran texts.[48]

Yet in spite of all Christ's pleading and that of his apostles, some will always continue to walk in darkness. "If we say that we have fellowship with him, and walk in darkness, we lie, and are not practicing the truth" (1 Jn. 1₆). The free and deliberate choice of darkness is the basis for God's ultimate judgment of man: "Now this is the judgment: The light has come into the world, yet men have loved the darkness rather than the light" (Jn. 3₁₉).

In summary, we find that in the Qumran texts, men are aligned under the banners of light and darkness, and this seemingly without much choice on man's part. Yet other passages suppose that man deliberately walks in either of the two ways. In John's terminology, too, man walks in the ranks of either light or darkness, but he does so freely inasmuch as he accepts or does not accept Christ, the light of the world.

*(e) The Sons of Light.* What ultimately constitutes a man one of the sons of light? (1 QS i, 9; iii, 24; and *passim*). It is clear from the above that, for Qumran, refusal to do God's will makes one a son of darkness. Yet if we are to say that doing God's will makes one a son of light, we must understand "God's will" in a very restricted sense. Apparently the sectarians felt that no one could do what God wanted unless he was acquainted with the Torah as explained in the Qumran Community. Nowhere is the question broached of those who do good works and are not members of the community. Thus, for all practical purposes, the sons of light are equated with the sectarians. Some citations from the Qumran literature make this quite clear.

In 1 QM we have a description of the forces of the sons of light in their ultimate struggle with the sons of darkness; the former consists of the sectarians. 1 QS i, 7-8, and 11, tells us: "All who dedicate themselves to do God's ordinances shall be brought into the covenant of friendship, to be united (or, to become a community) in God's counsel . . . All who dedicate themselves to his truth shall bring all their mind and their strength and their property into the Community of God." The short poetical citation of 1 QS viii, 5-8, describes the community as the "witnesses of truth" and "those chosen according to God's pleasure." They are the ones who have been set apart as a house of holiness in Israel (ix, 6). And so we see that the Qumran sons of light are marked by the exclusiveness typical of small sectarian movements whether in Israel or in Christianity.[49]

The precise factor in the community which sanctifies its members is their acceptance of, and obedience to, the teaching of the sect. The early chapters of 1 QS give the Covenant of the community. They are told that they have "to walk before him perfectly (in) all things that are revealed according to their appointed seasons . . ." (i, 8-9).[50] The idea of submissiveness to revealed teaching comes up again in the instruction of iii, 13: "For the wise man, that he may instruct and teach all the sons of light in the generations of all mankind with regard to all the varieties of their spirits. . . ." The hearts of the sectarians are illumined with the "wisdom of life"; and they can look upon the "light of life."[51]

Historically, God seems to have raised up the Teacher of Righteousness to instruct men in this marvelous wisdom. CD $1_7$ says: "And he raised them up a Teacher of Righteousness to lead them in the way of his heart."[52] Since this revealed wisdom is a special interpretation of the Torah, throughout the history of the sect there has been a strong emphasis on studying the Law. The enigmatic figure called "the Star" is described in CD $9^a_8$ as one who studied the Law. In the present circumstances the communication of such teaching is the function of the censor (mebaqqer, see p. 150) of the camp; it is he who "shall instruct the many in the works of God, and shall make them understand his wondrous mighty acts, and shall narrate before them the things of the world . . ." (CD $16_1$).

Acceptance of such teaching is not conceived of as purely passive; it implies that sectarians do good works in conformity with this instruction. 1 QS iv, 2, gives a list of the desirable virtues which are the way of the good spirits: truth, humility, patience, compassion, understanding, wisdom, zeal, purity—an interesting parallel to St. Paul's fruits of the Spirit (Gal. $5_{22ff.}$). Periodically the neophyte is to be examined "with respect to his understanding and his deeds in Torah, in accordance with the views of the sons of Aaron."[53] CD 10 ff. gives a detailed series of laws for the community to follow. And, as we see from 1 QS vi, 24 ff., backsliding or misbehavior was seriously punished. And so in general the sons of light, the Qumran Community, can truly be said to be "the doers of the Law in the house of Judah whom God will deliver from the house of judgment for the sake of their labor and their 'faith' in the Teacher of Righteousness."[54]

When we turn to the "sons of light" in St. John we find ourselves at a distance from Qumran. As we would expect, good men are attracted to the light of Christ. "But he who does the truth comes to the light that his deeds may be made manifest, for they have been performed in God" (Jn. 3$_{21}$). Yet it is not good deeds that constitute one a son of light—it is *faith in Christ, the light of the world!* ". . . believe in the light, that you may become sons of light."—"I have come a light into the world, that whoever believes in me may not remain in the darkness" (Jn. 12$_{36,46}$). This same idea is expressed in Jn. 8$_{12}$: "I am the light of the world. He who follows me does not walk in the darkness, but will have the light of life."[55]

Nevertheless, if by faith in Christ we are constituted sons of light, our obligations to perform good works have not ceased. Rather we are now expected to walk as sons of light, and to conduct ourselves virtuously.[56] Naturally, this includes all the virtues, but John stresses charity. "He who says that he is in the light, and hates his brother, is in the darkness still. He who loves his brother abides in the light, and for him there is no stumbling" (1 Jn. 2$_{9-10}$). And in the end, just as those who walk in the darkness are judged, so those sons of light who believe in Christ and keep his commandments are saved from their sins: "But if we walk in the light as he also is in the light, we have fellowship with one another, and the blood of Jesus Christ, his Son, cleanses us from all sin" (1 Jn. 1$_7$).

Summing up this point, we say that, while Qumran and St. John characterize good men in much the same way, they differ greatly in their notion of what brings one into the domain of light. For Qumran it is acceptance of the community's interpretation of the Law; for John it is faith in Jesus Christ. Both insist that sons of light live up to their name in virtuous behavior.

These five points of comparison should enable us to form an idea of the similarities and differences that exist between the modified dualistic concept of light and darkness in the Qumran and in the Johannine literature. In retrospect, it should be evident that *the basic difference between the two theologies is Christ.* Both believe in the creation of all things by God. Both conceive of the world as divided into the two camps of light and darkness, and see these camps arranged under personal leadership. For Qumran the leaders are the two created spirits or angels of light and darkness (truth and perversion); for St. John, however, the leader of light is the uncreated Word, while the leader of evil is the prince of this world. For Qumran the struggle between the forces is still on an equal plane, although light will shine victoriously at the end; for John light is already conquering darkness. Both the literatures maintain that all men are to be assigned to either of the two camps. Yet throughout the Qumran literature there is a curious mixture of determinism and free will, while John is quite clear that men remain in darkness because they obstinately turn away from light. And, finally, Christ is also the point of difference between John and Qumran with respect to the ultimate constituent of the sons of light. If the terminology and ideology are often the same, St. John's whole outlook has been radically reoriented by the revelation that is Christ.

Granting this all-important difference, we may ask if the similarities are sufficient to posit dependence of St. John's outlook upon Qumran ideology. We have considered only one point: modified dualism; in succeeding pages we shall take up others, e.g., the spirits of truth and perversion, the emphasis on charity, the fountain of living waters. With this added evidence the reader will be in a better position to make a judgment. Yet this much may be said of the dualism already discussed: in no other literature do we have so close a terminological and ideological parallel to Johannine usage.[57] Can such peculiar similarities between the two trains of thought (which were in existence in the same small region of the world at the same period of time) be coincidental?

## OTHER SIMILARITIES

*(a) Truth and Perversity.* For Qumran the terms "truth and perversity" are interchangeable with "light and darkness" as expression of modified dualism. In 1 QS iii, 19, the leaders of the forces of light and darkness are called the spirits of truth and perversion.[58] The way of the spirit of truth (iv, 2 ff.) is contrasted in detail with

the way of the spirit of perversion (iv, 9 ff.); and in one or the other way all men walk.

In the New Testament "the spirit of truth" is a term peculiar to St. John.[59] In his theology we notice a difference between the leader of the forces of light (Christ) and the Spirit of truth (the Third Person of the Trinity). There are three places where the latter term is used with a personal meaning. In Jn. 14₁₆₋₁₇, Christ says: "And I will ask the Father and he will give you another Advocate to dwell with you forever, the Spirit of truth whom the world cannot receive, because it neither sees him nor knows him." This is continued in 15₂₆: "But when the Advocate has come, whom I will send you from the Father, the Spirit of truth who proceeds from the Father, he will bear witness concerning me." And finally 16₁₃ says: "But when he, the Spirit of truth, has come, he will teach you all the truth." Thus, if St. John found "light" an ideal term for the revelation that is Jesus Christ,[60] he seems to have discovered in the "Spirit of truth" an apt description for the Holy Spirit, the true witness of Christ.[61]

Yet in 1 Jn. 4₁₋₆ one finds a different use of "the spirit of truth" in opposition to "the spirit of error": "Beloved, do not believe every spirit, but test the spirits to see whether they are of God; because many false prophets have gone forth into the world . . . We are of God. He who knows God listens to us; he who is not of God does not listen to us. By this we know the spirit of truth and the spirit of error."[62] Here we certainly find a remarkable similarity to the two spirits of 1 QS.[63]

The similarity grows even more striking when we compare sections of Qumran and Johannine phraseology. In 1 QS i, 5; v, 3; and viii, 2, the sectarians are urged "to practice" or "to do the truth." Jn. 3₂₁ says: "But he who *does the truth*[64] comes to the light that his deeds may be made manifest, for they have been performed in God." The same expression occurs in 1 Jn. 1₆: "If we say that we have fellowship with him, and walk in darkness, we lie, and are not *practicing the truth*."

The Qumran texts also share the idea of walking in truth[65] with John. "I rejoiced greatly that I found some of thy children walking in truth . . ." (2 Jn. 4) . An almost identical statement occurs in 3 Jn. 3: "I rejoiced greatly when some brethren came and bore witness to thy truth, even as thou walkest in the truth. I have no greater joy than to hear that my children are walking in the truth."

Because of their devotion to truth, the sectarians are called "witnesses of truth" (1 QS viii, 6).[66] Only in the Fourth Gospel, where it is used both of John the Baptist and of Christ, does this phrase occur in the New Testament: "You have sent to John, and he has borne witness to the truth" (5₃₃); and "I am a king. This is why I was born, and why I have come into the world, to bear witness to the truth" (18₃₇).[67]

In both the Qumran texts and St. John, truth is seen as a medium of purification and sanctification. 1 QS iv, 20-21, states: "And then God will purge by his truth all the deeds of man ... to cleanse him through a holy spirit from all wicked practices, sprinkling upon him a spirit of truth [Brownlee capitalizes "spirit"] as purifying water." This may be compared with Jn. 17₁₇₋₁₉: "Sanctify them in truth. Thy word is truth. Even as thou hast sent me into the world, so I also have sent them into the world. And for them I sanctify myself, that they also may be sanctified in truth."

Finally, we may compare two sentences which we have quoted in part before, but which are most effective when seen together: "According as man's inheritance is in truth and righteousness, so he hates evil; but in so far as his heritage is in the portion of perversity and wickedness in him, so he abominates truth" (1 QS iv, 24).—"For every one who does evil hates the light, and does not come to the light, so that his deeds may not be exposed. But he who does the truth comes to the light, that his deeds may be made manifest, for they have been performed in God" (Jn. 3₂₀₋₂₁).

*(b) Brotherly Love.* The Qumran literature (and, of course, the Bible itself) maintains the principles that one must hate evil and love good. 1 QS i, 3-4, urges those who seek God "to love everything that he has chosen, and to hate everything that he has rejected; to keep far from every evil and to cling to every good deed." (Also CD 3₁: ". . . to choose what he approveth, and to reject what he hateth.") As might be expected, however, we encounter difficulty when we pass from evil and good to persons who do evil and good.[68]

The Qumran texts inculcate a hatred of those who are not sons of light, i.e., are not members of the community.[69] 1 QS i, 10, requires one "to hate all the sons of darkness each according to his guilt in provoking God's vengeance!" The Levites of Qumran curse the sons of Belial: "Cursed be thou, without compassion, according to the darkness of thy deeds; and damned be thou in the gloom of eternal fire! May God not favor thee when thou callest; and may he not be forgiving to pardon thy iniquities" (ii, 7-8). The sectarian is admonished to separate himself from perverse men, and to conceal from them the community's special interpretation of the Law (v, 11, and ix, 17-18).[70]

Yet within the Qumran texts, as Grossouw remarks, "several passages struggle as it were to break through their narrow boundaries (of hatred)."[71] The hymn of 1 QS x, 18, is magnificent in its spirituality: "I will repay no man with evil's due; (only) with good will I pursue a man; for with God is the judgment of every living thing." Continuing in xi, 1, the author speaks of the duty "to teach the straying of spirit understanding, and to make murmurers wise through instruction; and to respond humbly before the haughty of spirit, and with broken spirit to men of injustice."

These two trends are puzzling. Certainly Qumran never reached the heights of Mt. 5₄₄: "But I say to you, love your enemies, do good to those who hate you, and pray for those who persecute and calumniate you, so that you may be children of your father in heaven, who makes his sun to rise on the good and the evil."[72] Christianity represents both a doctrinal and a moral development over all that went before. Yet, and we shall see this especially in the question of brotherly love, "One gets a strong impression that in these (Qumran) writings man's mind is preparing for the Christian precept of love."[73] The formulae of hate are found in the initiation ceremonies and formalized instructions of 1 QS: they may be ancient, stylized renunciations of evil as personified in the sons of Belial.[74] The hymns are, perhaps, more representative of the ideal of personal piety at Qumran.

Whatever may be the moral defects in the sectarians' dealing with outsiders, the fraternal affection is truly edifying. Over and over again 1 QS insists that there be a spirit of loving devotion in the community.[75] The instruction of i, 10, says that all who join the group have "to love all the sons of light, each according to his lot in God's counsel." This is made more practical in v, 26: "One shall not speak to his brother in anger, or in complaint, or with a (stiff) neck or a callous heart, or a wicked spirit; nor shall he hate him. . . ." If there are to be rebukes, they must be administered in the manner least calculated to offend.[76] Punishments for sins against one's brother are quite severe (vii, 4-8).

In the New Testament, while the Synoptics transmit Christ's command of universal charity, it is John who stresses love of one's brother within the Christian community.[77] Christ's great commandment for John is that of mutual love within the church: "A new commandment I give you, that you love one another: that as I have loved you, you also love one another. By this will all men know that you are my disciples, if you have love for one another" (13$_{34-35}$; also 15$_{12}$). This theme runs all through the Johannine Epistles, e.g., "He who loves his brother abides in the light, and for him there is no stumbling" (1 Jn. 2$_{10}$).[78] It reaches breathtaking heights in 1 Jn. 4$_{7-8}$: "Beloved, let us love one another, for love is from God . . . He who does not love does not know God, for God is love."

The prevalence of the theme of brotherly love in both the Qumran and the Johannine literature is not a conclusive proof of interrelationshhip. But it is certainly remarkable that the New Testament writer who shares so many other ideological and terminological peculiarities with Qumran should also stress the particular aspect of charity which is emphasized more at Qumran than anywhere else in Jewish literature before Christ.

(c) *Fountain of Living Waters.* The metaphorical use of this term occurs several times in the Old Testament. In Jer. 2$_{13}$ it refers to God: "For my people have committed two evils: they have forsaken me, the fountain of living waters, and hewed out cisterns for themselves, broken cisterns, that can hold no water." And again, in Ps. 36$_9$ "For with thee is the fountain of life; in thy light do we see light." Prov. 13$_{14}$ gives another application: "The teaching of the wise is a fountain of life."[79]

CD has its own use for the metaphor: the community's interpretation of the law is the well of living waters. 9$_{b28}$ warns: "So are all the men who entered into the New Covenant in the land of Damascus and yet turned backward and acted treacherously and departed from the spring of living waters." On the other hand, of those who stay in the community it may be said: "They digged a well of many waters: and he that despises them shall not live" (5$_3$). The most specific identification occurs in a commentary on Num. 21$_{18}$ (CD 8$_6$): "The well is the Law, and they who digged it are the penitents of Israel who went forth out of the land of Judah and sojourned in the land of Damascus."

In the New Testament this terminology occurs in only two books, the Fourth Gospel and Revelation. In his conversation with the Samaritan woman, Christ says, "He, however, who drinks of the water that I will give him shall never thirst; but the water that I will give him shall become in him a fountain of water, springing up into life everlasting" (Jn. 4₁₄). And again in 7₃₈ he cries out, "He who believes in me, as the Scripture says, 'From within him there shall flow rivers of living water.' "[80] Rev. 7₁₇ speaks of the Lamb guiding those who have suffered for Christ "to the fountain of the water of life." And toward the end of Revelation (21₆), Christ, the Alpha and Omega, promises, "To him who thirsts I will give of the fountain of the water of life freely."[81]

Because of the occurrence of the term in the Old Testament, this usage is not a conclusive proof of interrelationship between the Qumran and the Johannine literature. But it is interesting to notice that the metaphor betrays the characteristic interests of Qumran and of St. John. For Qumran the water of life comes from the community's discipline and lore; for John it is given by Christ to those who believe in him—the same difference we found in the discussion of "the sons of light."

(d) *Apostasy.* We now turn to a group of similarities which have been suggested by various authors, but for which, in our opinion, there is not at present any really conclusive evidence. The first of them concerns apostasy. In the Qumran literature particular stress is laid upon the heinousness of unrepented apostasy from the community. In many ways it is the unforgivable sin. The man who alienates himself from the community and then repents will be forgiven after two years.[82] But the backslider who says to himself, "Peace be to me, because I walk in the stubbornness of my heart," will be destroyed without forgiveness.[83] When "the prince of the congregation" rises, he will deliver to the sword all who have proved faithless (CD 9₄₁₀ff.).

In the New Testament there is an unforgivable sin against the Holy Spirit (Mt. 12₃₂; cf. also Heb. 6₄₋₆). Many have held that this sin is deliberate apostasy from Christ.[84] The fact that in Qumran Jewry apostasy was an "unforgivable sin" may lend plausibility to their theory. Yet we are concerned here primarily with St. John.

1 Jn. 5₁₆, in speaking about prayer, says: "There is a sin unto death; I do not mean that anyone should ask as to that." We have no indication what this "sin unto death" may be. It may be apostasy, but the Qumran texts so far contain no real parallel.

(e) *Seasons and Feasts.* In the Qumran literature there are many references to celebrating Sabbaths and festivals correctly: "God confirmed the covenant of Israel forever, revealing unto them the hidden things wherein all Israel had erred: his holy Sabbaths and his glorious festivals . . ." (CD 5₁₋₂).[85] 1 QS repeatedly urges the sectarians ". . . to walk perfectly in all God's ways, as he commanded for his appointed seasons."[86] We even find what seems to be a hymn about feasts and seasons in x, 1-8. The text is very difficult; but, according to Dupont-Sommer,[87] it constitutes a poem of liturgical and mystical inspiration. He sees two stanzas: the first deals with the holy hours of the day and the feasts of the year; the second, with the sabbatical and jubilee years.

Building on such observations, some have concluded that the sectarians were following a special calendar. A statement in CD 20₁ gives the most definite clue: "And as for the exact statement of their periods to put Israel in remembrance in regard to all these, behold, it is treated accurately in the Book of the Divisions of the Seasons according to their Jubilees and their Weeks." In opposition to the Hellenistic lunar calendar followed by most of the Jews, the Book of Jubilees presents a solar calendar[88] which God announced to Moses (1₂₆). Dupont-Sommer tells us: "Without doubt it is to this same calendar attested by Jubilees and Enoch that 1 QS refers."[89]

Accepting this evidence, Miss Mowry turns her attention to St. John's Gospel.[90] There is no doubt that this work mentions a great number of feasts, particularly in chaps. 5-12. "Why," asks Miss Mowry, "if the author of the Fourth Gospel was removed from the Palestinian environment, and the Jews no longer worshipped at the Temple and no longer constituted a threat to the early Church, did he bother with a cycle of Jewish feasts?" In the light of the Qumran texts, she suggests an answer: the feasts are for John a vehicle of Jesus' pronouncements which give them a higher meaning. "Thus it would seem that the writer of the Fourth Gospel, prodded by the calendar quarrel, used with remarkable creativity the cycle of festivals as a literary device to interpret the meaning of Christ for a

Christian group living in the midst of an Essene group in Syria."[91]

Unfortunately, Miss Mowry's evidence involves rather cryptic interpretations of the Gospel, and consequently is not really convincing. Although we admit that a calendar quarrel *may* have entered into the scope of the Fourth Gospel, we find no clear evidence for it within the Johannine literature. The simplest explanation of why John speaks of feasts is that Christ actually delivered discourses on such occasions.

(f) *Purifications and Baptism.* Josephus informs us of the purificatory baths of the Essenes.[92] And indeed there are suggestions within the Qumran literature that the sectarians attributed moral values to lustrations. 1 QS iii, 4-5, speaks of one who refuses to enter the covenant: "While in iniquity, he cannot be reckoned perfect. He cannot purify himself by atonement, Nor cleanse himself with water-for-impurity, Nor sanctify himself with seas or rivers, Nor cleanse himself with any water for washing!"[93]

Only through submission to God's ordinance can a man be cleansed "so that he may purify himself with water-for-impurity and sanctify himself with rippling water" (iii, 9). Again in iv, 21, the cleansing action of the spirit of truth is compared to purifying water. CD 12 is devoted to the law of bathing: "As to being cleansed in water. No man shall wash in water (that is) filthy or insufficient for a man's bath. None shall cleanse himself in the waters of a vessel. And every pool in a rock in which there is not sufficient (water) for a bath, which an unclean person has touched, its water shall be unclean like the water of the vessel." If we add to these citations the discovery of large cisterns at Qumran[94] which might have been used for bathing, we may well suspect that purifications played an important role in the community.

Of all the Gospels, St. John gives the greatest emphasis to the symbolism of water.[95] We can mention: the changing of water to wine (Jn. 2₁₋₁₀); the conversation with Nicodemus (3₁₋₁₅); the conversation with the Samaritan woman (4₁₋₂₆); the pool of Bethesda (5₁₋₉); the blind man and the pool of Siloe (9₁₋₁₂); the washing of feet at the Last Supper (13₁₋₁₆); the blood and water from the side of Christ (19₃₄; also 1 Jn. 5₆₋₇); the use of "living water," cited above. If we admit interrelationship between the Qumran and the Johannine literature, the importance of purification at Qumran may well be related to John's peculiar emphasis on water.

Miss Mowry proposes some examples of the relationship. In reference to the miracle of Cana, she thinks that the changing of water to wine may have been used to convey the idea that the Essene purifications (water) were to be abandoned as a means of approach to God. "Thus it is conceivable that the evangelist intended to say that Jesus takes the place of the water of purification used by this group of super-ritualists."[96] Likewise in the Nicodemus story she sees the command to be born again of water and the spirit directed against the Essenes: not only ritual purification but also spiritual reformation is necessary for Christ's kingdom. "The writer of the Fourth Gospel is virtually saying to the Essene sect that they are men who move on the material level of ordinances and commandments to achieve piety . . . But John maintains that one must be transformed into the other order by a power outside the self."[97]

These connections are possible, but the internal evidence adduced for such anti-Essene polemic is far from conclusive. The clear statement that Nicodemus was a Pharisee would be rather misleading if John's main purpose was to convince Essenes. Until we have more evidence, it seems to me that we must be cautious in introducing Qumran elements into every phase of the Johannine literature.

(g) *Messianism.* Brownlee has brought out two aspects of Qumran Messianism which have repercussions on the Johannine writings. The first concerns the text in one of the Qumran manuscripts to the Book of Isaiah (1 QIs$^a$).[98] The Masoretic text (the basis for our translations) of Is. 51₄₋₅ reads (RSV—italics mine): "Listen to me, my people, and give ear to me, my nation; for a law will go forth from me, and my justice for a light to the peoples. My deliverance draws near speedily, my salvation has gone forth, and *my* arms will rule the peoples; the coastlands wait for *me*, and for *my* arm they hope." But in 1 QIs$^a$ we have: ". . . and *his* arms will rule the peoples; the coastlands wait for *him*, and for *his* arm they hope."[99] Brownlee sees a reference to a person in these last lines, so that all the titles that go before now become personal names. For him the new Isaiah scroll "subtly converts the name 'salvation' where it occurs in Isaiah into a designation of the Servant of the Lord."[100] This is true also of the terms "Law" and "Righteousness" (Justice).

Now, as Brownlee points out, St. John has some texts which

would be affected if this hypothesis is true. If "salvation" is a personal name, we have ". . . salvation is from the Jews" (4₂₂). And if "New Law" is a personal name, we have, "A new commandment I give you . . ." (13₃₄). Without going into the merits of such applications, we would simply note that Brownlee's position rests largely on 1 QIsᵃ having *waw* instead of (or in addition to) the Masoretic *yodh*. There has been a good deal of discussion of the confusion of these two letters in the Scrolls.[101] In any case this difference in 1 QIsᵃ, which is not found in 1 QIsᵇ, could have arisen from many sources (confusion, difference of pronunciation). Therefore, without additional evidence, we do not believe it wise to fashion a theory of Qumran's personal messianic use of the names of this text, and to interpret the Johannine texts accordingly.

Brownlee raises another point of Qumran messianism that would affect St. John's Gospel. 1 QS ix, 11 reads: ". . . until the coming of a Prophet and the anointed ones (*meshihe*) of Aaron and Israel." In his note on this passage Brownlee comments: "The 'prophet' is doubtless the Messiah, whose followers ('anointed ones') will consist of two classes; priests (i.e., those of 'Aaron'), and laity (i.e., those of 'Israel')." In a recent article[102] he has developed this thought; and he sees that the coming of the Messiahs will be, as it were, an anointing of the two classes of his followers. This would resemble John's idea of the followers of Christ receiving his fullness (1₁₆) and being anointed with the Spirit (1₃₃).[103]

The value of such comparisons with the New Testament depends on the meaning of the 1 QS passage. On the basis of new evidence, K. G. Kuhn has challenged Brownlee's interpretation.[104] One of the longer fragments from Qumran (1 QSa) mentions two different people: a priest, and then the Messiah of Israel. Combining this with information from CD, Test. XII Patr., and rabbinic literature, Kuhn maintains that the sectarians expected two individual Messiahs—from Aaron and from Israel.[105] Because of this conflicting interpretation, the New Testament similarities to 1 QS ix, 11 proposed by Brownlee and Braun can hardly be regarded as definite.

We may summarize briefly the second part of our article. The parallels between the Qumran literature and St. John in reference to truth and perversity are perhaps the most striking yet advanced. John's theological outlook on the "Spirit of truth" is Christian, but terminologically other instances of his peculiar use of "truth" run close to Qumran. Again, in his emphasis on brotherly love John is stressing an aspect of charity which was especially advocated at Qumran. The use of the "fountain of living water" in the two literatures betrays the same theme we found in the discussion of dualism; the sectarians' interpretation of the Law *vs.* faith in Christ. In our opinion some of the other similarities suggested by various authors (apostasy, calendrical motifs, purifications, messianic passages) are lacking in sufficient evidence at this time. Indulgence in too much speculation would only weaken the force of well-attested parallels.

## CONCLUSIONS

Our primary purpose was to present enough evidence to enable the reader to draw his own conclusions. It would seem somewhat abrupt, however, to close without evaluating the parallels.

First, and of this there should be no question, there remains a tremendous chasm between Qumran thought and Christianity. No matter how impressive the terminological and ideological similarities are, the difference that Jesus Christ makes between the two cannot be minimized. Therefore, we would do well to avoid any policy of hunting for Christian parallels to every line of the Qumran texts. The Essene sectarians were not Christians, and the recognition of this will prevent many misinterpretations. On the other hand, it is even more incorrect to turn the early Christians into Essenes. In his second volume on the Scrolls, Dupont-Sommer rejects some of the wild conclusions that were based on his first work.[106] Yet he still states, "Christianity, I repeat, is not Essenism, it is *'an* Essenism' as Renan said." We do not think that the adaptation of Essene terminology and ideology to Christianity in the New Testament makes Christianity *an* Essenism any more than the use of Platonic terminology and ideology by the Fathers makes it a Platonism. Christianity is too unique to be classified as any earlier "ism."

Having made these very important reservations, we can turn to evaluate the evidence. If we add the similarities mentioned in Part II to what we saw about the modified dualism, the argument for interrelation between the Johannine writings and the Qumran literature is indeed strong. The resemblances do not seem to indicate immediate relationship, however, as if St. John were himself a sectarian or were personally familiar with the Qumran literature. Rather they indicate a more general acquaintance with the thought and style of expression which we have found at Qumran. The ideas of Qumran must have been fairly widespread in certain Jewish circles in the early first century A.D.[107] Probably it is only through such sources that Qumran had its indirect effect on the Johannine literature.

W. F. Albright has pointed out how important this interrelationship is for dating the Fourth Gospel.[108] We now realize that John's peculiar terminology (which was often the reason for a late dating of the Gospel) has parallels in a Palestinian tradition which flourished before the Christian Era. Therefore, even if we allow time for the oral transmission of the Gospel in the Diaspora, we may still date its writing well within the first century A.D.—a far cry from the very late  dating of some critics. As for authorship, the knowledge that the tradition of the Fourth Gospel is local Palestinian weakens the position of those who deny that it contains the memoirs of John the Apostle.

The reader may wonder how the Qumran parallels in John compare with those of other books of the New Testament. After the Johannine literature, the Pauline corpus shows the greatest affinities to Qumran. In the notes of the section on dualism, we mentioned Pauline passages which betray sectarian terminology; but a thorough study of all similarities would require another article just as long as the present one. (The importance of these similarities should not be neglected, Albright observes, for they show a closeness between Paul and John which has been too often denied.)[109] Certainly the parallels throw an interesting light on St. Paul's "mysteries" and on his theology of faith.[110] The Epistle to the Hebrews has also some interesting points of contact with the Qumran literature.[111] The remaining New Testament books show scattered Qumran affinities,[112] but not with the frequency of the Johannine or Pauline works.

These facts may cause us to wonder why similarities to Qumran thought are more frequent in some portions of the New Testament than in others.[113] At the present there are only indications toward a solution. For St. John the answer may lie in a verse of his own Gospel: "Again the next day John (the Baptist) was standing there and two of his disciples" (1₃₅). One of these disciples was Andrew; his anonymous confrère has traditionally been identified as John the Evangelist. Now virtually everyone who has studied the Qumran texts in the light of the New Testament has recognized the startling Qumran parallels in the narratives concerning John the Baptist;[114] almost every detail of his life and preaching has a *possible* Qumran affinity. From this it would seem likely that the Baptist, before his contact with Christ, was in relationship with Qumran or other Essenes (perhaps he was raised by the community;[115] or in contact with the community, or the head of a quasi-Essene group). If this is true, and if John the Evangelist was his disciple, we can explain very well the Qumran impact on the Fourth Gospel.

External evidence adds an interesting note. Tradition is almost unanimous that this Gospel was written at Ephesus.[116] Acts 18₂₄ speaks of the presence at Ephesus of disciples of John the Baptist who were not yet fully Christian.[117] An hypothesis might be constructed that John the Baptist was familiar with the Qumran Essenes and their thought, and that through him certain of these ideas passed on to his disciples, including John the Evangelist. The latter formed his ideas of Jesus in the light of this background, and, of course, remembered and stressed those *logia* of Jesus which were in close harmony with his own feelings. Later at Ephesus, an encounter with the disciples of the Baptist who had not completely accepted Christ prompted John to commit to writing his memories of Christ.[118] The language he used was familiar to these disciples and was intended to show how Christ fulfilled all their ideas. Christ is the light they speak of; true sons of the light are those who believe in him; the "spirit of truth" is the Holy Ghost, etc. Yet such an hypothesis,[119] while it fulfills the tradition of the origin of the Gospel, is based on so many surmises that it can remain only an interesting possibility for the present.

# XIII

## The Qumran Scrolls, the Ebionites, and Their Literature*

JOSEPH A. FITZMYER, S.J.

The importance of the Dead Sea Scrolls for both Old and New Testament study has become increasingly recognized as these texts are published and studied. Though it will be many years before their exact value can be fully assessed, constant efforts are being made by scholars to interpret these documents. It is not surprising that some interpretations find almost immediate acceptance in scholarly circles, while others are rejected or subjected to long debate. For it is only by a gradual sifting process that the value and importance of these texts can be ascertained.[1]

Shortly after the publication of three of the Qumran Scrolls by the American Schools of Oriental Research, J. L. Teicher of Cambridge wrote an article in the *Journal of Jewish Studies,* in which he maintained that the Qumran sect, in whose midst these scrolls originated, was Ebionite.[2] This interpretation has not been accepted by most scholars, who at present prefer to regard the group who lived at Qumran as Essenes (or at least as a branch of the Essenes). Nevertheless, the fact was recognized that Teicher had indicated a source from which further information might be drawn.[3] Teicher has continued to write a series of articles on the Ebionite sect of Qumran and the early church.[4] More recently, however, Oscar Cullmann published an article in *Neutestamentliche Studien für Rudolf Bultmann,*[5] claiming that the remnants of the Essenes went over to the Ebionite

* Reprinted, in slightly abridged form, from *Theological Studies* 16 (1955), pp. 335-72.

group after the destruction of Jerusalem in A.D. 70. Another recent article, by H. J. Schoeps, puts forth the theory that the Qumran sect, the Essenes of Philo and Josephus, the Ossaeans of Epiphanius, the disciples of John the Baptist, and the Ebionites (the last as the descendants of the Jerusalem church) all became representatives of an apocalyptic-gnostic Judaism.[6] The present article intends to review the evidence for this connection and to sift the valid from the invalid claims that have been made. A *mise au point* is obviously needed, to see whether the parallels in tenets and practices of both groups are such as to warrant the assertion that the Qumran sect was Ebionite or passed over into Ebionism or even influenced the latter group.

The matter will be discussed under three main headings: the identification of the Ebionites; their literature; and the comparison of Ebionites and the Qumran sect.

## The Ebionites

Relatively little is known about the Ebionites. Most of the data concerning them has been preserved in patristic literature, and it is not easy to interpret. Scraps of information are found in Justin, Irenaeus, Tertullian, Origen, Hippolytus, Eusebius, and Jerome, while Epiphanius devotes a full chapter to them in his *Panarion*. Literary borrowing took place in some cases, so that it is not always easy to tell when the patristic writer is supplying data gathered from independent sources.[7]

As the name of a sect, the word "Ebionites" appears for the first time in Irenaeus (*Adv. haer.* 1, 26, 2).[8] It seems to be a transliteration of an Aramaic/Hebrew word, meaning "the poor" (*ebyonim*). Irenaeus offers no explanation of its meaning or origin, but several were given in antiquity. They were called Ebionites: (*a*) because of the poverty of their intelligence; (*b*) because of the poverty of the law which they followed; (*c*) because of the poverty of the opinions they had of Christ; (*d*) because they were "poor in understanding, hope, and deeds." These are obviously pejorative afterthoughts, which scarcely give us a clue to the origin of the term.

The name of the sect was derived also from the name of a founder, named Ebion. Despite this tradition, which also ascribes to him certain fragments in the work, *Doctrina patrum de incarnatione*

*Verbi,* modern scholars are inclined to look on Ebion merely as an eponymous hero, a personification of the sect itself.[9] However, since preliminary reports about the contents of the thirteen Coptic codices from Chenoboskion, Egypt, have been indicating that the patristic data regarding the early heretics are more reliable than is often supposed, a word of caution is injected here.[10] Perhaps the name "Ebionite" actually does mean "follower of Ebion."

We know from the New Testament that certain early Christians were referred to as "the poor" (Rom. 15₂₆; Gal. 2₁₀). This may refer, of course, merely to the poor members of the community at Jerusalem. But it is possible that the name *Ebionaioi* grew out of a practice of referring to the first Christians in Jerusalem as "the poor," especially after the destruction of the city in A.D. 70. At some time during the first two centuries (it is impossible to be more precise), this designation was restricted to those who lived in Palestine and Syria, and who continued to observe the Mosaic Law. It seems likely that the original use of the word was in no way connected with a heretical sect.

The Ebionites were, then, a Jewish-Christian group, first mentioned by Irenaeus *ca.* A.D. 175, which flourished during the second, third, and early fourth centuries (at least). In the New Testament there is mention of Jewish Christians, who believed in Christ but also observed the Mosaic Law (Acts 15₁ff., 21₂₁; Gal. 2). This was the community at Jerusalem, headed by St. James. It is not unlikely that remnants of this group, after the destruction of Jerusalem, developed into the Ebionite sect, acquiring heterodox notions in time from other sources, such as Cerinthus and the Elchesaites. Eusebius (*Hist. eccl.* 3, 5) tells us: "The people of the church in Jerusalem were commanded by an oracle given by revelation before the war to those in the city who were worthy of it to depart and dwell in one of the cities of Perea which they called Pella. To it those who believed on Christ migrated from Jerusalem, that when holy men had altogether deserted the royal capital of the Jews and the whole land of Judaea, the judgment of God might at last overtake them for all their crimes against the Christ and his apostles" (K. Lake's translation).

It is important to note here that Eusebius does not call these emigrants by the name of Ebionites, nor have we any reason to assume that he was speaking of them specifically. They were merely some of the Christians of the original community of Jerusalem. Justin distinguished two sorts of Jewish Christians, those who observed the Mosaic Law but did not require its observance of all others, and those who maintained that this observance is necessary for salvation. Justin would communicate with the former, but not with the latter (*Dial.* 47; 48). Schoeps equates the Ebionites with the more intransigent group.[11] By the time of Irenaeus there was definitely a sect named Ebionites, who were considered heretical by him and were listed among the Gnostics (*Adv. haer.* 1, 26, 2). He mentions specifically that they rejected the virgin birth of Christ (5, 1, 3; 3, 21, 1) and denied the Incarnation (4, 33, 4).[12]

Tertullian adds no new details. He is one of the Fathers who speak of Ebion, not of the Ebionites. He mentions that this Ebion was influenced by Cerinthus, *non in omni parte consentiens* (*Adv. omn. haer.* 3).[13] It is generally agreed that the christological tenets of the Ebionites came from this Cerinthian influence. Hippolytus (*Philosoph.* 7, 34; 10, 22) adds a few details to our knowledge, but they are not important here (Cf. note 17).

It is Origen who first distinguishes for us two kinds of Ebionites: those who admit the virgin birth of Christ and those who reject it (*Contra Cels.* 5, 61). Both groups, however, reject the Epistles of St. Paul (5, 65). Eusebius has likewise recorded the fact of two groups of Ebionites: "But others, the wicked demon, when he could not alienate them from God's plan in Christ, made his own, when he found them by a different snare. The first Christians gave these the suitable name of Ebionites because they had poor and mean opinions concerning Christ. They held him to be a plain and ordinary man who had achieved righteousness merely by the progress of his character and had been born naturally from Mary and her husband. They insisted on the complete observation of the Law, and did not think that they would be saved by faith in Christ alone and by a life in accordance with it. But there were others besides these who have the same name. These escaped the absurd folly of the first mentioned, and did not deny that the Lord was born of a Virgin and the Holy Spirit, but nevertheless agreed with them in not confessing his pre-existence as God, being the Logos and Wisdom. Thus they shared in the impiety of the former class, especially in that they were equally zealous to insist on the literal observance of the Law. They thought that the letters of the Apostle ought to be wholly rejected and called him an apostate from the Law. They used only the Gospel called according to the Hebrews and made little account of the rest. Like the former they used to observe the sabbath and the rest of the Jewish ceremonial, but on Sundays celebrated rites like ours in commemoration of the Saviour's resurrection. Wherefore from these practices they have obtained their name, for the name of Ebionites indicates the poverty of their intelligence, for this name means 'poor' in Hebrew" (*Hist. eccl.* 3, 27; Lake's translation).

Epiphanius, who of all the patristic writers gives most space to the Ebionites, supplies names for the two groups. The more orthodox group, which probably admits the virgin birth of Christ (*Pan.* 29), is called *Nazoraioi;* the more heterodox group is labeled *Ebionaioi* (*Pan.* 30). The identification of the *Nazoraioi* as an orthodox group of Jewish Christians, related somehow to the Ebionites, is admitted by many scholars; but the identification has problems connected with it that we cannot discuss here.[14] It is complicated by the fact that Jerome equates *Ebionitae, Nazaraei,* and *Minaei.*[15] At any rate, we are sure that there was a definite group of christological heretics in the early centuries of the church who were called Ebionites.

Among the details supplied by Epiphanius, mention is made of the influence of the Elchesaites on the Ebionites (*Pan.* 30, 17). He goes to the trouble of indicating that this influence affected the followers of Ebion, not Ebion himself. Elchesai was a heretical leader who preached (*ca.* A.D. 100) a doctrine of baptism unto the remission of sins which was heavily infected with Gnostic ideas (so, at least, it is usually judged). Schoeps,[16] following C. Schmidt and others, maintains that Epiphanius has confused the Ebionites with the Elchesaites, so that his account of the Ebionites can be accepted only when there is outside control. It is true that Epiphanius adds details about the Ebionites not found elsewhere in patristic writings. A closer comparison of the Nazoraioi and the Ebionites with references to the source of our information[17] shows that dualism, various types of baths, peculiar ideas on the prophets, Christ—all of which have been associated with Jewish-Christian Gnosticism, are reported only by Epiphanius. Has he confused the Ebionites with the Elchesaites? We just do not know. It is just as reasonable to admit the explanation given by J. Thomas,[18] that the Ebionites were influenced by three groups: the Essenes, the early Christians, the Elchesaites.

Before terminating this section on the identification of the Ebionites, we shall mention briefly the opinion of J. L. Teicher regarding the Qumran sect, which he maintains is Ebionite. Teicher does not depend upon a discussion of the Pseudo-Clementines for his "proof" that the sect is Ebionite,[19] but the description thus far given of the Ebionites makes it natural to raise the question to which Teicher has given such an emphatic answer: Is there any connection between the Ebionites and the sect of Qumran? Certainly the climate of opinion in which the latter group lived was that of the Old Testament, as is evident to all who are acquainted with the Qumran literature.[20] The New Testament, on the other hand, is definitely the framework and background of the Ebionite way of life, even though they have retained the observance of the Mosaic Law. This we know from patristic information and from the Pseudo-Clementine writings. Yet for Teicher the Qumran sect is Ebionite,

Christ is the Teacher of Righteousness, and Paul is the "Man of Lies." The Ebionites, being Christians, were affected by Diocletian's edict of persecution, and so, rather than hand over their sacred books according to the royal decree, they hid them in the caves at Qumran. The Qumran sect is Ebionite: the term "poor" (*ebyonim*) is found in 1 QpHab xii, 3, 6; and Qumran is "in the vicinity" of the spot in Transjordan where the Ebionites lived. Efforts have been made to point out the weaknesses in the arguments and opinion of Teicher,[21] but he writes on undaunted. In an article such as this a detailed refutation is out of place.[22]

The most serious difficulty, of course, with Teicher's opinion is that of chronology. The latest possible date for the deposit of the manuscripts is the destruction of Qumran in A.D. 68-69.[23] Though our first explicit mention of the Ebionites dates from Irenaeus (*ca.* A.D. 175), and though it is quite probable that they existed as a sect much earlier, there is simply no evidence for their existence in the first century A.D., either before or after the destruction of Jerusalem. Consequently, the simple identification of the Qumran sect and the Ebionites is an untenable opinion.

### EBIONITE LITERATURE

By Ebionite literature we mean here the Pseudo-Clementine *Homilies* and *Recognitions*, often called merely the *Pseudo-Clementines* (PsC).[24] Various spurious works circulated in antiquity under the name of Clement of Rome, and among these was the romantic novel which exists today under the title of *Homilies and Recognitions*. The PsC contain five documents: (1) *Epistle of Peter to James*, instructing the latter that the accompanying writings are not to be entrusted to any but the initiated; (2) *Diamarturia* or *Contestatio*, the "oath" to be taken by the initiated concerning these writings; (3) *Epistle of Clement to James*, telling of Peter's martyrdom, Clement's ordination, Peter's instruction to Clement, his successor, and Peter's order to write down an epitome of his sermons in the various cities that it might be sent to James, the bishop of Jerusalem; this serves as an introduction to the *Homilies*, for Clement says that he is sending this very epitome; (4) twenty books of the *Homilies*; (5) ten books of the *Recognitions*.[25]

The *Homilies* (hereafter, Hom.) and the *Recognitions* (hereafter, Rec.) are two forms of a novel about the fate of the various members of the noble family of Clement of Rome. Clement himself is portrayed as a searcher for truth, going about to the various schools of philosophy for a solution of his doubts concerning the origin of the world, the immortality of the soul, etc. At length he hears that the Son of God has appeared in

distant Judea. After a long journey, which takes him to Egypt and Palestine, he meets Peter in Caesarea, is instructed in the doctrine of the True
Prophet, and becomes a Christian. He is invited by Peter to accompany
him on his missionary journeys in pursuit of Simon Magus. Meanwhile,
curious circumstances bring about the break-up of Clement's family: his
mother and two brothers leave Rome, because of a warning his mother
receives in a dream, and sail for Athens; but they are shipwrecked and
separated. Finally, father, mother, and the three sons set out to find each
other, and the successive recognitions of the members of the family, aided
by the efforts of Peter, give the title of "Recognitions" to one of the
versions of this novel. The greater part of the novel is given over, however,
to the sermons of Peter and his debates with Simon Magus. This is responsible for the title of the other extant version, "Homilies." Actually there is
as much homiletic material in the *Recognitions* as there is recognition in
the *Homilies*. Long passages parallel each other, sometimes with word-
for-word identity.

Popular in the last century as the basis of the Tübingen-School theory of
opposition between the Petrine and Pauline churches of early Christianity,[26]
the PsC have been subjected to extensive critical study and different strata
and sources have been identified.[27] The identification of a source called
*Kerygmata Petrou* ("Sermons of Peter"), of Ebionite origin, has been
accepted by many scholars[28] and is the basis for Schoeps' description of the
theology and the history of Jewish Christianity, and for Cullmann's comparative study of the Qumran sect and the Ebionites.[29] The existence of
such a source has been seriously challenged,[30] but since our discussion of
the relation between Ebionite and Qumran literature is to be carried out
in the context of works like those of Schoeps and Cullmann we shall
indicate, whether or not our references to PsC belong to the *Kerygmata
Petrou* (KP) as defined by Schoeps.[31]

### COMPARISON OF THE EBIONITES AND THE SECT OF QUMRAN

We shall discuss in detail various points of similarity and dissimilarity that exist between the Ebionites and the Qumran sect
to see whether there is any basis for the assertion that the latter
was or became Ebionite. It will be evident that we are not trying to
trace the history of each idea or practice that we take up; nor are
we trying to list all the possible sources from which either group
may have derived its tenets and customs. We are concerned merely
with the influence of Qumran on the Ebionites.

At the outset it should be noted that the PsC do not depict the
Ebionites as living a communal existence, as does the Manual of
Discipline with respect to the Qumran sect. There is nothing
"monastic"[32] about the group described in PsC. Hence the compari-

son will not be based on rules, ways of acting, punishments, etc., such as are found in 1 QS. But there are many other points that can well be compared.

*Dualism.* This term is used normally of those opposites which have been found in Gnostic literature, the Johannine and Pauline writings, Greek philosophy, and elsewhere. It should be obvious that the principle of contradiction, being a basic metaphysical principle, could be made the support for many sets of opposites which are not specifically "dualistic." Such notions as the Levitical contrast of clean-unclean, God's creation of the heaven and the earth, the tree of the knowledge of good and evil, could be forced into a system of dualism. But, we may ask, with what right? Consequently, we must beware of trying to interpret every set of opposites as dualistic (in the sense usually intended by those who treat this question).

We can summarize the dualism of 1 QS as follows: The members are to do good and avoid evil (i, 4-5), to turn to the truth and away from perversity (vi, 15; cf. i, 5-6; i, 15-17; v, 1). This simple contrast of good-evil, truth-perversity soon appears more complex; for the members are to love the sons of light and hate the sons of darkness (i, 10), to bless the men of God's lot and curse the men of Belial's lot (ii, 2, 5). These two groups of men are divided according to the divine appointment of two spirits (truth and perversity) which are to guide men until the period of visitation (iii, 17-19). These spirits are the "prince of light" and the "angel of darkness" (iii, 20-21). Truth is derived from the spring of light and perversity from the fountain of darkness (iii, 19-23). The angel of truth is on the side of the God of Israel (iii, 24), whose enemy is Belial (i, 21-23; vii, 1-3). For God loves the spirit of truth and hates the spirit of perversity (iv, 1). These two spirits are the source of all good and evil works of men in this world (iii, 26; iv, 2 ff.). God has set them up to reign in equal parts with eternal, mutual enmity until the time of his visitation (iv, 17-19). Then God will destroy the spirit of perversity and the Truth will prevail (iv, 19). The spirits of truth and perversity both strive within the heart of man (iv, 23).

Dualism is found as well in 1 QM, but the system does not appear to be as developed as that in 1 QS. This is slightly surprising, because 1 QM is a manual for the conduct of God's war, in which the sons of light are to battle against the sons of darkness. The opposition of light and darkness is frequent; likewise that of God's lot and Belial's lot. But we find little mention of the opposition between truth and perversity. Columns i and xiii in particular contain dualistic concepts. A war is to be waged against the "sons of darkness" (i, 1, 7, 10, 16; xiii, 16; xiv, 17) by the "sons of light" (i, 1, 3, 9, 11, 13), against the "lot of darkness" (i, 1, 5, 11; xiii, 5) by the "lot of light" (xiii, 5, 9) or "God's lot" (i, 5; xiii, 6, 12; xv, 1). We read of the "army of Belial" (i, 13; xi, 8; xv, 2-3, xviii, 3), the "lot of Belial" (i, 5; iv, 2; xiii, 2, 4, 12; xiv, 10); the "prince of light" (xiii, 10), "spirits of truth" (xiii, 10); "prince of the dominion of impiety" (xvii, 5-6). It is God's war (xi, 1) that the sons of light are waging. The period of darkness reigns now, but in God's time the sons of light will prevail (i, 8). For God has determined of old the day for the war to wipe out the sons of darkness (i, 10).

In 1 QH we read that both the just man and the evil man proceed from God the Creator (iv, 38).

It is noteworthy that this dualism is lacking in 1 QpHab and CD. Like the passage in 1 QS iii, 6, the contrast between clean and unclean might possibly be considered a manifestation of dualism (CD 8₁₄; 14₁ ff.; 15₁). But this is obviously an opposition known from the Levitical laws of the Bible.[33]

In the PsC there is also a dualism which can be compared with that of Qumran. God, the Sole Creator of all, has differentiated all principles into pairs of opposites from the beginning—heaven, earth; day, night; light, fire; sun, moon; life, death (Hom. 2₁₅ KP). This is the system that is known as *syzygies,* or combinations, according to which all things come in pairs (Hom. 2₁₅, 33 KP). The smaller precedes the larger, the female the male, the inferior the superior, and evil precedes good (Rec. 3₅₉ KP). Outside the passages thought to belong to the original KP we also find a dualism, the doctrine of the "two paths" presided over by Belief and Unbelief (Hom. 7₆-₇).

Another way of expressing this dualism is the contrast of two kingdoms. "The prophet of truth who appeared (on earth) taught us that the Maker and God of all gave two kingdoms to two, good and evil: granting to the evil the sovereignty over the present world along with the law, so that he (it) should have the right to punish those who act unjustly; but to the good he gave the eternal age to come. But He made each man free with the power to give himself up to whatsoever he prefers, either to the present evil or to the future good" (Hom. 15₇ KP). Elsewhere we learn that Christ is the ruler of the future age as the King of Righteousness, whereas the Tempter is the ruler of the present; that is why he tempted Christ saying, "All the kingdoms of the present world are subject to me" (Hom. 8₂₁ KP [according to Schoeps]). Truth and error are contrasted in Rec. 6₄ KP. We will recall that Epiphanius recorded this opposition or dualism (*Pan.* 30, 16).

From the summaries given above it should be obvious that there is a definite similarity in the dualisms of Qumran and of the PsC. Cullmann has pointed out that in both cases there is a subordination of the dualistic system to Jewish monotheistic ideas. God set up the kings of the two domains in the PsC just as he set up the spirits of truth and perversity of 1 QS.[34] Both K. G. Kuhn[35] and A. Dupont-Sommer[36] have related this Qumran dualism to Iranian sources. The latter maintains that precisely this subordination of the two spirits to the supreme God is found in the Iranian source.[37]

There seems to be some difference of opinion among the scholars. Quite recently H. Michaud has suggested an even more specific source of the Qumran dualism, i.e., Zervanism. Zervanism was a particular branch of Zoroastrianism, in which the protagonist, Ahura Mazda, and the antagonist in the dualistic system are both born of a superior deity, *Zurvan* or *Chronos*, "time." It dates from the time of the Achaemenian empire, and was regarded as heretical only in the time of the Sassanids, i.e., from the third century A.D. Michaud is of the opinion that the author of the Qumran theological system either knew the Zervanite myth of creation or was influenced by the system of thought that had been infected with it.[38] This Iranian source cannot be disregarded, but it is obvious that the full implication of this source has not yet been explored. There is certainly no obstacle, theologically speaking, which would prevent such a dualism subordinated to a Supreme Being from being adopted either into the Jewish or Jewish-Christian way of thinking.

Cullmann, however, has pointed out a difference between the Qumran dualism and that of the PsC. The opposition "light-darkness, truth-perversity" in 1 QS is never brought into line with the opposition "male-female, light-fire" as it is in the PsC.[39] This is true, but it seems that the difference is much more fundamental. Kuhn has already described the Qumran dualism as ethical and eschatological, akin to the Iranian source.[40] This is true, for no pair of opposites can be found which are not to be understood in an ethical sense.[41] Light and darkness are only symbols for the other pair, truth and perversity, good and evil, God and Belial. But in the PsC there are passages where the dualism is definitely physical. *All* principles have been divided into opposites (Hom. 2₁₅ KP); the *syzygies* dominate everything (Hom. 2₁₅₋₁₆. ₈₃; Rec. 3₅₉ KP): heaven, earth; day, night, light, fire; sun, moon—as well as good, evil. The opposition in the ethical sphere is expressed in the PsC in terms of two kingdoms, two paths, two beings, whereas in 1 QS it is a question of two spirits. This, of course, may be a mere manner of expression. But we can safely say that the dualism of Qumran, though similar in its general conception to that of the Ebionites, is of a simpler type. An ethical dualism, like that of Qumran, could have developed —especially under other influences—into a dualism that was both physical and ethical, like that of the PsC.

Before leaving this question of dualism, we must say a word about its possible Gnostic character. In the first article that Kuhn wrote on the ideas of the Qumran sect, he labeled its dualism as "Gnostic."[42] Later, in discussing its connection with Iranian religion, he showed how the ideas of 1 QS confirmed the thesis once put forth by Bousset and Gressmann that the Jewish apocalyptic ideas of the last centuries B.C. had been affected by Persian thought. He emphasized the fact that the ethical character of the Qumran dualism definitely connected it with old Iranian ideas and clearly separated it from Gnosticism.[43] Schoeps constantly rejected throughout his book the idea that the Ebionites were Gnostics.[44] He accused Epiphanius of confusing them with the Elchesaites and of erroneously ascribing to them the Gnostic ideas of the latter. For him the PsC dualism is nothing but a development of a trend, which has "a legitimate Jewish root . . . for the zugot (pair)-principle is very ancient in Judaism."[45] Yet in a later article Schoeps has apparently abandoned this fundamental position, for he claims that he has finally realized that the Gnostic syzygies-system of Book 6 of KP is derived from the 1 QS teaching of the two spirits.[46] This is a complete volte-face, the denial of a main contention in his book. Though the Qumran dualism could be the source of the Ebionite dualism of the PsC, we still have no real evidence for labeling either of them as Gnostic. It is to be hoped that the publication of the Gnostic Codices of Chenoboskion, mentioned earlier in this paper, will shed light on the dualism of the PsC and give us a better understanding of early Gnosticism. But there is certainly no reason to call the Qumran dualism Gnostic.[47]

*Teacher of Righteousness.* The *moreh ha-sedeq* in the Qumran and Damascus texts[48] has certain characteristics which resemble those of the "prophet of truth" or "true prophet" in the PsC (KP: Hom. 1₁₈₋₁₉; 2₆, and passim). The latter is sometimes called merely "the Prophet (Hom. 2₆) or "the Teacher" (Hom. 11₂₀, ₂₈). This last description is also found for the Teacher of Righteousness in CD 9₆₈. But it should be noted immediately that, whereas the identity of the Teacher of Righteousness in the Qumran documents is unknown (or at least has not yet been correctly and certainly established), there can be no doubt that Christ is the True Prophet of the PsC (cf. Epiphanius, *Pan.* 30, 18; Hom. 3₅₂₋₅₆ KP).

The function of the Teacher of Righteousness is to lead men in the way of God's heart (CD 1₁₁); his words come from the mouth of God (1 QpHab ii, 2), for God has revealed to him all the mysteries of the words of his servants the prophets (vii, 4). The men of the community are to listen to him (CD 9₆₈, ₇₁), and God will deliver from the house of condemnation all those who suffer for him and believe in him (1 QpHab viii, 23). He also seems to have been a priest (1 QpHab ii, 7),[49] "persecuted" by the "Man of the Lie," who rejected the Law (v, 10; xi, 5; CD 9₅₃). According to CD 8₁₃, he is still to come at the end of the days; but he precedes the Messiah awaited from Aaron and from Israel (CD 9₄₀).

The function of the True Prophet in KP is similar to that of the Teacher of Righteousness, at least, in that he too is looked upon as the leader of the group and the helper of a mankind which is enshrouded in darkness and ignorance, communicating to it knowledge.[50] "He alone is able to enlighten the souls of men, so that with our own eyes we may be able to see the way of eternal salvation" (Hom. 1₁₉ KP; cf. Rec. 1₁₅₋₁₆ KP). "This is peculiar to the Prophet, to reveal the truth, even as it is peculiar to the sun to bring the day" (Hom. 2₆ KP).

In this connection Cullmann speaks of an *Erlösergestalt* ("redeemer") found in both sets of documents, whose specific role is to reveal the truth.[51] One may question whether the Teacher of Righteousness is aptly described as an *Erlösergestalt*. 1 QpHab viii, 2-3, is apparently the only passage (doubtful at that) that would lend itself to such an interpretation. For, though "deliverance from the house of condemnation (or: judgment)" might conceivably be understood in the sense of redemption, yet this may refer as well to some contemporary political situation, described by this vague expression, as do others in 1 QpHab. As for the PsC, the True Prophet could be called an *Erlöser* ("redeemer"); but Bultmann is undoubtedly right in stressing that the Pseudo-Clementine christology is anything but soteriological in the Pauline sense, adopted by the early church.[52]

As a revealer of truth, then, the Teacher of Righteousness and the

True Prophet can be favorably compared, for their functions are definitely similar.[53] Nothing, however, warrants more than a possible connection between these two figures when we are trying to trace the influence of Qumran on the Ebionites.

*The Man of the Lie.* The antagonist of the Teacher of Righteousness is described as the "Man of the Lie" (cf. 1 QpHab ii, 1-2; v, 11; CD 9$_{53-54}$) or the "Preacher of the Lie" (1 QpHab x, 9; CD 9$_{29}$). In the PsC, however, the antagonist of Christ, the True Prophet, is Satan, the prince of evil (Hom. 8$_{21}$ KP). Peter, too, has an adversary throughout, Simon Magus. But there is the unnamed figure referred to as "the hostile man," "the one who leads astray," (*inimicus homo, ho echthros anthrōpos, planos tis;* Rec. 1$_{70, 71, 73}$; Hom. 2$_{17}$; 11$_{35}$; *Ep. Petri* 2$_{3}$), who is identified as the Apostle Paul on the basis of Rec. 1$_{71}$, alluding to Acts 22$_{5}$. But it should be noted that he is definitely considered to be the adversary of the bishop of Jerusalem, St. James. It is, therefore, a gratuitous assertion to equate the *inimicus homo* of PsC with the "man of the lie," and to maintain on this basis that Paul is the antagonist referred to in the Qumran literature. Both the Qumran scrolls and the PsC speak of a figure who is an adversary, but the differing details prevent any further identification or comparison.[54]

*Attitude toward the Old Testament.* Under this heading we will discuss the attitude of both groups toward the prophets, the Pentateuch, the sacrifice of the Temple, and the priesthood.

(*a*) The prophets. The Qumran sect not only held to the strict observance of the Torah, but also regarded the prophets of the Old Testament with great esteem. This is evident not only from statements of 1 QS (e.g., i, 3) and 1 QpHab (ii, 7; vii, 4), but also from the way they quote the prophets (CD 5$_{10}$; 9$_{5}$) and from the writings they composed to interpret the biblical prophets (e.g., the so-called *pesher*-commentaries on Habakkuk and Micah already published.[55]

As for the Ebionites, Irenaeus tells us that they had developed their own way of expounding the prophets: "As for the writings of the Prophets, they aim at expounding them *curiosius*" (*Adv. Haer.* 1 26, 2). What does *curiosius* mean? It has been explained (Schoeps 1, p. 159) in terms of the information supplied by the *Panarion* of Epiphanius (30, 17) where we learn that the Ebionites admitted Abraham, Isaac, Jacob, Moses, Aaron, and Joshua, but rejected all the prophets, David, Solomon, Isaiah, Jeremiah, Daniel, Ezekiel, Elijah, and Elisha together with their oracles.

This explanation, however, is not certain. *Curiosius* is the Latin translation of a lost Greek word. Since we have no reason to assume that it is not an accurate translation, we may legitimately ask what Irenaeus, writing *ca.* A.D. 175, could have meant by it. Epiphanius' statement about the rejection of the prophets remains, of course, a possible interpretation, but it represents more likely the attitude of a later stage of Ebionism. Between Irenaeus and Epiphanius (310-403), the Ebionites could have been subjected to other influences (Samaritan, for instance) with regard to the prophets. Certainly there is no foundation for the opinion of J. Thomas that *curiosius* shows that some Ebionites were Gnostics.[56] *Curiosius* means "bestowing care or pains upon a thing, applying one's self assiduously," as well as "curious, inquisitive."[57] It is just as likely that the Ebionites of Irenaeus' times had something like the *pesher*-method at Qumran and that *curiosius* is his way of describing this detailed, careful exegesis of the prophets.

In the PsC, Christ is the only true prophet. Owing to their peculiar christology, the Holy Spirit, who was believed to be in Christ, was also present in Adam, so that he too is called the "only true prophet." "The only true prophet gave names to each animal" (Hom. 3₂₁ KP). This probably refers, not to Christ as such, but to the spirit which made him the True Prophet. "Know then that Christ, who was from the beginning, and always, was ever present with the pious, though secretly, through all their generations; especially with those who waited for him to whom he frequently appeared" (Rec. 1₅₂ KP). This attitude toward Christ is responsible for the Ebionite rejection of the prophets of the Old Testament.[58] But an even stranger reason is found in the view of the Old Testament prophets as representatives of female prophecy, having been born of women. The True Prophet, being the Son of *Man,* represents male prophecy, and so is accepted on the principle of the *syzygies* (Hom. 3₂₂₋₂₃).

There are a few references to the Old Testament prophets in the PsC.[59] But it is hard to deduce anything from them, because they may have passed into Ebionite literature via works that were more acceptable to them. One clear case is found in Rec. 1₃₇, where Hos. 6₆ is cited: "For I delight in piety, not sacrifice." This text of Hosea, however, is used by St. Matthew (9₁₃, 12₇).

The attitude of the Qumran sect toward the Old Testament prophets, then, is entirely different from that of the Ebionites, at least as they are known to us from Epiphanius and the PsC. Consequently, we cannot look to the tenets of Qumran as a source for the Ebionite attitude.

(b) *The "False Pericopes."* Epiphanius (*Pan.* 30, 18) tells us that the Ebionites did not accept the whole Pentateuch, but rejected certain passages of it. The PsC, too, knew of falsehoods that have been added to the Law of Moses. "The Scriptures have had joined to them many falsehoods against God" (Hom. 2₃₈ KP). By labeling certain passages of the Pentateuch as false chapters, the Ebionites managed to eliminate those that seemed in conflict with their beliefs about God. Peter cites as examples the following: "Neither was Adam a transgressor, who was fashioned by the hands of God; nor was Noah drunken, who was found righteous above all the world; nor did Abraham live with three wives at once, who, on account of his sobriety, was thought worthy of a numerous posterity; nor did Jacob associate with four—of whom two were sisters—who was the father of the twelve tribes, and who intimated the coming of the presence of our Master; nor was Moses a murderer, nor did he learn to judge from an idolatrous priest . . ." (Hom. 2₅₂ KP).

There is not the slightest trace of such an attitude in the writings of the sect of Qumran.[60]

(c) *Sacrifice.* Though there was formerly some hesitation about the attitude of the Qumran sect with regard to sacrifice, it seems clear from the recently published War Scroll that they did not reject it. In 1 QM ii, 5-6, we read: "These shall be posted at the burnt-offerings and the sacrifices, to prepare an offering of incense, agreeable to the good pleasure of God, to make atonement on behalf of all his community, to burn flesh continually before him on the table of glory." According to J. Baumgarten, "We do not find in 1 QS any law concerning animal sacrifice. There are only figurative references to sacrificial offerings."[61] But "1 QS and CD tell us of a sect which looked with disfavor upon the priests of the Temple of Jerusalem. They accused them of violating the sanctity of the

Temple and the Holy City by failure to observe the laws of ritual purity and appropriating sacred property. The sectarians, who were themselves identified with the Zadokite priestly tradition, held that it was preferable, under such conditions, not to bring sacrifices to the altar. Consequently, they entered a covenant to avoid the Sanctuary. In support of their position, they turned to Prophetic denunciations of sinful offerings. The *halakah* of CD, however, preserved several laws relating to the Temple and the sacrifices."[62] This supports Josephus' testimony about the Essenes, who "do not offer sacrifices, because they profess to have more pure lustrations" (*Ant.* 18, 1, 5).

But the Ebionites did reject sacrifice without a doubt. "It is Jesus who has put out, by the grace of baptism, that fire which the priest kindled for sins" (Rec. 1₄₈ KP; cf. also 1₃₆.₃₇.₃₉.₅₅.₆₂; Hom. 3₄₅; all KP). Peter even preaches that the destruction of the Temple is due to the continuance of sacrifices at a time when they had been officially abolished (Rec. 1₆₄ KP). This evidence from PsC agrees with the testimony of Epiphanius (*Pan.* 30, 16).

The radical difference of outlook here between the two sects prevents us from saying that the Ebionite attitude developed out of that of Qumran.[63]

(*d*) *Priesthood.* The priesthood was a recognized group in the Qumran sect. Baumgarten has given a good summary of their attitude, as it is known from 1 QS. "To the priests, 1 QS assigns an exalted position within the community. As in CD, the sect is conceived as joining Aaron and Israel (1 QS v, 6), but while the Israelite sectaries formed a 'holy house,' the priests were to be established as a 'most holy institution' (1 QS viii, 5-6; cf. viii, 8-9; ix, 6). Legal decisions were made 'according to the sons of Zadok, the priests who keep the Covenant, and according to the majority of the men of the community' (1 QS v, 2-3; v, 9, 21-22; vi, 19; viii, 9). 1 QS ix, 7 provides that 'only the sons of Aaron shall have authority in matters of law and property.' In the council of the community there were twelve laymen and three priests (1 QS viii, 1). A priest was required to be present in every place where ten men formed a unit of the community. At the sessions of the sectarians the priests were given preference in seating and procedure. A priest invoked the blessing over the bread and wine before communal meals (1 QS vi, 5-6). The priests also played a significant role in the annual covenant ceremony, which was one of the important institutions of the sect."[64]

In 1 QM we learn that there are priests (vii, 10-15; viii, 2-7, 13ff.), but also "leaders of the priests" (ii, 1), a "chief priest" (ii, 1; xv, 4; xvi, 13; xviii, 5),[65] and "the priest appointed for the time of vengeance according to the vote of his brethren" (xv, 6). The robes of the priests in battle are described (vii, 9-11), and the role the priests are to perform in the course of the battle is detailed (vii, 12-18). They are to blow the trumpets (vii, 15), encourage the soldiers (vii, 12), bless God and curse Belial (xiii, 1-6), etc.[66]

Such passages leave no doubt as to the status of the priests in the sect of Qumran. Levites, too, are often mentioned as a specific class. This is in sharp contrast to the attitude of the Ebionites as manifested by PsC. Their rejection of the priesthood logically follows the substitution of baptism for sacrifice. The priesthood has its function and meaning in history, in the days when God *permitted* sacrifice, but that time has passed (Rec. I₄₈ KP). Cullmann looks upon this attitude as an extension of the attitude of the Qumran sect, adopted with reference to the official priesthood in the Temple.[67] 1 QpHab viii, 8ff., speaks of a "wicked priest," who rebelled against the statutes of God, and ix, 4 ff., of the "priests of Jerusalem," who gather wealth and loot. Consequently, Cullmann may well be right in relating the Ebionite rejection of the priesthood to such a movement in Palestine as the Qumran disapproval of the official priesthood in Jerusalem.

The general conclusion to be drawn from the treatment of the attitudes of these two sects with regard to the Old Testament and its institutions is that they differ considerably. It is only in the last point that there is a possible kinship of ideas. For the rest the difference is radical.

*Baths and Baptism.* Several passages in the Qumran literature have been interpreted as referring to the bathing practices of the sect. Cullmann[68] cites in 1 QS iii, 4, 9; v, 13 ff. It will be profitable to examine these and other texts: "He cannot be justified while he conceals his stubbornness of heart / and with darkened mind looks upon ways of light. / While in iniquity, he cannot be reckoned perfect. / He cannot purify himself by atonement, / nor cleanse himself with water-for-impurity / nor sanctify himself with seas or rivers / nor cleanse himself with any water for washing! / Unclean! Unclean! shall he be as long as he rejects God's laws / so as not to be instructed by the community of his counsel" (1 QS iii, 3-6).

It is not impossible that we have here a veiled reference to some bathing practice of the Qumran sect, to a purificatory bath perhaps. But it is just as possible that this is a rhetorical way of stressing the uncleanness and guilt of the man who rejects God's laws. The same could be said of 1 QS iii, 9. Similarly in 1 QS iv, 20 f., "Then God will purge by his truth all the deeds of man . . . to cleanse him through a holy spirit from all wicked practices, sprinkling upon him a spirit of truth as purifying water to cleanse him from all untrue abominations. . . ." However, the passage in 1 QS v, 13 f, may well allude to some bathing practice: "These (the perverse) may not enter into water to (be permitted to) touch the Purity of the Holy men, for they will not be cleansed unless they have turned from their wickedness. . . ." Two passages in CD ($12_{1-2}$; $14_2$) seem to be a mere repetition of the Levitical purity laws prescribed in Lev. $11_{40}$, $15_{10}$. There is also one passage in 1 QM xiv, 2-3, which may or may not refer to a purificatory bath. "After they have gone up from among the slain to return to the camp, they will intone the hymn of Return. In the morning they will wash their garments and cleanse themselves of the blood of the sinners' corpses."

Perhaps no special meaning would be attached to references such as these were it not for the fact that we know from other sources that the Essenes were a baptist sect (Josephus, *Bell.*, 2, 5). Baumgarten has emphasized the adherence to stringent laws of purity and purification among the Essenes of Qumran.[69] Contact with a member of lower grade necessitates a purification (Josephus, *ibid.* 2, 8; 2, 10). Excavations at Khirbet Qumran uncovered large "reservoirs," the nature of which has not yet been definitely established. They have been considered as the bathing places of the Qumran sect; A. Dupont-Sommer has called them "swimming-pools" in the Postscript (dated Feb. 10, 1954) to the English translation of his *Nouveaux aperçus sur les manuscrits de la Mer Morte*.[70] Partially roofed-over reservoirs, fitted with steps by which one could descend to reach the water level, are not unknown in Roman Palestine.[71] We are not trying to exclude the possibility of these installations as bathing places; it is merely a question of reserving judgment until more convincing evidence is had.[72]

The conclusion, then, regarding the sect of Qumran is that it probably was baptist, even though the evidence is not conclusive. Several factors point in that direction with a high degree of probability. Against the background of a general baptist movement, which is known to have existed in Palestine and Syria between 150 B.C. and A.D. 300, the suggestion is even more plausible.[73]

There is a great deal of evidence for the bathing practices of the Ebionites in both Epiphanius (*Pan.* 30, 21) and PsC. However, the one big difference in this regard is that they admitted Christian baptism as well. "This is the service he (God) has appointed: to worship him only, and trust only in the Prophet of Truth, and to be baptized for the remission of sins, and thus by this pure baptism to be born again unto God by saving water . . ." (Hom. 7$_8$, not KP; cf. Rec. 1$_{39}$ KP). "Unless a man be baptized in water, in the name of the threefold blessedness, as the true Prophet taught, he can neither receive the remission of sins nor enter into the Kingdom of Heaven" (Rec. 1$_{69}$ KP; cf. Hom. 11$_{27}$ KP). This baptism is necessary before Peter and his followers will partake of food with a man (Hom. 1$_{22}$, not KP; cf. 13$_{4-5}$, not KP).

But in addition to baptism, which is definitely considered an initiation-rite to be conferred only once in the PsC, there are other baths of a purificatory ritualistic character that remind one of the Essene practices mentioned above. These take place before meals and before prayers (Hom. 8$_2$, 9$_{23}$, KP; 10$_1$, not KP, etc.). "Peter rose early and went into the garden, where there was a great water-reservoir, into which a full stream of water constantly flowed. There having bathed, and then having prayed, he sat down" (Hom. 10$_1$, not KP; cf. 10$_{26}$, not KP: Peter bathes with others before a common meal; 11$_1$, not KP: Peter bathes before prayer; Rec. 4$_3$ KP: Peter bathes in the sea before eating). Washing with water was prescribed after sexual intercourse (Hom. 11$_{30, 33}$ KP). These baths are highly recommended by Peter in his preaching (Hom. 11$_{28}$ ff.; Rec. 6$_{11}$ KP).[74] Such baths could well have been received into the Ebionite group from the Qumran sect; but, in view of the fact of a general baptist movement in Palestine and Syria at this time, we cannot restrict the source of this practice to Qumran alone.

As a matter of fact, there seems to be evidence of other influence. Epiphanius mentions the Elchesaites as the source of some of the baths in vogue among the Ebionites. "Whenever any one of them is sick or bitten by a snake, he goes down into the water. There he makes use of all the invocations which Helxai composed, calling upon the heavens and the earth, salt and water, winds and the angels of justice (as they say), likewise bread and oil; then he says, 'Come to my aid, and free me from this pain'" (*Pan.* 30, 17). The similarity that exists between this practice and the "oath" to be taken by the neophyte before he is entrusted with the sacred books and traditions of the Ebionites (described in *Diam.* 2), support this contention of other than Essene influence on the Ebionites. There is certainly nothing like this oath, taken by a stream of water with an invocation of elements, in the Qumran literature. J. Thomas maintains that the Ebionites were influenced by the Christian church, the Essenes, and the Elchesaites.[75]

*The Communal Meal.* In 1 QS vi, 2, we learn about the Qumran sect that "they shall eat communally." "When they arrange the table to eat or (arrange) the wine to drink, the priest shall first stretch out his hand to invoke a blessing with the first of the bread and/or the wine" (vi, 4-6). "He (the neophyte) shall not touch the drink of the Many until his completion of a second year among the men of the Community" (vi, 20; cf. vii, 20). The room in which this communal meal was most likely taken has been found at Khirbet Qumran.[76] In the so-called "Two Column" Document (1 QSa), we hear of a Messiah of Israel sharing in the banquet of the sect, but he remains subordinate to the priest, whom Abbé Milik has identified as the Messiah of Aaron.[77]

As for the Ebionites of the PsC, we have already mentioned that they did not eat with the nonbaptized (Hom. 1$_{22}$, 3$_{4, 9}$; Rec. 2$_{71}$, not KP). But they too had a communal meal. References to it are vague at times, but there seem to have been fixed places at table.[78] Though the expression used to indicate that the meal is often merely "to partake of food" (Hom. 8$_2$ KP; 10$_{26}$, not KP; Rec. 4$_{37}$; 5$_{36}$, not KP), we meet on occasion a peculiar expression "to partake of salt" (Hom. 4$_6$, KP; cf. *Ep. Clem.* 9$_1$). Salt and bread are mentioned together in *Diam.* 4$_3$, and we even find "the communal partaking of salt" expressed by one single compound verb (*synalizesthai:* Hom.

13$_4$, not KP), a verb which is also used in Acts 1$_4$.[79]

There is another set of expressions, which indicate that the Ebionites of the PsC celebrated the Eucharist. The verb used in connection with "eucharist" to describe the celebration is "to break," as in "the breaking of the bread" in Acts 2$_{42}$, *et al.* (Hom. 11$_{36}$, not KP; Rec. 6$_{15}$, not KP; and in connection with the use of salt: Hom. 14$_1$, not KP). Connection with the Christian Eucharist seems clear from the following passage: "For I showed them that in no way else could they be saved, unless through the grace of the Holy Spirit they hastened to be washed with the baptism of the threefold invocation, and received the eucharist of Christ the Lord . . ." (Rec. 1$_{63}$ KP). Whether these were two separate types of communal meals is hard to say. The mention of bread and salt in Hom. 14$_1$ recalls the passage in *Diam.* 4$_3$, where there is no mention of the Eucharist. The question is further complicated by the fact that Epiphanius (*Pan.* 30, 16) mentions that the Ebionites celebrated the mysteries with unleavened bread and water.

The main fact, however, is certain, that a communal meal was found in both the Qumran sect and the Ebionites of the PsC. Whereas bread and wine figure in the former, bread, salt, and water (?) are found associated with the latter. In both cases the meal was only for the initiated. Neither similarities nor dissimilarities in this case should be overlooked in drawing conclusions.

*Sacred Books.* Mention of an enigmatic book of *Hagu* is found in CD 11$_2$; 15$_5$; and, possibly, in 17$_5$. As still unpublished fragments of the Manual of Discipline are said to prescribe that the members of the sect be instructed in this book from their youth, Dupont-Sommer thinks that this might refer to 1 QS itself.[80] This is by no means certain, and we have no indication that the Qumran sect treated this book as secret.

In the PsC the sermons of Peter were treated as secret writings, which were to be entrusted only to the initiated; cf. *Ep. Petr.* 1$_2$; 3$_1$; *Diam.* 1-3. It is in connection with these books that the period of probation is mentioned, which lasts for six years (*Diam.* 1$_2$; 2$_2$). This is the only connection in which a probation is mentioned, whereas in the Qumran sect an elaborate process of initiation is found. It has nothing to do with the receiving of sacred books, but leads up to the acceptance as a full member of the community.

Consequently, both on the score of sacred books and the probation or initiation connected with them, there is much more dissimilarity than similarity between the Qumran sect and the Ebionites of the PsC.

*Community of Goods.* Even though details may not be very clear, it is quite certain that the sect of Qumran practiced some sort of communal poverty. "All who dedicate themselves to his Truth shall bring all their mind and their strength and their property into the Community of God . . . to direct all their property according to his righteous counsels" (1 QS i, 11-13; cf. v, 2). After a year's probation the novice's property will be handed over to the Custodian of Property of the Many (vi, 20), but it will not be pooled with the rest until the second year of probation is completed (vi, 22). "If there be found among them a man who lies in the matter of wealth, and it become known, they shall exclude him from the Purity of the Many for one year, and he shall be fined one-fourth of his food allowance" (vi, 24 f.). No one may share in the property of those that transgress the laws of the community (vii, 25; viii, 23; ix, 22). The priests (sons of Aaron) will regulate the property (ix, 8).

Epiphanius (*Pan.* 30, 17) tells us that the Ebionites practiced poverty, selling their goods as was the custom in the days of the apostles. In the PsC poverty is praised and possessions are regarded as sinful (Hom. 15₇ KP). "To all of us possessions are sins" (Hom. 15₉ KP). Yet, as Cullmann has pointed out,[81] the fact is that we find no practice of poverty in the PsC and do not see the members pooling their wealth as does the sect of Qumran; it is thus an ideal rather than established practice. As previously mentioned, the Ebionites did not live a communal life (though they might have come together at times for communal meals). And though they might praise poverty, they could still judge as follows: "One is not unquestionably righteous because he happens to be poor" (Hom. 15₁₀ KP). This may be a bit surprising in view of the fact that the group was known as Ebionite, a name which has often been explained in connection with the Hebrew word for "the poor," as already discussed. Of course, Epiphanius' testimony stands as evidence to the contrary, but even here it is just possible that he or his sources have reasoned from the name to the practice, especially when the example of the apostles could be cited in favor of early church practices.

At any rate, this is another significant difference between the sect of Qumran and the Ebionites, at least as they are known from the PsC.

## CONCLUSION

To sum up, then, we can say that whereas there are many similarities between the sect of Qumran and the Ebionites, there are also striking dissimilarities. The Qumran dualism resembles the Ebionite in that it is subordinated to Jewish monotheism and both are ethical. But the Qumran dualism is ethical alone, whereas the Ebionite is also physical; the Qumran dualism is simpler (being a contrast merely of light-darkness, truth-perversity, good-evil, and two spirits), but the Ebionite is much more complex. In both groups we find two main figures, the Teacher of Righteousness and the Man of the Lie (or Prophet of Truth and "the hostile man"). In the Qumran literature they are protagonist and antagonist. The Ebionite Prophet of Truth has a role similar to that of the Teacher of Righteousness, whereas "the hostile man" can be compared to the Man of the Lie only in that he is an adversary. However, we do find a radical difference of outlook when we consider the attitude of the two groups toward the Old Testament and its institutions. Qumran esteems the Torah, the Prophets, their priests, and sacrifice (when their own rigid ideas of purity are observed by the priests and in sacrifice). But the Ebionites reject the "false pericopes" of the Pentateuch, reject the prophets of the Old Testament, reject priesthood, and claim that baptism has replaced sacrificial cult. Whereas the Ebionites admitted Christian baptism and had purificatory baths of different sorts, we find at Qumran only simple purificatory baths (at least most probably). Though both had some sort of communal meal, bread and wine were used at Qumran, while the Ebionites used bread, salt, and water (?) and celebrated the Christian Eucharist. Some sort of sacred book (*Hagu*) was used at Qumran, but we are not told that it was a secret writing, so that it can scarcely be compared with the Sermons of Peter, which were to be entrusted only to the initiated among the Ebionites, who had passed a long probation. Whereas communal poverty was definitely practiced at

Qumran, there is no evidence of its practice in the PsC, where it is, however, praised. Epiphanius tells us, however, that the Ebionites did practice poverty.

From the preceding survey of the main points,[82] which have served as the basis of our comparison between the sect of Qumran and the Ebionites, several conclusions can be drawn. First, as already stated, there is no real evidence for the identification of the sect of Qumran as Ebionite. This opinion is contrary to that of J. L. Teicher, but finds itself in good company.[83] Secondly, it does not seem possible to admit that the Essenes of Qumran became the Ebionites. Cullmann's conclusion is that "the remnant of the Essenes from the Dead Sea was absorbed into Jewish Christianity."[84] Such an opinion demands that the strict-living Qumran sect, adhering rigorously to the Torah, the teaching of the prophets, and their own ascetical rules of communal life, abandoned their main tenets and practices and became Christians. We have no evidence for this. As should be obvious to anyone reading this essay, we have utilized much of the material Cullmann has brought together in his enlightening article. Many of the similarities and dissimilarities here pointed out were indicated previously by him. Consequently, one is surprised to read at the end of his article that one group passed over into the other. It seems that the most we can say is that the sect of Qumran influenced the Ebionites in many ways; Essene tenets and practices were undoubtedly adopted or adapted into the Ebionite way of life. To try to state more than this is to overstep the limits set by the evidence we have at our disposal.[85]

In our discussion of dualism we rejected the idea that either the Qumran or the Pseudo-Clementine dualism was Gnostic. We do not intend to claim that there is no Gnosticism at all in the PsC. It is, moreover, quite conceivable that many of the ideas of the Qumran writings would easily lend themselves to Gnostic adaptation. To admit this is not at all the same as to speak of a "Gnostic Judaism" at Qumran, as Schoeps has done.

This discussion has tried to furnish a *mise au point* in the problem of the relationship between Qumran and the Ebionites. It is obvious that the last word has not yet been said, and that much more will be written when adequate studies have been made of the recently published Hebrew University Scrolls, and the fragments of Qumran Cave I.[86]

# XIV

## Hillel the Elder in the Light of the Dead Sea Scrolls

NAHUM N. GLATZER

It is still too early to evaluate the significance of the Dead Sea
sectarian writings in relation to contemporaneous normative Judaism. As matters stand today, we have learned of some of the sect's
teachings, its institutions, and its organizational detail. But as long
as the history of the sectarian movement cannot be written, consideration of its relationships to the official Judaism of the period
must remain fragmentary and provisional.[1] One point, however,
can be made with a degree of certainty: official Judaism must
have noted the exodus from Jerusalem and must have taken a stand
on the phenomenon; the zeal and determination of those who joined
the New Covenant invited response, or criticism. Such reasoning
becomes particularly pertinent if we keep in mind that much of the
thought, discipline, and way of life of the Early Hasidim (fourth
and third centuries) found its way into the Essene order and related
groups.[2] This hypothesis granted, it can be said that primarily those
among the leading teachers in Jerusalem whose concern was the
cultivation of the ancient *hesed*[2a] ideal, paid attention to the Dead
Sea brotherhood.

The talmudic tradition was aware of a critical *caesura* in the
Judaism of the early Maccabean period. Joseph, son of Joezer,
described as "the *hasid* (pious) in the priesthood,"[3] is considered the
last in the long chain of teachers "who studied the Torah like
Moses our master; from his time on, the Torah was no longer
studied in this manner."[4] Also: "The scholars up to the days of

Joseph, son of Joezer, were all without reproach; from his time on that could not longer be said."[5] The crisis to which the talmudic tradition alludes appears to have been overcome with the appearance of Hillel the Elder, who about 30 B.C. became the leading teacher in Jerusalem. In summing up his life's work, the rabbinic sources compare Hillel to Ezra the Scribe: both were active in periods when "the Torah was forgotten from Israel" and had to be re-established.[6]

The question arises whether Hillel, and his school, in attempting to reform religious life in Jerusalem, took into account the fact that not insignificant groups of Judeans had withdrawn into the wilderness "to prepare the way for the Lord." A brief analysis of some of Hillel's teachings, and the sayings and deeds attributed to him and his school, partly in legendary reports, may lead us in the direction of an answer, however preliminary.

*Hesed.* If the connection between Early Hasidism and the sect is accepted, then the not too frequent, but emphatically stressed, term *hesed*, and the references to the love for *hesed* (*ahavat hesed*, Mic. 6₈) in the Manual of Discipline[7] are no coincidence. It can be argued that the sectarians tried to realize the *hesed* ideal which was focal in the early hasidic communities. The social regulations and communal character of sectarian life make such a supposition probable, even though the sect did not call themselves *hasidim*.[8] However, the Manual speaks of "a covenant of *hesed*" into which those dedicated to following God's laws shall be brought.[9]

An examination of the terminology employed by the talmudic accounts of Hillel's teachings and his mode of life, and of the selection of scriptural verses applied to him, reveals a preference for the terms *hasid* and *hesed*.

" 'A man of mercy (*ish hesed*) benefits himself'[10]—this refers to Hillel the Elder."[11] Referring to his soul, Hillel said: "I am going to do kindness (*hesed*) to the guest in the house."[12] In discussing the issue of the Day of Judgment, the School of Hillel pointed to the divine attribute of mercy (*hesed*).[13] A leading saying of Hillel's on the importance of learning reads: "An ignorant man cannot be a *hasid*."[14] His reason for teaching "every man" is that even "the sinners, when drawn to the study of Torah, became parents of righteous men, *hasidim*, and worthy people."[15] When Hillel died, his disciples enumerated the master's three characteristics: "the *hasid*, the humble man, the disciple of Ezra."[16] Johanan, son of Zakkai, whom tradition regards to be Hillel's chief pupil, took as his motto, after the destruction of the Temple, Hosea's: "I desire mercy (*hesed*) and not sacrifice."[17]

In addition to direct references to the *hesed* motif there are stories of Hillel's life which illustrate his hasidic tendency. Returning from a journey he heard cries in the vicinity of his house, but he trusted in the Lord that the cries did not come from his house.[18] In contradistinction to the School of Shammai, which from the first day of the week prepared for the coming Sabbath, the School of Hillel was wont to quote: "Blessed be the Lord, day by day he beareth our burden."[19] And whereas the School of Shammai, for the sake of truth, described a bride "as she is," Hillel's disciples described every bride as "beautiful and graceful" and led the Sages to the formulation: "A man's heart should always be outgoing in dealing with people."[20]

During the "ceremony of Water-Drawing," held on the second day of the Festival of Booths, in which Hasidim and "men of good works" actively participated, Hillel is said to have admonished the easygoing and encouraged the contrite by saying that the people's joyful homage is dearer to the Lord than the praises of myriads of angels.[21] To his wife, who gave to a poor man a meal prepared in honor of a guest, he said approvingly: "All you have done was done for the name of Heaven."[22] A once wealthy, but now impoverished, man he provided with a horse and a servant; one day, when he could find no servant, he himself "ran before the poor man for three miles."[23] A hasidic trait is manifest also in Hillel's word on humility: "My humiliation is my exaltation; my exaltation is my humiliation."[24]

It is possible that Hillel, who was naturally inclined toward Hasidism, consciously cultivated the hasidic form of religion in Jerusalem in order to counterbalance the sect's emphasis on *ahavat hesed*. He might even have felt that the sectarians, by their extreme exclusiveness, deviated from the doctrines of Early Hasidism, and that only through contact with the simple people in Jerusalem could the ancient teachings be restored.

*Study.* The Manual of Discipline speaks of the rule that in a congregation of ten men "there shall not cease to be a man who expounds the Torah (*doresh*[24a] *ba-torah*) day and night, continually. . . ."[25] In addition, the community is to spend a third of the night in reading the Book, expounding the Law, and worshiping together.[26] "The way of the Lord"[27] to be cleared in the wilderness is interpreted to mean "the study of the Torah (*midrash ha-torah*) as He commanded through Moses, to do according to all that has been revealed throughout time and as the prophets revealed by his Holy Spirit."[28] Those "who choose the way" will be guided with knowledge and instructed in the secrets of marvel and truth so that they may walk perfectly each with his fellow in all that was revealed for them.[29] All those "who have offered themselves for his truth" have the duty to "purify their mind (or knowledge) in (or by) the truth of the laws of God."[30] This tenet makes study a pursuit of central importance for the Covenanter. The people of Israel are called, among other things, "the people of the saints of the covenant, taught in the law."[31]

The Teacher of Righteousness is looked upon as the man whom God has given a heart "to interpret all the words of His servants, the prophets"[32]; God had made known to him "all the secrets (or mysteries) of the words of the prophets."[33] The sectarian group is led by an "expounder (or searcher) of the Torah" (*doresh ha-torah*), who is called the Star and to whom Num. 24:17 is applied.

We knew already from Philo that the Essenes devoted much time and attention to study, especially on the Sabbath: "In synagogues . . . they sit decorously . . . with attentive ears; then one takes the books and reads aloud and another of especial proficiency comes forward and expounds what is not understood."[34] A "holy congregation" is to Philo a group "in which it is ever the practice to hold meetings and discussions about virtue"[35] as documented by the Torah. The study of the Torah should not be a mere application of the ear, but an understanding with the mind.[36]

It is true that there was a long tradition of study in postexilic Judaism.[37] But, with some notable exceptions, this endeavor, as far as the Law is concerned, was cultivated by the priests and directed mainly toward a mastery of established traditions; if held in ever-present readiness, these could be applied to any given situation. Although the traditions were ultimately based on *midrashim*, the chief concern of the schools was the correct preservation of the teachings, and their value lay in their practical application.

In the sectarian writings, however, we find (besides interest in the pragmatic side of scriptural exegesis) an emphasis on study for its own sake, on nonpractical, pure study, on study that approaches the character of worship.

It is this type of learning that found its way back to the Jerusalem schools through the activity of Hillel. Through Hillel the study of the Torah became an issue of great religious significance. It became a prerequisite of piety (*hasidut*).[38] It was understood as leading to life: "The more Torah, the more life . . . he who has gained knowledge of the Torah, has gained life in the world-to-come."[39] Study, therefore, was not to be postponed: "Say not: 'When I shall have leisure I shall study'; perhaps you will not have leisure."[40] Stagnation was impermissible: "He who does not increase (his knowledge) causes it to decrease."[41] The process of study had to be continual. Asked to explain the difference between the expressions "the righteous" and "he that serveth God" and their antithesis "the wicked" and "he that serveth him not" in Mal. 3[18], Hillel interpreted both "he that serveth him and he that serveth him not" as referring to people who were perfectly "righteous" in their actions; "he that serveth him not," however, was the man who had studied ("repeated his chapter a hundred times") but ceased to do so; only he who studied without cessation was the one "that serveth God."[42]

Long before Hillel there were students who received the teachings from their masters; Ben Sira uses the terms *beth ha-midrash*, house of instruction, and *yeshibah*, which, later, came to mean an academy of learning. But only in connection with Hillel do our sources first speak of a true community of disciples[43]; of a master's use of everyday events to start a conversation of religious or ethical importance[44]; of attempts to spread knowledge of the Torah beyond the immediate circle of disciples,[45] as an expression of love for one's fellow men. Be the function of the *sons* of Aaron the priest what it may, the task of the *disciple* of Aaron is defined by Hillel as "loving peace, pursuing peace, loving one's fellow men, drawing them near to Torah."[46]

This development can be interpreted as re-establishing in the Jerusalem school an element which was being cultivated in the sectarian community. However in defining the method of reading Scriptures and determining the laws, Hillel differed from the usage of both Pharisaism and the sect.

When, after an absence of years, Hillel reappeared in Jerusalem, he was invited, as a former student of Shemaiah and Abtalion, to quote a decision in a ritual question to which the Elders of Bathyra knew no answer. Instead of referring to a tradition, he employed hermeneutical rules (*middot*), logical principles of interpretation. This approach failed. "He sat and expounded (*darash*) to them the whole day long but they did not accept" his teachings. Finally, Hillel added: "I have received this tradition from Shemaiah and Abtalion." That authority was accepted.[47]

This talmudic report shows that Hillel's stress on *midrash* was a decisive act. It has been pointed out that only in Hillel's time did study become increasingly methodical, and the logical categories by which the Torah was to be expounded broadened.[48] The *midrash* method, with its constant reference to the text itself, resulted in the elimination of any authority which resisted rational examination; knowledge of the meaning of the scriptural word was no longer confined to the man to whom, as to the Teacher of Righteousness, God revealed the mysteries. It resulted, furthermore, in the restriction of the power of tradition as sole authority in the law.

Hillel's School, in which rabbinic modes replaced older Pharisaism, combined the theoretical, logical reading of Scripture with a worshiplike, inherently religious, "learning." The *midrash* cultivation of the sect seems accepted; in the method of *midrash*, however, Hillel differed from the sect.

*The Poor.* The Essenes are known to us as "despisers of riches."[49] The biblical term "the poor of the flock" is applied to members of the sect, "they that give heed unto Him."[50] Love of riches is a feature of the "men of the Pit."[51] A fragment of a commentary to Ps. 37 refers to the sectarians as "the community of the poor."[52] The laws of the sectarian group include one "to strengthen the hand of the poor and the needy."[53]

Hillel's personal regard for the poor is part of his hasidic outlook on life. What interests us more is his concern with the status of the poor in the official Judean community and in Jerusalem. In his school, Hillel opposed the Shammai trend which, continuing an older Pharisaic tradition, wanted school admissions restricted to students who, besides being wise and modest, came from good families and were rich. Hillel maintained that "everybody should be taught,"[54] rich and poor.

In discussing religious usage, Hillel was spokesman for the poor, or, at any rate, for the less privileged group, of the Judean population, while the Shammai school represented the interests of the conservative well-to-do.[55] According to Hillel, the benedictions sequence at the home service on the eve of the Sabbath or of a festival should be based on the living conditions of the poor; the Shammai school set the order according to the pattern of the well-to-do.[56] The so-called New Year for fruit trees is, according to Hillel, observed half a month later than the date set down by the Shammai school[57]; Shammai's regulation was based on the experience of the rich, who had better fields and gardens, the fruits of which matured earlier than the fruits in the gardens of the poor; Hillel's later date was for the accommodation of the poor. A quantity of food sufficient for a single meal is required for a ritual (known as *Erub tabshilin*) performed on the eve of a festival which is followed by a Sabbath; the Shammai school required two courses, the minimum apparently, of a rich man's meal; the Hillel group ruled that one course was sufficient, as that was the customary meal of the poor.[58] Hillelites accepted the benediction over bread as a blessing over the entire meal, for the bread was the main dish of the poor. The Shammai school, with the meal of the rich in mind, ruled differently.[59]

The actual care of the poor was an integral and undisputed part of the biblical tradition and needed no special emphasis. The adjustment of the minutiae of ritual life to the standards of the poor and the humble—due, no doubt, to a genuine internal development within Pharisaism—served, in Hillel's day, to counteract the sect's claim to being sole champion of the poor against the world of the rich.

*The Intermediate Group.* The polarity between the wicked, usually identified with the prosperous, and the righteous, usually detected among the poor and the humble, is not new in Judaism. However, in the period of Alexander Jannaeus, tension between the "sinners" and the "righteous" assumed extreme proportions. In sectarian thinking the world is to be understood in the light of an absolute dualism between good and evil. Against the vast realm dominated by sin stand the sons of the New Covenant, "the Elect of Grace." The Covenanter is obligated "to love everything that He has chosen, and to hate everything that He has rejected."[60] The Book of Enoch mirrors most forcefully the radical position of the "righteous" and their hope for the utter destruction of the sinners.[61]

It is against this background that a discussion on the Day of Judgment by the schools of Hillel and Shammai should be read.[62] Referring to the division in the Book of Daniel between those who "shall awake to everlasting life" and those doomed "to everlasting abhorrence,"[63] the schools assigned the "perfectly righteous" to the first group, the "perfectly wicked" to the second. However, they introduced the concept of an "intermediate group," people in whom good and evil are mixed and who, technically, are in an equilibrium. The strict Shammaiites insisted that such people would have to taste the fire of punishment (Gehenna) before being allowed to rise again, "for the Lord . . . bringeth down to the grave and bringeth up."[64] The lenient Hillelites maintained that the Lord who is "full of mercy (*hesed*) inclines the scales of judgment toward mercy"; i.e., there is no Gehenna for the "intermediates"; it was in their behalf that David said: "I was brought low and he saved me."[65]

It is obvious that in this discussion it is not the difference of opinion between the two schools that is of primary importance, but their postulation of the existence of an "intermediate group." This new doctrine reads like a response to the sharp juxtaposition of the righteous and the wicked in the Book of Enoch, the *Habakkuk Commentary* from Qumran, and other writings. Without denying the existence of the wholly wicked (who deserve their punishment), the schools of both Hillel and Shammai, in keeping with the *hesed* idea, restored the average man to his rightful place in the community and in theological thought. The term "intermediate," or "average," is used again in the Hillel texts in connection with his student body. Hillel designates as his successor not a member of the sixty outstanding disciples, but one from among the remaining twenty, whom he terms "average," or "intermediate."[66]

*"For the better order of the world."* The drive for the wilderness which motivated the sect is echoed in the Psalms of Solomon. The pious found that "there was not . . . one that wrought in the midst of Jerusalem mercy (*hesed*) and truth." Therefore, "they that loved the synagogues of the pious (*hasidim*) fled from them" and wandered in deserts "that their lives might be saved from harm."[67]

It was one of Hillel's principles not to separate from the community but to work within its framework. Our sources remember Hillel for his endeavors to improve the social conditions of the community and for initiating special legislative measures (*takkanot*) in its behalf ("for the better order (*tikkun*) of the world").[68] Adopting a Hellenistic institution, he introduced the *prosbul*, a ruling protecting the creditor against cancellation of a debt in the Sabbatical year and the borrower against possible resistance of the lender.[69] Another legal enactment concerned the sale of houses in a walled city; buyers of such houses used to circumvent the law of redemption by the original owner within a year[70] by absenting themselves around the time when that original owner was expected to make his bid. The ruling introduced by Hillel allowed the original owner to deposit the due amount in the court of law and thus obtain the right to renewed ownership.[71] We also hear of Hillel's effective opposition to certain Sages, whose inconsiderate ruling would have made bastards of some Alexandrians.[72] A legislation regarding usury was designed to prevent a lender from possible exploitation of a carelessly made arrangement at the time of the loan; precaution must be taken, Hillel ruled, that not even in minor transactions "they be found partakers in usury."[73] The School of Hillel, prompted by the Shammaiites, solved the awkward position of a man "who is half bondman and half freedman" by compelling the master to set him free and turn the remaining obligation into a bond of indebtedness.[74] The motivation for this law is, again, given as "for the better order (*tikkun*) of the world."

Thus—in a period in which many felt that Judean society was doomed and the only possible life would be to follow the orders[75] of "the exiles of the desert"[76]—Hillel's tendency seems to have been the correction of existing deficiencies, prevention of misuse of existing laws, restoration of the original meaning of the statutes, and work for a better functioning society.

*Proselytes.* The Damascus Document counts the proselyte (*ger*) among the groups of which the community is composed.[77] The duty of helping the poor and the needy is extended to the *ger*, which may refer to the stranger.[78] The Manual of Discipline does not mention the proselyte as a part of the community. Millar Burrows holds that the term *ger* in the Damascus Document may possibly refer only to probationary candidates for membership.[79] The spirit of exclusivism in the sects makes it improbable that the proselyte was considered a desirable addition to the community.

Hillel, on the other hand, is known as having had a friendly attitude toward proselytes. Our texts, which mingle facts with legend and stress primarily Hillel's forbearance as against Shammai's sternness, nevertheless reveal a pronounced interest in keeping the doors open for the Gentile. Hillel is said to have accepted a heathen who agreed to conversion only if taught "the whole Torah while standing on one foot," and another who originally refused to accept the Oral Law as valid.[80] Hillel even admitted a candidate who immodestly aspired to the office of high priest.[81] A later story refers to the two sons of the latter proselyte as "Hillel's proselytes."[82]

In all the instances mentioned, Shammai, representing a more conservative trend within Pharisaism, is said to have instantly rejected the prospective converts.[83] Even though Hillel's position is not unique in Pharisaic tradition, it acquires special significance in a period in which the Dead Sea sect considered an exclusive attitude necessary for the proper observance of Torah.

*Messianism.* Expectation of the coming of a Messiah, of the end of days, the tribulation to precede the end, of life in the world of light—all these have an important place in the sectarians' thinking. The Covenanters were to play a decisive role in the final drama: "Into the hand of his elect will God give the judgment of all the peoples and by their chastisement all the sinners of his nation will be punished."[84]

In the Hillel texts there is no reference to the messianic idea. There is mention of retributive justice on earth[85] and an affirmation of the life in the world-to-come, a portion of which is to be gained by the study of Torah.[86] The silence on messianism in a period in which it was a burning issue cannot be adequately explained by the paucity of our sources. It can be assumed that, in concentrating on learning, on *hesed*, on the reconstruction of the Pharisaic community, Hillel counteracted the challenge of eschatological thought. As quite indirect evidence, the fate of Jonathan, son of Uzziel, Hillel's most eminent disciple, may be cited. Jonathan, whom the sources made also heir to the prophetic tradition of Haggai, Zechariah, and Malachi, is said to have undertaken an Aramaic translation *(Targum)* of the prophetic books. A Voice reprimanded him for having "revealed God's secrets to mankind." He defended his work as being done "that dissension may not increase in Israel." When, continuing his labors, he came to the Book of Daniel, with its allusions to the messianic end, the Voice issued again and said: "No more!"[87] In this legendary report in which much is questionable, an antimessianic tendency in the Hillel circle seems at least indicated.

*Contacts.* Provided the preceding points are sufficient to suggest that Hillel had knowledge of the sectarian development, the question comes to mind whether he may have had direct contact with the Covenanters. Our sources speak of a Menahem who preceded Shammai as Hillel's associate. A difference of opinion persisted for generations on the question whether the customary laying of hands on the head of the sacrifice may, or may not, be performed on a festival (to which, with one exception, the same prohibition of work applies as to the Sabbath); only "Hillel and Menahem did not differ."[88] Then, however, "Menahem left his office and Shammai took his place."[89] Among the answers to the question "Whither did he go?" it is recorded that "he went over from one principle to another,"[90] that is, as some scholars interpret it, he left the Pharisees and joined the Essenes.[91] It is indeed possible that our Menahem is identical with Menahem the Essene who predicted a great future to young Herod and whom Herod rewarded by honoring all the Essenes.[92] A personal contact between Hillel and a representative of a sectarian group, or even a community, is not out of the question.

There may have been a period in Hillel's life spent in preparation for his Jerusalem activities. The gap between the time he spent in the School of Shemaiah and Abtalion[93] and his appearance before the Elders of Bathyra[94] has been explained by an assumption that he had gone back to his native Babylonia. More probable—yet by no means certain—would be to suggest that he studied the religious situation wherever he could best observe it. A legendary description of his learning suggests the widest possible range of observation and interest.[95] A Baraitha lets Hillel distinguish between "a generation to which the Torah is dear" when it is appropriate to spread its knowledge and a period in which it is more advisable only to gather.[96] At an enigmatic gathering of the Sages in the upper chamber of one Gurya's house in Jericho, a heavenly voice issued proclaiming that there was among those assembled "one who would be worthy of the holy spirit but his generation is not worthy of it." Thereupon all eyes were fixed upon Hillel the Elder.[97]

These statements, however vague, may reflect Hillel's situation before he returned to Jerusalem to start his work in "re-establishing the forgotten Torah." An early rabbinic source sees Hillel's activity as beginning "one hundred years before the destruction of the Temple,"[98] i.e., at 30 B.C., which roughly coincides with the earthquake in the spring of 31 B.C.,[99] a significant event for Judea proper and apparently also for the Dead Sea community.[100] It is difficult to decide whether this is more than a coincidence.

*Summary.* There are indications that in his teachings and activities Hillel the Elder took notice, among other religious and social issues of his time, of some doctrines and institutions current in the sectarian movement. Such reference may be found in his concept of learning, in his application of the *hesed* principle, and in his special regard for the poor. Shammai, in contradistinction to Hillel, represented, on the whole, the established traditions. Hillel's emphasis of an "intermediate group" may have been an attempt to counteract the sectarian dualism of good and evil. Hillelite institutions "for the better order" of society may, among other considerations, have been motivated by desire to counterbalance the sectarian drive to the desert.

Hillel's friendly attitude toward proselytes can be read in the context of his nonexclusivist concept of Torah and the community of Israel. The absence of the messianic motif in Hillel's thought may be due to an awareness of the perils dormant in an eschatological world outlook; the place of messianism is taken by the concept of the life in the world-to-come.

It is therefore possible that, in addition to other factors, Hillel—while adopting some of the sect's teachings, especially those it preserved as heirs to pre-Maccabean Early Hasidism—attempted to reform Pharisaic Judaism as an answer to the challenge of the sectarian movement. Here emerges classical, rabbinic Judaism.

True, Hillel's activity can be interpreted against the background of the religious, social, and political conditions in Jerusalem proper and in the official centers of Judaism. Singly, every source reference can be understood as referring to conditions created by the Sadducean opposition, by the Jerusalem priesthood, by the Herodian rule, the older traditions, etc. Such a procedure, however, would rest on the assumption that those concerned with Torah, and foremost among them Hillel the Elder, ignored the movement which created the sect and wrote off its members as heterodox extremists not worthy of consideration.

Yet, the approach I have chosen remains as a possibility. Were Hillel a mere cultivator of established traditions, it would be precarious, without explicit textual evidence, to presuppose his regard for conditions outside his immediate group. But Hillel was very early recognized as a second Ezra and many of his teachings and actions show a reformatory spirit. To such a man a wider view and a more general concern must be attributed. Then, however, a reading of the texts, as here attempted, suggests itself. Even so, no one point should be pressed; a revaluation of detail should be expected.

# Abbreviations; Editions of the Qumran Texts Referred to in this Volume

For the Qumran texts the abbreviations of the official edition (see *Qumran Cave I*, pp. 46 f.) are used. The number "1" indicates the cave in which they were found.

1 QS      The Manual of Discipline (*Serek ha-yahad*).
1 QH      The Thanksgiving Hymns (*Hodayoth*).
1 QM      The War Between the Sons of Light and the Sons of Darkness (*Milhama*).
1 QpHab The Habakkuk Commentary (*pesher*).
1 QSa     The Two-Column Document (*Serek ha-edah*).

Texts:

*The Dead Sea Scrolls of St. Mark's Monastery* [now the property of the Hebrew University in Jerusalem]: vol. I and II:2 (edited by M. Burrows). The American Schools of Oriental Research, New Haven, 1950-51. Contains 1 QIs$^a$ (a complete text to Isaiah), 1 QpHab and 1 QS.

*Osar: Osar ha-megilloth ha-genuzoth*, The Hebrew University, Jerusalem, 1955 (edited by E. L. Sukenik). Contains 1 QIs$^b$ (another, less complete, text to Isaiah), 1 QM and 1 QH.

*Qumran Cave I: Discoveries in the Judaean Desert, vol. I. Qumran Cave I* (edited by D. Barthélemy and J. T. Milik). Clarendon Press, Oxford, 1955. Contains 1 QSa and other longer or shorter fragments (with French translations).—*A Genesis Apocryphon,* ed. by N. Avigad and Y. Yadin, Jerusalem, Hebrew University Press, 1956. This edition gives the full text of cols. ii, xix-xxii, with translation and a summary of the rest of the document in English.

K. G. Kuhn, *Phylakterien aus Hohle von Qumran*. Abh. der Heidelberger Akademie der Wissenschaften 1957.

Translations:

*Brownlee* (W. H.): 1 QpHab: "The Jerusalem Habakkuk Scroll," *Bulletin of the American Schools of Oriental Research* 112 (1948), pp. 8-18. 1 QS: *The Dead Sea Manual of Discipline.* Bulletin of the American Schools of Oriental Research, Supplementary Studies 10-12, 1951.

*Burrows* (M.): *The Dead Sea Scrolls.* Viking Press, New York, 1955. Contains translations of the Damascus Document (see below), 1 QpHab, 1 QS and selections from 1 QH and 1 QM.—*More Light on the Dead Sea Scrolls,* ibm., 1958. Contains translations of the Genesis Apocryphon, 1 QSa, 1 QSb and some significant fragments, mainly from Cave 4.

*Wernberg-Moeller* (P.): The Manual of Discipline. Translated and Annotated with an Introduction (Studies on the Texts of the Desert of Judah, vol. I, E. J. Brill, Leiden, 1957).

*Gaster* (Th.H.): *The Dead Sea Scriptures.* Doubleday Anchor Books, Garden City, N.Y., 1956. The most complete edition available with translations of all texts and more extensive fragments so far published.

A few fragments from Cave IV have been published by J. M. Allegro in *Palestine Exploration Quarterly* 86 (1954), 69-75: 4 QpPs37; in *Journal of Biblical Literature* 75 (1956), pp. 89-95: 4 QpNah.; and *ibidem*, pp. 174-87: Patriarchal Blessings and Florilegium, etc.— "Fragments of a Qumran Scroll of eschatological Midrashim," ibm., 77 (1958), pp. 350-54.

## THE DAMASCUS DOCUMENT

CD: The Damascus Document (Covenanters of Damascus).

Text and Translation:

*Fragments of a Zadokite Work* (edited by S. Schechter). University Press, Cambridge, 1910.

*The Zadokite Documents* (edited by Ch. Rabin). Clarendon Press, Oxford, 1954; Second revised ed. 1958.

Translation only: in R. H. Charles, *Apocrypha and Pseudepigrapha of the Old Testament,* vol. II, Clarendon Press, Oxford, 1913.

The references are either to column and line (iv, 2) or chapter and verse (6₁). Rabin uses the former, Charles the latter; both are found parallel in L. Rost's edition of the text, *Die Damaskusschrift* (1933).

## OTHER WORKS AND ABBREVIATIONS

*Strack-Billerbeck:* H. L. Strack and P. Billerbeck, Kommentar zum Neuen Testament aus Talmud und Midrasch, I-V, C. H. Beck, München, 1922-56.

*LXX:* The Septuagint, i.e. the Greek translation of the Old Testament.

Josephus—*Ant.:* Jewish Antiquities; *Bell.:* The Jewish War. Most of Josephus' works are now available in the Loeb Classical Library (Harvard University Press).

In the translations of the Qumran and Damascus documents square brackets [ ] indicate that the translator (or the editor of the Hebrew text) has filled in a gap in the actual manuscript; parentheses ( ) contain clarifications or interpretative additions by the translator.

## ADDENDA

For the further study of the Scrolls, attention is drawn to the following works published after the first edition of this collection of essays:

Ch. Burchard, *Bibliographie zu den Handschriften vom Toten Meer*. (Beih. zur Zeitschr. f. d. alttest. Wissensch. 76 [1957], which lists and classifies not less than 1556 items on the Scrolls.)

M. Burrows, *More Light on the Dead Sea Scrolls* (1958), where Professor Burrows' capable report on the ongoing discussion is brought up to that date.

Frank M. Cross, Jr., *The Ancient Library of Qumran and Biblical Studies* (1958); and J. T. Milik, *Ten Years of Discovery in the Wilderness of Judaea* (Studies on Biblical Theology, 26; 1959). These two volumes give the most reliable and comprehensive introduction to the field, both written by men who have worked directly with the texts, published as well as unpublished ones.

# Notes

## I. THE SCROLLS AND THE NEW TESTAMENT

1. E. Wilson, *The Scrolls from the Dead Sea* (1955), p. 108.

1a. The first part of the first of these manuscripts has now been published with French, German, and English translations: *Evangelium Veritatis* (Gospel of Truth), ed. M. Malinine, H. Ch. Puech, and G. Quispel. (Zürich, Rascher Verlag, 1956); cf. F. L. Cross (ed.), *The Jung Codex* (1955).

2. This is the issue raised and discussed, e.g., by John Knox, *Criticism and Faith. The Role of Biblical Scholarship in the Life of the Church* (1952).

3. *The Dead Sea Scrolls* (Eng. trans., 1952), p. 99.

4. E. Renan, *Histoire du peuple d'Israël*, vol. V, pp. 70 ff.

5. *Op. cit.*, pp. 74 f.

6. *Op. cit.*, p. 34.

7. *The Dead Sea Scrolls* (A Pelican Book, 1956), p. 148.

8. See pp. 10 ff.

9. The strongly apologetic work of G. Graystone, *The Dead Sea Scrolls and the Originality of Christ* (1956), argues that all similarities between the Scrolls and the New Testament have their common root in the Old Testament. Although this is true in a general sense, the very fact that the Essenes and the Christians happened to emphasize the same Old Testament points, and do it in a similar fashion, makes Graystone's arguments less significant.

10. See especially Kuhn's essay on "New Light on Temptation, Sin and Flesh in the New Testament," p. 98.

11. New York, Doubleday Anchor Books, 1956. Gaster gives a rather free translation. The degree to which his translation differs from others alerts the reader to the fact that some similarities depend more on the translation than on the text itself. The interpretive element in all translations is especially important to have in mind in a context such as ours. Gaster's translation is also colored by his interpretation of the Scrolls as exponents of Jewish mysticism, a view which needs thorough testing before it can be accepted.

12. See K. Stendahl, *The School of St. Matthew and Its Use of the Old Testament* (1954).

13. See especially Joach. Jeremias, *Jerusalem zur Zeit Jesu*, vol. IIB (1937), pp. 115 ff.

14. Gaster, *op, cit.*, p. 52, takes "purity" in an abstract sense: ". . . he is to be regarded as outside the state of purity entailed by membership." His reading and translation indicate, however, in a different way, the significance of "membership." On Gaster's understanding of the communal meals, see note 19.

15. 1 QS vii, 1, 16, 17, 23. This punishment seems to apply primarily to officials and members of the Council, while the members of lower rank are dealt with somewhat less rigidly, except when they obstruct and murmur against the leaders and the Community as such.

16. See p. 14.

17. For the different stages of the term *sedaqah*, "righteousness" in the O.T.,

see C. H. Dodd, *The Bible and the Greeks* (1934), pp. 42-65.

18. The translation as well as the interpretation here followed is that of Frank M. Cross, Jr., *The Christian Century* 72 (1955), p. 969.

19. Gaster, *op. cit.*, p. 278, has objected to this interpretation and he tries to de-eschatologize the passage. He affirms that the text is "a Manual of Discipline for the future Restored Congregation of Israel." Once this is admitted, the fact that this future is the focus of the Qumran expectations makes it difficult to see how the passage can be taken just as a cold *halakah* for a future situation, where even smaller gatherings in the Age to Come are foreseen. The tension between the now and the future suggests an eschatological interpretation regardless of the reading: "When God begets the Messiah/When the Messiah is present," *ibid.*; cf. p. 256, note 13.

20. This leads us to raise questions for further consideration in connection with Kuhn's analysis of the traditions on the Lord's Supper. Must not the "future" motif be far more original with the meal than he intimates? See esp. p. 93.

21. The best listing of the material and the alternatives is found in W. Bauer, *Griechisch-Deutsches Wörterbuch* (1952⁴), now also in English translation edited by W. F. Arndt and F. W. Gingrich (1957).

22. There is a slight but important difference between these terms as a translation of the Greek *arrabon* and the more modern word "guarantee" in the RSV. *Arrabon* is not only the confirmation of the promise but the first installment of the heavenly power itself, the down payment.

23. J. M. Allegro, "Further Messianic References in Qumran Literature," *Journ. of Bibl. Lit.* 75 (1956), pp. 176 f; cf. note 7. There is the possibility that the "Interpreter of the Law" is rather identified with the Prophet, who will come together with the two Messiahs, 1 QS ix, 11, see p. 54. But even so he is a "messianic figure."

24. The translation as well as the interpretation here followed is that of J. V. Chamberlain, *Journ. of Near Eastern St.* 14 (1955), pp. 32-41 and 181-82. This passage has bearing on the expression "When God begets his Messiah," I QSa ii, 11, see n. 19. See the further discussion in *Journ. of Bibl. Lit.* 75 (1956), pp. 96-106, by L. H. Silberman with references to the studies of G. S. Glanzman, J. Baumgarten, and M. Mansoor.

25. See, e.g., V. Taylor, *The Names of Jesus* (1953), pp. 18-23; and the sharp distinction made in E. Stauffer, *"Messias oder Menschensohn?" Novum Test.* 1 (1956), pp. 81-102.

26. See Taylor, *op cit.*, pp. 25-35. The distinction which we emphasize has nothing to do with the discussion about the unified or the diverse origin of the terms "Messiah" and "Son of Man." See A. Bentzen, *King and Messiah* (1955), and H. Ringgren, *The Messiah in the Old Testament* (1956).

27. Sometimes this view is combined with an understanding of the term "Son of Man" as a device used by Jesus in order to indicate his human nature over against more celestial expectations, but of the two terms, "Son of Man" certainly was the more celestial: The Savior expected on the clouds of heaven at the end of time.

28. Two major contributions may suffice as a guide to further study and bibliography: J. Klausner, *The Messianic Idea in Israel* (1955) and E. Sjöberg, *Der verborgene Menschensohn in den Evangelien* (1955).

29. See now J. A. T. Robinson, "The Most Primitive Christology of All?" *Journ. of Theol. St.* 7 (1956), pp. 177-89; cf. Acts 1₃₀-31.

30. It is only in such a context that one can understand the story about how

"the graves were opened and many bodies of holy men and women who had died were raised." This tradition is found only in Mt. 2752ʳ.

31. For the fullest treatment of this question and its great significance for New Testament thought and the history of the primitive church, see J. Munck, *Paulus und die Heilsgeschichte* (1954); *Christus und Israel* (1956); and Joach. Jeremias, *Jesus' Promise to the Nations* (1958).

## II. The Significance of the Qumran Texts for Research Into the Beginnings of Christianity

1. *Le problème littéraire et historique du roman pseudo-clémentin. Étude sur le rapport entre le gnosticisme et le judéo-christianisme* (1930).

2. See. J. Thomas, *Le mouvement baptiste en Palestine et Syrie* (1935).

3. K. Elliger, *Studien zum Habakuk-Kommentar vom Toten Meer* (1953), p. 222.

4. See K. G. Kuhn in this volume, p. 65-93.

5. See the alternate phrases in 1 QS vi, 4-6, "bread *or* wine"; "bread *and* wine."

6. S. E. Johnson recognizes, however, that in the Manual of Discipline the emphasis is upon communal life and not on poverty as such; this volume, p. 133.

7. On the organization, see Bo Reicke's essay in this volume, pp. 143-56, and J. Daniélou, "La communauté de Qumran et l'organization de l'Eglise ancienne," *Rev. d'hist. et de philos. rel.* 35 (1955), pp. 104 f. Daniélou shows that there is a smilarity between both organizations in the coexistence of institution and charisma.

8. S. E. Johnson, *op. cit.*, p. 134.

9. K. G. Kuhn, "Die in Palästina gefundenen hebräischen Texte und das Neue Testament," *Zeitschr. f. Theol. und Kirche* 47 (1950), pp. 193 ff.

10. *Ibid.*

11. According to Philo, *Quod omnis probus liber* § 75, the Essenes rejected the sacrifices of animals. According to a not very clear passage in Josephus, *Ant.* 18, 1, 5, the Essenes sent gifts to the Temple but did not participate themselves in Temple worship. The new texts published so far do not contain passages explicitly rejecting Temple worship. However, see 1 QS ix, 3 f.

12. Especially *Ps.-Clem. Rec.* 154,60.

13. H. Lietzmann, *Sitzungsber. d. Berl. Ak. d. Wissensch.* (1930), refused to recognize the existence of any ancient source within the Mandean writings (especially against R. Bultmann, "Die Bedeutung der neuerschlossenen mandäischen und manichäischen Quellen für das Verständnis des Johannes-Evangeliums," *Zeitschr. f. d. neutest, Wissensch.* 24 (1925), pp. 100f. But more recent research confirms the former view according to which the Mandean literature contains very old material.

14. W. Baldensperger, *Der Prolog des vierten Evangeliums* (1898).

15. See O. Cullmann, *The Early Church*, p. 175-82. The Pseudo-Clementines go further in their polemic against the sect of John the Baptist. Whereas the Fourth Gospel rejects only the members of the sect, this Jewish-Christian writing attacks John the Baptist himself, considering him to be the false prophet in the line of Cain, Esau, the Antichrist. The whole Pseudo-Clementine theory of the "pairs" *(syzygiai)* aims at turning the chronological argument against John the Baptist, the forerunner always being the representative of false prophecy.

16. *Ibid.*

17. See F.M. Braun, "Le mandéisme et la secte essénienne de Qumran,"

*Orientalia et Biblica Lovaniensia* 1 (1957), pp. 193-230.

18. Perhaps we may also call attention to the prophetic text, "Prepare ye the way of the Lord," which is found in the Manual of Discipline.

19. R. Bultmann, *op. cit.*

20. See F. A. Schilling, "Why did Paul Go to Damascus?" *Anglican Theol. Rev.* 16 (1934), p. 199, and S. E. Johnson, *op. cit.*, p. 140.

21. In both passages, other witnesses read "Greeks."

22. Vol. V, pp. 59 f.

23. *The Early Church* (1956), pp. 183-92.

24. On the other hand, S. E. Johnson, *op. cit.*, pp. 129ff. has described the relationship between the Book of Acts and the Qumran sect.

25. K. G. Kuhn, *op cit.* (1950), pp. 193 f.

26. See H. Odeberg, *The Fourth Gospel* (1929).

27. S. E. Johnson, *op. cit.*, pp. 137ff., mentions interesting parallels between Stephen's speech and 1 QS.

28. See O. Cullmann in *Studi e Materiali di Storia delle Religioni* 29 (1958), pp. 3-21.

29. See Lucetta Mowry, "The Dead Sea Scrolls and the Background of the Gospel of John," *Bibl. Archaeol.* 17 (1954), pp. 78 f.

30. The Qumran texts which are known so far do not contain the title "Son of Man."

31. See my *Christologie des Neuen Testaments* (1957), pp. 189 ff.

32. On the disappearance of the Qumran sect, or rather its absorption into the gnostic Jewish-Christians, known through the Pseudo-Clementines, see my article: "Die neuentdeckten Qumrantexte und das Judenchristentum der Pseudoklementinen," in *Neutestamentliche Studien für Rudolf Bultmann* (1954), pp. 35 ff.—In his instructive essay (see p. 208 of this volume), J. A. Fitzmyer has at this point misunderstood my intention. I naturally do not mean that "the Essenes of Qumran became the Ebionites." What I say, however, is that after the dispersion of the community during the war of A.D. 70 the remnants of the sect were absorbed into the Jewish-Christian groups of the East Jordan district, which degenerated more and more into a Jewish sect, and were open to all kinds of syncretistic influence.

### III. John the Baptist in the New Light of Ancient Scrolls

1. An important study of Bo Reicke in Swedish discusses this side of John most excellently, "Nytt ljus över Johannes döparens förkunnelse," *Religion och Bibel*, xi (1952), pp. 5 ff. Locusts are listed among the clean foods in Lev. 11₂₁f.

2. For the scribe of this document, not even the word "Lord" could be written for Yahweh (corrupted sometimes today as Jehovah). Instead we have four dots here for the four letters of the ineffable Name. In the line just above, in the indirect quotation, there is a coined surrogate, HUHA. Cf. M. Delcor, "Des diverses manières d'écrire le Tetagramme sacré dans les anciens Documents hébraïques," *Rev. de l'Hist. des Rel.* 147 (1955), pp. 145-73.

3. C. H. Kraeling, *John the Baptist* (1951), p. 4. Our citations of modern criticism will be confined largely to him, in view of the fact that his book is the only recent critical work in English.

4. *Bell.* 2, 8, 2 (120), translation that of H. St. J. Thackeray in the Loeb Classical Library. Although Josephus mentions marrying Essenes (*op. cit.*, 2, 8, 13) as "another order," it may be that there was no sharp cleavage between them.

H. L. Ginsberg seems to suggest that both celibate and noncelibate Essenes belonged to the same society, "The Cave Scrolls and the Jewish Sects, New Light on a Scholarly Mystery," *Commentary*, 16 (1953), pp. 77-81.

5. The Essenes as represented in 1 QS accorded a large place to priests. It may be that Zechariah, his father, thought there was more future for John as a priest with the Essenes. In a group where celibacy was practiced, priests may have tended to become scarce. Not all the priests officiating at Jerusalem were Sadducees, but the piety of some of them leaned more to the Pharisees or even to the Essenes. It is to this pietistic group that Zechariah and Simeon belonged, and probably also those most easily converted to the Christian faith (Acts 67).

6. Cf. Kraeling, *op. cit.*, pp. 9 f.

7. *Ant.* 18, 1, 5. The translation is that of William Whiston.

8. *Harv. Theol. Rev.* 46 (1953), p. 155.

9. Precisely this is said of Cornelius' household in Acts 1047*t.*, when interpreted in the light of Acts 158*t.* In a kind letter from J. Jeremias of Göttingen (dated 10/25/55), I have received the keen and important query as to whether Josephus may have been influenced by his firsthand knowledge of Essenism and simply attributed Essene teaching to John the Baptist. See here the Life of Josephus, chap. 10 f., from which it is apparent that Josephus spent three years (beginning when he was sixteen years old) making trial of Pharisaism, Sadduceeism, Essenism, and the life of a hermit with Banus (perhaps only three months with this man, certainly not three years!). It is apparent that Josephus could never have been more than a novitiate among the Essenes, but long enough to have acquired accurate information concerning their basic tenets and rules of discipline. Jeremias' suggestion represents a real (though unprovable) possibility and is certainly a reasonable caution. Though Josephus was born after the death of John, he would have had many opportunities in the normal concourse of Palestinian life to have familiarized himself with the still-living first generation of the baptist movement and to have received accurate information concerning its baptismal faith. Hence we have no reason to question the substantial accuracy of Josephus' description of John's baptism, though one may entertain the possibility of some Essene coloring in his portrayal. In view of this suspicion, Jn. 325 may assume greater significance.

10. Cf. J. V. Chamberlain, "Another Qumran Thanksgiving Psalm," *Journ. of Near Eastern St.* 14 (1955), pp. 32-41; "Further Elucidation of a Messianic Thanksgiving Psalm from Qumran," *ibid.*, pp. 181 f.; A. Dupont-Sommer, "La mère du Messie et la mère de l'Aspic dans un hymne de Qoumran," *Rev. de l'Hist, des Rel.* 147 (1955), pp. 174-88; G. Vermès, "Quelques traditions de la Communauté de Qumran," *Cahiers Sioniens* 9 (1955), pp. 54-58.

11. *Op. cit.*, p. 117.

12. We cite here the translation of A. Dupont-Sommer, *The Dead Sea Scrolls* (1952), p. 73.

13. See my discussion in the *Bull. of the Amer. Schools of Oriental Research* 135 (1954), pp. 35-38; also Yigael Yadin, "A Note on DSD IV, 20," *Journ. of Bibl. Lit.* 74 (1955), pp. 40-43. G. Vermès, *op cit.*, pp. 56 f., accepts Yadin's translation but follows in this regard my interpretation.

14. R. H. Charles brackets the words "in the water," regarding them as a Christian interpolation; but this may have been quite wrong, as Dupont-Sommer observes.

15. See here my discussion in the *Bull. of the Amer. Schools of Oriental Research* 132 (1953), pp. 10 f. On the word "sprinkle," cf. the exegesis of J. Muilen-

burg in *The Interpreter's Bible,* vol. V, pp. 617 f. It is the opinion of the present writer that the syntax of Is. 52₁₄t. has not been properly understood or correctly translated. The protasis is to be limited to "Just as many were astonished at thee"—the second person referring to Israel, who is here alluded to as the corporate Servant of the Lord, but distinguished from the personal Servant referred to in the third person. What the passage says is that the experience of Israel is in many respects analogous to that of the Messiah. Both Isaiah texts from Qumran Cave I, the Septuagint, and the Masoretic text support the second person suffix. Hence it is an error to emend to the third person after the Syriac, which is but a slender attestation of an easier reading. There are two apodoses, each being introduced with *ken.* C. C. Torrey recognized this most natural interpretation of the first conjunction, but eliminated it through two emendations, the alteration of the pronominal suffix in the previous clause, and the correction of *ken* to *ki.* See Torrey's *The Second Isaiah* (1928), p. 415.

16. This and other quotations of the Pseudepigrapha, so called, are from R. H. Charles, *Apocrypha and Pseudepigrapha of the Old Testament,* vol. II.

17. Y. Yadin in *Israel Exploration Journal,* 6 (1956), pp. 158 f.

18. See 1 QSa ii, 11-22; 1 QSb v, 20-29; i, 21-iii, 21, and the discussions concerning them in *Qumran Cave I,* pp. 117 f., 120-25, 128 f.

19. See my article, "Messianic Motifs of Qumran and the New Testament," *New Testament Studies,* 3 (1956/57), pp. 12-30, to be continued in fasc. 3.

20. So Kuhn, see pp. 58-60.

21. Cf. N. Wieder, "The Doctrine of the Two Messiahs among the Karaites," *Journ. of Jewish St.* 6 (1955), pp. 14-25. It is to be hoped that the fragments of CD found in the Scroll Caves may shed light upon this reading. The original flight to the land of Damascus was probably earlier than the reign of Herod, and we should probably understand the existence of two distinct but closely related groups in the Covenanters of Qumran and Damascus. It is not at all unlikely that when the Qumran Community Center was destroyed by earthquake in 31 B.C. the sectaries of Qumran took refuge with their cousins in Damascus. When they returned and rebuilt, they brought the Damascus Covenant with them. Contrast Charles T. Fritsch, "Herod the Great and the Qumran Community," *Journ. of Bibl. Lit.* 74 (1955), pp. 173-81.

22. There is an easy harmonization here without erasing differences. Though John did not regard himself as Elijah, he was still in his mission one who heralded the coming Messiah, Jesus and the Synoptic Gospels do not overestimate his greatness in calling him Elijah. It is not satisfactory to say that John was denying merely the rigidly literalistic identity of himself with Elijah, whereas he reallly was Elijah in a spiritualized sense. We would expect John in that case to express himself more clearly.

23. Jn. 3₁₃; 17₁,₅.

24. Cf. J. Jeremias, *pais theou,* in Kittel's *Theol. Wörterb. z. N.T.,* vol. V, pp. 653 ff.

25. For the extent of the documentary discoveries, see *Rev. Bibl.* 63 (1956), pp. 49-67.

26. Cf. here the study of M. Black, "Servant of the Lord and Son of Man," *Scot. Journ. of Theol.* 6 (1953), pp. 1-11.

27. See the article "Elias" in *Theol. Wörterb. z. N.T.,* vol. II, pp. 942 f.

28. In consistency with this interpretation, Mark uses the same verb *paradidomi* for the delivering up of both John (1₁₄) and Jesus (9₃₁; 10₃₃; 14₄₁ff.;

151,10,15)—a verb employed twice in the LXX version of Is. 5312. Cf. also Rom. 425.

29. See note 10. The title "pregnant one" for the corporate mother probably comes from Is. 714: "Therefore the Lord himself will give you a sign; behold the young woman *is pregnant* and is about to give birth to a son, and she shall call his name Immanuel." In the *United Presbyterian*, Jan. 31, 1955, pp. 13, 15, I suggested that the LXX translated *almah* with *parthenos* in order to indicate their messianic interpretation by simulating the verse to references elsewhere to "the virgin daughter Zion" (Lam. 213, etc. Cf. Micah 410; 52*t*.); but I cautioned: "We must await *proof* that Isaiah 714 was interpreted messianically." This suggestion occasions a close examination of Rev. 12 in relation to Is. 714. In both passages the general picture would be the same, a "sign" consisting of a pregnant woman who gives birth to a son, the differences being accounted for by the pictorial influence of Gen. 379. The specific evidence (aside from striking similarities with the Qumran messianic hymn) narrows to a single, but troublesome word in Rev. 125 in the redundant statement: "She gave birth to *a son, a male*." The tautology was avoided in both the King James and the Revised Standard Versions by omitting the word "son"; but the American Standard Version renders correctly: "a son, a man child." It seems not at all improbable that the author of Revelation in the fullness of his biblical allusions has wished to conflate Is. 714 with Is. 667, combining "give birth to a son" with "give birth to a male." An analogy for "a son, a male" can be found only in the Hebrew of Jer. 2015, where the redundancy serves to emphasize the sex. This may possibly have served to provide the precedent for Rev. 125; but an allusion to the birth of Jeremiah does not seem apposite here, so that in the Greek texts of both Nestle and Westcott, only *arsen*, not *huion*, is printed in the heavier type to indicate quotation. In any case this combination is lacking in the LXX, and it is the LXX which is followed here in the citation of Ps. 29. Yet, with greater fidelity to the Hebrew original than the LXX, John of Patmos refers to the mother as a "woman" rather than a "virgin." But cf. 4 Ezra 938-1044 for this designation.

Assuming this background, Matthew has narrowed the application of Is. 714 from the virgin nation to the virgin Mary, interpreting the birth as physical rather than the endowment of a mature man for his messianic mission. Yet even here the travail of the corporate mother is to be seen in the figure of Rachel weeping for her children 218, cf. here 4 Ezra, *loc. cit.*! The virgin Mary probably represents the true Israel which gave birth, both physically and spiritually, to the Christ. Similarly in the Fourth Gospel, Mary, who precipitates Jesus earthly ministry, may possibly represent the true Israel whose sufferings give birth to the resurrected Christ (21-5; 1621*t*.). In this case, John would be truer to the Jewish background than Matthew, in that the birth of the Christ in both his earthly and heavenly ministry is spiritual rather than physical. This also brings John into close harmony with Rev. 12! By reason of this standpoint of John, there is no room for the nativity stories of Matthew and Luke in his narrative.

30. In his unpublished Ph.D. thesis, *An Ancient Sectarian Interpretation of the Old Testament Prophets: A Study in the Qumran Scrolls and the Damascus Fragments* (1955), pp. 32-61. The passage cited above is 1 QH viii, 10 f. This messianic interpretation is still possible in the translation of Millar Burrows (p. 411); but Chamberlain's syntax is preferable. It reads *SYTR (sether)* rather than *SWTR*, probably construed by Burrows as a *Qal* active participle. The use of the *Qal* of this verb is subject to question.

31. Cf. note 1. See now also A. S. Geyser, "The Youth of John the Baptist. A deduction from the break in the parallel account of the Lucan infancy story," *Novum Testamentum* 1 (1956), pp. 70-74.

## IV. THE TWO MESSIAHS OF AARON AND ISRAEL

1. Brownlee's translation.
2. E.g., the emendations in H. E. del Medico, *Deux manuscrits hébreux de la Mer Morte* (1951); K. Schubert, "Die jüdischen und judenchristlichen Sekten im Licht des Handschriftenfundes von 'En Fashcha,'" *Zeitschr. f. kathol. Theol.* (1952), p. 53, note 103. Cf. the more settled linguistic arguments in M. Black, "Theological conceptions in the Dead Sea Scrolls," *Svensk Exegetisk. Arsbok* 18-19 (1953-54), pp. 85-92.
3. M. Burrows comes to the same conclusion, "The Messiahs of Aaron and Israel," *Angl. Theol. Rev.* 34 (1952), p. 204.
4. *Qumran Cave I*, pp. 108-18.
5. See p. 70.
6. They do not differ significantly from Barthélemy's text (in *Qumran Cave I*) and never affect the meaning of the passage. At one place—namely, in the lacuna in line 21—I now make use of Barthélemy's insertion. I had suggested an insertion, which, however, was longer than the gap in the text would allow. For my Hebrew text see this article in its original edition.
7. *Reshit,* a technical term from the sacrificial vocabulary of the O.T.: "the best," "the first part," that which belonged to the priests. The retention of this term · (even though it does not any longer refer to sacrificial facts) is, besides other things, a sign of the priestly origin of the Essene community.
8. I.e., he "recites the benediction over."
9. Literally "according to his glory," a frequent expression in 1 QSa and synonymous with "according to his rank" in other writings of this strictly hierarchal sect.
10. Targ. Is. 161,5; Targ. Micah 48; cf. *Strack-Billerbeck*, I, pp. 6-11.
11. This expression notes subordination to him.
12. For the Hebrew text in my reconstruction, see this article in the original edition.
13. Namely, regarding the just-mentioned lacuna in the beginning of line 12, where I read *ha-kohen ha-mashiah.* Barthélemy agrees with me that line 11 gives the heading for what follows: "This is the order of the seating of the honored men, the conveners of the assembly [Barthélemy: *invités aux convocations*], for the session of the community's council."

We also agree that line 12 from the fourth word on speaks of the priestly Messiah. This agreement is decisive, since it means that we agree on the meaning of the entire passage. Thus a difference between us exists only with regard to the last two words of line 11 and the lacuna before the word at the beginning of line 12, where there could have been, at most, only two words. Barthélemy reads and amends these four or five words as follows: 'M YWLYD 'L ϙ 'T HMSHYH 'TM, and understands it as an addition to the heading in line 11. This then would read: "This is the order of the seating . . . , when God causes the Messiah to be born with them." As, however, this "with them" does not fit the sentence, Barthélemy has to avail himself of a conjectural alteration of the text. In accordance with the proposal of J. T. Milik he holds the verb, YWLYD for a scribal error in the place of an original YWLYK. Accordingly, he then translates: "au cas où Dieu mènerait le Messie avec eux." The way he continues from there essentially agrees with my reading, in that it understands the passage to speak of the priestly Messiah: "The priest shall come as the head of the whole Congregation of Israel."

My proposal *(HKWHN)* for the lacuna at the beginning of line 12 is just as possible as Barthélemy's suggestion. The decision, therefore, depends on the way the last two words of line 11 should be read. In the original text I could not, with the exception of the initial *aleph*, decipher anything with any degree of certainty there. Barthélemy, who was able to avail himself of better technical aids, claims that on careful examination the reading *YWLYD* is "practically certain." Nevertheless, I should wish to ask whether this is really so certain, especially as he has to make use of a conjecture in order to arrive at a usable text. Above all, it seems to me impossible that *ha-mashiah* "the Messiah" could have been used here in an absolute construction, as referring to the "Messiah of Israel"; the title appears in the texts always in the genitive construction. I suggest that both words under question (at the end of line 11) serve as a further apposition to the "honored men," and that this is thus the end of the heading. With line 12 a new sentence begins, with the subject of the sentence to follow.

14. These terms, which we encounter in 1 QSa several times, stem from Num. 16₂; 11₆; 26₉; Gen. 6₄; Sir. 44₃. (I QSa has, however, *QWR'Y* instead of the O.T. *QRY'Y*).

15. This refers to the camp order and marching formations of the whole people of Israel, divided according to its twelve tribes in Num. 2 and 10₁₂₋₂₈.

16. J. T. Milik comes to the same conclusion, *Rev. Bibl.* 60 (1953), pp. 290 f.

17. *Apocrypha and Pseudepigrapha*, vol. II. p. 294.

18. This view on the two Messiahs was convincingly established in 1947 by Beasly-Murray in an article in the *Journ. of Theol. St.*, 48, pp. 1-13. It was confirmed by B. Otzen, *Studia Theol.*, 7 (1954), pp. 151-54. The objections raised against this position by A. J. B. Higgins, "Priest and Messiah," *Vet. Test.* 3 (1953), pp. 321-36, are resolved by the Qumran texts now under discussion.

19. The best supported reading of Test. Rub. 6₈ is in my opinion the correct one, and not Charles' conjecture.

20. *Christos* in Test. Levi 10₂; Test. Ass. 7₂ is a Christian interpolation, as is shown by the weak support both of these readings get from textual criticism.

21. The added "God and man" is a Christian interpolation.

22. Excluding later Christian interpolations.

23. The same expectation is also shared by Jubil. 31₁₃₋₂₀. This is significant, since the Book of Jubilees belongs too to the cycle of Essene writings, as is shown by the discovery of fragments of Jubilees in original Hebrew text at Qumran.

24. I have shown this especially with regard to concepts as "spirit" and "flesh," See p. 105 and 101.

25. "Die in Palästina gefundenen hebr. Texte und das Neue Testament," *Zeitschr. f. Theol. u. Kirche* 47 (1950), pp. 196 ff., *et passim*.

26. R. de Vaux, *Rev. Bibl.* 60 (1953), p. 86.

27. Both of the CD manuscripts stem from around the tenth and twelfth centuries A.D. J. T. Milik arrives at the same conclusion, *Verbum Domini* 30 (1952), pp. 39 f.

28. The given text has *MSHYHW* instead of *MSHYHY*. Textual errors through the confusion of *Waw* and *Yodh* are not infrequent in CD (i, 16, 21; iii, 5; iv, 8 [cf. iv, 10], 12, 17; x, 7). This frequent confusion of *Waw* and *Yodh* shows that

the archetype from which the medieval copies of CD stem must have had the same form of writing as the Qumran texts, where it is usually impossible to distinguish between *Waw* and *Yodh*.

29. This is clear from the coins minted during the second insurrection, A. Reifenberg, *Ancient Jewish Coins* (Jerusalem, 1947), Table XIII, No. 169. The parallel has also been pointed out by J. T. Milik, *Rev. Bibl.* 60 (1953), p. 292.

30. His real name was Shimon ben Kosba, as is evidenced by the letter written by him which was found in 1952 in a cave in Waddy Murabbaat, see *Rev. Bibl.* 60 (1953), p. 277. Bar Kokba (Son of Stars) was a messianic interpretation of his name according to Num. 2417.

31. E. Schürer, *Geschichte des jüdischen Volkes*, vol. I (4th ed., 1901), p. 219.

32. *Ibid.*, p. 249.

33. *Ibid.* and F. M. Abel, *Les Livres des Maccabées* (1949), pp. 260 f., in reference to 1 Macc. 1441-47.

34. Josephus, *Ant.* 13, 11, 1 (§ 301).

35. Schürer, *op. cit.*, p. 269; Reifenberg, *op. cit.*, Table II, No. 8, 9, 12.

36. Schürer, *op. cit.*, p. 275; Reifenberg, *op. cit.*, Table II, No. 13.

37. Schürer, *op. cit.*, p. 285; Reifenberg, *op. cit.*, p. 15, ascribes these coins (Reifenberg, Table II, No. 18-20) to Hyrcanus II (63-40 B.C.), who really was only high priest. In this Reifenberg follows the thesis of E. Merzbacher, *Zeitschr. f. Numismatik* 3 (1876), pp. 201 ff. There is, however, the serious objection already stressed by Schürer (*op. cit.*, p. 349) that there are no sources to support the view that Jonathan stands for Hyrcanus II. Reifenberg, referring to J. Derenbourg, *Essai sur l'histoire et la géographie de la Palestine* (1867), pp. 146-48, writes that talmudic sources perhaps can support the suggestion that Hyrcanus' Hebrew name was Jannaeus, the equivalent of Jonathan. However, the story in bSanh. 19a, to which Derenbourg refers, is without any historical merit. It is a highly revised form of the events in 47 B.C., recorded in Josephus, *Ant.* 14, 9, 4: The young Herod is summoned by Hyrcanus II to answer before the Sanhedrin in Jerusalem for a murder committed by him. Nobody, however, dares to voice the accusation against him or to pass judgment against him. The only person who dares is the Pharisee Sameas, who rises against him and upbraids the Sanhedrin for its cowardice. In bSanh. 19a the point of the story is changed and all names are changed. Instead of Herod it is "a slave of King Jannaeus" who is accused of the murder, and the owner responsible for the slave under trial, the King (Alexander) Jannaeus is summoned before the Sanhedrin. It is impossible to claim from this that Hyrcanus II's Hebrew name was Jannaeus/Jonathan.

38. Schürer, *op. cit.*, p. 284; Reifenberg, *op. cit.*, Table II, No. 14 and 16.

39. Cf. the national decision in 141 B.C. (p. 60). In this sense the somewhat different title of John Hyrcanus on a few coins could be understood: "Johanan, the High Priest, the head of the Jewish Community"; cf. Schürer, *op. cit.*, p. 269; Reifenberg, *op. cit.*, Table II, No. 11, cf. No. 7.

40. Josephus, *Ant.* 13, 11, 1 (§ 301), uses an almost identical phrase concerning Aristobulus.

41. Cf. K. G. Kuhn, *Die älteste Textgestalt der Psalmen Salomons* (1937), pp. 57 f. and Plate viii.

42. Schürer, *op. cit.*, pp. 296, 300.

43. In Test. Levi 815 things are a little different; there it is said about the new priest of the eschatological times that "his coming will be as pleasant as that of a prophet of the Most High, a prophet from the seed of Abraham, our father."

44. In Jn. 614f. the new prophet and the king have coalesced into one figure.

45. It is noteworthy that this union of the three offices in one person is also expressed in the Epilogue over John Hyrcanus, Josephus, *Ant.* 13, 10, 7 (§ 299 f.): "He was deemed by God worthy of the highest three honors: of sovereignty over the people, of high priesthood and of the prophetic office, for the Divine was with him."

46. J. T. Milik calls our attention to another connection (*Rev. Bibl.* 60 (1953), p. 291): Hippolytus, in his commentary on the blessings of Isaac, Jacob and Moses, remarks that Jesus is both king and priest in one person, as he is descended from both the tribes of Judah and Levi. Evidence for the view that Hippolytus was familiar not only with the (Davidic) Messiah of Judah but also with a Levitic Messiah, and that he saw both of these messianic expectations as fulfilled in the person of Jesus has been carefully collected by L. Mariès, "Le Messie issu de Lévi chez Hippolyte de Rome," *Mélanges J. Lebreton*, I (*Rech. de Science Rel.* 39 (1951), pp. 381-96). At the end of his article, Mariès also shows that this "Messiah out of Levi" of whom Hippolytus speaks must be related to the *Testament of the Twelve Patriarchs*. This relationship was pointed out by N. Bonwetsch, in his translation of Hippolytus' exposition of the Blessings of Jacob, *Drei Georgisch erhaltene Schriften von Hippolytus* (Texte und Untersuchungen, N.F. 11.), 1904, p. 25; cf. the Introduction, *ibid.*, p. xii. Bonwetsch quotes still further evidence from patristic literature for this theory, such as two passages in Ambrose and *Epiph. Haer.* 78, 13. Mariès replies to this that these passages can certainly be traced back to the influence of Hippolytus, and he wonders whether any church father before Hippolytus had drawn on this tradition. Cf. Chrysostom, *hom.* 3, 7 in II Cor. 112 (Migne, *Patr. Gr.* 61, 417).

### V. THE LORD'S SUPPER AND THE COMMUNAL MEAL AT QUMRAN

1. Cf. p. 97.

2. See M. Burrows, *The Dead Sea Scrolls*, pp. 271 ff.

3. It is significant that the congregations of the sect found in their various locations are *magor*—"sojourning"; cf. *paroikia*, Ps.Sol. 1717; Mart. Polyc., inscr.; also 1 Pet. 117; 2 Clem. 51.

4. I.e., wherever several men of the community are together.

5. I.e., the man of lower rank in the community shall obey the man of higher rank.

6. This prescription that each person belonging to the Order must obey his superior in regard to his work agrees with Josephus (*Bell.* 2,8,6): "The Essenes do not undertake any work to which they are not assigned by their superiors."

7. Here *yahad* is not the substantive, "the community," but adverbial "in common," cf. my article in *Zeitschr. f. Theol. u. Kirche* (1950), p. 198, note 1.

8. This corresponds completely with the prescription of CD x, 23, which now becomes intelligible with the help of our passage in 1 QS. (This is further evidence for CD belonging to the writings of this sect; cf. note 10). CD x, 23 ff., provides in its prescriptions for the strict observance of the Sabbath: "To eat and to drink is permitted only when one is within the Community (camp). (But) if one is on a way travelling and goes down to bathe (the ritual bath is meant), one is allowed to drink while standing (in the water), but one is not to draw (water) into any vessel."

9. Women are never mentioned in 1 QS. This, too, is a significant point of agreement between it and the Essenes in Josephus.

10. Literally: "There shall not be lacking a priest"; the sentence has a literal parallel in CD xiii, 2. Josephus also mentions the "ten," *Bell.* 2,8,9.

11. I.e., the priest shall preside.

12. I.e., in this order of precedence.

13. The Qumran texts always describe the wine used at the cult meal by the word *tirosh*, which means "grape juice"; it is remarkable that they never use the word *yayin*, "wine"; cf. *Qumran Cave I*, p. 118: *Tirosh* as "une appellation rituelle poétique" preferred to the mundane expression *yayin*.

14. For *reshit*, "first portion," see note 22.

15. For their meals they naturally—being far from the Temple—did not have meat offered for sacrifices. Yet their meals, with their monastic singularity, were still subject to the regulations for ritual purity prescribed for the meals of the priests in the Temple. For this reason, their food was prepared only by priests, Josephus, *Ant.* 18, 1, 5; cf. E. Schürer *Geschichte des jüdischen Volkes*, II (4th ed., 1907), p. 666, n. 63. Thus they understood their meals as a substitute for the Temple sacrifices. This is what seems to me to be the meaning of Josephus' statement (*ibid.*): ". . . being excluded from the Common Court of the Temple they offer sacrifices by themselves."

16. See *Strack-Billerbeck,* vol. IV, pp. 621 and 628. This was my interpretation in the original edition of this essay.

17. See p. 71.

18. *Qumran Cave I*, pp. 108 ff.

19. This is an important parallel to Lk. 2230ᵃ, where Jesus gives his disciples this promise for the time of the eschatological consummation: "You shall eat and drink at my table in my Kingdom." Cf. also Lk. 1415.

20. Cf. for this my article, "The Two Messiahs of Aaron and Israel," in this volume.

21. The text is now available with a French translation in *Qumran Cave I*, pp. 111 ff; cf. this volume, pp. 56 f.

22. *R-sh-t* = *reshit* in 1 QS vi, 5, is the technical term in the sacrificial terminology of the Old Testament: "the best, the first portion," which went to the priests. The fact that the Essenes retained this sacrificial terminology for their cult meal is still another indication that the cult meal is originallly derived from the priestly meal in the Jerusalem Temple.

23. It may be pointed out as a marginal note that the last meal of Jesus with his twelve disciples—or, after the departure of Judas from the feast, with the eleven—complies with this requirement.

24. Cf. *Strack-Billerbeck,* vol IV, p. 634.

25. The unusual order "wine-bread" in Did. 9 is hard to explain. It contradicts, on the one side, the accounts of the institution at the last meal of Jesus (where the order is "bread-wine") and also the usage in the church, as the Didache itself knows: "But let no one eat or drink of your Eucharist. . . ." On the other hand, it also contradicts the parallels in the Qumran texts, where the order always is "bread-wine." The reference to the Jewish custom of the *passah-kiddush*, or the blessing of the cup, which preceded even the opening prayer of the meal proper, is not very helpful. According to Jewish custom, the meal itself began first with the opening grace over the bread. *Strack-Billerbeck,* vol. IV, pp. 616 ff; also H. Leitzmann, *Mass and Lord's Supper* (Eng. transl., 1954), pp. 166 ff.; M. Dibelius, "Die Mahlgebete der Didache," *Zeitschr. f. d. neutest. Wissensch.* 37 (1938), p. 33.

26. *Strack-Billerbeck,* vol. IV, p. 75.

**27.** *The Eucharistic Words of Jesus* (Eng. transl., 1955), p. 60.

**28.** *Op. cit.,* p. 60, n. 7; cf. p. 133.

**29.** Paul's use of the expression "the cup of the blessing" (1 Cor. 10₁₆) could also be understood as an indication that the blessing over the wine was the closing prayer at the end of the meal; this would be the case if this expression corresponded to the rabbinic terminus technicus *kos shel berakah,* which describes the cup of wine over which the thanksgiving after the meal was said. See *Strack-Billerbeck,* vol. IV, pp. 628 and 630 f., and Jeremias, *op. cit.,* p. 60. But this is by no means certain. The full formulation of Paul's "the cup of blessing which we bless" does not exactly suggest an established technical formula. We may as well think of the "blessing over the wine" together with "the blessing over the bread" in the above-cited passage from the Qumran texts as a parallel, whereby *barek,* "to bless," corresponds to the New Testament *eulogein.*

**30.** The Greek text was edited by P. Batiffol, *Studia Patristica* I (1889). There is an English translation by E. W. Brooks, *Joseph and Aseneth* (*Translations of Early Documents* II, 6, 1918). German translation by P. Riessler, *Theol. Quartalschrift* 103 (1922), pp. 1 ff. and 145 ff.; P. Riessler, *Altjüdisches Schrifttum ausserhalb der Bibel* (1928), pp. 497 ff.

**31.** "The Last Supper," *Exp. Times* 64 (1952/53), pp. 4-8; a reply by Joach: Jeremias (*ibid.*), pp. 91 ff.

**32.** There may be a literary parallel to such a novelistic adornment and enlargement of Genesis in the scroll from Cave I at Qumran, which was earlier téntatively and, as we now know, wrongly, called the Apocalypse of Lamech. This scroll was unrolled in Jerusalem the winter of 1955-56, and the first reports indicate that it contains a paraphrased and enlarged retelling of Genesis, especially chaps. 12-14. [Cols. ii, xix-xxii of this text and a summary of the whole document is now available with an English translation: *A Genesis Apocryphon,* ed. N. Avigad and Y. Yadin (Jerusalem, Hebrew University Press, 1956), Ed. note.]

**33.** A translation from Hebrew was conjectured by P. Riessler, *op. cit.* (1922), pp. 1 ff. However, already expressions like "immortality," "incorruption" and many other cannot really be translations from the Hebrew. In my opinion, *Joseph and Aseneth* was originally composed in Greek, as would be natural for a writing of the Jewish community in Egypt.

**34.** A Jewish writing which extols and propagates the conversion of pagans into Jewish proselytes must belong to the time before Hadrian's legislation against circumcision (*ca.* A.D. 135). The latest possible date is the beginning of the second century. A.D. The actual date may be considerably earlier, first century A.D.; cf. V. Aptowitzer, *Hebrew Union College Annual* (1924) pp. 239 ff. It seems, however, questionable to date the writing as far back as the first century B.C. (Kilpatrick, *op. cit.*: between 100 and 30 B.C.).

**35.** To this is added as a third characteristic, mentioned in three of the five passages, that he "is anointed with the blessed oil." Although this third element does not interest us in the present connection, it should be pointed out that it is significant for the understanding of the "anointing" in 1 Jn. 2₂₀, ₂₇.

**36.** Cf. Kohler in *The Jewish Encyclopedia,* II, cols. 172 ff.; Riessler, *loc. cit.*

**37.** This fact—apart from other reasons—invalidates Batiffol's hypothesis (*op. cit.,* pp. 7 ff.) that the repentance and conversion of Aseneth is a Christian insertion into an original story about the love and marriage of Aseneth and Joseph. The very part which he excludes as Christian has especially clear and specific Jewish traits.

38. For this reason, we cannot argue as, e.g., E. W. Brooks, *op. cit.*, p. xi, "that the book in its present shape is the work of a Christian writer will be at once recognized by every reader, the reference to the sacred bread and cup and chrism, by which the ceremonies of the Eucharist and Confirmation are clearly meant, being sufficient to place the fact beyond doubt."

39. To this must also be added the words of the archangel Michael immediately before he places a piece of the heavenly honeycomb into Aseneth's mouth, after he had first himself eaten a piece thereof (cf. the Qumran provision for the priest to eat the first portion): "This honeycomb is the spirit of life, and it has been made by the bees of the paradise of abundance out of the dew of the roses of life, which are in the paradise of God, and out of each blossom; of this the angels and all elect of God and all sons of the Most High do eat; and no one who eats of it will ever die" (16₁₄). There is nothing specifically Christian in this passage either. All of these expressions are to be understood as Jewish, belonging to this same kind of sectarian Judaism with its cult meal. The juxtaposition of "Angels" and "Elect" is found also in 1 QM xii, 1, 4-5. If this passage had been written by a Christian it should have contained some christological reference—whatever its form—instead of the reference to dew of roses in paradise as the source of the food.

40. *Op. cit.* (1922), pp. 4 ff., and (1928), p. 1303. With the Qumran material available, we find many more similarities between the Essenes and *Joseph and Aseneth*. In our context it may, however, suffice with the ones already mentioned.

41. Regarding the third element in our passage, the oil of anointing, the interpreting genitive is "of incorruption."

42. Cf. p. 68.

43. See pp. 80 f.

44. The hypotheses of Dupont-Sommer, lately restated in a similar form by John Allegro, that the Master of the Essene Order, the "Teacher of Righteousness," had, according to the Qumran texts, died upon a cross and was believed by the community to have risen from the dead, and that his return for the Last Judgment was expected, are constructions which have no basis in the new texts.

45. Extensive bibliographic references are naturally beyond the scope of this article. We will only refer to a few scholars whose work is of special interest for our question proper. An extensive bibliography is found in Joach. Jeremias, *The Eucharistic Words of Jesus*, pp. 177-83. It has to be especially noted that this article is a purely historical and literary New Testament study. It does not aim at taking a stand for or against an ecclesiastical interpretation of the Eucharist, be it Lutheran or Reformed. If our findings prove to be correct, they may well have bearing upon the foundations and interpretations implied in the doctrines of the churches concerning the Eucharist. Yet, what we have to say has, as historical research, no such aim, nor does the doctrine of the churches serve as our point of departure.

46. See especially M. Dibelius, *From Tradition to Gospel* (Eng. transl., 1935), pp. 205 ff.; J. Jeremias, *op. cit.*, pp. 102 ff.; R. Bultmann. *Theology of the N.T.* (Eng. transl., vol. I, 1951), p. 146.

47. The Matthean text (26₂₆–₂₉) is of less importance, being so close to the Marcan text.

48. This has been shown—in my judgment, irrefutably—by Jeremias, *op. cit.*, pp. 106-18.

49. W. Marxsen has lately tried to prove the Pauline text of 1 Cor. 11 to be closest to the original form, "Der Ursprung des Abendmahls," *Evang. Theologie* 12 (1952/53), pp. 293 ff. I do not find his evidence convincing.

50. This, too, seems to me to have been well proved by Jeremias, *op. cit.*, pp. 118-32. We may strengthen his evidence by pointing out that the expression "*polloi* (many)" = "the whole, all" is paralleled in the Qumran texts by the frequent word *rabbim* or *ha-rabbim* = "the whole." In 1 QS often *ha-rabbim* = "the entire community."

51. Cf. Jeremias, *op. cit.*, pp. 68 and 108. Since this is an editorial remark by Mark, there is no force in the argument that the blessing over the bread and the wine and thus the words of institution were spoken first after the meal had begun. If we isolate the original cult formula, the blessings could just as well have been pronounced at the beginning of the meal.

52. Jeremias, *op. cit.*, pp. 133 ff.

53. King James Version has the word "new" also in Mk. 14₂₄, but RSV follows the more dependable manuscripts in leaving it out. [Ed. note.]

54. *Op. cit.*, p. 146.

55. This is an example—in its simplest form—of the law in folk composition to lay the emphasis on the last of the elements in a doublet or triplet. Dibelius, *op. cit.*, p. 251.

56. The strictly parallel form of the words of institution, as later given by Justin, *Apol.* 66₃ ("this is my body—this is my blood") is, therefore, not original, as Bultmann argues (*op. cit.*, p. 146), but is a later liturgical adjustment.

57. So also Jeremias, *op. cit.*, pp. 64 ff. and 68.

58. The Jewish Passover has a double aspect, looking back at the deliverance from Egypt and—reassured thereby—looking forward to the coming messianic deliverance; the eschatological twin saying of Jesus relates itself to this latter aspect.

59. *Op. cit.*, pp. 115-18.

60. Luke had before him the text of Mk. 14₂₃, the words introducing the cup, and he used it (Lk. 22₂₀) in the form of the liturgical tradition he had inherited. It is hard to imagine that he would have created deliberately a second similar saying in v. 17.

61. This conclusion is further supported by the different position of the eschatological sayings in Mark and Luke: in the former, it follows the words of institution; in the latter it precedes them. Cf. Jeremias, *op. cit.*, p. 69.

62. See Lk. 22₁₄-₂₃ in the RSV, where vv.19ᵦ-20 are taken out of the text proper. This is "the longer text," missing in some manuscripts. If the longer text is accepted, its removal is due to a scribal tradition where one wanted to avoid what wrongly appeared to be a repetition. [Ed. note]

63. Cf. Dibelius, *op. cit.*, p. 211.

64. Yet, let me emphasize that my concern is not to refute Jeremias' thesis that the Last Supper was a Passover meal, nor is it my concern to prove that the words of institution proper exclude the possibility of a Passover setting. Neither can be claimed. I want rather to show how nothing in the formula of institution itself speaks for or requires such a setting. We approach the formula with an *exegetical* question. The *historical* question whether Jesus' Last Supper really was or was not a Passover meal is thereby not in focus.

65. R. Jirmeja; jPes. 10, 37c 27, with two parallel passages; see *Strack-Billerbeck*, vol. IV, p. 61; Jeremias, *op. cit.*, p. 145. The exegetical remark of Raba (fourth century A.D.), cited also by Jeremias, *loc. cit.*, says nothing about such a Passover rubric.

66. I take this example as one of the many mentioned by Jeremias, but what is true about this one applies to all.

67. The two interpretive statements in rabbinic literature, which are closest

to those in the words of institution are the ones already quoted: (a) the old Aramaic statement about the unleavened bread of Passover: "This is the bread of affliction"; (b) Rab's statement (third century A.D.) at a meal on the 9th of Ab, the day commemorating the destruction of Jerusalem: "He took a piece of decayed bread, strew ashes on it and said: 'This is the meal of the 9th of Ab'" (see Jeremias, op. cit., p. 36). If these were really to correspond, in form, to Jesus' words: "This is my body" and "this is my blood," the first would be, "This is the affliction," instead of "This is the bread of affliction," and the second, "This is the 9th of Ab," instead of "This is the meal of the 9th of Ab." Vice versa, Jesus' words would be, "This is the bread of my body" and "This is the wine of my blood."

68. Nor is it possible to find a reflection of the so-called "Haburah-meal" in the cult formula; see Jeremias, op. cit., pp. 25 f.

69. Cf. ibid., pp. 18 ff.

70. Cf. Strack-Billerbeck, IV, pp. 72 and 628. Where there was no such person present, it is natural to suppose that it was the pater familias himself who would say the closing prayer. There was no call for this at Jesus' last meal with the disciples.

71. At Qumran, this leader has to be a priest, i.e., of Aaronic descent, a fact in accord with the priestly origin of the Order (cf. p. 68). At his last meal, Jesus presides over the Twelve as Master. Yet, the company of his disciples, and thus also the meal, is definitely of lay character. The aspect of priestly descent is totally missing, all in accordance with the entire teachings of Jesus. Consequently, the community of disciples of Jesus is no "Essene Community," but is a new community of its own.

72. See E. Lohmeyer, Theol. Rundschau, N.F. 10 (1938), pp. 92 ff., and Jeremias, op. cit., pp. 42 and 137.

73. For "many" = "all"; cf. note 50.

74. So also Jeremias, op. cit., p. 132: this piece of tradition can be traced at least back to the early forties A.D., i.e., one decade after the death of Jesus.

75. Cf. p. 80.

76. "Die Mahlgebete der Didache," Zeitschr. f. d. neutest. Wiss. 37 (1938), pp. 32 ff.; cf. also Jeremias, op. cit., pp. 84 f.

77. The same sequence was apparently followed at the celebration of the Quartadecimans: Agape and Eucharist (Ep. Apost. 15); see B. Lohse, Das Passafest der Quartadecimaner (1953), p. 86. In this connection see especially H. Schürmann, Biblica 32 (1951), pp. 364 ff. and 522 ff.; idem, Quellenkritische Untersuchungen des lukanischen Abendmahlberichtes (Lk. 22₇-₃₈), N.T. Abhandl. 19-20 (1953-56). According to Schürmann, the Lucan juxtaposition of the Passover meal with an eschatological twin saying and the cult formula with the words of institution (cf. p. 80) reflects the structure of the cult meal in the church at this time: first the meal (vv. 15-18), then the adjoining Eucharist (vv. 19-20). This seems probable to me, especially since Luke otherwise (both in the Gospel and in Acts) tries to avoid doubtlets. When he accepts such an obvious "doublet" at this point, it indicates that he actually did not consider it a doublet. Thus Lk. 22₁₅-₂₀ is another instance where the Christian cult meal in the time of Luke must have been celebrated along the lines of 1 Cor. 11 and Did. 9-10.

78. The other texts all prove to belong to later synoptic strata. As for the "renunciation" in Mk. 14₂₅, it is worth observing that, while Luke unequivocally speaks of the Passover, there is no such reference in Mark. This is the more

important, since the eschatological saying of Jesus here is attached to the Marcan cult formula.

79. See Jeremias, *op. cit.*, p. 117. The Greek behind "I have earnestly desired" actually reads "With desire I have desired," an expression which is a Hebraism, not an Aramaism. The Qumran texts have now shown that the use of Hebrew, as a religious language, was much more common in the New Testament period than has been hitherto assumed. Thence the possibility that in Luke's source this text might have been Hebrew. The Qumran texts also make frequent use of this type of emphatic construction. Granted a Hebrew source, the expression is not due to the Lucan imitation of Septuagint style.

80. Cf. note 77.

81. Jeremias, *op. cit.*, pp. 165 ff., understands these words of Jesus as a "vow of abstinence." I question, however, whether it is possible to deduce this from the text. Essentially, however, it makes little difference whether it is a vow or simply an emphatic renunciation.

82. This conclusion is not Lohse's, nor could it be, since he takes the Passover character of Jesus' last meal for granted—thereby only referring to Jeremias— and considers the saying in Lk. 22:15-18 as genuine words of Jesus, spoken at that occasion. Nevertheless, he has clearly recognized the basic connection between Lk. 22:15-18 and the Passover of the Quartadeciman sect.

## VI. NEW LIGHT ON TEMPTATION, SIN, AND FLESH IN THE NEW TESTAMENT

1. See p. 113. The reader of this essay will soon be aware of why the Greek term *peirasmos* is retained, instead of "temptation." *Peirasmos* has, in fact, a double or triple sense (temptation—trial—tribulation—test) which is impossible to hold together in any English translation. It is this complexity of the word which is the key to a proper understanding of the passages where it occurs. [Ed. note]

2. See pp. 111 f.

3. See p. 111.

4. "Paraenetic" is the technical term for ethical teaching and exhortations as found, e.g., toward the end of Paul's Epistles. It comes from the Greek verb *paraineo* = "exhort." [Ed. note]

5. See p. 110.

6. In its origins the sect certainly reaches back as far as the second century before Christ. The community center was built at Khirbet Qumran around 130-120 B.C., and the sect lived there until A.D. 68, when Qumran was taken and occupied by the Romans. *All* texts from Qumran were written *before* this time. The original date of the writings, especially 1 QS and 1 QpHab, goes back definitely to the first century B.C. and possibly even to the second.

7. I supposed, and expressed the opinion from the beginning, that these finds contained the writings of the Essenes, and this has been confirmed anew by every publication. On the basis of the excavation at Qumran, which R. de Vaux has been leading since 1951, there can be no more doubt as to this. Cf. R. de Vaux, "Fouilles au Khirbet Qumran," *Rev. Bibl.* 60 (1953), pp. 83-106 and 61 (1954), pp. 206-36. [Now also *ibid.* 63 (1956), pp. 533-77. Ed. note.]

8. Or: "Everything that is and has been." The participle *nifal* can have perfect as well as future meaning.

9. "To come from the source of light" means "to be a man of the spirit of truth" and "to come from the source of darkness" means "to be a man of the

spirit of perversion," just as in, e.g., 1 Jn. 4₆ there are only two sorts of men, those who are "of God" and those who are "not of God," parallel with the distinction between "the spirit of truth and the spirit of error." 1 John renders in content as well as in expression the conception of this Jewish-Palestinian sect. This explains the fact that "spirit of truth" appears here really as an anthropological concept. The fact that the antithesis is here not the "spirit of perversion" but the "spirit of error" is not a difference from the terminology of the writings of the sect. On the contrary: already two lines farther on in 1 QS it says, "And through the angel of darkness comes *error* . . ." Having recognized that "spirit of truth" is part of a terminology taken over from the sect gives us the key to the understanding of the description of the Paraclete as "spirit of truth" (Jn. 14₁₇, 15₂₆, 16₁₃), an important connection which, however, cannot be further developed here.

10. My essay in *Zeitschr. f. Theol. u. Kirche* 47 (1950), p. 211, had already pointed out that the texts of the sect indicate clearly how the preaching of Zarathustra affected Judaism. At that time the writings of the sect were not yet at our disposal. They now completely confirm what I said at that time. This decisive connection for the history of religion can be only briefly presented here. My article on the Manual of Discipline and Iranian Religion *(Zeitschr. f. Theol. u. Kirche* 49, 1952, pp. 296-316) handles the problem more closely.

11. Here is the equivalent to the "ruler" or "prince" (archon) of the New Testament, e.g., Mk. 3₂₂, Mt. 9₃₄, Jn. 12₃₁, 1 Cor. 2₆₋₈, Eph. 2₂. God as well as Satan has such in his army, or (in another image) in his court, always with specific duties. In the Qumran texts and in Jewish apocalyptics—and not in the gnosis—is the place of origin of this idea. See the collection of supporting passages in K. G. Kuhn, *Sifre Numeri*, (Rabbinical Texts II, 2; 1954), p. 514, note 83, and in the appendix pp. 698-700. The "Prince of lights" is to be found also in CD v, 18; as "Prince of light" in 1 QM xiii, 10; cf. Dan. 8₂₅.

12. *Mastema*, "hostility" of the devil; in the *Book of Jubilees*, "Mastema" is used as a proper name of Satan.

13. This refers to the army of Satan, his elect ones, those who are by predestination allotted to him; cf. further my article in *Zeitschr. f. Theol. u. Kirche* 47 (1950), p. 200.

14. For this "helping" and its correspondence in the New Testament, see pp. 108 ff.

15. Here I can only point to the significance of these dualistic catalogues of "deeds" for the "catalogue of virtues and of vices" of the New Testament (especially Gal. 5₁₆₋₂₃, Eph. 5₇₋₁₁). See further Siegfried Wibbing, on the catalogues of virtues and vices in the New Testament (Thesis, Heidelberg, 1956). Cf. also my article in *Zeitschr. f. Theol. u. Kirche,* 1950, pp. 206 ff. What was said there about Barn. 18-20 and Did. 1-6 is now confirmed by this passage from the writings of the sect, which was not yet known at that time.

16. The text now published in the *Osar.*

17. Ten members is the minimum number for an independent congregation.

18. *Ha-rabbim*, "the many," as often in the New Testament *hoi polloi*, the "entirety" (here: of the members of the congregation).

19. I suppose it means: in turns, one-third of the congregation watching each night.

20. This means: to speak the prayers which are prescribed for special times.

21. In the collection of regulations for punishment of the congregation it says in 1 QS vii, 10: "He who lies down and falls asleep in the meeting of the

members of the congregation (shall be given reformatory measures) for thirty days." Here they are not, I suppose, thinking of "watching" in its meaning of the required attitude for the fight with "Belial and the people of his lot," but simply taking a necessary precaution for the discipline of the congregation. The punitive measures probably consist of exclusion from the common meals, which in the Essene religion have the nature of a service of worship, tied together with the reduction of the food rations by one quarter, and of exclusion from the council meetings of the congregation. For the proper evaluation of the magnitude of the punishment for falling asleep in the meeting, thirty days, let us compare other punishments: there is the possibility of imposing such measures for ten days, thirty days, three months, six months, a year, two years, and beyond that of complete exclusion forever. For example: "The man, whose spirit (note again the characteristic concept of "spirit") sways (so that he strays) from the basic order of the congregation, and sins against the truth, and walks in a closed heart, but turns back from these ways again" (1 QS vii, 18 f.) is punished with two years' exclusion. But he who does not turn back (cf. the New Testament *metanoein*, "repent") is excluded forever. Lighter transgressions: "He who shows himself naked before another, unless he is severely ill: six months" (1 QS vii, 14).

22. See also the New Testament, e.g., Mk. 16₁₇, 1 Cor. 15₅₀, Gal. 1₁₆, Eph. 6₁₂, Hebr. 2₁₄.

23. It is most significant that the terminology used by Paul in Rom. 8₃, "flesh of sin," corresponds to this. In both passages it means the existence of man as such, the sphere of the human. It is the fact that Christ became man which is stated in Rom. 8₃: "God sent him in the form of the *flesh of sin*."

24. This refers to the angels.

25. This means: to the community of flesh, which the worms will eat; cf. 1 QS xi, 21. See also the hymn which the Sons of Light sing as a song of battle and of victory (1 QM xii, 11-12): "Your (God's) sword devours the sinful flesh."

26. 1 QH iii, 21 ff.

27. Hebrew *belial* (1 QH ii, 22) need not be taken as the personal name "Belial," the devil. This personal meaning is ascertained for other passages, especially in 1 QS, but the term can be taken abstractly, as it is in the Old Testament: "being good for nothing." This abstract meaning seems more meaningful here and elsewhere in 1 QH 1, e.g. iv, 10.

28. What this usage of the "righteousness of God" means for contrast to the Pauline concept cannot be discussed here; it requires a separate presentation.

29. In 1 Jn. 2₁₆ "flesh" has the same meaning: "the lust of the flesh" does not mean specifically the sexual urge, but generally the striving of the natural man, which—because he is "flesh"—is directed toward sin.

30. Cf. further Eph. 5₉, "the fruit of light," and note 15.

31. This context of dualism of "light-darkness" with the *Ethic* of the "doing of righteousness" in contrast to "sinning" which is so characteristic of Paul as well as of the texts of the sect, *is lacking in the gnosis*. This is why Ernst Fuchs (*Die Freiheit des Glaubens*, 1949, pp. 39 ff.), in his interpretation, taking gnosis as the origin, can do nothing with the concept "weapons of righteousness" in Rom. 6₁₂ ff. He says: the "weapons of error" are wrong weapons, and the "weapons of righteousness" are right weapons. How meaningful in contrast to this is the concept when seen with the texts of the sect as background! The fact that Paul calls the ungodly power Sin and includes in this word both the power and the deed is also understandable from the point of view of the gnosis, whereas it is really characteristic for the connection with this Jewish-Palestinian sect.

This becomes particularly clear in Rom. 5:12: "Wherefore, as by one man (through the fact that he sinned!) sin entered into the world, (as a *power*) and death by sin (as a necessary consequence)." Here, too, it is seen that Fuchs (*op. cit.*, pp. 18 ff.) in his interpretation from gnosis does not reach the real meaning of the Pauline thought. He says: "Death should be the subject in the first phrase rather than sin . . . Paul substitutes first in Rom. 5:12 *sin for death* . . . but by so doing he loses the basis of the Gnostic comparison of the one (Adam) with the other as his real self (Christ)." To be sure, if one interprets from the point of view of gnosis, the "basis" for the Pauline comparison is missing. But there is nothing "substituted" here. Here, if anywhere, the word "sin" has its original meaning and strength.

32. Even in the "I"-style; cf. p. 102.

33. 1 QS ii, 20; iii, 14; iv, 6-26; v, 21-24; vi, 17; vii, 18-23; ix, 14, 15, 18.

34. Completely different is the sense of the "dwelling" of the "spirit" in the pious man in the quotation of unknown origin in Jas. 4:5: "the spirit he has made to dwell in us." Here spirit is not, as is seen from the parallels in the Shepherd of Hermas and especially in Herm. mand. 3:1, the spirit of God in the Christian sense, but the spirit of man, that is, the good spirit, certainly given by God, but given in creation, which man *has*, "his good I, that must assert itself against the bad I," as M. Dibelius rightly says in his commentary to the passage. That corresponds exactly to the view of the Qumran texts of the pre-destined "spirit of truth" which takes the pious man to itself at the time of creation, of "*his*, the pious man's, spirit" which stands in battle with the "spirit of perversion."

35. In Mt. 7:16–20, the way of thinking of the Jewish sect is quite unbroken, and in sharp contrast to Paul: as the tree, so the fruit. A good tree *cannot* bear bad fruit, and a bad tree *cannot* bear good fruit. On the other hand, 1 Jn. 3:9 also speaks in this deterministic way: every man who is born of God *cannot sin*. John here makes use of traditional deterministic language. Nevertheless, in the writings of John, as in those of Paul, this determinism is broken through and over-come—in spite of the retention of the terminology—by the concept of "faith," and that means: by the christology. According to the Gospel of John, man is not irrevocably determined through his origin either "from above," "from God," or "from below," "from the world," "from the devil" (even though John uses this terminology widely); rather, man becomes another through the fact that he believes in Jesus as the Saviour sent by God. Through this "he is born" (Jn. 3:3 ff.), he receives a *new origin;* from being one "born of the flesh" he becomes one "born of the spirit," because he believes in Jesus (Jn. 3:6 in connection with 3:14–16).

36. "To become unsteady," 1 QS vii, 18; xi, 12.

37. Only in 1 Cor. 5:5 does Paul speak differently of "spirit" in relation to "flesh": the exclusion of the sinner from the congregation means that he is given over to Satan, and results in the annihilation of his "flesh," that is, of his body, his earthly life, so that the "spirit" (which possesses him irrevocably, and which he *has*) may be saved in the final judgment. Here Paul remains in the traditional scheme, similar to that of the texts of the sect, and thereby stands in considerable tension with his real concept of "spirit."

38. More details in R. Bultmann, *New Testament Theology*, vol. I (1951), p. 233.

39. According to the context, the phrase concerns solely the "wicked priest," and not the "Teacher of Righteousness, as was the false conclusion of Dupont-Sommer, who then proceeded to attach the most fantastic consequences to it as

regarded the Teacher of Righteousness: "Without doubt he was a divine being, who became flesh to live and die as a man," Dupont-Sommer, *The Dead Sea Scrolls* (1953), p. 34.

40. Enoch 102₅. Jeremias had already referred to this passage, *Zeitschr. f. d. neutest. Wiss.* 38 (1939) pp. 112 ff., which M. Philonenko, "Sur l'expression 'corps de chair' dans le Commentaire d'Habacuc," *Semitica* 5 (1955), pp. 39 ff., has neglected.

41. The passive form *apentethe* stands here for an active form with God as subject, as is common in late Jewish writings.

42. This is the correct form of the Ethiopic text (in opposition to R. H. Charles, *The Apocrypha and Pseudepigrapha of the Old Testament*, vol. II, p. 198).

43. *Op. cit.*, p. 235.

44. See p. 100.

45. Luther's explanation of the sixth petition in his Small Catechism hits the meaning exactly, then: "God of course tempts no one, but we ask in this prayer, that God should shield and preserve us, so that the devil, the world and our flesh should not deceive us nor lead us into false faith, despair and other great shame and vice; and so that if we are attacked with these, that we should nevertheless win in the end and hold the victory." From this point there are important lines which run through the entire theology of Luther.

46. Cf. the statement in K. G. Kuhn, *Achtzehngebet und Vaterunser und der Reim* (1950), pp. 37 ff. and 45 ff.

47. Cf. Mt. 19₂₈.

48. For this eschatological "now," cf. further the proofs in *Zeitschr. f. Theol. u. Kirche* 47 (1950), pp. 208 ff.

49. Only from the basis of this thought can the parables of the heavenly kingdom, especially the parables of the mustard seed and the unleavened bread (Mt. 13₃₁₋₃₃ par.), be properly interpreted: that which happens *now breaks through*; it is the *coming*.

50. "To fall" as quasi passive for "to be dashed down," is a Hebraism; cf. 1 Sam. 5₃₋₄, Hag. 2₂₂ *et passim* in the Old Testament. The same is true of Rev. 12₁₂, "the devil was dashed down," as Rev. 12₉ correctly says.

51. The interpretation which Hans Conzelmann gives of this passage, in his article, "Zur Lukasanalyse," *Zeitschr. f. Theol. u. Kirche* 49 (1952), p. 29, seems to me to be on the wrong track. It is out of the question that there should be an increase in the use of the word *peirasmos* in the Gospel of Luke from 22₁₀ on to the end, as he maintains. Certainly: it is right that Luke, with his editorial remark in 4₁₃ at the end of the story of the temptation ("And the devil left him alone for a while"), which intentionally points to 22₃ ("And then Satan entered into Judas Iscariot"), wishes to communicate a special meaning: *only* the story of the temptation at the beginning and the story of the suffering of Jesus at the end stand under the pressure of satanic attack (cf. 22₅₃: "the power of darkness)." The time between, the actual course of his teaching and works, is free from this. According to the presentation in Luke, his teaching and acting occur in a realm that is free from the interference of Satan, in a pure, unendangered, divine atmosphere. Even though it is certain that this is the opinion of Luke, nevertheless, one cannot interpret the saying of Lk. 22₂₈₋₃₀ from this point of view; this saying is *older* than the work of Luke, only *taken over* by Luke and arranged in his work. Here we must stick to the principle of every synoptic exegesis, that every single piece of tradition must be interpreted in itself and out of itself and not in the editorial framework in which it

appears. Then it becomes clear that in the saying of Lk. 22₂₈ (in contrast to the editorial frame of Luke) *peirasmoi* means the time of Jesus' life as the situation under attack.

52. Cf. my essay, "Jesus in Gethsemane," *Evang. Theol.* 12 (1952/53), pp. 260-85.

### VII. "Peace among Men of God's Good Pleasure" Lk. 2₁₄

1. The different forms in which the Song of the Angels at Bethlehem is quoted is a matter not only of translation and interpretation but of textual criticism. The King James Version, as well as all older Protestant translations, follows the vast majority of Greek manuscripts: *en anthropois eudokia* (nominative), translating it "good will toward men." However, the more reliable Greek manuscripts which we now have at our disposal make it quite clear—as D . Vogt points out in this essay—that the correct reading is that which has been preserved all the time in the Vulgate's *pax hominibus bonae voluntatis=eirene en anthropois eudokias* (genitive). This is the reading followed by the Revised Standard Version. Nevertheless, their translation: ". . . peace among men with whom he is pleased" (taking *eudokia* to mean God's acceptance of man), is now challenged by the Qumran texts. Dr. Vogt suggests the following Hebrew retranslation: "*kabod bammeromim lelohim ubaares shalom leanshe rason.*" [Ed. note]

2. For this reason the pronoun *autou* (his) must be implied: *eudokias autou*. It may even be that *en anthropois eudokias* stands for the suffixed form *leanshe resono* (so in F. Delitzsch's translation of the New Testament into Hebrew), for in Sirach 15₁₅ and 39₁₈ *resono* is translated by *eudokia* alone. But even in the Hebrew it could have been omitted, as in 1 QS viii, 6: *behire rason*, "the elect of (his) good pleasure."

3. "Neues Licht auf Lc 2₁₄," *Zeitschr. f. d. neutest. Wissensch.* 44 (1952/53), pp. 85-90. This article also has an extensive apparatus with references to the voluminous exegetical discussion of Lk. 2₁₄. The complete text of 1 QH is now available in the *Osar*, plates 35-58.

4. The same words are found almost identically in 1 QS xi, 2.

5. These words lend support to the emendation of Ps. 30₆: "For affliction (read: *naega* for *raega*, moment) is in his anger, life in his good pleasure (*biresono*)."

6. In the Qumran texts hitherto published the word "mystery" (*raz*) occurs about forty times. "The mysteries of God" are his secret decrees on the impending destruction of all wickedness and the eternal glorification of the men of his good pleasure who enter and persevere in the covenant; cf. my article, "Mysteria in textibus Qumran," *Biblica* 37 (1956), pp. 247-57, where all the texts mentioning the "mysteries" are collected.—Because the words "in excelsis" ("in the highest"=*bammeromim*) occur in Lk. 2₁₄, in this connection two Qumran texts may be mentioned where they are found: "Your wonderful mysteries are *bammeromi[m]*" (1 QM xiv, 14); "righteousness will rejoice [*b*]*ammeromim*" (1QM xvii, 8).

### VIII. The Sermon on the Mount and the Qumran Texts

1. Shabbath 116a, b.

2. Lit. "blank spaces," "margin." This is probably an abusive designation for the Gospels.

3. H. J. Schoeps, *Theologie und Geschichte des Judenchristentums* (1949), p. 318 properly connects this whole controversy with Ebionite writings.

4. Lit. "a philosopher." In view of the context there is no doubt that it means a Jewish Christian.

5. This is perhaps the best translation of the uncertain *by nshy*.

6. Cf. Num. 27₈.

7. Lit. "pages of sin."

8. Such a statement is not to be found in the canonical Gospels. In contrast, cf. Lk. 12₁₄

9. J. Klausner, *Jesus of Nazareth* (1929), p. 45, prefers reading *welo* "and not," to *ala* "but rather," which corresponds fully to the Greek *alla*. Still, Klausner's reading ought not to be accepted, because it is also to be found in the censored editions of the Talmud and likely represents a censor's change.

10. Cf. J. Klausner, *Historia shel ha-bait ha-sheni*, vol. IV (1951), p. 229: "The Pharisees did not agree with the *halakoth* and usages of Jesus, especially not with the relief which he gave his pupils."

11. *Op. cit.*, p. 146.

12. *Ibid.*, p. 112.

13. *Ibid.*, pp. 166f.

14. Cf. *Strack-Billerbeck*, vol. I, p. 353.

15. Cf. K. Schubert, *Zeitschr. f. kath. Theol.* 74 (1952), pp. 31-37. To reiterate, I do not hold [as G. Molin, *Judaica* 7 (1951), pp. 210f.; and *Die Söhne des Lichtes* (1954), p. 221] both sects to be fully indentical. The term "Essenism" must not be made too narrow. It probably was much more a group of sects with several patterns of doctrine varying somewhat among themselves than a sharply determined and delineated community. In this sense we can also understand Josephus, *Bell.* 2, 8, 13, and Hippolytus, *Adv. haer.* 10, 26. I, therefore, maintain that if one disregards all those characteristics peculiar to Qumran (e.g., the Teacher of Righteousness), the pattern of teaching of the Qumran texts, above all of 1 QS, can be used to complement the picture which Josephus, Philo, and Pliny give us of the Essenes. On the other hand, one must be careful not to expand the Qumran material on the basis of the ancient sources about the Essenes. There is, however, the further question of how the peasants and hand workers of Galilee came to know Essene teachings. On the basis of 1 QS viii, 12-14, I have already pointed to the possible connection with John the Baptist (*op. cit.*, p. 31). In the meantime this suspicion has become more substantial in my sight. In another place I hope to treat it and the manner of the intellectual contact between the Judaic Essenes and the Galilean Zealots in a more thorough-going fashion.

16. The so-called War Scroll also belongs to the realm of eschatological bellicosity. Cf. also Enoch 91₁₂. Elsewhere I hope to treat the relationship between the Ten Week Apocalypse and the Qumran literature. (Cf. further Enoch 95₃₋₇; 96₁; 98₁₂.) For the motive of hatred for enemies is yet clearer in iii, 5f.: "And upon the trumpets of their columns they inscribe, 'The Strength of God,' in order to scatter the enemy and to put to flight all those who hate justice and those who show mercy to them that hate God." The motif which dominates the whole of 1 QM is the militant eschatological zeal against the enemies of God. The vengeance of God is executed by the members of the community. See particularly iii, 6, 8, 9; iv, 3, 11-14; vi, 3, 5, 6. The members of the community refer to themselves as the "called of God," e.g., iii, 2; iv, 10f.

17. Mt. 5₄₄ indicates that this interpretation may be correct, since, according to 1 QpHab, it is the evil powers of the Last Time who persecute the members of the sect. Jesus commands his listeners to pray for these enemies.

18. Cf. *Strack-Billerbeck*, vol. I, p. 241.

19. An early Christian sublimation of hatred for the agents of evil into hatred for evil as such is to be found in the Didache, esp. 12; 28; 31. Cf. J. P. Audet, *Rev. Bibl.* 59 (1952), p. 219-38.

20. Cf. p. 127.

21. L. Harding, *Palest. Expl. Quart.* 84 (1952), p. 104; R. de Vaux *Rev. Bibl.* 60. (1953), p. 95.

22. Josephus, *Bell.*, 5, 4, 2.

23. It is remarkable that almost all scholars accept the opinion that only the settlement of Khirbet Qumran is to be identified with the Essene Community described by Pliny in his *Hist. nat.* 5, 17. It was certainly one of the settlements "below which the town of Engadda was located." Pliny also cites Masada as an Essene locality, "a fortress on a cliff not far from the Dead Sea." Accordingly, there must have been Essene settlements farther south than Engedi. B. Maisler's report in *Bull. of the Jewish Palest. Expl. Soc.* 15 (1949), pp. 25-28, on the experimental excavations in Engedi, coincides generally with the archaeological findings of Khirbet Qumran. In both spots there is a central edifice. According to Maisler's assumption (p. 28), that of Engedi too belongs in the Roman era of Palestinian history. The four thousand Essenes, whom Josephus mentions in *Ant.* 18, 1, 5, can, according to the letter of the text, only have been the monastic Essenes.

24. Vol. I, p. 190.

25. Cf. 1 QS i, 11f., and vi, 19f., with *Bell.* 2, 8, 3; further see 1 QS v, 16, 20; 1 QpHab viii, 10-12; ix, 5f.; cf. CD 8₁₇; 9₂₁, ₂₃; 13₅, ₂₅. The term "poor in spirit," "poor with inner agreement," is found also in 1 QM xiv, 7; cf. for this—and for the Qumran studies at large—Dr. Flusser's provocative article, "The Sect in the Judean Desert and its Ideas" (in modern Hebrew) *Zion* 19 (1955), p. 89-103, esp. p. 93.

26. The problems of this passage are admirably handled by K. Elliger, *Studien zum Habakuk-Kommentar vom Toten Meer* (1953), pp. 221ff.

27. 1QH ii, 32.

28. Cf. Schubert, *op. cit.*, pp. 27f.

29. The question as to what extent the teachings of Mt. 5 belonged to the original Sermon on the Mount may be left untouched here.

30. In this meaning the word "prophet" e.g., in Mt. 23₃₄.

31. *Ant.* 15, 10, 5.

32. *menosh deah* (stat. constr.). Consequently it may refer to one who indeed seeks knowledge, but who, because he does not belong to the community, stands outside of the area where such can be granted to him.

33. Cf. Schubert, *Theol. Lit. Zeit.* 78 (1953), cols. 505f.

34. "Holy ones" and "sons of heaven" may be references to angelic beings. The idea that the angels make common cause with the community is unambiguously substantiated in the more recently published texts: "In that day the congregation of the Elim and the congregation of men will enter the field for the great battle" (1 QM i, 10f.) "And no man, who is not pure from his origin, may descend with them on the Day of War, for angels of holiness are together with their armies" (vii, 6). "These (i.e., the impure and the palsied) may not come to place themselves in the midst of the congregation of the men of the 'Name,' for angels of holiness are in their assembly" (1 QSa ii, 8f.).

35. Cf. P. Riessler, *Altjüdisches Schrifttum ausserhalb der Bibel* (1928), p. 1300. K. Galling, *Orient. Lit. Zeit.* 33 (1930), puts the date of the Jewish layer of Asc. Is. in the second century B.C.

36. Flusser in *Bull. of the Isr. Expl. Soc.* 17 (1952), pp. 28-46; also *Isr. Expl. Journ.* 3 (1953), pp. 30-47; the Teacher of Righteousness was in fact mercilessly persecuted and fought by the Priest of Wickedness, as is apparent from the allusions of 1 QpHab, e.g., xi. 4-6.

37. If Flusser's identification is retained, this passage would indicate the martyrdom of the Teacher of Righteousness. The decisive passage in CD does not give unambiguous evidences for this, although it leaves the possibility open; Schubert, *Zeitschr. f. kath. Theol.* 74 (1952), p. 25.

38. *Theol. Lit. Zeit.* 78 (1953), cols. 495-506.

39. In the third century of our era a copy of Asc. Is. could easily have fallen into the hands of Rabba.

40. The problem of the related passages Mt. 23$_{29-37}$ and Lk. 11$_{47-51}$ cannot be discussed here; cf. 2 Chron. 24$_{20-22}$.

41. Cf. my discussion of the concepts "man of lies" and "men of violence" in *Zeitschr. f. kath. Theol.* 74 (1952), p. 16, and *Theol. Lit. Zeit.* 77 (1952), cols. 334f.

42. *Bell.* 2, 8, 6; cf. *Ant.* 15, 10, 4.

43. An interesting parallel is offered in Shebuoth 4, 13 (35a).

44. So with G. Molin, *op. cit.,* p. 32.

45. This is not intended as an argument concerning the literary conception of the Sermon on the Mount, as found in Matthew. Nevertheless, it is remarkable that the Essene parallels are found almost exclusively in Mt. 5.

46. The same negative attitude toward money is found in Enoch 63$_{10}$ and even more in 94$_{7-8}$.

IX. THE DEAD SEA MANUAL OF DISCIPLINE AND THE JERUSALEM CHURCH OF ACTS

1. W. H. Brownlee, in his *Translation*, notes some of the parallels. I have quoted from his translation.

2. Cf. G. W. H. Lampe, *The Seal of the Spirit* (1951), pp. 25-27. In a recent publication Brownlee understands 1 QS iv, 19-21, as containing an allusion to Is. 52$_{14f.}$, which in the Isaiah scroll contains a peculiar reading, *The United Presbyterian*, Dec. 14, 1953, p. 7; cf. Brownlee, *Bull. of the Amer. Sch. of Oriental Res.* 132 (1953), pp. 8-15; cf. this volume, p. 43.

3. Josephus, *Ant.* 18, 5, 2. Cf. K. Stendahl's note on *Axios* in *Nuntius* 7 (1952), pp. 54f.

4. Mk. 14 describes John's baptism as "a baptism of repentance to the remission of sins"; Professor Cadbury points out that Matthew, in the parallel passage (Mt. 3$_2$) omits "to the remission of sins" but adds the phrase in the account of Jesus' words at the Last Supper (26$_{28}$). Thus Matthew believes that complete remission of sins is found only in connection with Jesus.

5. 1 QS ix, 20, contains an interpretation, itself somewhat obscure, of this text: now is the time to clear the way of the Lord by teaching men true and marvelous mysteries. Cf. K. Stendahl, *The School of St. Matthew* (1954), p. 215.

6. Cf. K. G. Kuhn, *Theol. Lit. Zeit.* 75 (1950), cols. 71ff.; Joh. Hempel, *Deutsches Pfarrerblatt* 51 (1951), p. 482, n. 17; J. Coppens, *Les documents du Désert de Juda et les Origines du Christianisme*, p. 29; G. Molin, *Die Söhne des Lichtes* (1954), p. 211.

7. On the date of this see K. S. Gapp, "The Universal Famine under Claudius," *Harv. Theol. Rev.* 28 (1935), pp. 258-65.

8. On the other hand, there is nothing to indicate that Luke thought of Zacchaeus as giving up all his property (Lk. 19₈ƒ.). Cf. the discussion of the poor in E. Percy, *Die Botschaft Jesu* (1953).

9. E. Lohmeyer, *Galiläa und Jerusalem* (1936), pp. 68-74. Although the "Son of Man" in James' martyr-speech is obviously borrowed from the account of Stephen's martyrdom in Acts, there is no reason to doubt that this title goes back to the early Palestinian church. Note its occurrence, e.g., in Lk. 6₂₂. The metaphors of "a spring of light" and "a fountain of darkness" (1 QS iii, 19) have a formal similarity to James 3₁₁.

10. See especially H. J. Schoeps, *Theologie und Geschichte des Judenchristentums* (1949); and Fitzmyer's essay in this volume.

11. Cf. K. Elliger, *Studien zum Habakuk-Kommentar vom Toten Meer* (1953), pp. 222 f., but also A. Dupont-Sommer, *The Dead Sea Scrolls*, p. 40, n. 1. Schoeps, *Zeitschr. f. d. alttest. Wiss.* 63 (1951), pp. 249 ff., gives parallels between 1 QpHab and the Psalms of Solomon which seem highly significant. The Ps. Sol. and the canticles of Luke belong to the same species of literature.

12. Cf. E. Stauffer, *Theol. Lit.-Zeit.* 77 (1952), cols. 201 ff.

13. M. H. Shepherd, Jr., *Munera Studiosa* (1946), p. 104, assigns the Matthias story to the Antiochian-Hellenistic source, which is interested in the Twelve, the Seven, and ordination or appointment to office. The great heroes of this source are the prophets, and it is significant that Matthias must be appointed by the Holy Spirit.

14. O. Cullmann, *Peter* (1953), pp. 35-46.

15. Cf. Molin, *op. cit.*, pp. 142 ff. Professor A. D. Nock, in a personal letter, dissents.

16. Other translations: G. Vermès, *Les Manuscrits du Désert de Juda* (1953), p. 145: "Les Grands"; Molin, *op. cit.*, p. 26: "die Vollversammlung."

17. See K. G. Kuhn, in this volume, esp. on 1 QSa, pp. 70 ff.

18. See especially W. H. Brownlee, "Biblical Interpretation among the Sectaries of the Dead Sea Scrolls," *Bibl. Arch.* 14 (1951), pp. 54-76; K. Stendahl, *op. cit.*, pp. 183-202. Stendahl shows that the principles of interpretation of 1 QpHab are similar to those employed by Matthew in his Old Testament quotations and allusions. Cf. also Joh. Hempel *Zeitschr. f. d. alttest. Wissensch.* 62 (1950), p. 264.

19. S. E. Johnson, "Laodicea and Its Neighbors," *Bibl. Arch.* 13 (1950), pp. 17 f.

20. J. B. Lightfoot, *Comm. Col.* (3rd ed., 1879), pp. 71-111.

21. B. W. Bacon, *The Gospel of the Hellenists* (1933). Cf. "Samaria and the Origins of the Christian Mission," in O. Cullmann, *The Early Church* (1956), pp. 183-92.

22. W. D. Davies, "Knowledge in the Dead Sea Scrolls and Matthew 11₂₅-₃₀," *Harv. Theol. Rev.* 46 (1953), pp. 113-39.

23. W. H. Brownlee, *Transl.*, p. 23, n. 3.

24. This passage is more probably the deliverance of a Christian prophet than an historic word of Jesus; the same is true of most of the special Matthean passages which we consider here. The term "brothers" is also characteristic of the Jerusalem traditions of Acts which center in Peter; cf. Shepherd, *op. cit.*, p. 103.

25. It should be noted that Brownlee and Samuel Iwry emend *librith mishpat* to *likroth mishpat*, cf. Brownlee, *Transl.* p. 33, n. 19. The hypothesis of B. H. Streeter, *The Four Gospels* (4th impression, 1930), p. 232, that the M source, containing much of the special Matthean material, was written in Jerusalem,

appears to be strengthened by the parallels to 1 QS; at least a Judean origin is suggested. I would, however, restrict the dimensions of M more narrowly; cf. *The Interpreter's Bible*, vol. VII (1951), pp. 238 f.

26. This passage, which has puzzled commentators and caused much controversy, seems to me to be clearer when we consider it in the light of Jerusalemite suspicion of the Samaritans; cf. further G. W. H. Lampe, *op. cit.*, pp. 66-75.

27. F. A. Schilling, "Why did Paul Go to Damascus?" *Anglican Theol. Rev.* 16 (1934), pp. 199-205.

28. F. M. Cross, "The Manuscripts of the Dead Sea Caves," *Bibl. Arch.* 17 (1954), pp. 2-21, particularly pp. 4-6; R. Marcus, "Philo, Josephus and the Dead Sea Yahad," *Journ. Bibl. Lit.* 71 (1952), pp. 207-9; M. Burrows, "The Discipline Manual of the Judaean Covenanters," *Oudtestamentische Studiën* 8 (1950), pp. 156-92; but see S. Lieberman, "The Discipline in the So-called Dead Sea Manual of Discipline," *Journ. Bibl. Lit.*, 71 (1952), pp. 199-206.

29. I. Rabinowitz, "A Reconsideration of 'Damascus' and '390 Years' in the 'Damascus' ('Zadokite') Fragments," *Journ. Bibl. Lit.* 73 (1954), pp. 11-35.

30. Josephus tells us nothing about James except that, after the death of Festus and before Albinus' arrival, the younger Ananus persuaded the Sanhedrin to have him and some others stoned (*Ant.* 20, 9, 1). The leading figures among the Jews who protested this judicial murder may well have been Pharisees. Because of his loyalty to the Law they probably regarded him as an ally rather than an enemy. The action of Ananus can be understood if James protested against the Sadduccean priesthood.

31. Josephus, who claims to be a Pharisee (*Vita* 2, 12) approves of the "virtue" and "righteousness" of the Essenes (*Ant.* 18, 1, 5; *Bell.* 2, 8, 2-14). J. Klausner, *Jesus of Nazareth* (1927), p. 202, understands "the first Hasidim" of the Talmud to refer to the Essenes; cf. pp. 206-12, in which he argues, following Derenbourg. that there is nothing in Essenism that cannot be paralleled among the stricter Pharisees.

32. Klausner, *op. cit.*, pp. 202 f.

33. On the Qumran attitude toward sacrifices, see J. M. Baumgarten, "Sacrifice and Worship among the Jewish Sectarians of the Dead Sea (Qumran) Scrolls," *Harv. Theol. Rev.* 46 (1953), pp. 141-59.

34. Cf. Klausner, *op. cit.*, pp. 211 f.; S. E. Johnson in W. Schmauch, ed., *In Memoriam Ernst Lohmeyer* (1951), pp. 80 f.

### X. THE CONSTITUTION OF THE PRIMITIVE CHURCH IN THE LIGHT OF JEWISH DOCUMENTS

1. K. E. Kirk, ed., *The Apostolic Ministry* (1946), pp. vi and 10; T. G. Jalland, "The Doctrine of the Parity of Ministers," *ibid.*, p. 311. Note, however, that other authors in the same work, particularly A. M. Farrar and G. Dix, give a less one-sided picture of the "apostolic succession" and attribute a prominent place to the Presbyterial office in primitive Christianity.

2. W. Michaelis, *Das Aeltestenamt der christlichen Gemeinde im Lichte der Heiligen Schrift* (1953), pp. 26-65, 171. It is emphasized that elders were often installed by the apostles, not always by the congregation, pp. 74-79. The elders are supposed to have formed a college, and this collegiate system was the normal one in New Testament times.

3. E. Schweizer, *Das Leben des Herrn in der Gemeinde und ihren Diensten* (1946), pp. 23, 59, 86 *et passim*.

4. Aristotle, *Polit.* 3, 5, 1b (1279a): "Either one or a few or the many must rule." In fact Aristotle here treats "oligarchy" and "democracy" as degenerate forms of "aristocracy" and "polity." Since, however, the former have been accepted as descriptive terms without any pejorative tinge, while the latter are no longer used to mean governmental systems, we can speak of "oligarchy" and "democracy" here in an entirely neutral sense. Cf. Plutarch, *Praec. ger. reip.*

5. *Strack-Billerbeck,* vol. II, pp. 594 f.

6. O. Linton, *Das Problem der Urkirche in der neueren Forschung* (1932), pp. 189-94.

7. As soon as 1 QS was closely inspected, striking relationships to CD were discovered. This latter document had been known to scholars since 1910, and belonged to a pietistic group, which had emigrated from Palestine to Damascus. These two texts contain chiefly a congregational order of certain Jewish sectarians. The correlations between the texts are so far-reaching that it is necessary to attribute them by and large to the same religious movement. This has been confirmed by the recent discovery of a fragment of CD at Qumran (*Rev. Bibl.* 63 [1956], pp. 55 and 61). This essay cannot go deeply into the question of the historical background of the two texts. I have suggested that the emigration to Damascus, mentioned in CD, took place about 90 B.C. (in the introduction to my Swedish translation of Qumran texts, *Symbolae Biblicae Upsalienses* 14 [1952], p. 57, cf. pp. 20 and 46). There are, however, a good many other theories about the chronology of the Damascus Document. As for 1 QS, its text contains nothing which could be definitely dated. Only the agreement with the Essene movement described by Josephus and other historians allows us to place the Manual in the end of the pre-Christian period or at the beginning of the Christian Era. In addition, however, certain external circumstances contribute to a similar dating of the two texts. Above all, the new archaeological investigations make it seem certain that 1 QS, as the other Qumran texts—among them the CD fragments—were deposited in this area at the latest in A.D. 70, where they have remained until modern times. Probably the texts in question are older, and they may date from the first or partially from the second century B.C. But this is not important here. We are, in any case, right in saying that these texts belong to a milieu chronologically and geographically very near to early Christianity, and in utilizing them for the explanation of New Testament problems.

8. Thus it was also with the Essenes: Josephus, *Bell.* 2, 8, 5 (131); see this volume, pp. 67 ff.

9. See p. 154.

10. *Ho epimeletes,* Josephus, *Bell.* 2, 8, 3 (123).

11. Literature in B. Reicke, *The Damascus Documents and the New Testament* (1946), p. 16, note 40. See also G. Dix, "The Ministry in the Early Church," in *The Apostolic Ministry,* p. 252.

12. So also Dix, *loc. cit.,* concerning the *mebaqqer* in CD: ". . . its casual evidence is again an illustration of how naturally the priestly and pastoral duties of the *episkope* might be developed upon one man in Syrian Judaeo-Christian surroundings . . ."

## XI. PAUL AND THE DEAD SEA SCROLLS: FLESH AND SPIRIT

1. See A. Schweitzer, *Paul and his Interpreters* (Eng. trans., 1912); J. Klausner, *From Jesus to Paul* (Eng. trans., 1942); W. D. Davies, *Paul and Rabbinic Judaism* (1948, 2nd ed., 1955).

2. E.g., W. L. Knox, *St. Paul and the Church of the Gentiles* (1939); W. D. Davies, *op. cit.*

3. See, especially, E. R. Goodenough, *Jewish Symbols in the Greco-Roman Period* (1953-    ); S. Lieberman, *Greek in Jewish Palestine* (1942); and, for other bibliographical notes, W. D. Davies, *op. cit.*, p. 354 and also p. 16.

4. A. Schweitzer, *op. cit.*

5. The literature on this is already large. For a convenient summary, J. Schmitt in *Rev. des Sciences Rel.* 29 (1955), pp. 381 ff. 30 (1956), pp. 55 ff.

6. See W. H. Brownlee in this volume.

7. See O. Cullmann in this volume, p. 29.

8. *Ibid.*, pp. 25 ff. But it is difficult to accept Cullman's view that Christian universalism owes much to the sectarians or that the term "Hellenists" is likely to point to representatives of anything like what we have at Qumran.

9. H. J. Schoeps, *Urgemeinde, Judenchristentum, Gnosis* (1956), pp. 69 ff. But see J. A. Fitzmyer's essay in this volume.

10. See Cullmann, *op. cit.*, p. 25, and references in note 20. The meaning of the term "Damascus" is in dispute, however; R. North holds it to refer not to the city of Damascus but to almost all the area around the Dead Sea, including Damascus, *Pal. Expl. Quart.* 87 (1955), pp. 34-38. Rabinowitz has rejected the geographic interpretation of Damascus, *Journ. of Bibl. Lit.* 73 (1954), pp. 11 ff. See also Charles T. Fritsch, *The Qumran Community* (1956), pp. 21 ff., on Damascus as a place of refuge.

11. For this, see his various articles in *Journ. of Jewish St.*, since the treatment in these articles is always greatly rewarding even though we may not accept the main positions advanced.

12. *Op. cit.*, p. 219. For the ease with which terminology can mislead, I may refer to a dissertation by my former student, G. R. Edwards, *The Qumran Sect and the New Testament*, Duke University, 1955 (unpublished). He rejects the view that *yahad* and *koinonia* are identical.

13. For these and other parallels, see especially W. Grossouw, "The Dead Sea Scrolls and the New Testament," *Studia Catholica* 27 (1952), pp. 1-8; the notes in W. H. Brownlee's translation of I QS are invaluable; S. E. Johnson, "Paul and the Manual of Discipline," *Harv. Theol. Rev.* 48 (1955), pp. 157 ff. Also the relevant pages in F. M. Braun, "L'arrière-fond judaïque du quatrième évangile et la Communauté de l'Alliance," *Rev. Bibl.* 62 (1955), pp. 5-44.

14. W. Grossouw, *op. cit.*, p. 1; S. E. Johnson, *op. cit.*, pp. 160 ff.

15. For a rich treatment, see the three articles by S. Lyonnet, "L'étude du milieu littéraire et l'éxegèse du Nouveau Testament," *Biblica* 35 (1954), pp. 480-502; 36 (1955), pp. 202-12; 37 (1956), pp. 1-38. For the Synoptics, see L. Cerfaux, in *New Testament St.* 2 (1955/56), pp. 238 ff.

16. See, e.g., E. Earle Ellis, "A Note on Pauline Hermeneutics," *New Testament St.* 2 (1955/56), pp. 127 ff.; E. Dinkler, *Journ. of Rel.* 36 (1956), pp. 121 ff., finds possible Essene influence on Paul's conception of predestination and individual responsibility in Rom. 9-11; see also M. Burrows, *The Dead Sea Scrolls* (1955), p. 336.

17. *Op. cit.*, pp. 19 ff.

18. Our translation is that of Danby, *The Mishnah* (1933). Israelstam's comment is found in the Soncino Talmud. Contrast R. T. Herford, *Pirqe Aboth* (1945), pp. 48-49.

19. Translation by J. W. Etheridge, *The Targums of Onkelos and Jonathan ben Uzziel* (1862).

20. *The Dictionary of the Talmud, ad. loc.*

21. The basic treatment is by K. G. Kuhn. See this volume, pp. 101 ff.

22. Compare on all this J. A. T. Robinson, *The Body* (1952), for the "flesh" in Paul.

23. Cf. Gen 63. For other references in the Scrolls, see Ph. Hyatt, "The View of Man in the Qumran Hodayot," *New Testament St.* 2 (1955/56), pp. 276 ff.

24. E.g., 1 QS x, 11; cf. Ps. 513t.

25. See W. H. Brownlee, "The Servant of the Lord in the Qumran Scrolls," *Bull. of the Amer. Sch. of Oriental Res.* 135 (1954), pp. 36-38; Y. Yadin in *Jour*. *of Bibl. Lit.* 74 (1955), pp. 40-43; G. Vermès in *Cahiers Sioniens* 9 (1955), pp. 56 ff.

26. M. Burrows, *The Dead Sea Scrolls*, p. 393. The interpretation of 1 QM has a bearing on the meaning of the struggles in which Christians are engaged. This may confirm the views on the forces fought by the early church suggested by A. N. Wilder, "Kerygma, Eschatology and Social Ethics"; Davies and Daube (ed.), *The Background of the New Testament and its Eschatology* (1956), pp. 527 ff.

27. See G. Friedrich in *Theol. Wörterb. z. N.T.* (ed. Kittel), vol. II, p. 705, on "good 'good news.' "

28. So also Kuhn, *op. cit.*, p. 101.

29. *Ibid.*, p. 104.

30. So. W. H. Brownlee's translation, *ad loc.* S. E. Johnson rejects this apparently, *op. cit.*, p. 159, where he writes that "the newly discovered literature does not mention angels." This position can hardly be maintained in the light of the sources now available, apart from 1 QS xi, 6 ff. Angelology is very marked in 1 QM especially. The angelology of the sect illuminates much in the New Testament. See Barthélemy and Milik, *Qumran Cave I*, p. 117, comments to 1 QSa ii, 8.

31. See, e.g., *Encycl. of Rel. and Ethics*, vol. II, p. 66b.

32. *Op. cit.*, pp. 19, 25, and 31.

33. W. D. Davies, *op. cit.*, pp. 22 ff.

34. On the problem of whether the "I" of the Psalms is to be taken individually or corporately, see K. G. Kuhn, *op. cit.*, pp. 102 f. We take them individually at least in 1 QS x and xi. The fact that they could be used publicly does not militate against this, cf. Ph. Hyatt, *op cit.*, p. 276.

35. *The Jewish Sect of Qumran and the Essenes* (Eng. trans., 1954), pp. 118 ff.

36. K. G. Kuhn, "Die Sektenschrift und die iranische Religion," *Zeitschr. f. Theol. u. Kirche* 49 (1952), pp. 296-316.

37. Davies, *op cit.*, p. 27. On the Evil Impulse in the Scrolls, see Ph. Hyatt, *op cit.*; also E. Schweizer, "Gegenwart des Geistes und eschatologische Hoffnung," *The Background of the New Testament and its Eschatology*, pp. 489 ff.

38. See the commentaries on Colossians.

39. For bibliographical details, consult the studies in *Biblica* by S. Lyonnet already mentioned; P. Benoit, "Corps, tête et plérôme dans les Épitres de la Captivité," *Rev. Bibl.* 63 (1956), pp. 5 ff.

40. The term "body of flesh" occurs also in Greek in Sir. 2317, Enoch 1024-5. In 1 QpHab it apparently merely means the physical body or flesh. We are not to understand here a rigid distinction between "flesh" and "body." So too in Paul "body" *(soma)* and "flesh" *(sarx)* are often synonymous (Gal. 617, 1 Cor. 927, etc.). The anthropology of the Scrolls has not been sufficiently examined. Hyatt has dealt in a broad way with the view of man in 1 QH, *op. cit.*, but does not

think a strict anthropology possible because the Hymns are "not a theological work," (p. 278). But we may ask the question whether the Scrolls throw any light on the Pauline doctrine of the "body." The term *gewiyyah* may mean in Mishnah Mikwaoth 10₇ "the inner part of the body" (so Jastrow); in the Jerusalem Targum on Gen. 7₂₃, it seems identical with "flesh." In the Old Testament the term occurs mostly in the sense of corpse, but is also used of the form taken by visionary creatures (Dan. 10₆). In Gen. 47₁₈, Neh. 9₃₇, K. Grobel (in *Neutest. St. für Rudolf Bultmann*, 1954, p. 56), takes it to stand for the "self." (See H.D.B., p. 156). The evidence is too meager to connect the fully developed Pauline concept of the "body" with *gewiyyah*, however. There are passages which suggest that, in part, what Paul calls the "body" is in the Scrolls designated by "spirit"—if we take "body" as a designation of the "self." (See references in J. A. T. Robinson, *op cit.*, pp. 26 ff.) This is another instance of the distance that separates the sectarian conceptual milieu from Paul. See, further, Marc Philonenko, "Sur l'expression 'corps du chair' dans le Commentaire d'Hababuc," *Semitica* 5 (1955), pp. 39-40. He concludes: "It is of interest to observe that this expression . . . which is rather rare, is found both in one of the Qumran Scrolls, in the Book of Enoch, fragments of which are found in the Qumran caves, in Ecclesiasticus and also in the New Testament."

41. See W. D. Davies, *Harv. Theol. Rev.* 46 (1953), pp. 113 ff.; Bo Reicke, "Traces of Gnosticism in the Dead Sea Scrolls," *New Testament St.* 1 (1954/55), pp. 137 ff.

42. See note by C. Rabin, *The Zadokite Documents* (1954), p. 16.

43. On this see further C. G. Howie, "The Cosmic Struggle," *Interpretation* 8 (1954), pp. 206 ff. It is not irrelevant to note the marked affinities between the "Ephesian Gospel" and "Qumran" tendencies ?t this point. Those influences may have been strong in Asia Minor. See, e.g., W. F., Albright in *The Background of the New Testament and its Eschatology*, pp. 164 ff.

44. *Commentary, ad loc.*

45. *Abingdon Commentary, ad loc.*

46. 1 Cor. 2₈; Rom. 8₃₈f.; Gal. 4₃,₉.

47. See W. Grossouw, *op. cit.*, p. 3.

48. See the commentaries. The Scrolls do not present us strictly with *Haustafeln*, but we do find something not dissimilar in 1 QSa i, 6-18.

49. See D. Daube, *The New Testament and Rabbinic Judaism* (1956), pp. 90 ff., especially p. 101.

50. The structure of CD is instructive here, as is the combination in 1 QS of "Theology" and "Ethics."

51. See p. 169.

52. Cf. Dupont-Sommer, *op. cit.*, p. 120.

53. On "their designs," cf. 1 QS xi, 11. Burrows translates "and before they came into being he established all their designing." Erich Dinkler, *op. cit.*, p. 125, n. 23, finds here a parallel to the "purpose of God" in Rom. 8₂₈, 9₁₁. He refers, among others, to J. Dupont, *Gnosis* (1949), pp. 88 ff., where other New Testament parallels are given. See also *Strack-Billerbeck*, vol. II. pp. 335 ff. Ph. Hyatt, *op. cit.*, 280, n. 1, sees a parallel idea in a familiar passage on the Torah as the plan of the world in GenRabbah 1₁.

54. Cf. E. Schweizer, *op. cit.*, p. 491.

55. See references in note 25.

56. We can think of the spirit of truth in the Scrolls as eschatological, in the sense that it forwarded the victory of the Good and thus hastened the "End."

We should not, however, too certainly assume that the "End" was expected soon, as Matthew Black pointed out to me. The phrase "When these things come to pass . . ." is vague. On the other hand, the interim ethic which seems to mark the sect (e.g., 1 QS ix, 21 ff.) would suggest the nearness of the "End." It is difficult to agree with Cullmann, *op. cit.*, p. 32, that the sect did not know the Spirit. The warmth of its piety is inexplicable otherwise. Cullmann writes: "Instead of the Spirit, the Qumran movement had an organization." This is to introduce a false antithesis. Daniélou's view that we have both "order" and "ardor" at Qumran is to be preferred. See *Rev. d'Hist. et de Phil. Rel.* 35 (1955), pp. 104-15.

57. See Moore, *Judaism*, vol. I, p. 237.

58. *Op. cit.*, p. 8, n. 4. Cf. above on 1 QS viii, 14 ff.

59. *Op. cit.*, p. 264.

60. In *Journ. of Jewish St.* 5 (1954), pp. 139-40. Teicher translates "and He has imparted to them knowledge through His Christ His Holy Spirit, who is the truth," which he asserts contains "the germ of the doctrine of the Trinity." His translation demands a reading which, according to Rabin, is impossible to substantiate in the manuscript. Rabin then claims that, on the ground of 1 QM xi, 7-8 (". . . by thy anointed ones, seers of testimonies . . ."), there can be no doubt that *mashiah* can mean prophet and need not refer to a messianic figure in CD ii, 12. On Kuhn's solution, in the context of the Two Messiahs, see p. 59. The interpretation of MSHYHW must remain doubtful and so too much cannot be built upon it. The discussion is summarized by P. Wernberg-Møller in *Journ. of Semitic St.* 1 (1956), pp. 116 ff. He deals with previous translations and suggests his own: ". . . and He made known to them, through those who were anointed with the holy spirit of His true community . . ."

61. See Brownlee's translation, p. 35.

62. Perhaps we have underestimated the possible messianic significance of the term "man" in 1 QS iv, 20. See the discussion in W. H. Brownlee, "The Servant of the Lord in the Qumran Scrolls," *Bull. of the Amer. Sch. of Oriental Res.* 135 (1954), pp. 36-38. G. Vermès, *Cahiers Sioniens* 9 (1955), pp. 57 ff., finds in the term a messianic significance which had not in the sect been synthesized with other elements of the messianic expectation. But even if the Spirit is to be more closely related to the messianic hope than we have allowed above, its role is still not emphasized.

63. *Op. cit.*, p. 493.

64. Should we understand the Pauline emphasis on "liberty" in Galatians partly in the light of this, if, as was suggested above, there were possibly sectarian influences at work in the Galatian churches? A particularly bad instance of inquisitorial methods occurs in 1 QS i, 11, where the wife is to bear witness against her husband.

65. Rom. 14; 8₁₅; 1 Cor. 4₂₁; 2 Cor. 4₁₃; Gal. 6₁; Eph. 1₁₇.

66. See R. Bultmann, *Theology of the New Testament*, vol. I (Eng. trans., 1951), pp. 205 ff.

67. We cannot doubt that Paul regarded Old Testament prophecy, like prophecy in the church, as the gift of the Spirit: 1 Cor. 12₈, *et al.*

68. See W. D. Davies, *Paul and Rabbinic Judaism*, pp. 200 ff.

69. *Ibid.*, pp. 188 ff. Contrast E. Schweizer, *op. cit.*, p. 485, n. 1.

70. See *Paul and Rabbinic Judaism*, pp. 217 ff. The Scrolls add force to our contention there that Paul was not the first to "ethicize" the Spirit. Cf. G. R. Edwards, *op. cit.*

71. No account is here taken of the phrase *diakriseis pneumaton*, 1 Cor. 12$_{10}$, 14$_{14,32}$.

72. It does denote evil dispositions elsewhere, as was above noted.

73. *Op. cit.*, pp. 247-61.

74. See W. D. Davies, *Harv. Theol. Rev.* 46 (1953), pp. 121 ff.

75. See Robertson and Plummer, *Intern. Critic. Com. I Cor.* (1911), pp. 45 f.

76. Brownlee: "From the spring of light (issue) the generations of truth . . . but from a fountain of darkness (issue) the generations of perverseness." His reading requires an emendation which Burrows avoids in translating: "In the abode of light . . ."

77. See E. Schweizer, *op. cit.*

78. *Paul and Rabbinic Judaism*, pp. 177 ff.

79. In this Paul is in line with the whole of the New Testament: the Christian Dispensation is regarded as a new creation.

80. See J. Daniélou, *op. cit.*, pp. 104-16.

81. It is instructive to note how often the term "all" occurs, for example, in 1 QS. I counted 73 instances. See, further, H. Braun, "Beobachtungen zur Tora-Verschärfung im häretischen Spätjudentum," *Theol. Lit. Zeit.* 79 (1954), cols., 347 ff.

82. So S. E. Johnson, *op. cit.*, p. 159.

83. 2 Cor. 37,13.

84. *Op. cit.*, p. 225.

85. See our caveat to this in note 62.

86. There is, however, a caveat to be issued here. We stated above that "Law" and "Spirit" coexist in the Scrolls. Is their juxtaposition easy or are they uneasily yoked? Explicitly there is no reference to any tension between them; but if we look closer perhaps we can discern such. Is it possible that the Scrolls reveal the kind of tension within Paul's experience and within Judaism which issued in or rather found its resolution in the gospel? There are passages which imply that "the Law" under which the sect is living is not completely adequate. The prevailing view in Judaism was that the Law given on Sinai was perfect and eternal. Passages referring to a New Law are late and difficult to assess. In the Scrolls we do find, however, along with an unmistakeable and intense awareness that the days of the Messiahs would introduce changes, one explicit description of these as the coming of the New. In 1 QS iv, 25, we read: "For in equal measure God has established the two spirits until the period which has been decreed and the making new" (Burrows' translation). Brownlee renders: ". . . and the making of the New." When this new epoch dawns, there will be a change in the laws governing the community. The pertinent passage reads: "When these things come to pass in Israel (I QS ix, 3) . . . They shall not depart from any counsel of the Law, walking in all the stubbornness of their hearts; but they shall judge by the first judgments by which the men of the community began to be disciplined, until there shall come a prophet and the Messiahs of Aaron and Israel" (9-11). There can be little doubt that the term "first judgments" refers to the law of Moses, as understood by the sectarians; this is mentioned in 1 QS viii, 15, 22. Does the passage contemplate changes in the Law or merely in the application of the Law in the ideal future? Is the "making of the New" to include the *mishpatim* ("judgments") themselves? On this term, see *Qumran Cave I*, p. 113, on line 11 (1 QSa i, ii).

Whatever the answer to this question, we are justified in finding here perhaps a sign of tension under the Law. The concentration, relentless and rigid, on obedience to the Law in the sect we have already noticed. The awareness of sin which accompanied this concentration shines equally clear. In no other sources is failure to achieve the righteousness of the Law more recognized and at the same time its demands pressed with greater ruthlessness. May it be that this condition may have led to the hope that the Age of the Messiahs would bring relief? (See, further, W. D. Davies, *Torah in the Messianic Age* [1952].) This possibility we can perhaps further discern in the yearning of the sect for the "fullness" of knowledge in the Messianic Age. The passage in 1 QS iv, 18 ff., is pertinent here. In iv, 22 ff., the outcome of the sprinkling of the spirit of truth is "to make the upright perceive the knowledge of the Most High and the wisdom of the sons of heaven, to instruct those whose conduct is blameless. For God has chosen them for an eternal covenant, and theirs is all the glory of man; and there shall be no error, to the shame of all works of deceit" (Burrows' translation).

The chief end of man, if we so term the matter, is here defined in terms of knowledge of God; it is to share in the wisdom of the angelic hosts. Note that there is no suggestion of absorption in God as in Hellenistic sources. Contrast, for example, the frequently quoted words from the *Corpus Hermeticum* 1, 26: "This is the good end *(telos)* of those who have knowledge: To be deified." Knowledge of God, which is the aim and end *(telos)* of the perfect of way, implies that the distinction between creature and creator is preserved; it has a parallel in 1 Cor. 13₁₂ and Jn. 17₃. How is this knowledge to be understood? Is it more knowledge in and through the Law, or is it knowledge beyond the Law? I have cited evidence elsewhere that the "knowledge" about which the Scrolls speak as marking the final time is eschatological not only in the sense that "it belongs to the final time, but in the sense that it gives insight into the meaning of the events of that time" *Harv. Theol. Rev.* 46 (1953). Should we go further and find among the sectarians a yearning for a knowledge which itself constitutes "life eternal," which transcends the knowledge supplied by the "Law" as known in this present age? Of this we cannot be sure, because the Law itself for people such as the sectarians would be the sum of all wisdom and knowledge. But it does seem that in the yearning for "knowledge" which we find here, we see Judaism straining at the leash of the Law. Is it too much to say that the Scrolls reveal Judaism at "boiling point"? Much that we have written will recall Paul's cry in Rom. 7₂₄. The life under the Law which Paul describes echoes much in the Scrolls, so that these must be taken into consideration in any future discussion of Paul's experience, which it is now customary to treat without much reference to his struggles under the Law in his pre-Christian days.

87. Gal. 1₁₄; Phil. 3₄ff.

## XII. The Qumran Scrolls and the Johannine Gospel and Epistles

1. Similarities between the Scrolls and the New Testament can be gleaned from the various articles we shall cite, but especially valuable are W. H. Brownlee's notes in his *Translation* of 1 QS. For the Damascus Documents, see Bo Reicke, "The Jewish 'Damascus Documents' and the New Testament," *Symbolae Biblicae Upsalienses* 6 (1946).

2. We do not intend to treat the Apocalypse (Revelation), not primarily because of the authorship problem but because this literary genre has so many stereotyped qualities that it offers great difficulties for establishing interrelationship. F. M. Braun, O.P., "L'arrière-fond judaïque du quatrième évangile et la Communauté

de l'Alliance," *Rev. Bibl.* 62 (1955), pp. 27-31, considers similarities to the Apocalypse (Revelation) without discovering anything decisive. Braun's article appeared when ours was virtually finished (the topics treated and the conclusions are, by coincidence, quite similar), but we have been able to take advantage of his observations in notes.

3. This article is the outgrowth of a seminar paper presented in February of 1955 at Johns Hopkins University. The writer is indebted to Professor William F. Albright for his kindness in reading the manuscript and for his helpful suggestions. New Testament quotes from the transl. ed. by the Confraternity of Christian Doctrine (1941) or, in a few places where the Greek has important differences, from the RSV; in 1 QS and 1Qp Hab. I follow mainly *Brownlee.*

4. *The Dead Sea Scrolls* (Eng. transl., 1952), pp. 33-44 and 98 f.

5. H. H. Rowley, *The Zadokite Fragments and the Dead Sea Scrolls* (1952), p. 20, n. 3, lists some of the wilder statements. Dupont-Sommer, *op. cit.,* p. 99, says that Jesus Christ appears in many respects "as an astonishing reincarnation of the Master of Justice [Teacher of Righteousness]." Then he goes on to list the similarities.

6. The list is indeed long, and the complete references can be found in Rowley, *op. cit.,* p. 20, n. 4. It includes Lambert, Vermès, de Vaux, Goossens, Bonsirven, Delcor. We found of particular value J. Coppens, "Les Documents du Désert de Juda et les Origines du Christianisme," *Cahiers du Libre Examen* (1953), pp. 23-39.

7. Teicher's articles constitute a long series, chiefly in the *Journ. of Jewish St.* from 1951 on. [On Qumran and the Ebionites, see Fitzmyer's essay in this volume pp. 208 ff. Ed note.]

8. Some still opt for another group. S. Lieberman, *Journ. of Bibl. Lit.* 71 (1952), pp. 199-206, shows similarities to the rabbinic *Haberim* (members of a society which observed ritual cleanliness more strictly).

9. *Op. cit.,* pp. 26-27.

10. K. G. Kuhn, "Die Sektenschrift und die iranische Religion," *Zeitschr. f. Theol. u. Kirche* 49 (1952), p. 303: "This dualistic ideology is totally alien to Old Testament thought, nor can it be explained as an outgrowth of the Old Testament." There is dualism in the Pseudepigrapha, especially in the Test. XII Patr. (cf. Judah 20, Asher 5). Yet here one must beware of interpolations, both sectarian and Christian. Fragments of the Pseudepigrapha (Jubilees, Enoch, and Test. XII Patr.) have been found at Qumran; these indicate use of the Pseudepigrapha by the sectarians, but not necessarily authorship.

11. The first article, "Die in Palästina gefundenen hebraïschen Texte und das Neue Testament," *Zeitschr. f. Theol. u. Kirche* 47 (1950), pp. 192-211, was written before the most important Qumran texts were available. It should be modified by the later article mentioned in note 10. [Cf. Kuhn's essay in this volume, pp. 98 f. Ed note]

12. This religion has undergone many important changes in its long existence (cf. J. Finegan, *The Archaeology of World Religions* (1952), chap. II). In the period of Sassanian restoration, beginning of the third century A.D., it became strongly mythological. The reference here is to the much purer teachings of Zoroaster himself (tenth or sixth century B.C.) as represented in the Gathas.

13. Kuhn, "Die Sektenschrift," p. 307. Finegan, *op. cit.,* p. 90.

14. Kuhn, *ibid.,* p. 304: "As for the terminology, and, even more, the whole pattern of thought, there is an obvious parallelism between the Manual of Discipline and this Iranian ideology."

15. *Ibid.*, p. 310.

16. There are about forty treatises in Coptic from about the third or fourth century. They reflect Greek manuscripts of the second or third century. For an accurate but popular account, cf. Victor Gold, *Bibl. Archaeol.* 15 (1952), pp. 70-88. [Cf. p. 249, n. 1a. Ed.]

17. W. F. Albright, "The Bible After Twenty Years of Archaeology," reprint from *Religion and Life* (1954), p. 548. I enjoyed the privilege of reading in manuscript Professor Albright's article on "Recent Discoveries in Palestine and the Gospel of St. John," now published in *The Background of the New Testament and its Eschatology* (Studies in Honor of C. H. Dodd, ed. by W. D. Davies and D. Daube, 1956), pp. 153-71.

18. Kuhn, "Die Sektenschrift," p. 303: "This dualism is, however, not of a physical nature, as was later that of Gnosticism." Again, p. 315, of the Qumran dualism: ". . . that it actually is not of a physical and substantial, but of an ethical nature. This links the texts of the sect with primitive Iranian ideology and distinguishes it clearly from Gnosticism." Bo Reicke, "Traces of Gnosticism in the Dead Sea Scrolls?" *New Testament St.* 1 (1954/55), pp. 137-41, also clearly distinguishes between later Gnosticism and Qumran thought. It is at the most pre-Gnostic. For the nature of St. John's dualism, independently of the Qumran question, cf. E. K. Lee, *The Religious Thought of St. John* (1950), p. 109: ". . . it has no point of contact with metaphysical dualism"; p. 112: "The dualism is, however, an ethical dualism, and is neither absolute nor final."

19. For an interesting schema of all this, cf. Lucetta Mowry, "The Dead Sea Scrolls and the Background for the Gospel of John," *Bibl. Archaeol.* 17 (1954), p. 86. We might add a note on one special aspect of the Gnostic thesis, i.e., that the background of the Johannine Gospel was Mandean Gnosticism. In 1930 there were found some Manichean codices (published by Polotsky) which establish that Mandeanism is secondary in relation to Manicheanism. Thus W. F. Albright says that a fifth-century date for the Mandean sect (although its sources may be earlier) is probable, and its influence on John's Gospel is out of the question; cf. *The Bible After Twenty Years*, pp. 540-41 and 548.

20. This statement seems to have been an important axiom; cf. 1 QH x, 9, and also i, 20.

21. We might note that Qumran says things were made through "His knowledge" and John says through the Logos. To this, see Reicke, *op. cit.*, p. 140: "It is evident that what the Qumran text calls 'the knowledge' and 'the thought' of God is actually his creative intellect, or very much the same as what the Fourth Gospel calls the Logos of God."

22. Mowry, *op. cit.*, p. 83. St. Irenaeus, *Adv. Haer.*, 3, 11, states that the Prologue was against Cerinthus and his dualism.

23. For other New Testament texts, cf. Col. 1₁₆; 1 Cor. 8₆; Heb. 1₂.

24. 1 QS iii, 18, 20, 24; CD 7₁₉.

25. I QS iii, 19, 21; iv, 12; CD 24. The name "Mastema" comes up too—1 QS iii, 23; CD 20₃—and it seems to refer to the evil spirit. In QM xiii, 11, a difficult text, Gaster (*The Dead Sea Scriptures*, 1956, p. 298) reads: "But for corruption thou hast made Belial, an angel of hostility [i.e., Mastema]."

26. Kuhn, "Die Sektenschrift," p. 301, n. 4: "Here (1 QS iv, 23), however, it is a dualism within and not between individuals: the two spirits, that of truth and that of perversion, join battle within man, and the pious attains ultimate salvation when God frees man from the spirit of perversion within him . . ."

27. So also Braun, *op. cit.*, p. 13.

28. Jn. 12₄₆: "I have come a light into the world." Also 1₄ and 9.

29. As Fr. Braun points out, *op. cit.*, pp. 13-17, Satan and Mastema are variations of the same root *(STM)*.

30. Lk. 22₅₃: "But this is your hour, and the power of darkness." Also 2 Cor. 6₁₄-₁₅: "Or what fellowship has light with darkness? What harmony is there between Christ and Belial?" Notice the parallelism: Christ-light versus Belial-darkness. On this point cf. also 2 Cor. 11₁₄: ". . . for Satan disguises himself as an angel of light."

31. Jn. 12₃₁, 14₃₀, 16₁₁. (In the Prologue notice that the world is almost equated with the darkness.) The "prince of this world" has no power over Christ, is judged by Christ, and will be cast out by him. St. Paul in 2 Cor. 4₄ speaks of the "god of this world."

32. I QS iv, 17 and 25: "For God has set them in equal parts until the final period . . ."

33. CD 6₉: "And during all these years Belial shall be let loose against Israel . . ."

34. CD 9a; 1 QS iv, 12; 1 QH iii, 28 ff.

35. A fragment translated in G. Vermès, *Les Manuscrits du Désert de Juda* (2nd ed., Paris, 1954), p. 199. [Now published in *Qumran Cave I* as no. 27 (1 Q Myst.: *Livre des mystères*.) Ed. note]

36. This victory theme is echoed in Col. 1₁₃: "He has rescued us from the power of darkness and transferred us into the kingdom of his beloved Son, in whom we have our redemption, the remission of our sins."

37. Cf. Coppens, *op. cit.*, p. 35: "To the men at Qumran the end of time has not come; they await it. They live in expectation of the Judgment Day. For the Christians, especially St. John, 'the world is already judged'."

38. *Ibid.*, p. 33.

39. "The Dead Sea Scrolls and the New Testament," *Studia Catholica* 26 (1951), pp. 289-299, and 27 (1952), pp. 1-9. Cf. p. 293.

40. *Ibid.*, p. 297. Also Braun, *op. cit.*, p. 13. Kuhn, "Die Sektenschrift," p. 312: "For each individual, God has determined beforehand to which side he shall belong, and once he is in existence his acts and destiny are unchangeable." Of interest is the comment of Josephus, *Ant.* 13, 5: "But the sect of the Essenes affirm that fate governs all things, and that nothing befalls man but what is according to its determination."

41. These are the Jamnes and the Mambres of 2 Tim. 3₈. In relation to the sinful generation of the desert, CD has some strong phrases—2₆-₈: "For God chose them not from the beginning of the world, and ere they were *formed* he knew their works. And he abhorred *their* generations *from of old* and hid his face from *their* land until they were consumed" (italicized words emended by Charles). 2₁₀: "But them he hated he made to go astray." However, this language reflects a certain Hebrew idiom of thought. Compare the Johannine quote of Is. 6₁₀ (Jn. 12₄₀): "He has blinded their eyes, and hardened their hearts, lest they see."

42. 1 QS viii, 6. Brownlee translates this "the chosen of grace"; but this seems a little too Christian, influenced by Rom. 11₅, "A remnant, chosen by grace." [Cf. this volume, p. 115. Ed.] We might also quote 1 QS xi, 7, "To those whom God chose he has given them as an eternal possession," and CD 9a: "Moses said, 'Not for thy righteousness or for the uprightness of thine heart dost thou go in to inherit these nations, but because he loved thy fathers and because he would keep the oath.'" The whole of 1 QH i stresses man's dependence on God. These texts seem deterministic; yet they can have perfectly orthodox meanings. What

they actually meant to their sectarian authors is difficult to say.

43. 1 QS iii, 1: "For his soul has refused instruction and knowledge of righteous laws."

44. The words are "hidden" and "with a high hand." Brownlee translates them as unconscious and conscious sins.

45. Kuhn, "Die Sektenschrift," p. 300, n. 4, sees these two trends in Qumran thought.

46. Cf. Mk. 13₂₀; 1 Pet. 2₉; and esp. Eph. 1₄: "Even as he chose us in him before the foundation of the world."

47. The leading of men from light to darkness is also the mission of St. Paul, Acts 26₁₈: "I am now sending thee, to open their eyes that they may turn from darkness to light and from the dominion of Satan to God." Note the parallelism: darkness-dominion of Satan *versus* light-dominion of God. Grossouw, *op. cit.,* p. 6, sees this as one of the strongest New Testament similarities to Qumran.

48. Of course we must remember Is. 50₁₀: ". . . his servant who walks in darkness and has no light."

49. This Qumran exclusiveness is seen in their consideration of themselves as princes. CD 8₆: ". . . the penitents of Israel who went forth out of the land of Judah and sojourned in the land of Damascus, all of whom God called princes." And again in the *pesher*-commentary on Ps. 37, published by J. M. Allegro in the *Pal. Expl. Quart.* 86 (1954), p. 72 (ii, 4a): ". . . The Congregation of His Elect will be the Chieftains and Princes." Reicke, *op. cit.,* in note 1, sees in this a similarity to St. Peter's "chosen race, a royal priesthood" (1 Pet. 2₉).

50. There are numerous citations in the Qumran literature about a special revelation. CD 2₁: "And now, hearken unto me all you who have entered into the covenant, and I will disclose to you the ways of the wicked." Again CD 51–2: "God confirmed the covenant of Israel forever, revealing unto them the hidden things wherein all Israel had erred: his holy Sabbaths and his glorious festivals." Charles and others see a possible reference to the calendar of the Book of Jubilees which the sectarians are thought to have followed.

51. The passages are 1 QS ii, 3, and iii, 7; Brownlee translates: "life-giving wisdom" and "life-giving light."

52. In 1 QpHab ii, 8, those are condemned who will not accept what they hear from the mouth of the priest whom God has sent "to give the meaning of all the words of his servants the prophets."

53. 1 QS v, 21. The idea of examination is found also in 1 QS v, 24, and vi, 17. We may say that ix, 13, sets the ideal of the community: ". . . to do God's will according to all that has been revealed for any time at that time, and to learn all the wisdom found with reference to the times."

54. I QpHab viii, 1—a commentary on Hab. 2₄; the famous verse quoted in Rom. 1₁₇; cf. Gal. 3₁₁ and Heb. 10₃₈𝑓. Brownlee remarks (*op. cit.,* note 57): "Interestingly enough this commentator agrees with Paul in interpreting *æmunato* as a personal faith which brings salvation." Undoubtedly the *pesher* offers an interpretation of Habakkuk which is intermediary between the literal Old Testament sense and that of Paul, but does the Qumran document mean any more than fidelity to the Teacher's exposition of the Law? CD 9₅₀–₅₁ says that God will reward all those "who hold fast by these judgments in going out and coming in according to the Law, and listen to the voice of the Teacher and confess before God (saying), 'We have done wickedly . . .'"

55. Note the parallelism of the term "the light of life" here and at Qumran. For "sons of light," cf. 1 Thess. 5₅: "For you are all children of the light and

children of the day. We are not of night, nor of darkness." Eph. 5₈: "For you
once were darkness, but now you are light in the Lord." Also there is the
difficult Lk. 16₈: ". . . for the children of this world are in relation to their
own generation more prudent than are the children of the light." Could
"children of the light" have a definite sectarian meaning here?

56. Eph. 5₉ continues, "Walk, then, as children of the light (for the fruit of
the light is in all goodness and justice and truth), testing what is well pleasing
to God; and have no fellowship with the unfruitful works of darkness." The
RSV translates the Greek (dokimazontes) as "try to learn what is pleasing to the
Lord." Compare this to the Qumran quote in note 53. Also Rom. 13₁₂: "The day
is at hand. Let us therefore lay aside the works of darkness, and put on the
armor of light. Let us walk becomingly as in the day."

57. Cf. Braun, op. cit., p. 31.

58. In CD 2₁₀ a striking sentence occurs: "And through his Messiah (anointed
one) he shall make them know his holy spirit, and he is truth." [Cf. p. 59.] It
is not inconceivable that our present copy of CD (tenth century A.D., according to
Schechter) contains Christian interpolations. However, we should note that such
a text can have a perfectly clear sectarian interpretation: through his anointed
one, the Teacher or some other Qumran figure, God will make men follow the
spirit of truth. There is absolutely no evidence of Trinitarian belief at Qumran.

59. Cf. Jas. 1₁₈: "He has begotten us by the word of truth."

60. The term "truth" is also applied to Christ: "I am the way, and the truth
and the life" (Jn. 14₆); "And the word was made flesh, and dwelt among us.
And we saw his glory . . . full of grace and truth" (1₁₄). It is interesting to
take a concordance and see the number of times "truth" is used in John in a
sense obviously more meaningful than "veracity."

61. John never uses the term "spirit of perversion." However, he clearly regards
the devil as diametrically opposed to truth: "He was a murderer from the
beginning and has not stood in the truth because there is no truth in him.
When he tells a lie, he speaks from his very nature, for he is a liar and the
father of lies" (8₄₄).

62. Notice in this passage the peculiar phrase "test the spirit." A similar
expression occurs in 1 QS v, 20-21: "Now, when he (the neophyte) enters into
the covenant to do according to all these ordinances, to be united to a holy congregation, they shall examine his spirit in the community . . ." (Also v, 24, and
vi, 17). The term is roughly the same; but John seems to refer to charismata,
the gifts of the Spirit, while Qumran is talking about a way of behavior.

63. Another interesting combination of spirit and truth occurs in Jn. 4₂₃:
"But the hour is coming, and is now here, when the true worshipers will worship
the Father in spirit and in truth . . . God is spirit, and they who worship him
must worship in spirit and in truth."

64. This expression is peculiar to St. John. Rev. 22₁₅ speaks of "everyone who
loves and practices falsehood."

65. 1 QS iv, 6 and 15, speaks of walking in the ways of the two spirits, as
compared to walking in truth.

66. Brownlee suggests a cross reference to Is. 43₁₀₋₁₂: "You are my witnesses
and my servant whom I have chosen."

67. Also cf. 3 Jn. 3 in the preceding paragraph.

68. The Old Testament is quite clear about love for one who has offended:
Lev. 19₁₈ commands, "Take no revenge and cherish no grudge against your
fellow countrymen. You shall love your neighbor as yourself." Yet, in practice,

love of enemy does not seem to have received great emphasis in Old Testament morality.

69. Kuhn, "Die Sektenschrift," p. 306, sees close parallels to this in the Zoroastrian *Yasna*. These Qumran passages may well be adopted formulae which had lost some of their original venom.

70. Grossouw, *op. cit.*, p. 292, sees in this a resemblance to the Christian *disciplina arcani*.

71. *Ibid.*

72. Also Mt. 19₁₉ and parallels. Coppens, *op. cit.*, p. 32, points out that, even at its height, Qumran never attained to the paternity of God: "We seek in vain a text recalling the one where St. Paul asserts the presence of the Spirit in the heart of the believers, inviting and urging them to speak to God as their Father with a note of the intimacy of family relations."

73. Grossouw, *op. cit.*, p. 292.

74. Braun, *op. cit.*, pp. 17-18, suggests that this opposition to the sons of Belial may be echoed in John's opposition to the world: "Do not love the world, or the things that are in the world. If anyone loves the world, the love of the Father is not in him" (1 Jn. 2₁₅). This distrust of the world demands that the Christian, to a certain extent, separate himself from the world: "They are not of the world, even as I am not of the world" (Jn. 17₁₆). If Braun is correct in seeing a parallel to Qumran in this, St. John's theology still presents a great clarification: our hatred is for evil as represented in the world, and not for the people who do evil. However, even John speaks of "the children of the devil" (1 Jn. 3₁₀), which is not too far from "the sons of Belial."

75. ii, 24; v, 4 and 25; viii, 2; x, 26. Braun, *op. cit.*, p. 19, sees in this communal spirit an approach to the *agape* of John.

76. CD 10₁₀ff. outlines a process of rebuking before witnesses, and states that a sinner on the testimony of reliable witnesses can be excluded from "the Purity of the Community." As many have noticed, the process bears a resemblance to Mt. 18₁₅-17 on fraternal correction. Josephus, *Bell.* 2, 8, says of the Essenes: "They dispense their anger after a just manner and restrain their passion."

77. Grossouw, *op. cit.*, p. 298: "It is St. John who in the New Testament speaks exclusively, and very often, of the love of one's brothers or the love of each other, but never of the love of one's neighbor (in the Christian sense of the word neighbor)."

78. Cf. Cf. also 1 Jn. 3₁₁, 18, 23; 2 Jn. 5. And, of course, there is the *koinonia* ("fellowship") of 1 Jn. 1₃ and 6-7.

79. For similar usage, cf. Jer. 17₁₃; Prov. 14₂₇; 16₂₂; Sir. 21₁₆(13). Cant. 4₁₅ compares the beloved to "a well of living waters." In this connection, C. H. Dodd, *The Interpretation of the Fourth Gospel* (1954), p. 312, tells us: "In rabbinic tradition water was a frequent symbol of the Torah, as cleansing, as satisfying thirst, and as promoting life."

80. The reference is to Is. 58₁₁; but neither the Hebrew nor the Greek text has "living" water. Braun, *op. cit.*, p. 25, has noticed this similarity of the "fountains of living water," and he mentions the use of the Well of the Oath and the Well of the Vision in Jubil. 16₁₁ and 24₁.

81. Rev. 21₆; also 22₁ and 17.

82. 1 QS vii, 18-19: "And the man whose spirit is alienated from the institution of the community so as to be a traitor to the truth and walk in the stubbornness of his own heart, if he repents (and returns), he shall be fined for two years."

83. 1 QS ii, 13-14: "But his spirit will be destroyed, the thirst with the satiety, with no forgiveness."

84. This finds some support in Heb. 1026: "If we sin willfully after receiving the knowledge of truth, there remains no longer a sacrifice for sins." Cf. C. Spicq, *L'Épitre aux Hébreux*, (1952-53), vol. II, p. 167, excursus 4.

85. Also CD 815: "And to observe the Sabbath according to its true meaning and the feasts and the day of the Fast according to the utterances (or: ordinances) of them who entered into the New Covenant in the land of Damascus."

86. 1 QS iii, 10. Also i, 8-9.

87. *The Jewish Sect of Qumran and the Essenes* (Eng. transl., 1954), pp. 110-11. Mowry, *op. cit.*, p. 89, n. 12, "Dupont-Sommer's translation of the passage clarifies many of its obscurities." Undoubtedly true; however, it may be well to remember that his translations are often phrased in accordance with the theory he is trying to prove.

88. Jubil. 623-32; I Enoch 824-6. This calendar had four seasons of three months each, (30, 30, 31 days—91 in each quarter—364 in a year). Cf. J. Morgenstern, "The Calendar of the Book of Jubilees," *Vetus Test.* 5 (1955), pp. 34-76.

89. *Op. cit.*, p. 110. Of course, Charles already suggested this in reference to CD 51.

90. Mowry, *op. cit.*, pp. 87-89. She depends on B. W. Bacon, *The Gospel of the Hellenists* (1933).

91. If so, we may receive some light on "the 14th of Nisan problem" [i.e., the dating of the Last Supper and the Crucifixion; see e.g., J. Jeremias, *The Eucharistic Words of Jesus*, and this volume, p. 90—Ed.]. Could Jesus and his followers have followed this sectarian calendar? Morgenstern, *op. cit.*, p. 64, sees affinities between the calendar of the Galileans and that of Jubilees.

92. *Bell.* 2, 8, 5: at the fifth hour they bathe their bodies in water for purification; 8, 10: if the seniors are touched by the juniors, they must wash themselves; 8, 13: both women and men (of the marrying Essenes) bathe partially clothed. Especially noteworthy is 8, 7, where joining is described as being made a partaker of the waters of purification.

93. "Water-for-impurity" (cf. Num. 194).

94. Cf. R. de Vaux, *Rev. Bibl.* 60 (1953), pp. 88-106. Conceivably the cisterns could also have been used for storing water, in which case the steps allowed easier access.

95. Cf. Braun, *op. cit.*, p. 23.

96. Mowry, *op. cit.*, pp. 90-91.

97. *Ibid*, p. 92. Also Braun, *op. cit.*, p. 24.

98. W. H. Brownlee, in a series of articles on Qumran and Christ as Salvation, the New Law, and our Righteousness, *The United Presbyterian* (Nov. 29, Dec. 6, 13, 20, 27, 1954).

99. The LXX supposes the Masoretic reading. 1 QIs$^b$ is not preserved for the first case; but in the last two it is the same as the Masoretic text.

100. Brownlee, Nov. 29 art., p. 6.

101. Cf. the articles by Dewey Beegle, *Bull. of the Amer. Sch. of Oriental Res.* 123 (1951), pp. 26-30, and M. Burrows, *ibid.* 124 (1951), pp. 18-20.

102. "John the Baptist in the New Light of Ancient Scrolls," this volume, pp. 44 ff.

103. Brownlee's translation, p. 50. He suggests also 1 Jn. 220 (and 27): "But you have an anointing from the Holy One and you know all things." Braun, *op. cit.*, p. 23, accepts Brownlee's view: "In other words, the members of the Community shall bear the Messianic name since they shall share in his unction, which in the prophetic tradition is the Holy Spirit."

104. "Die beiden Messias Aarons und Israels," *New Testament St.* 1 (1954/55),

pp. 168-79. [The article found in revised and somewhat enlarged form in this volume, pp. 54-64. Ed. note]

105. Kuhn, *op. cit.*, p. 178. [This volume, p. 63. Ed.] As he observes, this is an interesting parallel to the patristic conception of Christ as prophet, priest, and king. L. H. Silberman, "The two 'Messiahs' of the Manual of Discipline," *Vetus Test.* 5 (1955), p. 82, disagrees with Brownlee also. His interpretation is that a prophet will come who will put in office an anointed high priest of Aaron and will restore the Davidic dynasty of Israel.

106. *Op. cit.*, chap. 9. For the effects of his first work, see notes 4, 5, and 6. In our opinion, Dupont-Sommer himself offered sufficient basis for some of these exaggerations.

107. Josephus, *Bell.* 2, 8, speaks of the Essenes: "They have no certain city, but many of them dwell in every city."

108. "Recent Discoveries . . ." (note 17), pp. 170-71.

109. *Op. cit.*, p. 167.

110. Grossouw, *op. cit.*, pp. 1-4, and Braun, *op. cit.*, pp. 32-34, give examples.

111. Braun, *op. cit.*, p. 37: "Among the New Testament writings, Hebrews is the one which gives the fullest answer to the basic tendencies of the Sect." C. Spicq, *L'Épitre aux Hébreux*, vol. I, pp. 109-38, points out the proximity of Hebrews to the Johannine literature; consequently, Qumran similarities should not be surprising. May not the principal argument of the Epistle, i.e., that Christ is a priest although he is from Judah, be directed against the expectation of the two Messiahs, from Aaron and from Israel?

112. We have given some in footnotes; Grossouw, pp. 5-8, and Braun, pp. 39-40, give others. Sherman E. Johnson, "The Dead Sea Manual of Discipline and the Jerusalem Church of Acts," *Zeitschr. f. d. alttest. Wissensch.* 66 (1954), pp. 106-20 [this volume, pp. 129 ff. Ed.], mentions these parallels between Qumran and the early church as described in Acts: baptism, communal sharing, poverty, communal meals, organization. These suggestions need to be critically evaluated.

113. As Albright wisely remarks, *op. cit.*, p. 170, it is not a question of a fundamental difference between the Synoptics and John; the latter has simply emphasized certain aspects of Christ's teaching, including certain aspects that resembled the teaching of the Essenes most closely.

114. Cf. especially two articles by Brownlee: the one published in this volume, pp. 33 ff., and "A Comparison of the Covenanters of the Dead Sea Scrolls with pre-Christian Jewish Sects," *Bibl. Archaeol.* 13 (1950), pp. 69-72. Also Grossouw, *op. cit.*, p. 5, on the Benedictus.

115. Suggested by Brownlee, see p. 35.

116. St. Irenaeus, *Adv. Haer.* 3, 11, 1 (PG 7, 879-880), tells us that it was directed against Cerinthus. St. Jerome, *In Evang. Matt. Prol.* (PL 26, 18-19), adds the name of Ebion to John's adversaries. Victorinus Petaviensis, *In Apocalypsin*, 11, 1 (PL 5, 333D), mentions Valentinus, Cerinthus, and Ebion. This is significant because, as we mentioned, there are similarities between Ebionite doctrines and those of Qumran. [Cf. in this volume, pp. 208-31. Ed. note]

117. We should note that some of the Pauline Epistles which have affinities to the Qumran literature are centered around Ephesus (Eph. 1 and 2 Corinthians, written at Ephesus or shortly after his departure; Timothy to his disciple at Ephesus). Spicq, *op. cit.*, I, chap. 7, attributes the authorship of Hebrews, which has Qumran influences too, to Apollos (the disciple of John the Baptist), who was at Ephesus.

118. There were, most likely, other causes too—whence our hesitancy to inter-

pret all details of the Gospel in anti-Essene terms.

119. Braun, *op. cit.*, pp. 42-44, proposes a theory similar to ours.


### XIII. THE QUMRAN SCROLLS, THE EBIONITES, AND THEIR LITERATURE

1. This essay has been developed out of the first of the papers delivered at the 1955/56 Seminar on the Qumran Scrolls, conducted by Professor W. F. Albright at Johns Hopkins University. To him the author wishes to express deep gratitude for his interest, his corrections, and the time taken to read the final copy.

2. "The Dead Sea Scrolls—Documents of the Jewish Christian Sect of Ebionites," *Journ. of Jewish St.* 2 (1951), p. 67-99.

3. A. Dupont-Sommer, *The Jewish Sect of Qumran and the Essenes* (London, 1954), p. 159. W. F. Albright, "Chronology of the Dead Sea Scrolls," Postscript to W. H. Brownlee's translation of the Dead Sea Manual of Discipline, *Bull. of the Amer. Sch. of Oriental Res., Suppl. Stud.* 10-12 (1951), p. 58, n. 3.

4. Cf. *Journ. of Jewish St.* 3 (1952), pp. 53-55, 111-18, 128-32, 139-50; 4 (1953), pp. 1-13, 49-58, 93-103, 139-53; 5 (1954), pp. 38, 93-99.

5. "Die neuentdeckten Qumrantexte und das Judenchristentum der Pseudo-klementinen," *Beiheft zur Zeitschr. f. d. neutest. Wiss.* 21 (1954), pp. 35-51.

6. "Das gnostische Judentum in den Dead Sea Scrolls," *Zeitschr. f. Religions-und Geistesgeschichte* 6 (1954), pp. 276-79 (hereafter referred to as Schoeps 2).

7. In the preface to his *Theologie und Geschichte des Judenchristentums* (1949; hereafter referred to as Schoeps 1), H. J. Schoeps claims to set a new landmark for scholarly research in the study of the Ebionites by being the first to take into account rabbinic literature and the translation of the Old Testament by Symmachus, the Ebionite. The data from Symmachus are quite fragmentary and do not really concern us here. See also H. J. Schoeps, *Aus frühchristlicher Zeit, Religionsgeschichtliche Untersuchungen* (1950), pp. 82-119. The questions and problems connected with Symmachus and his translation of the Old Testament are so numerous that it is too hazardous to try to draw any definite conclusions from this source. Important as is the study made by Schoeps, one may still ask whether he has really proved his point; cf. the reviews of his books by R. Bultmann in *Gnomon* 26 (1954), p. 180, and by G. Bornkamm in *Zeitschr f. Kirchengeschichte* 64 (1952/53), p. 197. The interpretation of the material in the rabbinic sources is so intimately connected with the question of the identity of the Minim that anything which might be gathered from such a discussion would remain quite problematical. Cf. Schoeps 1, pp. 21-25. Also J. Thomas, *Le mouvement baptiste en Palestine et Syrie* (1935), pp. 161-62. This author identifies the Minim with Ebionites and the Nazoraioi. But Ralph Marcus, "Pharisees, Essenes and Gnostics," *Journ. of Bibl. Lit.* 73 (1954), p. 159, remarks: ". . . it has become clearer in recent years that while the term Minim in the rabbinic and patristic literature of the third century and afterwards may refer to Jewish Christians, in Tannaitic writings it chiefly designates Jewish Gnostics." Professor Marcus quotes L. Ginzberg: "I may state with certainty that only in a very few places does Minim refer to Judeo-Christians, while in most cases it describes Jewish Gnostics" (*ibid.*, note 4). Cf. also Bultmann, *op. cit.*, p. 179; and G. Bornkamm, *op. cit.*, p. 197, speaks of the "rabbinic witness to Jewish Christianity, only hypothetically useful." Consequently, in a discussion of the relationship between the sect of Qumran and the Ebionites, we prefer not to use these sources for information concerning the latter.

8. For the different forms of this word in patristic writings, see this article in its original form.

9. Cf. J. Thomas, *op. cit.*, p. 160; Schoeps 1, p. 9. The latter maintains that this idea of Ebion as a founder is due to Hippolytus, but he gives no references for this statement (cf. p. 9, n. 2). This is but one example of the carelessness that is found in this book amid an otherwise mammoth display of erudition, which makes it necessary to use Schoeps' work only with the greatest caution. Cf. Bornkamm's review, p. 196: "many mistakes in quotations and bibliography." Similarly, Bultmann, *op. cit.*, p. 189. In the light of such criticism it is quite surprising to read the highly laudatory review of Schoeps' books written by P. Benoit, O.P., *Rev. Bibl.* 57 (1950), pp. 604-9.

10. Cf. G. Quispel, "Neue Funde zur Valentinianischen Gnosis," *Zeitschr. f. Religions- und Geistesgeschichte* 6 (1954), pp. 289-305; H.-Ch. Puech et G. Quispel, "Les écrits gnostiques du Codex Jung," *Vigiliae christianae* 8 (1954), pp. 1-51; V. R. Gold, "The Gnostic Library of Chenoboskion," *Bibl. Arch.* 15 (1952), pp. 70-88; W. F. Albright, "The Bible after Twenty Years of Archeology," *Religion in Life* 21 (1952), p. 548. [*The Jung Codex.* Three Studies by H. C. Puech, G. Quispel, W. C. van Unnik. Trans. and ed. by F. L. Cross (1955). Cf. p. 249, n. 1a.]

11. Schoeps 1, p. 8.

12. It is important to remember that the type of patristic writing in which the Ebionites are usually mentioned is heresiography. They were classed as christological heretics; such a classification, although important to the theologian, leaves us with a paucity of details for our comparison with the Qumran sect.

13. Perhaps it would be better to describe this work as Pseudo-Tertullian; it is generally held today that chaps. 46-53 of the *De praescriptione* are actually a digest of Hippolytus' lost *Syntagma*; cf. J. Quasten, *Patrology* II (1953), pp. 169-70.

14. Cf. J. Thomas, *op. cit.*, pp. 156-70, for a detailed discussion and references to the literature on the subject. Schoeps (1, pp. 8 ff.) likewise discusses the problem briefly.

15. Cf. Ep. 112, 13 (PL 22, 924): "What shall I say of the Ebionites, who pretend that they are Christians? Even to this present day there is a heresy amongst the Jews throughout all the synagogues of the East, which is called that (i.e., the heresy) of the Minaei and which is even now condemned by the Pharisees: they call them popularly Nazarenes, who believe in Christ the Son of God, born of the Virgin Mary, and assert that it was he who suffered under Pontius Pilate and was raised up again, in whom we also believe; but while they desire to be both Jew and Christian, they are neither Jew nor Christian."

16. Schoeps 1, p. 11; Schoeps is continually stressing throughout his book that the Ebionites were not Gnostics. He finds it convenient for his thesis to attribute all Gnostic elements that might be found in the Ebionite tenets to the Elchesaites. This may well be true, but it does not follow that Epiphanius has confused the Elchesaites and the Ebionites. Later Ebionites may well have been Gnostics, precisely because of the Elchesaite influence. Does not this seem to be indicated by the fact that Epiphanius notes a distinction between Ebion and later Ebionites?

17.                          I. The Ebionites

a) They depend on Cerinthus and Carpocrates (Iren, Tert, Hipp);
b) they believe in one God, the creator of the world (Iren, Tert, Hipp);
c) they use the Gospel of Matthew only (Iren, Tert[?], Epiph);
d) they reject Paul as an apostate from the Law (Iren, Orig, Epiph);

e) they expound the prophets *curiosius* (Iren);

f) they practice circumcision (Iren, Orig, Epiph);

g) they observe the Sabbath (Euseb, Epiph);

h) they live according to the Jewish way of life, according to the Law (Iren, Tert, Hipp, Orig, Euseb, Epiph);

i) they face Jerusalem when they pray (Iren);

j) they hold the observance of the Mosaic Law as necessary for salvation (Hipp, Euseb);

k) they reject the virgin birth of Christ (Iren, Tert, Orig, Euseb, Epiph);

l) they hold Christ to be a mere man (Iren, Tert, Hipp, Euseb, Epiph);

m) they maintain Jesus had to merit his title, Christ, by fulfilling the Law (Hipp, Epiph);

n) they reject virginity and continence (Epiph);

o) they use purificatory baths (Epiph);

p) they use remedial baths (Epiph);

q) they admit baptism (Epiph);

r) they celebrate the mysteries with unleavened bread and mere water (Epiph);

s) they hold that Christ came to abrogate sacrifice in the Temple (Epiph);

t) they believe that God set the devil and Christ to rule over this world and the world to come, respectively (Epiph);

u) they give up all goods and possessions (Epiph);

v) they permit divorce (Epiph);

w) they admit Abraham, Isaac, Jacob, Moses, Aaron, Joshua, but none of the prophets [David, Solomon, Isaiah, Jeremiah, Daniel, Ezekiel, Elijah, Elisha] (Epiph);

x) they claim that Christ alone is the True Prophet (Epiph);

y) they use the book, *Periodoi Petrou dia Klementos* (Epiph);

z) they abstain from meat like Peter (Epiph).

## II. The Nazaraioi

a) They believe in one God, creator of the world (Epiph);

b) they use the Gospel of Matthew only (Euseb, Epiph);

c) they reject Paul as an apostate from the Law (Orig, Euseb);

d) they practice circumcision (Epiph);

e) they observe the Sabbath (Euseb, Epiph [Euseb says they observed Sunday too]);

f) they follow the Jewish way of life according to the Law (Euseb, Epiph);

g) they do not reject the virgin birth of Christ (Orig, Euseb, Jerome; Epiph is not sure about this);

h) they deny Jesus' pre-existence as God (Euseb);

i) they call Jesus the Son of God (Epiph, Jer);

j) they believe in the resurrection of the dead (Epiph).

18. *Op. cit.*, pp. 171-83; cf. Bultmann, *op. cit.*, p. 185.

19. In his first article on the Ebionites and the Dead Sea Scrolls (cf. note 1) Teicher gives one reference to two places in the Pseudo-Clementines; cf. p. 98, n. 4. This is supposed to support his contention that Paul is the adversary referred to in 1 QpHab and in the Pseudo-Clementines.

20. Cf. K. G. Kuhn, "Die in Palästina gefundenen hebräischen Texte und das Neue Testament," *Zeitschr. f. Theol. u. Kirche* 47 (1950), p. 207.

21. Cf., for example, G. Vermès, "Le 'Commentaire d'Habacuc' et le Nouveau Testament," *Cahiers Sioniens* 5 (1951), pp. 337-49; K. Elliger, *Studien zum Habak-kuk-Kommentar* (1953), p. 244; H. J. Schoeps, "Der Habakkuk-Kommentar von

Ain-Feshka—ein Dokument der hasmonäischen Spätzeit," *Zeitschr. f. d. alttest. Wiss.* 63 (1951), pp. 249-50. Also Schoeps, "Handelt es sich wirklich um ebionitische Dokumente?" *Zeitschr. f. Religions- und Geistesgeschichte* 3 (1951), p. 322 (hereafter, Schoeps 3).

22. Cf. note 4 for references to his articles. Just a few points will be mentioned here. For the identification of Jesus as the True Teacher and Paul as the "Man of Lies" Teicher is relying on the article of G. Margoliouth, "The Sadducean Christians of Damascus," *Athenaeum* 4335 (Nov. 26, 1910), pp. 657-59, where the identification is merely asserted. Teicher does little more when he says, "T ∴ 'True Teacher' is, in fact, Jesus. He is addressed as such in Mk. 12:14, 'Master (Teacher) we know that thou art true.' " This is the only evidence given that the Teacher of Righteousness of the Qumran literature is Jesus. Another point is the problem of the Jewish Christians mentioned by Eusebius (*Hist. eccl.* 3, 5; quoted above). All we know is that they were early Christians from Jerusalem, most likely Jewish. Pella, the place to which they went according to Eusebius, is about 50 to 60 miles away from Qumran, as the crow flies, and on the other side of the Jordan; hardly "in the vicinity of the Ain Feshka cave" (JJS 2:93). Another gratuitous statement is the assertion that the Ebionites are mentioned by name in the 1 QpHab xii, 3, 6. K. Elliger (*op. cit.*, p. 244) has pointed out that the article would be necessary before *ebyonim* for this word to be capable of meaning "the Ebionites." Unfortunately for Elliger, the word has turned up with the article in the recently published 4 QpPs 37 (i, 9, and ii, 10). Cf. J. M. Allegro, "A Newly Discovered Fragment of a Commentary on Psalm 37 from Qumran," *Pal. Explor. Quart.* 86 (1954), pp. 69-75. This still does not prove that *ebyonim* means "Ebionites," for the word is obviously used in all places in the sense found so often in the Old Testament, "God's poor." 1 QpHab xii, 10, can easily be translated, "who robbed the possessions of the poor," meaning "what little they had." The parallelism between the "poor" and the "simple" in 1 QpHab xii, 3-4, cannot be disregarded. For other passages in the Qumran literature where *ebyonim* means the "poor," cf. 1 QM xi, 9, 13; xiii, 14.

23. Cf. A. Dupont-Sommer, *The Jewish Sect of Qumran and the Essenes* (London, 1954), p. 158: "The excavations of Khirbet Qumran, by establishing that the manuscripts were conveyed to their hiding-place about A.D. 66-70, show that Dr. Teicher's dates are too late, and accordingly suffice to undermine the whole of his theory." Cf. G. Vermès, *Les Manuscrits du Désert de Juda* (2nd ed., 1954), p. 36; Schoeps 2, p. 1. These authors' remarks are all based on the report of R. de Vaux, "Fouilles au Khirbet Qumran," *Rev. Bibl.* 60 (1953), p. 94; *Comptes rendus de l'Académie des Inscriptions et Belles Lettres* (1953), p. 317.

24. For the purpose of this paper we do not have to consider the translation of the Old Testament by Symmachus, nor the Gospel According to the Hebrews, which are generally judged to be Ebionite compositions. The latter is "some sort of reworking and extension of the Hebrew original of the canonical Gospel of Matthew" (J. Quasten, *op. cit.*, vol. I, p. 112). Cf. the remarks of Bornkamm, *op. cit.*, p. 197.

25. The *Homilies* are extant today in Greek; the text has recently been edited by B. Rehm, *Die Pseudoklementinen: I, Homilien,* in the series *Die griechischen christlichen Schriftsteller der ersten Jahrhunderte* 42 (Berlin, 1953). The *Recognitions* are extant only in a Latin translation (or, according to many scholars, a Latin adaptation) by Rufinus (*ca.* A.D. 405). A new edition has been promised for the Berlin Corpus. For the time being we must use the text found in Migne, PL 1, 1158-1474. There is also a Syriac manuscript, dated A.D. 411, which con-

tains the text of Hom. 10-14 and Rec. 1-4; cf. W. Frankenburg, *Die syrischen Clementinen mit griechischem Paralleltext* (1937; *Texte und Untersuchungen* 48:3). A few other fragments are also extant; cf. J. Quasten, *op. cit.*, vol. I, p. 61. An English translation (which must now be checked against the new critical edition of the Homilies) can be found in A. Roberts and J. Donaldson, *Ante-Nicene Christian Library*, vol. III (*Recognitions*, 1875), XVII (*Homilies*, 1870).

26. In the PsC Paul is alluded to, frequently under the designation "the hostile man," being depicted as the adversary of James, the bishop of Jerusalem. Though Peter is identified with the camp of James, we do not find Paul pictured as the enemy of Peter; the latter role is played by Simon Magus throughout. But the critics of the nineteenth century found no difficulty in asserting that the figure of Simon Magus was really a literary mask for the real opponent, Paul; cf. J. Chapman, "On the Date of the Clementines," *Zeitschr. f. d. neutest. Wiss.* 9 (1908), p. 150-51.

27. For an extensive survey of the problem of PsC source criticism, see this article in its original form.

28. See H. Waitz, *Die Pseudoklementinen* (1904, *Texte und Untersuchungen* 25:4); O. Cullmann, *Le problème littéraire et historique du roman pseudo-clémentin* (1930); Schoeps 1, pp. 37-61.

29. O. Cullmann, in *Neutest. Studien f. R. Bultmann* (1954), pp. 35-51; Cullman takes no account of Rehm's critical analysis of KP.

30. J. Chapman, *op. cit.*, pp. 147 ff.; Ed Schwartz-M. Goguel, "Unzeitgemässe Beobachtungen zu den Clementinen," *Zeitschr. f. d. neutest. Wiss.* 31 (1932), pp. 151-99; B. Rehm, *op. cit.*, and "Zur Entstehung der pseudoclementinischen Schriften," *Zeitschr. f. d. neutest. Wiss.* 37 (1938), pp. 77-184.

31. Schoeps 1, pp. 38 and 45-53, expands the list of KP passages; for a list of the passages which also indicates Schoeps' additions, see this article in its original form.

32. Cf. Cullmann in *Neutest. St. f. R. Bultmann* (cf. this volume, pp. 18 ff.), p. 42; unless otherwise noted, henceforth all references to Cullmann will be to this article.

33. Charles, *Apocrypha and Pseudepigrapha*, vol. II, p. 184, compares CD 814 with Ezek. 2226.

34. *Op. cit.*, pp. 38-39.

35. "Die Sektenschrift und die iranische Religion," *Zeitschr. f. Theol. u. Kirche* 49 (1952), pp. 296-316.

36. *The Jewish Sect of Qumran and the Essenes*, pp. 118-30.

37. *Op. cit.*, p. 129: "The point that strikes anyone reading the teaching of the Manual is that the Two Spirits remain subordinate to God as they do in the Gathas. The Spirit of God is not confused with God, whereas in the later specula-tions of Mazdaism he is identified with Ahura Mazda."

38. Kuhn, *op. cit.*, pp. 311-12, asserts that the subordination to God in the Qumran literature is a feature not found in the Iranian source. That an Iranian source had influenced, as well as the PsC, seems indicated by the interest shown in these writings by Nimrod-Zoroaster. Cullmann, *op. cit.*, p. 38, n. 14, pointed out the passages: Hom. 94, Rec. 130; to these we may add Rec. 427-29 (all KP). For the ideas of Michaud, see "Un mythe zervanite dans un des manuscrits de Qumran," *Vetus Test.* 5 (1955), pp. 137-47.

39. *Ibid.*, p. 39.

40. *Op. cit.*, p. 305.

41. This we maintain against W. Baumgartner, "Die Bedeutung der Höhlen-

funde aus Palästina fur die Theologie," *Schweiz. theol. Umschau* 24 (1954), p. 62, who thinks that the opposition between the sons of light and the sons of darkness is physical. What the basis of this physical interpretation is, Baumgartner does not tell us.

42. "Die in Palästina gefundenen hebraïschen Texte und das Neue Testament," *Zeitschr. f. Theol. u. Kirche* 57 (1950), p. 210, cf. p. 207.

43. "Die Sektenschrift", *op. cit.*, p. 315, cf. this volume, p. 97.

44. Cf. Schoeps 1, pp. 305-6: "As a matter of fact, the Ebionites were never Gnostics; on the contrary, they were their sharpest opponents" (emphasis supplied by Schoeps). Cf. Bultmann's review, p. 188.

45. *Ibid.*, p. 161. To be fair, we must indicate that he does admit in a footnote the possibility of the Persian source. The proof advanced for the *uralt* Jewish root is rabbinic literature, whose antiquity is very hard to determine.

46. "The doctrine (of the Two Spirits) is rather a product of Qumran theology at its best. It is now finally clear to me from where this Ebionite KP got its doctrine of the two spirits when it deals, in Book Six, with the highly Gnostic *syzygies*-doctrine of pairs of contrast." Schoeps 2, p. 277.

47. Cf. Heinrich Schlier, "Das Denken der frühchristlichen Gnosis," *Neutest. St. f. R. Bultmann, op. cit.*, pp. 67-92, for an example of how different early Christian Gnosticism was from Qumran ideas. Bo Reicke has also recently pointed out another difference in that the God of Qumran is a *personal* God, "Traces of Gnosticism in the Dead Sea Scrolls," *New Testament St.* 1 (1954/55), p. 140.

48. 1 QpHab i, 13; ii, 2; v, 10; 4 QpPs 37 ii, 15; CD 111; 813; 940, 53, 68, 71.

49. This point seems to be confirmed by 4 QpPs 37 ii, 15: "Its interpretation concerns (the) priest, the teacher of righ[teousness]." Cf. J. M. Allegro, *op. cit.*, pp. 71-72. J. L. Teicher denies, of course, that the Teacher of Righteousness was a priest, *op. cit.*, 3 (1952), p. 54, and 5 (1954), p. 96: "But he (the Teacher of Righteousness) was a teacher, not a sacrificing priest, and the term 'priest' applied to him in the Fragments is merely a metaphor." "The term *kohen* (priest) is the equivalent of the term *doresh ha-torah* (he who searches the Scriptures)."

50. K. Elliger, *op. cit.*, p. 285, and J. L. Teicher, *op. cit.* 2 (1951), p. 97, point out that the words *sdq* and *'mt* are really synonymous, so that we could well speak of the "Teacher of Truth" or the "True Teacher." The other expression, however, has become customary already, so that it is retained here.

51. *Op. cit.*, p. 39.

52. *Op. cit.*, pp. 183-86.

53. Cullmann, *op. cit.*, p. 40, points out a dissimilarity in that the Teacher of Righteousness is a priest, whereas the True Prophet is not. See, however, note 49 and compare 1 QpHab ii, 7, with vii, 4. As for the PsC, the situation is not clear. From the general context we would not expect the True Prophet to be a priest, yet Rec. 146-48 KP are difficult, certainly, to understand if he were not one.

54. Cullmann, *op. cit.*, p. 40, speaks of a "prophet of lies" in 1 QpHab vii, 9. I can find no such character in the 1 QpHab, unless that is the translation he is proposing for the "Preacher of the Lie" in x, 9.

55. For Micah see the article of J. T. Milik, "Fragments d'un Midrasch de Michée dans les manuscrits de Qumran," *Rev. Bibl.* 59 (1952), pp. 412-18.

56. *Op. cit.*, p. 169.

57. *Harper's Latin Dictionary* (1907), p. 502; cf. also *Thesaurus Linguae Latinae*, vol. IV, p. 1493.

58. Rec. 159, 68-69 KP.

59. Cf. Schoeps 1, p. 160.

60. Cf. G. Vermès, *op. cit.*, pp. 109-12. Bultmann, *op. cit.*, p. 187, maintains that this rejection of the false pericopes by the Ebionites presupposes a Gnostic rejection of the Old Testament and is merely another example of the compromise made by the Ebionites between Gnosticism and Jewish-Christian tradition. The theory of the false pericopes represents a "mysterion" transmitted by Peter to the Ebionite community. This is sheer speculation.

61. "Sacrifice and Worship among the Jewish Sectarians of the Dead Sea (Qumran) Scrolls," *Harv. Theol. Rev.* 46 (1953), p. 149.

62. *Ibid.*, pp. 153-54. Cf. also p. 155 for a discussion of the following text of Josephus.

63. Bultmann, *op. cit.*, p. 187, would derive the Ebionite outlook from the attitude found in the primitive community of the Christian church itself, not as dependent on passages in Mk. 12₃₃, Mt. 9₁₃, 12₇ but rather as coming from the attitude of the Jews among whom Christ lived. Jesus was not the opponent of the priests, as the prophets of the Old Law had been, but of the scribes. As far as Jewish piety was concerned, the synagogue had pressed the cult of the Temple into the background, and so sacrifice had lost its meaning for early Christianity.

64. *Op. cit.*, p. 152; cf. G. Vermès, *op. cit.*, p. 78.

65. Cf. H. L. Ginsberg, "The Hebrew University Scrolls from the Sectarian Cache," *Bull. of the Amer. Sch. of Oriental Res.* 112 (1948), pp. 20-21.

66. This brief description shows that the function of the priest can hardly be that as described by Teicher in his recent article, *op. cit.*, p. 96; see note 55 above. According to 1 QM vii, 11, at the end of the description of the robes of the priests in battle, it is prescribed that this battle dress shall not be worn in the *sanctuary.* This same word is used in 1 QM ii, 3, in a context where sacrifices are also mentioned; so there is no reason to maintain that the priests of Qumran had nothing to do with sacrifice.

67. *Op. cit.*, p. 41.

68. *Ibid.*, p. 44. Are we sure that 1 QS vi, 13 ff., refers to baths? M. H. Gottstein has gone to an opposite extreme in maintaining that the Qumran sect was not a baptist sect, whereas the Essenes are known to have been definitely such; cf. "Anti-Essene traits in the DSS," *Vetus Test.* 4 (1954), pp. 141-47. Even Schoeps, who thinks that the identification of the "Zadokites from Qumran" with the Essenes of Philo and Josephus is highly problematical, admits that Gottstein has gone too far; cf. Schoeps 2, p. 4; but compare the recent study by R. North, S.J., "The Qumran 'Sadducees,'" *Cathol. Bibl. Quart.* 17 (1955), pp. 44-68.

69. *Op. cit.*, p. 155.

70. *The Jewish Sect of Qumran and the Essenes,* pp. 167-68; Cullmann, *op. cit.*, p. 44, refers to these same excavated reservoirs or cisterns as proof that "the monastery of Qumran was an actual baptismal center."

71. A stepped reservoir was found at Gezer; cf. R. A. S. Macalister, *Excavation of Gezer* (1912), vol. I, pp. 274-76; III, pl. LIV. Cf. also F. J. Bliss and R. A. S. Macalister, *Excavations in Palestine during the years 1898-1900* (1902), p. 21. Mention is made here of a "vaulted cistern" at Tell Zakariya. "Similar stepped cisterns were excavated by me at Jerusalem" (*ibid.*). "It is quite possible that we have here an ancient cistern vaulted over during the brief Roman occupation" (*ibid.*).

72. F. M. Cross, Jr., most recently reports as follows: "The cisterns are structurally identical with contemporary Roman cisterns. Although there has been

some speculation that these were baptisteries, there is little reason to connect these cisterns with the well-known practice of the sect; more probably 'living water' was used for baptisms. In any case the aridity of the region requires extensive conserving installations, if a community of any size is to survive," *Archaeology* 9 (1956), p. 44.

73. Cf. J. Thomas, *op. cit.*

74. The question of baths in the PsC is one that is involved in the discussion of sources. Most of the cases cited above of Peter's bath before meals and prayer are found in non-KP passages; the scene is in Tripoli. Cullmann maintains that these passages represent later Ebionite practices (*op. cit.*, p. 45). It is precisely because of the bathing practices that J. Thomas decided to revise the usual theory of PsC sources and present his own (cf. *op. cit.*, p. 175). This cannot be discussed at length here. But it indicates once again the tenuous nature of this entire comparison.

75. *Ibid.*, p. 181.

76. Cf. R. de Vaux, "La seconde saison de fouilles à Khirbet Qumran," *Comptes rendus de l'Académie des Inscriptions et Belles Lettres* (1953), pp. 310-11.

77. "Une lettre de Simeon bar Kokheba," *Rev. Bibl.* 60 (1953), p. 291; see *Qumran Cave I*, pp. 110, 117-18.

78. "Each one finds, according to custom, the place of his proper rank" (*unusquisque ex more recognoscens proprii ordinis locum*, Rec. 4 87 not KP).

79. Here it is variously interpreted, cf. W. Bauer, *Wörterbuch zum Neuen Testament* (4th ed., Berlin, 1952), col. 1425. Philo (*Vita Contemp.* 4, 9) mentions the use of salt at the meals of the Therapeutae, who have been generally considered as related to the Essenes.

80. *Op. cit.*, pp. 60-62, 88-89; cf. Vermès, *op. cit.*, p. 176.

81. *Op. cit.*, p. 47

82. One main point has been purposely omitted: this is the question of "knowledge" in the Qumran and Ebionite sects. To treat this point adequately would demand a separate paper in itself. From the standpoint of Qumran, we already have a good treatment of the question in the Scrolls previously published, written by W. D. Davies, "'Knowledge' in the Dead Sea Scrolls and Matthew 11 25-30," *Harv. Theol. Rev.* 46 (1953), pp. 113-39. See especially pp. 129 ff., where he rejects the identification of Qumran "knowledge" with any of three ways of understanding "Gnosticism" or "gnosis." Strangely enough, Cullmann has not considered this point. Cf. W. Baumgartner, *op. cit.*, p. 62, where the Qumran emphasis on wisdom and intelligence is labeled "Gnostic." Cf. also Bo Reicke, *op. cit.*, pp. 137-41.

83. Cullmann, *op. cit.*, p. 35; A Dupont-Sommer, *op. cit.*, pp. 156-60, 201-6; K. Elliger, *op. cit.*, pp. 242-45; Schoeps 3, pp. 322-28.

84. *Op. cit.*, p. 50. [See Cullmann's note, this volume, p. 252. Ed. note]

85. It seems, too, that Cullmann has overemphasized the importance of the destruction of Jerusalem to the Ebionites of the PsC and to the sect of Qumran. We must await fuller publication of the details of the excavation of Khirbet Qumran before we can judge adequately the effect of this destruction.

86. I.e., the *Osar* and *Qumran Cave I*.

## XIV. HILLEL THE ELDER IN THE LIGHT OF THE DEAD SEA SCROLLS

1. On some significant parallels between the sectarian and rabbinic writings, see S. Lieberman, "Light on the Cave Scrolls from Rabbinic Sources," *Proceed-*

*ings of the American Academy for Jewish Research,* 20 (1951), and "The Discipline in the So-Called Dead Sea Manual of Discipline," *Journ. of Bibl. Lit.* 71 (1952).

2. See I. F. Baer, "The Historical Foundations of the Halacha," *Zion* 17 (1952); "The Ancient Hassidim in Philo's Writings and in Hebrew Tradition," *Zion* 18 (1953); *Israel among the Nations* (1955), all in Hebrew.

2a. This Hebrew word has many shades of meaning when translated into English: mercy, kindness, steadfast love, etc. Therefore it is used in its transliterated form in this essay. The adjective form is *hasid* (pl. *hasidim*) and often means "pious." [Ed. note]

3. Mishnah Hagigah II. 7.

4. Temurah 15b.

5. *Ibid.* Another report, referring to the martyrdom of the Sages under Alexander Jannaeus, says, "the world was desolate until Simeon, son of Shetah, came and restored the Torah to its former authority" (Kiddushin 66a).

6. Sukkah 20a; a third period of decline was said to have ended by Hiyya and his sons.

7. ii, 24; v, 4, 25; viii, 2; x, 26. See Brownlee's trans., Appendix B.

8. I. F. Baer pointed to a possible relationship of the name *essenoi* to *essenes,* the Artemis priests of Ephesus who took upon themselves "to live as Essenes (*esseneuein*) in purity and piety." "The Historical Foundations of the Halacha," *Zion 17* (1952), pp. 43 f.

9. i, 7-8.

10. Prov. $11_{17}$.

11. Lev. Rabbah XXXIV. 3.

12. *Ibid.*

13. Tosefta Sanhedrin XIII. 3; Rosh ha-Shanah 16b quoting Ex. $34_6$, a verse rarely cited by the Tannaites.

14. Aboth II. 6.

15. Aboth de R. Nathan I, ch. III.

16. Yer. Nedarim 39b; Sanhedrin 11a.

17. Aboth de R. Nathan I, ch. IV.

18. Berakhoth 60a, quoting Ps. $112_7$.

19. Betzah 16a, quoting Ps. $68_{20}$.

20. Kethuboth 16 bf.

21. Mishnah Sukkah 53a; Yer. Sukkah 55b; Aboth de R. Nathan II, ch. XXVII.

22. Derekh Eretz VI.

23. Kethuboth 67b.

24. Lev. Rabbah I. 5. Cf. Mt. $23_{12}$; Lk. $18_{14}$.

24a. *Doresh*=he who expounds. *Darash*=he expounded. From the same stem comes the noun *midrash*=commentary. [Ed. note]

25. vi, 6-7.

26. vi, 8-9. Sir. $51_{23}$, "Spend the night in my *beth ha-midrash*" cannot be understood literally.

27. Is. $40_3$.

28. 1 QS viii, 14-16.

29. *Ibid.,* ix, 18-19.

30. *Ibid.,* i, 11-12.

31. 1 QM x, 10.

32. 1 QpHab ii, 8-9.

33. *Ibid.,* vii, 4-5.

34. *Probus* 80-82, in the translation by F. H. Colson. The motif of concentrated

study and exposition, and "transmitting the knowlege of the laws from husband to wife, from father to his children, from master to his slave" as in Philo's idealistic sketch of the Mosaic constitution; *Hypothetica* 7, 13.

35. *Quod Deus Sit Immutabilis* 24.

36. *De Specialibus Legibus* 4, 26.

37. E.g., "Raise up many disciples," attributed to the men of the Great Assembly (Aboth I. 1); Abtalion's admonition to the wise (*ibid*. II).

38. Aboth II. 6.

39. *Ibid*., 8. This is possibly the earliest reference to the connection between the pursuit of learning and man's part in the world-to-come. The term "gain life in the world-to-come," used by Hillel, also Aboth de R. Nathan II, ch. XXVI.

40. Aboth II. 5.

41. *Ibid*., I. 13.

42. Hagigah 9b. Some scholars have doubted the identity of Hillel in this text with Hillel the Elder.

43. Hillel recognized among his students thirty, like Moses, worthy of prophecy, thirty, like Joshua, worthy of miracles, and twenty "average" men. Sukkah 28a.

44. E.g., Lev. Rabbah XXXIV. 3, on the duty to care for one's body "since man has been created in the divine image," and on the soul as a guest in the body.

45. Aboth de R. Nathan II, ch. XXVI.

46. Aboth I, 12.

47. Yer. Pesahim 33a.

48. L. Ginzberg, "The Significance of the Halachah for Jewish History," *On Jewish Law and Lore* (1955), p. 95; Ginzberg lets this development start with "the great expounders" Shemaiah and Abtalion.

49. Josephus, *Bell.* 2, 8, 3.

50. CD, vii, 20c. For the relationship between poverty and piety, see e.g., Ps. Sol. 10⁷.

51. 1 QS ix, 21 f. See also 1 QpHab xii, 6 where the members are called "the poor ones" (*ebyonim*).

52. Fragment A, col. II.

53. CD vi, 21, and xiv, 14.

54. Aboth de R. Nathan I, ch. III.

55. L. Finkelstein, *The Pharisees*, applies to the two groups the terms "Plebeians" and "Patricians," respectively.

56. Mishnah Berakhoth VIII, 1. This and the following interpretations of the laws follow Ginzberg, *op. cit.*, pp. 104 ff.

57. Mishnah Rosh ha-Shanah I. 1.

58. Mishnah Betzah II. 1.

59. Mishnah Berakhoth VI. 5.

60. 1 QS i, 3-4.

61. E.g., 948, 10, 957, 961, 971, 983, 10, 13, 9910–16, 1024, 1033, 1042.

62. Tosefta Sanhedrin XIII. 3; Rosh ha-Shanah 16b f.

63. Dan. 122.

64. 1 Sam. 26.

65. Ps. 1166.

66. Sukkah 28a; Yer. Nedarim 39b.

67. Ps. Sol. 1717ff.

68. Gittin 34b.

69. Mishnah Shebiith X. 3.

70. Lev. 25.

71. Mishnah Arakin IX. 5.
72. Baba Metzia 104a.
73. Mishnah Baba Metzia V. 9.
74. Mishnah 'Eduyot I. 13.
75. 1 QS uses the term *tikkun* (spelled with a *kaf*), viii, 13 and *passim*.
76. 1 QM i, 2.
77. CD xiv, 4, 6 (ed. Rabin, p. 69).
78. *Ibid.*, vi, 21 (ed. Rabin, p. 25).
79. *The Dead Sea Scrolls*, p. 263.
80. Shabbath 31a.
81. *Ibid.*
82. Aboth de R. Nathan I, ch. XV.
83. Hillel is said to have generally displayed a nonrestrictive attitude; he is pictured standing at the gate of Jerusalem, trying to convince "people" going out to work that they would do better to forsake their worldly interests and devote themselves to the Torah. Aboth de R. Nathan II, ch. XXVI.
84. I QpHab. v, 4-5.
85. Aboth II. 7.
86. *Ibid.*, 8; Aboth de R. Nathan II, ch. XXVI.
87. Megillah 3a.
88. Mishnah Hagigah II. 2.
89. *Ibid.*
90. Yer. Hagigah 77d.
91. Ginzberg maintains that there was already a spiritual affinity between him and the Essenes even before he joined them; and that there was the Essene influence upon him that motivated his concurrence with Hillel's opinion regarding the sacrifice ritual, *op. cit.*, p. 101.
92. Josephus, *Ant.* 15, 10, 5.
93. Yoma 35b.
94. Yer. Pesahim 33a.
95. Soferim XVI. 9.
96. Berakhoth 63a.
97. Tosefta Sotah XIII. 3; Sotah 48a.
98. Shabbath 15a.
99. Josephus, *Ant.* 15, 5, 2.
100. C. T. Fritsch, "Herod the Great and the Qumran Community," *Journ. of Bibl. Lit.* 74 (1955), pp. 175 f.

# Index of Authors

Abel, F. M., 258
Albright, W. F., 186, 206, 279, 283 f., 290 ff.
Allegro, J. M., 5, 250, 262, 286, 294, 296
Aptowitzer, V., 261

Bacon, B. W., 138, 275, 289
Baer, I. F., 299
Baldensperger, W., 251
Barthélemy, D., 56, 256
Batiffol, P., 261
Bauer, W., 250, 298
Baumgarten, J. M., 38, 222 f., 225, 250, 275
Baumgartner, W., 295 f., 298
Beasly-Murray, G. R., 257
Beegle, D., 289
Benoit, P., 278, 292
Bentzen, A., 250
Billerbeck, P., 73
Black, M., 254, 256, 280
Bonsirven, J., 283
Bonwetsch, N., 259
Bornkamm, G., 291 f., 294
Bousset, W., 218
Braun, F. M., 186, 204, 277, 282 f., 284 ff., 289 f.
Braun, H., 281
Brooks, E. W., 261 f.
Brown, R. E., 5
Brownlee, W. H., 139, 176, 186, 203 ff., 273 f., 277 f., 280 ff., 285 ff., 289, 291
Bultmann, R., 79 ff., 107, 219, 251 f., 262 f., 268, 280, 291 ff.
Burrows, M., 175, 241, 256, 259, 275, 277 f., 289

Cadbury, H. J., 135
Cerfaux, L., 277
Chamberlain, J. V., 51, 250, 253
Chapman, J., 295
Charles, R. H., 48, 57, 269, 285 f., 289
Conzelmann, H., 269
Coppens, J., 184, 189, 273, 283, 285
Cross, F. M., Jr., 249 f., 275, 292, 297 f.
Cullmann, O., 208, 214, 217, 219, 224, 229, 231, 251 f., 274, 277, 280, 295 ff.

Daniélou, J., 251, 280 f.
Daube, D., 170, 279

Davies, W. D., 5, 16, 139, 274, 27~ T., 298
Delcor, M., 252, 283
Delitzsch, F., 270
Derenbourg, J., 258, 275
Dibelius, M., 260, 262 f., 268
Dinkler, E., 277, 279
Dix, G., 275 f.
Dodd, C. H., 168, 250, 288
Dupont, J., 279
Dupont-Sommer, A., 4 f., 49, 164, 183, 201, 205, 217, 225, 228, 253, 262, 268 f., 274, 279, 283, 289 ff., 294, 298

Edwards, G. R., 277, 280
Elliger, K., 251, 274, 293 f., 296, 298
Ellis, E. E., 277
Etheridge, J. W., 277

Farrar, A. M., 275
Finegan, J., 283
Finkelstein, L., 300
Fitzmyer, J. A., 252, 274, 277, 283
Flusser, D., 123, 273
Foakes-Jackson, F. J., 26
Frankenburg, W., 295
Friedrich, G., 278
Fritsch, C. T., 254, 277, 301
Fuchs, E., 267 f.
Funk, X., 69

Galling, K., 273
Gapp, K. S., 273
Gaster, T. H., 5, 249 f.
Geyser, A. S., 256
Ginsberg, H. L., 253, 297
Ginzberg, L., 291, 300 f.
Glanzman, G. S., 250
Gold, V., 284, 292
Goodenough, E. R., 277
Goossens, G., 283
Gottstein, M. H., 297
Graetz, H., 52
Graystone, G., 249
Gressman, H., 48, 218
Grobel, K., 279
Grossouw, W., 190, 198, 277, 279, 286 ff., 290

Harding, L., 272
Hempel, J., 273 f.

Herford, R. T., 277
Higgins, A. J. B., 257
Howie, C. G., 279
Hunzinger, C. H., 114
Hyatt, Ph., 278 f.

Israelstam, J., 159, 277
Iwry, S., 274

Jalland, T. G., 275
Jastrow, M., 160
Jeremias, J., 73, 79 ff., 88, 93, 249, 251,
    253, 261 ff., 269, 289
Johnson, S. E., 8, 251, 274, 277, 281,
    290

Kilpatrick, G. D., 74, 261
Kirk, K. E., 275
Klausner, J., 250, 271, 275 f.
Knox, J., 249
Knox, W. L., 277
Kohler, K., 261
Kraeling, C. H., 41 f., 252 f.
Kuhn, K. G., 3, 10, 16, 22, 27, 161 f.,
    164, 185 f., 204 f., 217, 249, 251 ff.,
    258, 266, 269, 274, 278, 280, 283 ff.,
    290, 293

Lake, K., 26
Lambert, G., 283
Lampe, G. W. H., 273, 275
Lee, E. K., 284
Lidzbarski, M., 20
Lieberman, S., 275, 277, 283, 298 f.
Lietzmann, H., 251, 260
Lightfoot, J. B., 137, 168, 275
Linton, O., 146 f., 276
Lohmeyer, E., 133, 264, 274
Lohse, B., 90 f., 264 f.
Lyonnet, S., 277 f.

Macalister, R. A. S., 297
Maisler, B., 272
Malinine, M., 249
Mansoor, M., 250
Marcus, R., 275, 291
Margoliouth, G., 294
Mariès, L., 259
Marxsen, W., 262
del Medico, H. E., 256
Merzbacher, E., 258
Michaelis, W., 144, 275
Michaud, H., 217, 295
Milik, J. T., 49, 227, 256 ff.
Molin, G., 271, 273 f.
Moore, G. F., 280
Morgenstern, J., 289

Mowry, L., 186 f., 201 ff., 252, 284, 289
Muilenberg, J., 253 f.
Munck, J., 251

Nock, A. D., 274
North, R., 277, 297

Odeberg, H., 252
Otzen, B., 257

Percy, E., 274
Philonenko, M., 269, 279
Polotsky, H. J., 284
Puech, H. C., 249, 292

Quasten, J., 292, 295
Quispel, G., 249, 292

Rabin, Ch., 280, 283
Rabinowitz, I., 140, 275, 277
Reicke, B., 8, 52, 186, 251 f., 276, 279,
    282, 284, 286, 298
Reifenberg, A., 258 f.
Rehm, B., 294 f.
Renan, E., 4, 18, 205
Riessler, P., 75, 261, 273
Ringgren, H., 250
Robertson, A., and Plummer, A., 281
Robinson, J. A. T., 162, 278 f.
Rowley, H. H., 283

Schechter, S., 49, 287
Schilling, F. A., 140, 252, 275
Schlier, H., 296
Schmidt, C., 212
Schmitt, J., 277
Schoeps, H. J., 119 f., 209, 211 f., 214,
    220, 231, 271, 274, 277, 291 ff.
Schubert, K., 256, 271 ff.
Schürer, E., 258, 260
Schürmann, H., 264
Schuré, E., 18
Schwartz, E., 295
Schweitzer, A., 7, 12, 159, 276 f.
Schweizer, E., 144, 177, 275, 278 ff.
Shepherd, M. H., Jr., 274
Silberman, L. H., 250, 290
Sjöberg, E., 250
Spicq, C., 289 f.
Stauffer, E., 250, 274
Stendahl, K., 249, 273 f.
*Strack-Billerbeck*, 122, 256, 260 f., **263 f.**,
    271 f., 276, 279
Streeter, B. H., 274

Taylor, V., 250
Teicher, J. L., 158, 175 f., 184, 208,
    212 f., 231, 280, 283, 293 ff.

Thomas, J., 212, 221, 227, 251, 291 ff.,
298
Torrey, C. C., 254

van Unnik, W. C., 249, 292
de Vaux, R., 39, 257, 265, 272, 283, 289,
294, 298
Vermès, G., 253, 274, 278, 280, 283,
285, 293 ff., 298

Waitz, H., 295
Weiss, J., 7, 12
Wernberg-Møller, P., 280
Wibbing, S., 266
Wieder, N., 254
Wilder, A. N., 278
Wilson, E., 1 ff., 16, 249

Yadin, Y., 278

# Index of passages from the Qumran Literature and the New Testament

**1 QS**

i, 3:220/3-4:197, 300/4:120/4-5:215/5: 196/5-6:215/6:126/7-8:192, 299/8-9: 193, 289/9:115, 192/10:120, 149, 197 f., 215/11:192, 280/11-12:272, 299/ 11-13:229/12:131/14:167/15-17:215/ 16:149/17 ff.:100/18:149/21-23:149, 215

ii, 2:115, 215/3:286/4:120/5:215/5-9: 120/7-8:198/13:136/13-14:288/16: 115/19-25:149/20:135, 268/24:117, 288, 299/25:115/26:161

iii, 1:161, 286/2:161/3:136, 161/3ff.:40, 68, 224 f./4:68, 161, 224/4-5:202/ 5:161/6:216/6ff.:160ff./7:286/9:68, 106, 202, 224f./10:289/11:117/11f.: 41/13:115, 193/13ff.:164, 167f., 179f./13-iv, 26:97, 164, 171f./14:268 /15:117, 186/15ff.:98, 116, 190/17-19:215/18:115, 284/18f.:98/19:195, 274, 284/19ff.:179, 215/20:115, 125, 284/20f.:99, 215/21:284/21f.:187/22: 115/22-25:100/23:284/24:108, 110, 115, 192, 215, 284/24f.:187/25:98, 187/26:215

iv, 1:215/2:193/2ff.:195, 215/3:176/5ff. 115/6:130, 287/6-26:268/7:117/9ff.: 170, 196/11:136/12:284f./15:190, 287/15-26:116/16-19:100/17:285/17-19:215/18ff.:139, 173, 188, 282/19ff.: 273/20:161f., 176, 280/20f.:197, 225 /21:43, 106, 130, 202, 281/22:191/ 22ff.:282/23:105, 215, 284/23f.:187/ 24:190, 197/25:110, 285

v, 1:117, 215/2:229/2-3:149, 223/3:196/ /4:228, 299/5:136/6:223/8-10:149/ 9:117, 223/10:117/10f.:131/11:191, 198/13:68

vi, 1:126/1-6:67, 71/2:227/2f.:135, 150 2-23:150/3:135/4:69/4-6:10, 55, 135, 227, 251/5:69, 260/5f.:224/6ff.:101, 299 / 8f.:299 / 10:69 / 13ff.:297 /14f.: 150/15:215/16:68, 150/16-20:131/ 17:268, 286f./18-20:150/19:115, 223 /19f.:272/20:227, 229/20-23:150/22: 229/24ff.:193, 229/24-vii, 25:151/25:

8, 132

vii, 1:249/1-3:215/4-8:199/10:266f./14: 267/16, 17:249/18:177, 268/18ff.: 267f., 288/20:227/23:177, 249/25: 229

viii, 1:133f., 151, 223/2:196, 288, 299/ 3:105, 176/5ff.:68, 152, 176, 192, 223/6:17, 115, 152, 197, 270, 285/ 6f.:120/7f.:136/8f.:223/9:137, 139, 223/10:152/10f.:120/12:177/12-14: 271/13:301/13-16:34/14:131/14ff.: 175, 280, 299/15:281/17-ix, 2:153/ 17, 20:115/22:281/23:229

ix :p. 55/3:281/3f.:251/4:160/4-6:137/ 5:117/6:193, 223/7:153, 223/8:115, 229/9-11:281/10f.:54, 139/11:44, 59, 63, 204, 250/13:286/13ff.:117/14: 115, 268/14ff.:176/15:268/17:179/ 17ff.:115, 198/18:268/18f.:299/20: 273/21ff.:120, 133, 280, 300/22:176, 179, 229/23:117, 120/24:117

x :p. 278/1-8, 9:138, 167, 201/11:278/ 17f.:126f./18:198/19:127/26:288, 299

xi :p. 278/1:105/2:176, 270/5-7:123/6 ff.:103, 162/7:161, 285/7ff.:102, 116f. /9:102, 161/11:9, 22, 186, 279/11f.: 103/12:161, 268/16:115/21:267

**1 QSa**

i, 1:54/6-18:279/11:281/ii, 8:278/8f.: 272/11:250/11-22:254/12-17:56f./17-22:71/18ff.:55, 70

**1 QSb**

i, 21-iii, 21:254/v, 20-29:254/24:51

**1QH**

i :p. 285/20:284/ii, 22:267/32:272/iii, 9f.:12/21:267/23-25:102/28ff.:42, 285 /iv, 10:267/29:101/30-38:114f./38, 216 /v, 27f.:37/viii, 5:177/10f.:51, 255/x, 5-7:116/5-10:110/9:284/xi, 7-10:114f.

**1 QM**

i :p. 215/2:301/5:110/10f.:272/ii,1:224 /3:297/5f.:222/iii, 2, 5, 6, 8, 9,:271/ iv, 2:216/3:102, 271/10f., 11-14:271

/vi, 3, 5, 6:271/vii, 6:272/9-11:224/
10-15:224/11:297/12-18:224/viii, 2-
7, 13ff.:224/x, 10f.:167, 299/ xi, 1:
216 /2, 3:60 /7:59f./7f.:280 /8:216/
9, 13:294/xii, 1, 4-5:262/11-12:267/
xiii:p. 215/1-6:224/10:187, 266/11:
284 /14:294 /xiv, 2f.:225 /7:272 /10:
216/14:270/17:215/xv, 1, 2f.:216/4,
6:224 /xvi, 13:224 /xvii, 5f.:216 /8:
115, 270/xviii, 3:216

**1 Qp Hab**

i, 13:296/ii, 1f.:220/2:219, 296/7:219f.,
296/8:286/8f.:299/iv, 29:160/v, 3-5:
120, 301/7:126/10:219, 296/ 11:219/
vii, 1f.:12/2f.:219/4:219f., 296/4f.:
299/9:296/10:115 /viii, 1:286/8ff.:
224 /10-12:272 /13ff.:166 /23:219 /ix,
2:107/4ff.:224, 272/x, 9:220, 296/xi,
4-6:273/5:219/xii, 3f.:122, 212, 294/
6:122, 212, 294, 300/10:122, 294

**1 Q Myst**
p. 285

**4 Qp Ps 37**
i, 9:294/ii, 4:286/10:294/15:296

**CD**

i, 16, 21:257/ii, 9ff.:175f./12:59, 280/
12f.:44/iii, 5:257/13-16:167/iv, 2f.:
135/8, 10, 12:257/13ff.:174/17:257/
v, 16ff.:174/18:266/vi, 1:59/7:12/
18:138, 167/21:300f./vii, 1:107, 160/
11ff.:136, 138 /14f.:136 /18:12 / 20:
300/viii, 6:107, 160/ix, 17-22:154/
21, 23:68/x, 4-10:154 / 7:257 /14-xi,
18:167/23ff.:259/xi, 13ff.:22/xii, 23:
58/xiii, 2:260/3:153/6, 7-10, 11-12:
154/xiv, 3-6:153/4, 6:301/9, 11, 12-
16:154/14:300/19:58/xv, 7ff,11:154/
xvi, 2:138/4:174/xix, 9:107/10:58/
xx, 1:58

1₇:193/11:219, 296/2₁:286/4:284/6-8:285/
10:285, 287/3₁:197/3:126/7:191/4₉-
10:125, 191/51:289/1f.:201, 286/3:
199/10:220/6₉:285/72f.:126/19:191,
284/84:125/6:199, 286/13:219, 296/
14:216, 295/15:289/17:272/9ₐ:285/5:
220/8:193/10ff.:200/21: 127, 272/23:
272/28:199/29:220/40:219, 296/50f.:
286 / 53:219, 296 / 53f.:220 / 68:218f.,
296/71:296/10ff.:193/10ff.:288/112:
228/121f.:202, 225/135:272/23f.:127/
25:272 / 26f.127 / 141ff.:216, 225/ 5:
187/151:216/5:228/161:193/175:228/
19₁:126/20₁:201/3:284

**Mt.**
2₁₅,₁₈:255/3₁:34/2:273/7:37/11-12:42/43-
10:112/5:p. 272/3:121f./12:122, 124/
14-16:125 /17:59, 118ff./20ff.:125 /28,
31f.:126/32:132/33-37:125f./ 38f.:127,
136/43f.:120f., 198, 272/6₁3:109/24:
127/7₁6-20:268/8₁₁:10/9₁3:222, 297/
34:266/10₅:140/34:11/11₁₁:24/11₁4:
46 / 11₂5-30: 119, 274, 298/12₇: 222,
297 /9-14:127 /29f.:111 / 32:200 / 13₂1:
108/31-33:269/16₁8f.:136, 139, 152/
21f.:255/18₁5ff.:126, 139, 288/19₃-9:
126/9:139/19:288/28:134, 139, 269/
23:p. 139 /12:299 /29-37:273 /34:272 /
24₂6:34/26₂6-29:73, 262, 273/27₅2f.:
251/28₁9f.:139.

**Mk.**
1₂:46/4:40, 273 / 8:43₁2-13:112 /3₁-6:127 /
14f.:85 /22:266 /27:97 /43:95 /17:108 /
67, 30:85/35ff.:86/7:p. 129f./20ff.:
169/81ff.:86/28:63/9₁2f.:46, 50/10₂1,
28:132/12₁4:294/33:297/13₂0:286/
14₂2-24:73, 78ff., 81, 88f., 263/25:81,
264/38:94, 105/15₄0:83/16₁:83/17:
267

**Lk.**
1₁₇:35, 46/76:46/80:35/2₁4:114ff./3₁:34/
2:24 / 7:37 / 43-12 : 112 / 13:269 / 6₆-11:
127₂0: 122 / 22: 274 / 38:132 / 7₁6: 63 /
26f.:46/8₁2f.:95f., 108/10₁8:111/11₂0:
97, 111/23:111/47-51:273/12₁4:271/
16-22:132/54:111/14₁5:260/33:132/
15₁6:33 /16₈:287 /19-31:59, 132/18₁4:
299 /19₈f.:274 /22₃, 10:269 /15-18:81,
90ff., 263ff./19-20: 73, 79, 82, 263/
28-30:10, 112, 134, 139, 260, 269f./
53:285/24₂1:15/27:58/30:86, 135/35:
135

**Jn.**
1₃:186f. / 4:285 / 5:189 / 9:285 /14:28, 254,
287/15:47/16:204/19-22: 46, 63/23:34,
47/26:51/28:36/29:49/30:47/33:35,
44, 51, 204/35:207/51:28/2₁-10:202/
31-15:202, 254, 268/19f.:191f./20f.:
194, 196f./23:36/25:40/41-26:202/14:
200 / 22:204 / 23:287 /38:27 /51-9:202/
33:197/6:p. 76/14f.:259/51-58:76/73s:
200 / 40f. 52:63 / 8₁2:194 / 44:287 / 9₁-
12:202/5:188/17:63/31:254/10₁8:31/
12₃1:189, 266, 285/33:254/35:191/36:
194/40:285/46:194, 285/13₁-16:202/
24:69/34f.:199, 204/14₁6f.:196, 266/
30:285/41ff.:254/151, 10:254/12:199/
15:254/16: 191/26:266/16₁1:285/13:
266/33:189/17₁:254/3:282/5:254/16:

288/17-19:197/18$_{37}$:197/19$_{34}$:202/20$_{30}$f.: 212$_5$:53

**Acts**

14:228/15-26:134, 145/233f.:15f./38:43, 130/42-47:86, 131, 135f., 151, 228/3$_1$:137/6:132/11:137/15, 19-21:14/22:63/411:136 3$_2$:151/34-37:131/51-11:8, 131, 151/17:7/6:pp. 26, 29, 145, 158/1:26/2:133, 135/5:135/7:29, 134, 158, 253/7:p. 28/37:63/44-51: 136/56:13/8:p. 27/1:26/14-18:27, 140/9$_{29}$: 26/104$_7$f.: 253/112$_0$:26/30:145/15:pp. 130, 145/1ff.:210/5:7/6-21:133, 146/8f.:253/16:136/1612, 30:135/1730-31: 250/18:24ff.:135, 207/191-4:135/21 18-26:86, 134, 137, 210/22$_5$:220/24$_5$, 14: 7/26$_{18}$:286/22:59/2735:81

**Rom.**

1:p. 163/3:163/4:280/17:286/2:p. 163/28: 163/3$_{20}$:163/41:107, 163/25:255/5:p. 163/12:268/6:pp. 96f., 104/12ff.:267/19:163/7:pp. 102ff./5, 18:163/24:282/8:p. 103, 163f./8:267/9f.:105/15:280/23f.:11/28:279/9-11:p. 277/9:106, 163/5, 8:163/11:279/115:285/14:107/1312:104, 287/152$_5$:132/26:210

**1 Cor.**

12$_6$, 29:163/26-16:178f., 266/421:280/5$_3$-5:139, 147, 268/616:163/75:95/28: 106, 163/8$_6$:284/927:278/10-11:p. 78/106-13:95f., 108/16f.:89, 261/18: 163/1123ff.:73, 79, 82, 89/128-10: 280f./1312, 1414, 32: 281f./1539:163/50:163, 267/161:132/18:96/22:87

**2 Cor.**

117:163/22:11/34-9:181, 281/13:281/17: 16/44:285/11:163/13:280/55:11/16: 11, 163/18:152/614f.:169, 285/71, 5: 163/91:132/103:163/1114:285/18:163/127:106, 163/131:139

**Gal.**

16:267/14:282/16:163/18f.:134/2:p. 210/9f.:21, 132, 152, 210/12:134/16, 20: 163/3$_3$:163/11:286/410:167/13f.:96, 106, 163/23, 29:163/5:p. 163f./13-24: 104f. 169, 193/61:95, 280/8, 12f.: 163/17:278

**Eph.**

14:286/14:11/17:280/21-3:163, 178f., 266/

11, 14:163/57-11:266f., 287/29, 31: 163/65:163/11:96, 179/12:163, 267

**Phil.**

122:163/24:106, 163/3$_3$:163/4ff.:163, 282/20:11

**Col.**

113, 16:168, 284f./18:15/20:168/22:107, 163, 167/21, 5:163/8:167/11-23:138, 163, 166/3$_5$:169/22:166

**1 Thess.**

3$_5$:95f./5$_5$ff.:96, 286f.

**1 Tim.**

37:95/15:152/69:95

**2 Tim.**

3$_8$:285.

**Philem.**

16:163

**Heb.**

12:284/214:267/17-18:96, 112/415:96/64-6:200/1026:289/38f.:286/1117:95/1315f.:137

**Jas.**

12, 12:95, 97/13:95/18:287/311:274/4$_5$: 268

**1 Pet.**

16:96/17:259/24f.:136f./9:286/412ff.:96/58:96

**2 Pet.**

29:108

**1 Jn.**

1$_3$:288/5:188/6f.:192, 194, 196, 288/28-10:189, 194, 199/15:288/16:267/20, 27:261, 289/39-23:268, 288/41-6: 196, 266/7-8:199/56-7:202/16:201

**2 Jn.**

4:196/5:288

**3 Jn.**

3:196/287

**Rev.**

113:13/210, 310:95, 109/717:200/115f.: 49ff./12$_5$:12, 255/9, 12:269/14:14:13/21$_6$:200, 288/14:152/221, 15, 17: 287f./20:87

# SELECTED BIBLIOGRAPHY:
# THE SCROLLS AND THE NEW TESTAMENT

The following bibliography is focused on books that have appeared from about 1960 to the present. This list is thus designed to assist the interested reader in understanding the chapters of this volume in light of recent developments.

## GENERAL WORKS

Betz, O. *Offenbarung und Schriftforschung in der Qumransekte*. Tübingen, 1960.

Black, M. *The Scrolls and Christian Origins: Studies in the Jewish Background of the New Testament*. Chico, CA, 1983, reprint from 1961.

———. *The Dead Sea Scrolls and Christian Doctrine*. London, 1966.

Braun, H. *Qumran und das Neue Testament*. 2 volumes. Tübingen, 1966.

Casciaro, J.M. *Qumran y el Nuevo Testamento*. Coleccion teologica, 29. Pamplona, 1982.

Cross, F.M. *The Ancient Library of Qumran and Modern Biblical Studies*. New York, 1961. See especially pp. 195–243.

Fujita, N.S. *A Crack in the Jar: What Ancient Jewish Documents Tell Us About the New Testament*. New York, 1986.

Garcia, Martinez, F. and E. Puech. *Memorial Jean Carmignac: Études Qumrâniennes*. *Revue de Qumran*, 13. Paris, 1988. See especially pp. 597–656.

Gärtner, B.E. *The Temple and the Community in Qumran and the New Testament*. Cambridge, 1965.

La Sor, W.L. *The Dead Sea Scrolls and the New Testament*. Grand Rapids, MI, 1972.

Schelkle, K.H. *Die Gemeinde von Qumran und die Kirche des Neuen Testaments*. Düsseldorf, 1960.

### John the Baptist and Qumran

Badia, L.F. *The Qumran Baptism and John the Baptist's Baptism*. Lanham, MD, 1980.
Wink, W. *John the Baptist in the Gospel Tradition*. SNTS Monograph Series, 7. London/Cambridge, 1968.

### Qumran Messianism

Charlesworth, J.H., *et al.*, eds. *The Messiah*. Minneapolis, in press. See especially the chapters by Charlesworth and Shiffman.
Dahl, N.A. *The Crucified Messiah, and Other Essays*. Minneapolis, 1974.

### Qumran and the Lord's Supper

Badia, L.F. *The Dead Sea Peoples' Sacred Meal and Jesus' Last Supper*. Washington, D.C., 1979.
Jauber, A. *The Date of the Lord's Supper*. Tr. by I. Rafferty. Staten Island, 1965.
Klinzing, G. *Die Umdeutung des Kultus in der Qumrangemeinde und im Neuen Testament*. SUNT, 7. Göttingen, 1971.

### Qumran Theologies

Becker, J. *Das Heil Gottes: Heils- und Sündenbegriffe in den Qumrantexten und im Neuen Testament*. SUNT, 3. Göttingen, 1964.
Bruce, F.F. *A Mind for What Matters: Collected Essays of F.F. Bruce*. Grand Rapids, MI, 1990.
Delcor, M., ed. *Qumran: Sa piété, sa théologie et son milieu*. BETL, 46. Paris, 1978.
Fabry, H.-J. *Die Wurzel Šub in der Qumran-Literatur: Zur Semantik eines Grundbegriffes*. Bonner biblische Beiträge, 46. Köln, 1975.
Garnet, P. *Salvation and Atonement in the Qumran Scrolls*. Tübingen, 1977.
Jefford, C.N. *Some Observations on the Concept of Sin at Qumran*. Claremont, CA, 1989.
Kimbrough, S.T. *The Concept of Sabbath at Qumran*. Paris, 1966.
Lichtenberger, H. *Studien zum Menschenbild in Texten der Qumrangemeinde*. SUNT, 15. Göttingen, 1980.
Merrill, E.H. *Qumran and Predestination: A Theological Study of the Thanksgiving Hymns*. Leiden, 1975.
Osten-Sacken, P. von der. *Gott und Belial: Traditionsgeschichtliche Untersuchungen zum Dualismus in den Texten aus Qumran*. SUNT, 6. Göttingen, 1969.

Ringgren, H. *The Faith of Qumran: Theology of the Dead Sea Scrolls.* Philadelphia, 1963.

Sekki, A.E. *The Meaning of Ruah at Qumran.* Atlanta, 1989.

### Qumran and the Sermon on the Mount

Davies, W.D. and D.C. Allison. *A Critical and Exegetical Commentary on the Gospel According to Saint Matthew.* ICC. Edinburgh, 1988.

Luz, U. *Matthew: A Commentary,* Volume 1. Tr. by W.C. Linss. Minneapolis, 1989.

Przybylski, B. *Righteousness in Matthew and His World of Thought.* SNTS, 41. Cambridge/New York, 1980.

### Qumran and the Palestinian Jesus Movement in Jerusalem (Acts)

Del Verme, M. *Comunione e condivisione dei beni: Chiesa primitiva e giudaismo esseno-qumranico a confronto.* Brescia, 1977.

Eisenman, R.H. *James the Just in the Habukkuk Pesher.* Studia post-Biblica, 35. Leiden, 1986.

Keck, L.E. and J.L. Martyn, eds. *Studies in Luke-Acts: Essays Presented in Honor of Paul Schubert.* Nashville, 1966. See especially the chapter by J.A. Fitzmyer.

Mowry, L. *The Dead Sea Scrolls and the Early Church.* Sound Bend, IN, 1966.

Thiering, B.E. *The Qumran Origins of the Christian Church.* Sydney, 1983.

### Qumran and Paul

Murphy O'Connor, J. and J.H. Charlesworth, eds. *Paul and the Dead Sea Scrolls.* New York, 1990.

Nebe, G. *'Hoffnung' bei Paulus: Elpis und ihre Synonyme im Zusammenhang der Eschatologie.* SUNT, 16. Göttingen, 1983.

Newton, M. *The Concept of Purity at Qumran and in the Letters of Paul.* Cambridge/New York, 1985.

Sabugal, S. *La Conversion de San Pablo. Damasco: ¿Ciudad de Siria o region de Qumran?* Barcelona, 1976.

Sanders, E.P. *Paul and Palestinian Judaism: A Comparison of Patterns of Religion.* Philadelphia, 1977. See especially pp. 233–328.

Scharlemann, M.H. *Qumran and Corinth.* New York, 1962.

Stuhlmacher, P. *Gerechtigkeit Gottes bei Paulus.* FRLANT, 87. Göttingen, 1965.

### Qumran and John

Betz, O. *Der Paraklet: Fürsprecher im häretischen Spätjudentum, im Johannes-Evangelium und in neu gefundenen gnostischen Schriften*. AGSU, 2. Leiden, 1963.

Böcher, O. *Der johanneische Dualismus im Zusammenhang des nachbiblischen Judentums*. Gütersloh, 1965.

Charlesworth, J.H. and R.E. Brown, eds. *John and the Dead Sea Scrolls*. New York, 1990.

Jeremias, J. *Die theologische Bedeutung der Funde vom Toten Meer*. Göttingen, 1962.

Johnston, G. *The Spirit-Paraclete in the Gospel of John*. SNTS Monograph Series, 12. Cambridge, 1970.

Leaney, A.R.C. *The Rule of Qumran and Its Meaning*. London/Philadelphia, 1966.

Schnackenburg, R. *The Gospel According to St. John*. Tr. by K. Smyth. 2 volumes. New York, 1968. See especially I, 105–111 and 128–35.

Stauffer, E. *Jesus and the Wilderness Community of Qumran*. Tr. by H. Spalteholz. Philadelphia, 1964.


### Alia

Coppens, J. *Les affinites qumrâniennes de l'Epitre aux hebreux*. Bruges, 1962.

Horton, F.L. *The Melchizedek Tradition: A Critical Examination of the Sources to the Fifth Century A.D. and in the Epistle to the Hebrews*. Cambridge/New York, 1976.

Spicq, C. *L'Epitre aux Hebreux*. Paris, 1977.